D0741861

BREACH OF TRUST

BREACH OF TRUST

Sexual Exploitation by
Health Care Professionals
and Clergy

Edited by
John C. Gonsiorek

SAGE Publications
International Educational and Professional Publisher
Thousand Oaks   London   New Delhi

Preface

The very first all women's group that I conducted in about 1970 contained a young woman who told of being sexually abused by her previous therapist. She had never spoken of this to anyone before telling the group. Initially, she told her story with much hesitation and fear. At the time, I had never before heard of such an event or even imagined that it ever happened.

The current literature then spoke of seductive patients, and a new report from the American Psychological Association Insurance Trust stated that

> the greatest number of actions are brought by women who lead lives of very quiet desperation, who form close attachments to their therapists, who feel rejected or spurned when they discover that relations are maintained on a formal and professional level, and who then react with allegations of sexual improprieties. (Brownfain, 1971)

Nevertheless, I believe this woman and tried to help her. I assisted her in taking her case to the local (Los Angeles) Ethics Committee; however, nothing significant happened as a result. She also presented her story to the American Psychological Association Convention in April 1972.

I did not know at the time that what was happening was history in the making, but it turned out that way. Members of the Association for

Women in Psychology heard this presentation, held a rump caucus, and then went to an open meeting conducted by then APA President Leona Tyler and asked for action. It was as a result of this that the APA Task Force on Sexual Abuse and Sex Role Stereotyping in Psychotherapy was formed. The task force surveyed psychologists and found that sexual exploitation, especially of women clients, was indeed a major problem (Holroyd & Brodsky, 1977). This was the beginning of the American Psychological Association's involvement in this important issue. I believe the American Psychological Association was the first major national professional association to take up the subject.

While conducting a preconvention workshop at the APA convention in around 1980, I met Gary Schoener and John Gonsiorek and began to learn of the work that was being done by them and others in Minneapolis. Slowly, a group of interested and involved professionals was forming. In 1984 I published my first annotated bibliography on the subject (Lerman, 1984), a tiny volume next to the second edition published in 1990 (Lerman, 1990).

I attended both the first Minneapolis conference on the topic in 1986 and the one in 1992. In 1986 the group of interested professionals was still small. If you were doing anything in this area, it was likely that your work was known by everyone in this courageous band. Victims/survivors also attended, told their stories, and received support and encouragement in their healing processes.

By 1992 the group was larger, more scattered geographically as well as more diverse. More people were initially strangers to one another and to one another's work or involvement. By now, of course, many changes have taken place in the legal and ethical arenas through which abused clients can sometimes achieve a measure of redress. Such meetings as the one this book is based on are crucial so that the small but growing number of involved professionals and victims/survivors can meet and interchange ideas and experiences. We all have very much to learn from each other in this branch of the mental health field, which, paradoxically, we all wish did not need to exist.

This volume is the result of the 1992 conference. Although it contains some of the individual presentations, much information to assist victims in becoming survivors, and reviews of the present legal and ethical state of affairs, it does not render the sense of excitement and interpersonal exchange that took place in the conference setting. I think that there is much here for professionals learning about the subject, professionals who have already become active in this area, as well as victims who are seeking ways in which to become survivors.

On a personal note, I have assumed the role of bibliographer of this subject. I already have two file drawers full of material that I have accumulated since 1990. I would like to enlist the help of the readers of this volume to send me copies of new relevant material that appears. Please send it to

Hannah Lerman, Ph.D.
10623 Rose Avenue
Los Angeles, CA 90034

I would also like people's suggestions about methods to get my bibliographic material on-line through an easily accessible source. The 1990 volume was 800 pages; the likelihood of written publication of anything much longer seems diminished (see the References for current availability information).

Hannah Lerman

Introduction

The impetus for this book was the Second International Conference on Sexual Misconduct by Clergy, Psychotherapists and Health Care Professionals held in Minneapolis in early October 1992 and sponsored by the Walk-In Counseling Center of Minneapolis.

All conference presenters were invited to contribute to this volume. However, some had previous publication commitments for their work, others felt their work was too much "in progress" and not ready for publication, and some had never before published and were perhaps daunted by the prospect. I am pleased that a number of contributors in this volume had never been previously published and were willing to accept the challenges of putting their work and ideas into written form.

This volume, however, is not the proceedings of that conference. Some contributors did not submit for reasons noted above. Other contributors, most notably for the chapters on legal concerns, discuss topics that are in such an extraordinary rate of flux that substantive revisions were being made to reflect these changes up to the week this manuscript was sent to the publisher. For other, more research-oriented chapters, the contributions were amended to incorporate new data or research available after the conference. Generally, the material in this manuscript is current as of approximately January 1, 1994.

More important, I believe the conference itself had a powerful impact on presenters. Contributors met and interacted with colleagues whose work they had heard about, or met new colleagues whose work they never knew existed. This volume unfortunately cannot capture the palpable sense of energy that existed at that conference—a critical mass of many people who worked, often in isolation, on this difficult topic, coming together and being catalyzed by each others' ideas.

I encouraged all contributors to incorporate their own or others' responses to their conference presentations and to produce chapters that reflect not only their presentations but the evolution of their thinking as the conference affected it. Chapters vary considerably in how much or little they depart from the conference presentations. Some depart hardly at all; others contain considerable revisions as new data or developments have occurred; and others bear only an ancestral relationship to the presentations. In a paradoxical way perhaps, this departure from the conference presentations more accurately captures the spirit of the conference, as it may partially reflect how the conference affected the presenters.

This book is organized into four parts. The first part contains background on this topic. It grounds readers in the history and basic facts about abuse by clergy and health care professionals. The second part focuses on the experiences of victims. There are first person accounts by victims and reflections on victim experience, discussions of support and advocacy by and for victims, and contributions on treatment of victims and their families.

Part III addresses the perpetrators of professional abuse, with descriptions of who perpetrators are, how to understand and assess them, and the organizational systems in which they operate. Special emphasis is given to situations other than abuse by men of women. While this latter dyad is most common, there are other variants; the typical silence on these is troublesome. Of all the subtopics in this field, the study of perpetrators of professional sexual abuse has been most marred by simplistic thinking. The contributions here can begin to flesh out professional perpetrators in all their complexity and diversity.

Part IV focuses on responses to this problem on all levels and from all perspectives; legal remedies, advocacy, prevention, employee liability, and the institutional church are all discussed. An epilogue closes the volume.

The contributions can best be seen as works in progress. As Hannah Lerman notes in the Preface, this area of study began about 20 years ago, in a number of different locations, arising independently as groups of dedicated individuals determined that professional abuse could not continue unchallenged. Virtually everything known about professional abuse, except its reality and unnerving frequency, is tentative or conditional.

This volume, I believe, contains some of the most creative and courageous thinking on this topic. This volume's authors hope that these contributions will energize readers as much as the conference energized us.

The references for all chapters, except the two on legal issues by Linda Jorgenson, are contained in one central reference list at the end, with some additional readings listed. The legal chapter references are at the end of those chapters. Legal and social science citation systems can be merged, but the result is often unsatisfactory to all. It is hoped this arrangement preserves the comprehensibility of each system and also allows for a unified bibliography for the nonlegal chapters, a resource in its own right.

John C. Gonsiorek

PART I

Background

It might appear, after the long silence about sexual abuse by health care professionals and clergy, and prior to its recent "discovery" in the last 20 years, that such abuse is a "new" problem. Nothing could be further from the truth.

Gary Schoener provides an overview on the extensive history of this problem. It has occupied the concerns of ethicists in the health care professions and clergy as long as these professions have existed. It has also served as a sort of projective technique, or cultural repository for a society's sex and gender myths, fears, and underlying power structure, for equally as long. Schoener's contribution places this topic in a rich context.

The contribution by Nanette Gartrell and her colleagues discusses prevalence of physician-patient sexual contact and is an important empirical study in establishing the frequency of this problem. Available research suggests that from 5% to 13% (depending on what posttherapy period is counted) of mental health professionals admit to sexual contact with patients (see Schoener, 1989b, for a review of this literature).

An analogy can illustrate the seriousness of this problem. The U.S. Food and Drug Administration (FDA) uses a cutoff of between 1% to 2% of adverse effects to ban a drug. Sexual contact between a mental health professional and patient is predominantly adverse, often seriously so, in its effects. Simply stated, if psychotherapy were a drug, the FDA would be required to ban it simply on the basis of the high prevalence of sexual exploitation by mental health professionals. Readers interested in basic information on sexual exploitation by psychotherapists are directed to Schoener, Milgrom, Gonsiorek, Luepker, and Conroe (1989).

Rev. Marie Fortune has written a timeless and eloquent chapter on sexual abuse by clergy, outlining the fundamental assault on the church and all it stands for, that such behavior represents. Gary Schoener, Dr. Gartrell and colleagues, and Rev. Fortune represent some of the earliest and most consistent contributors to this area from psychology, psychiatry, and clergy, respectively. It is fitting that these three provide background for the rest of this volume.

1

Historical Overview

Gary Richard Schoener

Before examining the history of sexual misconduct by professionals, it is important to remind ourselves about how uneasy the relationship is between the helping professions and the law. There is an old joke in which three passengers on a sinking ship—an attorney, a health care professional, and a bishop—find themselves in the same life raft. Unfortunately, the life raft is not very seaworthy and begins taking on water, and it becomes clear that it will not make it to an island visible in the distance. The attorney, noting that the raft could handle two but not three of them, suggests that they draw straws and that the one who gets the short straw has to swim to shore. They do so and the attorney gets the short straw. She is preparing to dive in and swim for the island when suddenly dorsal fins are everywhere—the raft is surrounded by sharks.

The attorney surveys the situation and grimly says, "Better one than three," and dives in and swims frantically. The sharks pull back and form a corridor to the island. The bishop says, "Heaven be praised, it's a miracle." The health care professional says, "Miracle my eye! That's professional courtesy."

3

This joke can serve as a useful metaphor. Those of us in the helping professions are the crew of the ship. We are the captain, the navigator, and the other crew members. The passengers are our clients and parishioners. It is our job to check the charts before we sail, to make sure where the hidden reefs lie. It is our job to check the weather before sailing so as to avoid, or at least be prepared for, storms. It is our job to make sure we have enough life jackets and life rafts, and that they are seaworthy, in case trouble happens. It is our job to make sure that we have procedures for emergencies and that all of the crew understand them. It is when we fail in these duties that the ship goes down, the passengers are endangered, and the sharks come around. The sharks are not the problem, they simply clean up the mess.

This metaphor can be further extended to examine how we may respond when a complaint is made against a professional—that is, a member of the crew. First of all, even if the crew member who is accused of dereliction of duty works in another part of the ship, he or she is one of "us." As such, when a complaint is made, we may choose to minimize it or attack the complainant, feeling ourselves attacked as a member of the crew and believing that the crew is a fine crew. Or we may take the "bad apple approach," deny any group responsibility, and attack the "bad" crew member as a "bad apple."

The problem with the "bad apple" approach is that it prevents us from looking at community and institutional problems, not to mention our own vulnerability to misconduct. Furthermore, to judge from the available research data, there are quite a few thousand "rotten apples" to deal with each year.

As a prelude to the examination of our current knowledge and understanding of sexual misconduct by professionals in this volume, a brief recapitulation of some history seems in order. Beyond the normal wish to learn from history so as to avoid reliving it, we may now be in a position to understand it in a new light.

HISTORICAL BACKGROUND

Although there are earlier medical codes and texts, such as the *Code of Hammurabi*, which was compiled around 2000 B.C., the first concerns about physician-patient sex in a written text are to be found in the *Corpus Hippocratum*. This was a body of about 70 medical texts compiled by the Library of Alexandria during the fourth and fifth centuries B.C. (Lloyd, 1983).

It is not known how many of these works can actually be attributed to Hippocrates, who lived from 460 to 370 B.C., although it is quite likely that he did not write the most famous item in the *Corpus*, the Oath that is usually attributed to him (Lloyd, 1983). In both the "Oath" and "The Physician," doctor-patient sexual intimacy is discussed. In "The Physician," the intimacy of the physician-patient relationship is described thus:

> The intimacy also between physician and patient is close. Patients in fact put themselves into the hands of their physicians, and at every moment he meets women, maidens and possessions very precious indeed. So towards all these self-control must be used. Such then should the physician be, both in body and in soul. (Translated by W. H. S. Jones, cited in Reiser, Dyck, & Curran, 1977, p. 5)

The original Greek version of the "Oath," usually referred to as the Hippocratic Oath, states in part: "and I will abstain from all intentional wrong-doing and harm, especially from abusing the bodies of man or woman, bond or free" (translated by W. H. S. Jones, cited in Reiser et al., 1977, p. 5).

When the "Oath" was rewritten for Christian physicians some centuries later, this section read as follows:

> with purity and holiness I will practice my art.... Into whatever house I enter I will go into them for the benefit of the sick and will abstain from every voluntary act of Mischief and Corruption and further from the seduction of females or males, of freemen and slaves. (Braceland, 1969, p. 236)

During the Middle Ages, the treatise "De Cautelis Medicorum," thought to have been written by Arnald of Villanova, read in part:

> Let me give you one more warning: Do not look at a maid, a daughter, or a wife with an improper or a covetous eye and do not let yourself be entangled in woman affairs for there are medical operations that excite the helper's mind; otherwise your judgment is affected, you become harmful to the patient and people will expect less from you. And so be pleasant in your speech, diligent and careful in your medical dealings, eager to help. And adhere to this without fallacy. (Braceland, 1969, p. 236)

During the Middle Ages, sexual contact between clergy and counselees or parishioners was known but not widely reported. A recent review of child sexual abuse by Roman Catholic priests notes:

Child sexual abuse involving priests is not a new phenomenon within the Catholic Church. Renaissance history reveals evidence of an awareness of this problem within the Church. During that period the Church took a traditional stance that clerics were the responsibility of the Church and, in theory, were not subject to secular law. The prosecutions that took place were tried in ecclesiastical courts under Canon Law. (Stark, 1989, p. 793)

The issue of professional-patient sex again emerges in the literature near the end of the eighteenth century. Concern about physicians taking sexual advantage of their patients through the misuse of mesmerism (hypnosis) was voiced in 1784 by a Commission of Inquiry headed by Benjamin Franklin, which, in a secret report to the French King Louis XVI, stated:

> The danger exists . . . since the physician can, if he will, take advantage of his patient. . . . Even if we ascribe to him superhuman virtue, since he is exposed to emotions which awaken such desires, the imperious law of nature will affect his patient, and he is responsible, not merely for his own wrong-doing, but for that he may have excited in another. (Franklin et al., 1784/1965, p. 6)

The King had appointed the commission due to his distrust of physicians. Perry (1979) notes that at "the time the report was written . . . medical doctors enjoyed a bad reputation in the eyes of a significant segment of the lay public" (p. 188).

A book widely thought to be America's first psychological novel, *The Scarlet Letter* by Nathaniel Hawthorne, was published in 1850. It described the shame of a young woman who was required to wear the scarlet letter "A" (for adulteress) after having been made pregnant by a clergyman, Arthur Dimmesdale, who escaped public disgrace but not emotional consequences. In a meeting with Hester in the forest, Rev. Dimmesdale tells Hester, when asked if he has found any peace in the preceding seven years, that he has found "None! Nothing but despair" (Hawthorne, 1991). When Hester inquires as to whether the good works he has done in the church among those who revere him have brought comfort, Dimmesdale replies:

> As concerns the good which I may appear to do, I have no faith in it. It must needs be a delusion. What can a ruined soul, like mine, effect towards the redemption of other souls?—or a polluted soul, towards their purification? And as for the people's reverence, would that it were turned to scorn and hatred! Canst thou deem it, Hester, a consolation, that I must stand up in my

pulpit, and meet so many eyes turned upward to my face, as if the light of heaven were beaming from it!—and then look inward, and discern the black reality of what they idolize? I have laughed, in bitterness and agony of heart, at the contrast between what I seem and what I am! And Satan laughs at it! (Hawthorne, 1991, p. 134)

Henry Ward Beecher (1813-1887), son of famous clergyman Lyman Beecher and brother of the author of *Uncle Tom's Cabin*, Harriet Beecher Stowe, was "one of the premier preachers in the late nineteenth century," according to the *Dictionary of Christianity in America* (Reid, Linder, Shelley, & Stout, 1990). A short summary of his career is presented thus:

Under his preaching (1847-1887) Plymouth church became one of the first large middle class suburban churches in America. As editor of two well-read journals, the *Independent* (1861-1863) and the *Christian Union* (1870-1881) Beecher's influence reached well beyond the confines of his own church's membership. Yale University invited him to deliver the prestigious Lyman Beecher Lectures for three years straight (1872-1874). (Reid et al., 1990, p. 123)

Though omitted from many summaries of church history, at the height of his distinguished career and pastoral influence, Beecher undertook pastoral counseling of Elizabeth Tilton, the wife of a friend, who was grieving the death of her infant. Beecher reportedly convinced her to engage in an intimate relationship with him, cautioning her not to tell anyone about it (Morey, 1988). In 1872 journalist Victoria Woodhull published the story of the relationship and was jailed but subsequently released (Fortune, 1989, p. 120). Theodore Tilton sued Beecher. A congregational investigating committee, ignoring "almost irrefutable evidence," not only exonerated Beecher but expressed toward him "sympathy more tender and trust more unbounded" than before (Morey, 1988, p. 868). Elizabeth Tilton was excommunicated in 1878. Beecher's career was not significantly affected (Waller, 1982).

Romance novels of the late nineteenth and twentieth centuries often portrayed ministers as boyish and innocent men, pursued by women who sought to seduce them but whose clutches they managed to escape (Morey, 1988). For example, Corra Harris's *A Circuit Rider's Wife*, published in 1910 (and serialized in the *Saturday Evening Post* the same year), includes the following narration by Mary, wife of a Methodist minister:

When we hear of a minister who has disgraced himself with some female member of his flock, my sympathies are all with the preacher. I know exactly what has happened. Some sad-faced lady who has been "awakened" from a silent, cold, backslidden state by his sermons goes to see him in his church study. (They who build studies for their preachers in the back part of the church surround him with four walls of moral destruction and invite it for him. The place for a minister's study is in his own home, with his wife passing in and out, if he has female spiritual invalids calling on him.)

This lady is perfectly innocent in that she has not considered her moral responsibility to the preacher she is about to victimize. She is very modest, really and truly modest. He is a little on his guard till he discovers this. First, she tells him that she is unhappy at home . . . .

. . . He sees her reduced to tears over her would-be transgressions, and before he considers what he is about he has kissed the "dear child." That is the way it happens nine times out of ten, a good man damned and lost by some frail angel of the church. (Harris, 1988, pp. 81-83)

Mary nipped one such potential relationship—that between a parishioner and her minister husband William—in the bud by privately confronting the woman, after having noticed with chagrin that "William was always cheered and invigorated by her visits. He would come out of his study for tea after her departure, rubbing his hands and praising the beautiful, spiritual clearness of her mind, which he considered very remarkable in a woman" (Harris, 1988, pp. 83-84).

Mary proposes a solution to this problem:

Someone who understands real moral values ought to make a new set of civil laws that would apply to the worst class of criminals in society—not the poor, hungry, simple-minded rogues, the primitive murderers, but the real rotters of honor and destroyers of salvation. Then we should have a very different class of people in the penitentiaries, and not the least numerous among them would be the women who make a religion of sneaking up on the blind male side of good men without a thought of the consequences. (Harris, 1988, p. 85)

At the turn of the century, *women* were "the problem." In case one is tempted to relegate this account of the 1880s published in 1910 to the past, it should be noted that it was reissued as *The Circuit Rider's Wife* (Harris, 1988) in 1988 and had a second printing in 1990. Furthermore, *The Bishop's Mantle*, written by Agnes Turnbull in 1948, contained similar sentiments, describing the struggles of Hilary Laurens, a young minister, who was barely able to escape the clever plotting of predatory women in his congregation:

In spite of himself he thought of the ministers, from Beecher down, who had had trouble with women. Every city clergyman had to recognize this menace.

A few to his own knowledge through the years, in spite of their utter innocence, had yet escaped by a hair's breadth. A few here and there had not even escaped. There were always the neurotic women who flocked not only to the psychiatrists but also in almost equal numbers to ministers, pouring out their heart confessions and their fancied ills; there were those pitiable ones in whose minds religion and sex had become confused and intermingled; there were those who quite starkly fell in love with a clergyman and wanted love from him in return. Yes, a man of God had to be constantly on his guard in connection with *this problem of women*. (Turnbull, 1948, p. 235, italics added)

Erotic feelings between therapist and client also are found in the earliest reported cases of psychotherapy—the "talking cure." Anna O. was treated using hypnosis by Joseph Breuer in 1880; subsequently, the case became one of Freud's most widely discussed models of psycho-therapeutic treatment. Ernest Jones (1953), Freud's first biographer, reported, on the basis of Freud's account of the case,

that Breuer had developed what we should nowadays call a strong counter-transference to his interesting patient . . . his wife became bored at listening to no other topic, . . . jealous . . . unhappy and morose. It was a long time before Breuer . . . divined the meaning of her state of mind. It provoked a violent reaction in him, perhaps compounded of love and guilt, and he . . . [brought] the treatment to an end . . . that evening he was fetched back to find [Anna O.] in the throes of an hysterical childbirth . . . the logical termination of a phantom pregnancy . . . he managed to calm her down . . . and then fled the house in a cold sweat. The next day he and his wife left for Venice to spend a second honeymoon. (pp. 224-225)

Although this experience deterred Breuer from further experiments with hypnosis to treat hysterical symptoms, Freud went on to experiment with the "talking cure" and, eventually, to develop psychoanalysis. In his classic *Introductory Lectures in Psychoanalysis*, published in 1917, Freud noted the romantic and erotic feelings his female patients exhib-ited toward him, labeling it *transference*. In writing on this topic, Freud (1958) clearly indicated that the therapist should not take advantage of the patient's "longing for love" and should abstain from sexual involve-ment. Freud also noted that the therapist had to struggle with his own countertransference love feelings.

Despite Freud's warnings of the potentially erotic atmosphere of the psychoanalytic relationship, some of his followers experimented with physical contact with clients. When Freud learned that Ferenczi, one of his followers, had engaged in kissing and other physical contact with

clients, he wrote a challenging letter on December 13, 1931, warning
Ferenczi about this practice (Groskurth, 1991, p. 206).

Wilhelm Reich (1945, pp. 126-127) believed that the therapist should
allow the client's overt sexual feelings to develop until they are "con-
centrated, without ambivalence, in the transference." Although he never
advocated ongoing sexual relationships between therapist and client,
at times "[he] physically manipulated . . . [some clients] to 'appropriate'
responses" (Marmor, 1970, p. 12), using sexual touch as a treatment
technique. Reich (1945, p. 133) cited two measure of whether sensual
genital striving was freed from repression: "phantasies of incest without
guilt feeling" and "genital excitation during analysis." While explaining Reich's theories and behavior as, in part, symptoms of paranoid
schizophrenia, Marmor (1970) accused Reich's students and followers
of using "the prestige of this unfortunate psychoanalytic pioneer to act
out their own countertransference needs" (p. 12).

In recent years it has come to light that psychoanalyst Carl Jung had
a romantic affair with Sabina Spielrein, whom he treated from 1905 to
1909. She had been 19 years old when she began her analysis. Subsequently she became a physician and in 1912 joined the Vienna Psychoanalytic Society (Carotenuto, 1984). Gay (1988), in his biography of Freud,
described Spielrein as

> "one of the most extraordinary among the younger analysts," who "had gone
> to Zurich to study medicine and in desperate mental distress, went into
> psychoanalytic treatment with Jung." "She fell in love with her analyst, and
> Jung, taking advantage of her dependency, made her his mistress. After
> painful struggle in which Freud played a minor but not admirable part, she
> freed herself from her involvement and became an analyst." (p. 396)

Her relationship with Jung was discussed in letters between Freud,
Jung, and herself and later was discussed in a book by Aldo Carotenuto,
first published in Italy in 1980. It then appeared in English translation
(Carotenuto, 1982) as *A Secret Symmetry: Sabina Spielrein Between Jung
and Freud.* The book generated reviews such as Bettelheim's (1983)
"Scandal in the Family." In terms of physical contact, the romantic
involvement may have gone no further than kissing and talk of love,
but Spielrein has been referred to as Jung's "mistress," implying greater
sexual involvement. The rumors generated and the subsequent inter-
changes between Freud, Jung, Spielrein, and others are discussed by
Masson (1988, pp. 170-177), Groskurth (1991), and others.

In a letter to Freud dated June 4, 1909, Jung mentions the relationship and indicates that Spielrein was "systematically planning [his] seduction" (McGuire, 1988, p. 228). Freud's response, dated June 7, 1909, was supportive and noted that, while Freud himself had "never been taken in quite so badly," he had "come very close to it a number of times and had a narrow escape" (McGuire, 1988, p. 230). Freud focused all blame on Spielrein: "The way these women manage to charm us with every conceivable psychic perfection until they have attained their purpose is one of nature's greatest spectacles" (McGuire, 1988, p. 231).

On June 21, 1909, Jung wrote to Freud that he had met with Spielrein and discovered that she had not been the source of the rumors about their relationship and indicates remorse about "the sins" he had committed:

> When the situation had become so tense that the continued preservation of the relationship could be rounded out only by sexual acts, I defended myself in a manner that cannot be justified morally. Caught in my delusion that I was the victim of the sexual wiles of my patient, I wrote to her mother that I was not the gratifier of her daughter's sexual desires but merely her doctor, and that she should free me from her. In view of the fact that the patient had shortly before been my friend and enjoyed my full confidence, my action was a piece of knavery which I very reluctantly confess to you as my father. (McGuire, 1988, p. 236)

Jung had written to Sabina Spielrein's mother, indicating that he had moved from doctor to friend "the more easily" because he had not charged a fee, and then made a proposition that he would come to regret—that if she wished him "to adhere strictly to [his] role as doctor," she should pay him "a fee as suitable recompense for [his] trouble" (Donn, 1990, p. 93).

In his letter of June 30, 1909, Freud reports that he had written to Sabina Spielrein's mother, as Jung asked him to, and that "the matter has ended in a manner satisfactory to all." He asks Jung not to fault himself for drawing Freud into the situation, asserting that "it was not your doing but hers" (McGuire, 1988, p. 238). Again we can see what *the problem* is—it is *seductive women*. As for the harmful impact of such behavior on the client, Bettelheim wrote:

> Whatever may be one's judgment of Jung's behavior toward Spielrein . . . one must not disregard its most important consequence: he cured her. . . .
>   In retrospect we ought to ask ourselves: what convincing evidence do we have that the same result would have been achieved if Jung had behaved toward

her in the way we must expect a conscientious therapist to behave toward his patient? However questionable Jung's behavior was from a moral point of view—however unorthodox, even disreputable, it may have been—somehow it met the prime obligation of the therapist toward his patient: to cure her. True, Spielrein paid a very high price in unhappiness, confusion, and disillusion for the particular way in which she got cured, but then this is often true for mental patients who are as sick as she was. (Carotenuto, 1984, p. 38)

A disturbing footnote was added to this seemingly incongruous defense of Jung after Bettelheim's suicide when former patients, trainees, and staff from his famed Orthogenic School came forward with stories of emotional and psychological abuse by Bettelheim (Angres, 1990; Schoener, 1991, 1992). Kerr (1993) has further extended the understanding of the Freud-Spielrein-Jung triangle in his book *A Most Dangerous Method*, which argues that these relationships had a profound impact on the development of psychoanalysis.

In 1913 Ernest Jones, one of Freud's inner circle, had become the subject of a complaint by a former patient to the president of the University of Toronto, where he was a faculty member. This patient, who alleged sexual advances by Jones, had come forward with the help and support of her general practitioner. Jones claimed that the general practitioner, a woman, had a lesbian relationship with the complainant, but the credibility of his defense was undermined by his admission that he had paid money to the patient in an attempt to buy her silence (Grosskurth, 1991, p. 56).

Popular literature of the first half of the twentieth century also examined doctor-patient sex. F. Scott Fitzgerald's novel *Tender is the Night*, published in 1933, dealt with a psychiatrist, Dr. Diver, who became romantically involved with a woman who was a patient. In one scene she asks Dr. Diver if he finds her attractive: "He was in for it now, possessed by a vast irrationality. She was so near that he felt his breathing change but again his training came to his aid in a boy's laugh and a trite remark" (Fitzgerald, 1933, p. 174). During the next 50 years, a number of novels and movies would include plots involving sexual and/or romantic involvement between professional and client. Most involved male professionals and female clients.

Despite the fact that the ranks of physicians and clergy were overwhelming male, such transgressions were not limited to male professionals, even in the early days. Karen Horney, one of the leading figures in psychoanalysis, was quoted as saying: "As a rule it is better not to have social relationships with a patient, but I am not terribly rigid about it. Generally, I have none or a restricted relationship" (Wolff, 1956, p. 87). However, in her biography of Horney, *A Mind of Her Own*, Susan Quinn notes that in her later years Horney had a romantic relationship with a young man who was in treatment with her, something Quinn (1988) attributed to "old impulsive ways [which] survived into middle age" (p. 378). Quinn claims that this relationship, begun during the second half of the 1940s, lasted until the end of Horney's life in 1952.

During the 1960s the human potential movement blurred some of the distinctions between traditional psychotherapy and new methods such as encounter groups. The taboo against touch in psychoanalysis was questioned, with, for example, one female analyst arguing: "It seems absurd that any qualified psychoanalyst should be so carried away by contact with a patient, however attractive, that he (or she) could not refrain from complete gratification" (Mintz, 1969, p. 371).

Despite experimentation with nudity in sensitivity groups (see, for example, Bindrum, 1972, p. 160, or Maslow, 1965), only one author argued for sexual contact with clients. J. L. McCartney, a psychoanalyst, claimed to have experienced "overt transference" with 30% of his female patients, including undressing, genital touch, or sexual intercourse with 10% (McCartney, 1966). Although no clients complained, McCartney was widely attacked within the profession and was expelled from membership in the American Psychiatric Association.

The next decade opened with the publication of Masters and Johnson's classic *Human Sexual Inadequacy* in 1970, inaugurating the development of the new field of sex therapy. Ironically, in a widely reported address to the American Psychiatric Association convention in 1975, these authors reported that a sizable number of their clients had reported sexual contact with a previous therapist and had labeled such conduct "rape" (Masters & Johnson, 1975). However, media accounts of "sex therapy," focusing on the use of sexual contact in research and "sexual surrogates" in therapy, left many consumers less clear about what might constitute acceptable therapy for sexual difficulties.

Martin Shepard's (1971) book *The Love Treatment*, based on interviews with 11 clients who reported sexual relationships with their therapists, fueled major controversy when popular articles such as "Should You Sleep With Your Therapist? The Raging Controversy in American Psychiatry" in *Vogue* (Weber, 1972). Shepard's (1972) second book, *A Psychiatrist's Head*, which described an orgy during a group therapy session, resulted in the revocation of Shepard's medical license, despite the absence of client complaints (Simon, 1992c).

Feminist perspectives began to play a key role with the publication of Phyllis Chesler's *Women and Madness* in 1972. One of its chapters discussed sex between male therapists and female clients based on interviews with 10 women who reported such an experience. This was followed by two widely discussed Ph.D. dissertations involving case studies of women who reported sex with their therapists (Belote, 1974; D'Addario, 1977).

The 1970s also saw the advent of the self-report survey of various professional groups with the publication of Kardener, Fuller, and Mensh's (1973) study of a sample of 1,000 physicians in Los Angeles County. Their finding that 10% of psychiatrists and other physicians acknowledged erotic contact with clients, and that 5% acknowledged sexual intercourse, established the seriousness of the scope of the problem and presaged the ensuing professional debate, not to mention a large number of self-report surveys (Schoener et al., 1989, pp. 25-45).

In March 1974 the case of *Roy v. Hartogs* was tried in New York City. It was widely reported in newspapers around the United States and Canada. Julie Roy, the plaintiff, charged that Dr. Renatus Hartogs, a psychiatrist with good credentials and the author of a column for *Cosmopolitan* magazine, had sexually exploited her. Ms. Roy won the suit and the next year coauthored a book, *Betrayal*, which was later made into a made-for-TV movie of the same title (Freeman & Roy, 1976). Although not the first such case, its broad publicity led to many other clients coming forward and presaged the local and national coverage of other cases by news media.

A major discussion of therapist-client sex occurred in May 1976 at the annual convention of the American Psychiatric Association. The next year a national survey of psychologists was published whose findings mirrored those of Kardener, Fuller, and Mensh (Holroyd & Brodsky, 1977), and in 1978 a California Psychological Association Task Force undertook a large-scale survey of psychologists concerning their knowledge of such cases (Bouhoutsos, Holroyd, Lerman, Forer, & Greenberg, 1983).

The remainder of the 1970s through the present have been characterized by many theoretical articles and discussions at professional conferences, continuing research (largely involving surveys), and repeated efforts to refine the language of professional codes of ethics (so as to have more specific prohibitions against sex with clients). Complaints to ethics committees and licensure boards and malpractice actions related to sexual misconduct by therapists steadily increased during the 1970s and 1980s. There is no evidence that all of this study and discussion, or even the refinements in the ethics codes, changed professional behavior. Frustrated consumers who had been sexually exploited and concerned professionals began seeking remedies through media attention and changes in public policy. In 1984 Wisconsin criminalized therapist-client sex and the Minnesota legislature created a Task Force on Sexual Exploitation by Counselors and Psychotherapists. In 1985 Minnesota criminalized therapist-client sex, including sexual contact by clergy who were providing counseling for emotional problems. In 1993 the scope of this statute was expanded to include *clergy doing spiritual counseling*. To date 13 states have criminalized therapist-client sex, and others have bills pending or task forces studying the problem. Several have special civil statutes covering suits against therapists for sexual misconduct (Jorgenson, Randles, & Strasburger, 1991; see also Chapters 20, 21, and 24 in this volume).

In October 1984 the indictment of Father Gilbert Gauthe Jr. for sexual abuse of children in Lafayette, Louisiana, sent shock waves around North America. The criminal case was followed by a $12 million lawsuit against the church, both of which received wide publicity. In May 1985 a secret report was made to the Conference of Catholic Bishops at their annual meeting, held that year at St. John's University in Collegeville, Minnesota. The report warned that the church had to deal more effectively with priests who sexually molest children (Berry, 1992).

Numerous other lawsuits followed, many of them involving alleged sexual abuse of children by clergy. However, interdenominational task forces in several states examined sexual misconduct by clergy with both child and adult counselees/parishioners. The Washington Council of Churches issued a report, *Sexual Contact by Pastors and Pastoral Counselors in Professional Relationships,* in 1984 and the Minnesota Interfaith Committee on Sexual Exploitation by Clergy published *Sexual Exploitation by Clergy: Reflections and Guidelines for Religious Leaders* in 1989.

In 1989 two cases of alleged sexual misconduct by priests with young people received considerable publicity throughout North America— Father Bruce Ritter, the founder of Covenant House Charity in New York (Sennott, 1992), and the Mount Cashel Orphanage case in Newfoundland (M. Harris, 1990). That same year Rev. Marie Fortune's book *Is Nothing Sacred?*—challenging the religious community to deal more effectively with sexual misconduct in the church—was published. Dr. Peter Rutter's *Sex in the Forbidden Zone,* also published in 1989, generated considerable discussion and media coverage in North America and elicited an extraordinary response from many victims/survivors of sexual misconduct by professionals. For example, hundreds of people contacted the Walk-In Counseling Center in Minneapolis alone about misconduct by therapists and clergy as a result of reading this book.

By the end of the 1980s and beginning of the 1990s, a number of church denominations had developed or were working on policies and guidelines for handling complaints of sexual misconduct by clergy. Workshops, conferences, and training programs were under way in some denominations and communities to help address this problem.

Sexual misconduct by nonpsychiatric physicians and other health care professionals, by contrast, has received considerably less attention until recently. Burgess and Hartman's (1986) *Sexual Exploitation of Patients by Health Professionals* received little attention in contrast to the books about sexual misconduct by therapists and clergy. The case of Dr. John Story, a family practitioner who was criminally convicted of sexual misconduct with female patients in 1988, was the subject of a major book, *DOC: The Rape of the Town of Lovell* (Olsen, 1989) and has been featured on a number of TV shows. There also has been media coverage of local cases in a number of cities, although nothing in the United States has had the impact and visibility of the debate in Canada over the past two years in response to *The Preliminary Report* and *The Final Report* of the Special Task Force on Sexual Abuse of Patients of the College of Physicians and Surgeons of Ontario (1991a, 1991b). Other provincial colleges have undertaken similar studies and are examining the need for change as not only physicians but other regulated health professions examine the problem of sexual misconduct within their own professions. It is my belief that complaints involving physicians in specialties other than psychiatry as well as complaints involving other health care professions will increase throughout the 1990s.

CONCLUSION

What have we learned from this brief recapitulation of the history and evolution of our concern about sexual misconduct by various professional groups? It seems that a certain critical level of visibility is necessary before either the profession itself or the community attempts to intervene in a major fashion to prevent or remedy sexual misconduct with clients. It is also apparent that sexual misconduct by professionals is a very old problem and one that has evaded solution for many centuries. Our history also tells us that ethics codes, discussion, and research alone have failed to significantly change the situation. We have tried "Plan A"—self-regulation in concert with codes of ethics—and it has not solved the problem. Twenty-four centuries is probably long enough to try any one solution. Now it is time for new initiatives.

2

Physician-Patient Sexual Contact

PREVALENCE AND PROBLEMS

Nanette K. Gartrell

Nancy Milliken

William H. Goodson III

Sue Thiemann

Bernard Lo

Whatever houses I may visit, I will come for the benefit of the sick, remaining free of all intentional injustice, of all mischief and in particular of sexual relationships with both female and male persons, be they free or slaves.

"Hippocratic Oath,"
Fourth Century B.C.
(Campbell, 1989, p. 300)

AUTHORS' NOTE: This chapter is adapted from the article of the same title that appeared in *The Western Journal of Medicine* (1992), Vol. 157, pp. 139-143. Reprinted by permission of *The Western Journal of Medicine*.

Sexual contact which occurs concurrent with the physician-patient relationship constitutes sexual misconduct. Sexual or romantic interactions between physicians and patients detract from the goals of the physician-patient relationship, may exploit the vulnerability of the patient, may obscure the physician's objective judgement concerning the patient's health care, and may ultimately be detrimental to the patient's well-being.

American Medical Association Council
on Ethical and Judicial Affairs,
December 4, 1990 (McMurray, 1990, p. 1)

Concern about physician-patient sexual contact dates as far back as the Hippocratic treatise. Most investigations into the prevalence of this problem have focused on psychiatric abuse. Of the psychiatrists responding to anonymous surveys, 5% to 8% have acknowledged sexual involvement with their own patients (Borys, 1988; Gartrell, Herman, Olarte, Feldstein, & Localio, 1986; Gartrell, Herman, Olarte, Localio, & Feldstein, 1988; Hamilton & DeRosis, 1985; Kardener, Fuller, & Mensh, 1973; Len & Fischer, 1978; Perry, 1976). Offending psychiatrists are predominantly male, and the patients are predominantly female. Psychiatrists who later treated such patients reported that the sexual contact was harmful to the patients (Gartrell, Herman, Olarte, Feldstein, & Localio, 1987).

Although the damage done by sexual involvement between patients and physicians who are not psychiatrists also has been well documented (College of Physicians and Surgeons of Ontario, 1991a; Felman-Summers & Jones, 1984; Schoener, Milgrom, Gonsiorek, Leupker, & Conroe, 1989; VanTuinen, McCarthy, & Wolfe, 1991), the prevalence of such contact has never been reliably established. Existing estimates are based on two small, geographically restricted surveys (Kardener et al., 1973; Perry, 1976). To document the current prevalence of physician-patient sexual contact, we surveyed randomly selected national samples of family practitioners, internists, obstetrician-gynecologists, and surgeons. We defined sexual contacts conservatively, excluding spouses, significant others, and sexual partners who later became patients. The survey was designed to address the following questions: How prevalent is physician-patient sexual contact? What are the opinions of physicians regarding sexual contact with patients? How are patients affected by sexual contact with physicians?

METHODS

The 33-item anonymous questionnaire in this study contained 7 items on demographic characteristics, 4 items on respondents' opinions and 2 items on their education concerning physician-patient sexual contact, and 20 items on respondents' personal experiences with their own patients. The questions on personal experience included 4 items regarding patients who had been sexually involved with previous physicians and who were subsequently treated by the respondents. The remainder of the personal experience questions focused on the respondents' sexual contacts with their own patients.

Sexual contact was defined in behavioral terms as physical *contact that arouses or satisfies sexual desire in the patient, physician, or both.* The word *patient* referred to anyone the respondent had ever treated. However, respondents who had treated spouses, significant others, and sexual partners who later became patients were excluded from the pool of those who acknowledged sexual contact with patients. We decided on this exclusion because many physicians believe that treating one's spouse or significant other is not unethical. Therefore our definition was conservative, and we studied only physician-patient sexual contact that began during or after medical treatment.

The study population consisted of 10,000 U.S. physicians (3,000 family practitioners, 2,000 internists, 2,000 obstetrician/gynecologists, and 3,000 surgeons). All surveyed physicians had completed training and were currently practicing clinical medicine.

The questionnaire and a one-page cover letter explaining the procedures for establishing complete confidentiality and anonymity were mailed out in May 1990 to 10,000 physicians. The respondents were asked to return the questionnaire by July 30, 1990. Of the physicians surveyed, 19% (1,891) responded to the deadline. (For additional details about the methodology and statistical analysis, the reader should refer to Gartrell et al., 1992.)

RESULTS

Sexual Contact With Patients

A total of 176 (9%) respondents acknowledged sexual contact with one or more patients. An additional 56 respondents reported that in the most recent case their sexual partners later became their patients; these respondents were not counted as involved physicians even though more than half had sexual contact with multiple patients.

Of the total, 164 male physicians (10% of male respondents) and 12 female physicians (4% of female respondents) acknowledged sexual contact with a total of 332 patients. Of the contacts for which both the physician's and the patient's gender were specified, 89% occurred between male physicians and female patients, 6% between female physicians and male patients, 4% between male physicians and male patients, and 1% between female physicians and female patients.

Involved physicians offered various explanations for their conduct, typically focusing on their own needs or concerns rather than the health and well-being of their patients. For example, a 44-year-old male family practitioner wrote that "she [the patient] viewed the sexual contact with me as therapeutic for me since I was somewhat depressed at the time." Others felt that sexual attraction justified sexual involvement with patients. "We're human also!" said a 40-year-old male family practitioner who had been involved with three female patients. Two male obstetrician-gynecologists wrote that it was difficult for both the physician and the patient not to be aroused in gynecology—"a sexually charged field."

Of the involved physicians, 42% had sexual contact with more than one patient. The largest number of contacts reported by a single physician was 11. When asked about their most recent patient contact, involved physicians indicated that the duration of the sexual involvement ranged from one "sexual encounter" (17%) to "more than 5 years" (15%). However, 62% of those involved with one patient and 58% of those involved with two or more patients reported that the sexual relationship lasted less than 12 months. Of those involved, 72% indicated that the most recent contact involved a current patient, and 28% indicated that the most recent contact was a "former" patient, using their own definitions of *former*. Two physicians who were involved with "former" patients wrote that the sexual contact began within three months of a surgical procedure. Of those whose most recent contact was a "former" patient, 35% had been involved with multiple patients. Finally, 7% sought consultation with a colleague concerning their sexual involvement with the most recent patient.

Respondents' Opinions Concerning Sexual Contact With Patients

Virtually all respondents (94%) opposed sexual contact with current patients. In addition, 37% opposed sexual contact with former patients.

Respondents rejected the use of physician-patient sexual contact to treat sexual dysfunction (97%), to enhance the patient's self-esteem (98%), or to change the patient's sexual orientation (99%). Numerous respondents considered it highly inappropriate for the sexual contact to occur during a consultation. "The physician's genitals have no reason to be uncovered in the work place," stated a 32-year-old female obstetrician-gynecologist. Some respondents described physician-patient sexual contact as a breach of trust. "The physician-patient relationship is based on trust, care, and the patient's best interest. Sexual contact exploits and violates that trust," said a 43-year-old male family practitioner. A 44-year-old male family practitioner made an analogy with incest: "Physician-patient sexual behavior is a form of incest: [It] breaks the trust bond and destroys boundaries." A 60-year-old family practitioner wrote that he learned about the negative effects of physician-patient sexual contact through his own personal experience: "This [relationship] was disturbed; I didn't understand how or to what depth until years later when she [the patient] committed suicide."

Physicians who had been sexually involved with patients were significantly more likely than uninvolved physicians to approve of sexual contact with patients and to oppose regulations prohibiting such contact. Involved physicians were also more likely to approve of sexual contact when the physician "falls in love" with the patient.

Concerning policy recommendations, over 50% of respondents favored state licensing board regulations prohibiting physician-patient sexual contact. "State licensing prohibition would have deterred me [from dating a patient], and I would support it wholeheartedly," said a 40-year-old female family practitioner. "It [physician-patient sexual contact] should be forbidden in state license applications which doctors sign. There are too many temptations and vulnerable people out there for this subject to be closeted the way it has been," commented a 61-year-old male internist.

Medical Treatment of Sexual Partners

Of the survey respondents, 39% considered it professionally acceptable to *become the physician* of a current or former sexual partner. Male respondents (41%) were more likely than female respondents (26%) to consider it acceptable. However, a 32-year-old male family practitioner cautioned, "I feel that it would be very difficult to remain objective in medical treatment with a sexual intimate. Are we not taught the hazards of treating our own family members?"

Patients' Sexual Contacts
With Other Physicians

Of the respondents, 23% had had at least one patient report sexual contact with another physician. A total of 1,085 female and 54 male patients reported such contact. Respondents who were involved sexually with their own patients were more likely than uninvolved respondents to hear from patients about their sexual involvement with other physicians.

When asked about the effect on their patients of sexual contact with other physicians, 63% of respondents (including 38% of involved physicians) indicated that it was "always harmful." No respondent found it "always helpful." Female respondents and respondents who were not sexually involved with their own patients were more likely to assess sexual contact with other physicians as harmful to their patients. A 45-year-old male surgeon commented on the four patients he had seen who had been sexually involved with other physicians: "The patients felt betrayed; however, most were too ashamed to press charges."

Respondents' Education Concerning
Physician-Patient Sexual Contact

Of the respondents, 56% indicated that physician-patient sexual contact had never been addressed during medical school or residency. Only 3% of respondents had participated in a continuing education course that addressed this issue. Some were frustrated about such lack of education. For example, a 42-year-old male family practitioner wrote, "During residency the issue was never addressed. When [as a resident] I fell in love with a patient and refused to continue as her doctor (before any sexual contact), the faculty would not discuss the matter with me." A 35-year-old female family practitioner commented that "there are too many complex issues of power/dependence, sexuality, trust and confidentiality involved in the physician-patient relationship to allow [it] to develop into a romantic relationship. These are issues that medical school didn't address at all!"

Several younger respondents expressed gratitude that their training programs had addressed the issue. "I have been invited to become involved with female patients on 3 or 4 occasions, but medical school training helped me to handle these situations appropriately," wrote a 26-year-old male family practitioner.

COMMENT

Nearly one out of ten physicians responding to this anonymous survey acknowledged sexual contact with their own patients. The prevalence of physician-patient sexual contact among our male respondents is consistent with a previous smaller study (Kardener et al., 1973). This survey's prevalence of sexual contact between female physicians and their patients is higher than previously reported. Only one of the California and New York female physicians surveyed by Perry in 1976 had engaged in erotic contact with a patient.

While our response rate of 19% may limit the generalizability of our findings, inquiring about behavior that might be punishable as felony sexual assault may have diminished our returns. Some respondents commented that no physician living in a state that actively prosecuted physician-patient sexual involvement would ever return such a questionnaire. Other respondents may not have reported sexual involvement with their own patients out of a concern that such information might damage the credibility of the profession. The percentage acknowledging sexual contact with patients might have been higher if the physicians who received questionnaires had felt less inhibited. Even in the unlikely case that none of our nonrespondents had had sexual contact with patients, the prevalence of such contact among all 10,000 physicians surveyed would still be 2%. Furthermore, 23% of respondents reported sexual contact between their patients and other physicians—which suggests that self-reporting may underestimate the true prevalence of this problem.

Sexual contact between physicians and their current patients violates the fiduciary nature of the physician-patient relationship, which requires physicians to act for the benefit of patients who entrust their care to them (Beauchamp & Childress, 1989). When seeking medical care from physicians, patients are vulnerable because of their illnesses and dependent upon their physician's medical expertise. To receive the care they need, patients must provide intimate information in the medical history, undress for a physical examination, and, for surgical procedures, allow their physician to violate bodily integrity. During this process, patients develop feelings of trust and respect for their physicians as well as gratitude for the physician's willingness to listen and ability to heal. Because feelings of trust, dependency, gratitude, and intimacy are inherent in the doctor-patient relationship, patients may find it difficult to decline sexual initiatives from their physicians. Some patients, because of their vulnerability, may interpret their physician's professional caring as personal intimacy and even initiate sexual advances. However, it is the physician's responsibility to prevent the harm that may result from physician-patient sexual contact (Beauchamp & Childress, 1989).

Sexual contact between physicians and their current patients may seriously harm patients (McPhredan, Armstrong, Edney, Marshall, Roach, & Long, 1991). In our study, two thirds of uninvolved physicians whose patients reported sexual contact with other physicians believed that such contact was "always harmful." This belief that sexual contact with physicians can harm patients is supported by the recent Ontario College of Physicians and Surgeons Task Force on Sexual Abuse of Patients (1991a). The task force documented 174 cases of "clear substantive abuse" of patients who were sexually involved with physicians. Many of these patients felt exploited or betrayed when the sexual contact ended. Some reported that they were unable to trust subsequent physicians. Because a sexual relationship may interfere with professional objectivity, a patient who is sexually involved with her or his physician may receive inadequate medical care especially with issues regarding pregnancy, sexually transmitted diseases, or psychological health (Schoener et al., 1989). The task force concluded that these violations of trust in the physician-patient relationship were "devastating for the victim, usually in many aspects of her or his life, for the families affected, for the trust we place in the medical profession and for society as a whole" (College of Physicians and Surgeons, 1991a, p. 10). We concur with the majority of our respondents, the AMA Council on Ethical and Judicial Affairs, and the Ontario College of Physicians and Surgeons that sexual contact between physicians and current patients is unethical.

While almost all respondents in our study condemned sexual contact with current patients, they disagreed about the appropriateness of sexual contact between physicians and former patients. Of the respondents, 63% felt that physician-patient sexual contact was permissible if the treatment had stopped and the patient had been referred to another physician. Some indicated that feelings of trust, dependency, or gratitude do not arise in all patient-physician relationships or may diminish over time. Even though our data do not support the contention that physician-patient sexual contact generally leads to long-term relationships (43% of involved physicians had sexual contact with more than one patient; the majority of physician-patient sexual relationships lasted less than 12 months), several respondents cited personal knowledge of successful long-term relationships between physicians and their former patients. Others felt that doctor-patient relationships should be judged on a case-by-case basis. They suggested that some patients could make autonomous choices to have sexual relationships with former physicians and would be no more likely to be harmed than by any other sexual partners. The remaining 37% of respondents opposed sexual contact with former patients. The AMA Council on Ethical and Judicial Affairs agrees: "Sexual or romantic relationships with former patients are unethical if the physician uses or exploits trust, knowledge, emotions or influence derived from the previous professional relationship" (McMurray, 1990, p. 1). Patients have been documented to be seriously harmed by sexual relationships with previous physicians (College of Physicians and Surgeons, 1991a; Felman-Summers & Jones, 1984). Thus such relationships need to be considered carefully.

The issue is not how inconsequential the physician considered a previous interaction but how significant the patient considered it. A given patient's problem may seem routine or trivial to the physician, but not to the patient. Suppose a physician meets a patient at a social gathering two years after a single clinic visit. The physician may have forgotten the original care, but can one be certain that the patient's dependency and gratitude have been extinguished or that she or he is no longer vulnerable? For many patients, feelings that arise in a therapeutic relationship persist long after the episode of medical care (Schoener et al., 1989). Furthermore, in a brief visit, most physicians are unlikely to have time to determine whether a patient had some special vulnerability, such as a prior history of sexual abuse, which might complicate relationships with authority figures. Thus it may be impossible for physicians to be sure that they are not taking advantage of the prior doctor-patient relationship to gratify their own needs.

To minimize harm to the patient, we suggest that physicians consider two guidelines before becoming sexually involved with former patients. First, the professional relationship must have been terminated without intention of future sexual involvement or a continuing social relationship. By termination, we mean that, in the previous two years, there have been (a) no office visits, (b) no prescriptions written, (c) no telephone consultations, and (d) no return appointment reminder postcards.

We agree with the recommendation of the Ontario College Task Force (1991a) that at least two years must have elapsed since the last episode of patient care, with no social contact in the interim. The key issue is not time but a discontinuous relationship. A dating relationship between a physician and patient that began a month after termination would be inappropriate therefore, even if the involved parties had refrained from consummating it for two years.

Second, the physician and former patient should meet again in a context entirely unrelated to the previous professional encounter. This helps ensure that the former patient is no more likely to be harmed than by any other potential sexual relationship.

It is difficult to be objective during the early phases of a new relationship. Thus both the physician and the patient may wish to discuss the incipient involvement confidentially with an adviser who will provide an honest appraisal of the potential harm to the patient, the physician, and the medical profession. Such counsel is a safeguard for physicians who might be inclined to act only on their impulses. Discussing such an intimate decision with a adviser—even anonymously—may seem intrusive. It may, however, remind physicians that such decisions are not completely private if they undermine public trust in the profession.

An unexpected finding in our study was that many respondents indicated that they treated their spouses, significant others, and former sexual partners. We did not ask whether such treatment involved major medical illness. Although treatment of intimates for major medical problems is not unethical, it is unwise (Bass & Wolfson, 1978). As one respondent stated, "You can't be objective when you are emotionally involved."

Our finding that physician-patient sexual contact had never been addressed during the medical training of more than half of our respondents is disturbing. The need for education on this issue is made evident by the fact that 23% of respondents had encountered patients who had been sexually involved with other physicians. The Ontario College of Physicians and Surgeons' Task Force (1991a) recommends comprehensive training on physician-patient sexual contact. We believe that curricula should include the following topics:

Recognition and management of nontherapeutic emotional responses to patients

Implications of the power dynamics between physicians and patients, women and men

The adverse effects of physician-patient sexual contact

The impact of physician-patient sexual contact on public trust in the medical profession

The legal implications of physician-patient sexual contact (civil and/or criminal statutes)

In conclusion, our study demonstrates that physician-patient sexual contacts occur despite professional ethical prohibitions. The potential for patient harm from such contacts is serious. Physician-patient sexual involvement ultimately affects the credibility of the entire medical profession. We urge medical school, residency programs, and continuing education courses to include teaching about this topic. A substantial educational effort will be required to prevent nearly 10% of the next generation of physicians from compromising patient welfare and public trust in the profession.

3

Is Nothing Sacred?

WHEN SEX INVADES
THE PASTORAL RELATIONSHIP

Marie M. Fortune

A ll clergy and ministers have friendships with parishioners and
clients; all clergy and ministers have experienced sexual attraction
to parishioners and clients; all clergy and ministers have experienced sexual "come-ons" from parishioners and clients; to some extent, all clergy
and ministers have violated the boundaries of our pastoral relationships, if not sexually, then emotionally.

At first reading, these may seem like powerful indictments against
the ministry. Yet to deny these assertions is to fail to comprehend that

AUTHOR'S NOTE: This chapter is reprinted from *Sex and Religion: Religious Issues in Sexological Treatment, Sexological Issues in Pastoral Care*, edited by Jacques H. N. Kerssemakers, proceedings of the first major conference on the relationship between sex and religion, part of the 10th World Congress of Sexology, Amsterdam, The Netherlands, June 20, 1991. Copyright © 1992 by Editions Rodopi B.V., Amsterdam–Atlanta, GA. Reprinted by permission.

these realities are facts of life in the ministry. Our profession, unlike many others, brings us in an ongoing way into some of the most intimate, sacred, and fragile dimensions of others' lives. Paradoxically, it is because of these intimate connections that ministers face the risk of engaging in inappropriate or unethical behavior with those persons whom they serve or supervise.

From the perspective of the institutional church, which carries responsibility for the professional conduct of its clergy, the task is twofold: to maintain the integrity of the pastoral relationship and, in so doing, to protect those persons who are vulnerable to clergy, that is, parishioners, clients, staff members, students, and so on—those who are vulnerable due to a variety of life circumstances.

SCOPE OF THE PROBLEM

Pastoral violation of boundaries involving sexualization of a relationship takes place in the pastoral relationship or the counseling relationship as well as the staff supervisory or mentor relationship. When the pastor sexualizes the pastoral or counseling relationship, it is similar to the violation of the therapeutic relationship by a therapist. When the pastor sexualizes the supervisory or mentor relationship with a staff member or student, it is similar to sexual harassment in the workplace and the principles of workplace harassment apply. When a child or teenager is the object of the sexual contact, the situation is one of pedophilia or child sexual abuse, which is by definition not only unethical and abusive but criminal.

Sexual contact by pastors and pastoral counselors with parishioners/clients undercuts an otherwise effective pastoral relationship and violates the trust necessary in that relationship. It is not the sexual contact per se that is problematic but the fact that the sexual activity takes place within the pastoral relationship. The crossing of this particular boundary is significant because it changes the nature of the relationship, and the potential harm that it causes is enormous.

The behaviors that occur in the sexual violation of boundaries include but are not limited to sexual comments or suggestions (jokes, innuendos, invitations, and so on), touching, fondling, seduction, kissing, intercourse, molestation, rape, and so on. There may be only one incident or a series of incidents or an ongoing intimate relationship over time.

Sexual contact by pastors or pastoral counselors in pastoral, professional relationships is an instance of professional misconduct that is often minimized or ignored. It is not "just an affair," although it may involve an ongoing sexual relationship with a client or parishioner. It is not merely adultery, although adultery may be a consequence if the pastor/counselor or parishioner/client is in a committed relationship. It is not just a momentary lapse of judgment by the pastor. Often it is a recurring pattern of misuse of the pastoral role by a pastor who neither comprehends nor cares about the damaging effects it may have on the parishioner/client.

Actual research on clergy sexual involvement with parishioners is sparse. A recent study, however, provides some data: 12.67% of clergy surveyed reported that they had had sexual intercourse with a church member (United Church of Christ, 1986).

This percentage is statistically equal across denomination, theological orientation, and gender. This figure does not compare favorably with other helping professions. Among clinical psychologists, 5.5% of males and 0.6% of females reported sexual intercourse with clients (Holroyd & Brodsky, 1977). Thus twice as many clergy self-report sexual intercourse with parishioners. In addition, 76.51% of clergy in this study reported that they knew of another minister who had had sexual intercourse with a church member (Blackmon, 1984). But the research that is most needed to give us a clear picture of the extent of this problem is a survey of the laity themselves. Research on sexual harassment in the workplace of the church is also limited. In 1985 the United Church of Christ in the United States asked its clergywomen if they had experienced sexual harassment in the church by senior ministers, supervisors, and so on: 47% responded affirmatively. When laywomen were asked the same question about their secular workplaces, only 20% had been sexually harassed there (United Church of Christ, 1986).

Although the vast majority of pastoral offenders in reported cases are heterosexual males and the vast majority of victims are heterosexual females, it is clear that neither gender nor sexual orientation excludes anyone from the risk of offending (pastors/counselors) or from the possibility of being taken advantage of (parishioners/clients) in the pastoral relationship.

CONSEQUENCES

The psychological effect on a parishioner/client of sexual contact with his or her pastor/counselor is profound. Initially, the person may feel flattered by the special attention that feels positive, and the parishioner/client may even see him- or herself as "consenting" to the activity. Frequently, however, the parishioner/client has sought pastoral care during a time of crisis and is very vulnerable. (It seems very common that persons who are exploited by a minister have some history of childhood sexual abuse, which may or may not have been addressed. Being a survivor of child sexual abuse only increases their vulnerability to further exploitation.) Eventually, the parishioner/client begins to realize that she or he is being denied a much-needed pastoral relationship and begins to feel taken advantage of. Such persons feel betrayed, victimized, confused, embarrassed, fearful, and blame themselves; at this point, they are not likely to discuss this situation with anyone and so remain isolated. When anger finally surfaces, they are then ready to break the silence and take some action on their own behalf and on behalf of others.

Spiritually, the consequences are also profound; the psychological pain is magnified and takes on cosmic proportions. Not only is the parishioner/client betrayed by one representing God but also betrayed by God and the church. For this person, the pastor/counselor is very powerful and can easily manipulate the victim not only psychologically but morally. The result is enormous confusion and guilt: "But he said that love can never be wrong; that God had brought us together." This psychological crisis becomes a crisis of faith as well and the stakes are very high.

AN ETHICAL ANALYSIS

It is a violation of professional ethics for any person in a ministerial role of leadership or pastoral counseling (clergy or lay) to engage in sexual contact or sexualized behavior with a parishioner, client, employee, student, and so on (adult, teen, or child) within the professional (pastoral or supervisory) relationship. Why is it wrong for a pastor to be sexual with someone whom he or she serves or supervises? It is wrong because sexual activity in this context is exploitative and abusive.

It is a violation of role. The pastoral relationship presupposes certain role expectations. The pastor/counselor is expected to make available certain resources, talents, knowledge, and expertise that will serve the best interest of the parishioner, client, staff member, student intern, and so on. Sexual contact is not part of the pastoral, professional role.

It is a misuse of authority and power. The role of pastor/counselor carries with it authority and power and the attendant responsibility to use this power to benefit the people who call upon the pastor/counselor for service. This power can easily be misused, as is the case when a pastor/counselor uses (intentionally or unintentionally) his or her authority to initiate or pursue sexual contact with a parishioner, client, and so on. Even if it is the parishioner who sexualizes the relationship, it is still the pastor/counselor's responsibility to maintain the boundaries of the pastoral relationship and not pursue a sexual relationship. It is taking advantage of vulnerability. The parishioner, client, employee, student intern, and so on is by definition vulnerable to the pastor/counselor; that is, in multiple ways, she or he has fewer resources and less power than the pastor/counselor. When the pastor/counselor takes advantage of this vulnerability to gain sexual access to her or him, the pastor/counselor violates the mandate to protect the vulnerable from harm. The protection of the vulnerable is a practice that derives from the Jewish and Christian traditions of a hospitality code.

It is an absence of meaningful consent. Meaningful consent to sexual activity requires a context of not only choice but mutuality and equality; hence meaningful consent requires the absence of fear or the most subtle coercion. There is always an imbalance of power and thus inequality between the person in the pastoral role and those whom he or she serves or supervises. Even in the relationship between two persons who see themselves as "consenting adults," the difference in role precludes the possibility of meaningful consent.

The summary of an ethical analysis of clergy sexualizing a pastoral relationship is the measure of harm caused by the betrayal of trust that is inherent in each of these four factors. Important boundaries within the pastoral relationship are crossed and, as a result, trust is betrayed. The sexual nature of this boundary violation is significant only in that the sexual context is one of great vulnerability and fragility for most people. However, the essential harm is that of betrayal of trust.

Traditional sexual ethics, whether conservative or liberal, have fallen woefully short in addressing the problem of clergy sexual activity with parishioners, clients, and so on. For conservatives, the issue is always framed in terms of adultery, that is, the pastor being involved in sex outside of marriage. This view of the ethical problem misses the point and is analogous to framing a father's incestuous abuse of his child as adultery. While it is certainly the case that a married pastor who engages in sexual activity with a parishioner is committing adultery, the adultery should be seen as the consequence of the primary ethical problem, which is the professional misconduct and violation of pastoral boundaries. Adultery is an issue and one that causes great pain for the pastor's family; but it is secondary to the harm caused by the pastor in his or her professional role.

Liberals, on the other hand, have hesitated to frame the issue at all. In recent years, some denominations have made a well-motivated effort to limit the church's involvement in a clergy person's personal, sexual life. Here the predominant norms have been "judge not that you not be judged" and "sex is God's gift to be shared with someone you love." Unfortunately, one consequence of this stance has been a laissez-faire sexual ethic, which has meant that the liberal church has had no professional ethic regarding clergy sexual involvement with parishioners, clients, and so on.

In both cases, because the church has approached the reality of clergy sexual involvement with parishioners, clients, and so on as a "sexual" issue, it has been devoid of resources with which to adequately address what is in fact an issue of professional misconduct.

A PROGRESS REPORT

Since 1983 the Center for the Prevention of Sexual and Domestic Violence has been addressing the issue of professional ethics and sexual abuse by clergy. That was the year we received our first call for help from a survivor of clergy sexual abuse. Between 1983 and 1991, we have had some contact with more than 450 cases in the United States and Canada. We have served as advocate, pastor, or consultant with victims, survivors, offenders, judicatory administrators, and lawyers.

In 1986 the first U.S. conference on abuse in helping relationships was held in Minneapolis. There we shared questions and strategies across professional disciplines. The title of the conference was significant: "It's Never O.K." By the end of the conference, we wanted to add a subtitle: "And It's Always Our Responsibility." This is the bottom line—and it's never simple.

In 1989 *Is Nothing Sacred? When Sex Invades the Pastoral Relationship* (Fortune, 1989) was published. This book was the first critical appraisal of the violation of the pastoral relationship that named it an issue of professional ethics and sexual abuse. The discussion of the problem has expanded; disclosures by victims/survivors have increased; lawsuits against churches and denominations have multiplied. A can of worms has been opened that now challenges our religious institutions. A number of denominations at the national and regional levels are moving to develop policy and procedures and they are being faced with an increasing number of complaints. More research projects are under way. More attention is beginning to be focused at the seminary level of theological education on preparing ministers to lessen their risk of violating the integrity of the pastoral relationship.

What Is the Status of These Efforts?

The good news is that some denominational leaders are moving swiftly and carefully to name the problem and to remove offending pastors in order to protect the church from further harm and erosion of credibility. They also are moving effectively to bring healing to victims, survivors, and congregations. The bad news is that others, although often now informed and prepared with policy and procedures, are still not acting to stop offending pastors.

In these situations, it would appear that the doctrine of the church that prevails is that it is the church's mission to

protect the perpetrator from the consequences of his or her behavior,

keep the abusive behavior a secret,

preserve the facade of pleasantry and normalcy in the church,

play the priest and Levite, passing by the injured person by the side of the road, ignoring the victim of sexual abuse or harassment by a pastor.

The best example of this doctrine of the church occurs in cases where a victim of clergy professional misconduct finally sues the church for damages. Frequently the church, at the urging of its lawyers, has sought to settle out of court for significant sums of money *if* the victim(s) agrees to silence, that is, not to discuss the particulars of her or his experience ever again. This church is more interested in secrecy than justice and is willing to pay people off to preserve its public image.

The effect of this doctrine and practice is never healing but is deevangelization: People are leaving or being driven out of the church because of the professional misconduct of some of our clergy and lack of response to parishioners' complaints. For these people, trust in the clergy and the church is forever shattered. The credibility of the church as a community of faith and as an institution is on the line.

There are some in leadership who deny the ability of the church to act in this situation: "We don't really have the authority to act"; "our polity does not provide a means for us to really address this"; and so on.

In 1990, while I was speaking at Luther Northwestern Seminary in St. Paul, the students were commenting on the action that the Evangelical Lutheran Church in America was taking in regard to the ordinations of three openly gay and lesbian pastors in San Francisco. They observed how the church moved with lightning speed and single-minded resolve to prevent these persons from serving as pastors. And their question was this: Why cannot the ELCA seem to move at all to prevent offending pastors (i.e., pastors who regardless of their sexual orientation have violated the pastoral boundaries of their office and sexually abused parishioners or clients) from continuing to serve?

Perhaps it is here that we can begin to discern the church's doctrine of sin: It would seem that it is a greater sin to *be* a gay or lesbian clergy member than to sexually molest, harass, and otherwise abuse those persons with whom a pastor supposedly has a relationship of trust and protection.

Why so little action? Why does it seem to be so difficult for judicatories, those bodies that in many denominations are empowered to act on behalf of the whole church, to act swiftly and unequivocally on behalf of those harmed by offending clergy?

I used to think that the primary reason for the lack of action was ignorance: Church leaders lacked information, analysis, and tools with which to act. So I, of course, assumed that education and training would provide the information, analysis, and tools and then, having girded their loins with truth and having put on the breastplate of righteousness, these church leaders would walk into the breach, name and confront the violations of professional ethics that they encountered, and remove offending pastors from positions of trust.

My assumption that, when prepared, church leaders would be eager to act has not been borne out. In fact, some judicatory administrators who know better continue to circumvent the process or are stymied when an offending pastor flatly denies the charges even in the face of multiple complaints. I have concluded that the primary reason for these occurrences is that, for some, there is little will and less courage.

There certainly are some judicatory administrators and local church leaders with strong commitment and great courage who have acted effectively to put policy in place and to use it to make justice in the church. It is clear that education and preparation have empowered them. But they remain few in number. And they run the risk of being marginalized for their actions.

The lack of will has to do primarily with an unwillingness to challenge the pastoral privilege of sexual access to parishioners, clients, or staff members that seems all too commonplace within a patriarchal church.

The lack of courage has emerged in the face of legal anxieties: Offending pastors are threatening to sue the church for slander, libel, or loss of livelihood. These threats have in many cases halted church proceedings. Yet an offending pastor has no basis on which to win such a suit and has not yet succeeded in doing so in the United States.

Ironically, it is another legal threat that may eventually embolden the church to act. In lieu of any effective action from their church, many victims/survivors are turning to the courts for redress, for justice. People do not want to sue their church, but they will if they find themselves not only mistreated by the church but stonewalled in their attempts to find justice.

Legally, the cost is high. The Roman Catholic Church in the United States expects to spend $1 billion by the year 2000 in settlements for cases of professional misconduct by clergy (Stark, 1989). Recent U.S. case law is unequivocal; the church is responsible for the hiring and supervision of its personnel. If the church credentials its representatives, it must also be accountable for their actions.

Development and consistent implementation of prevention and intervention strategies are fundamental steps toward maintaining the integrity of pastoral relationships. In short, the church has the right and responsibility to remove pastors who are a danger to the well-being of church members and the church as a whole. The cost for *not* acting is enormous—morally, spiritually, and legally.

Theology and Faith

Our theology and our faith are more than adequate to guide our response to an offending pastor. The church is to be a place of sanctuary, a place of hospitality for the vulnerable who seek it out. It is our responsibility to ensure the integrity of pastoral relationships that provide sanctuary and hospitality—not betrayal and collusion in victimization.

God promises vindication to the victimized when they seek justice. God also promises judgment and accountability for harm done to others, not for its own sake but for the sake of repentance and restoration.

God takes sides with the vulnerable—those within our ministerial care—against the powers and principalities, even when the church is the principality. Justice-making is the only means we have to bring about healing and restoration. It is the only context in which words of forgiveness are linked to acts of repentance with some authenticity.

Justice made frees persons to forgive, which makes possible restoration with memory: to forgive and remember. The church can be the vehicle for justice where harm has been done by one of its representatives—not just in theory or on paper but in the concrete reality of people's lives. In this effort, everyone's best interests are served: the victim's, the congregation's, and the offender's.

The progress that I report here is the result primarily of the courage of survivors who have come forward and told their stories. These survivors, far more than judicatory administrators, committee members, or workshop leaders, have broken the silence that has allowed clergy and other ministers to misuse their religious offices for years. They have dared to speak the truth of their experience even, as Audre Lorde (1984) has said, "at the risk of having it bruised or misunderstood" (p. 40).

Survivors of abuse by clergy and other ministers have blessed the church with a gift and deserve the church's gratitude. They have called us back to our mission: "to name and confront the powers of evil within and among us, to work for justice, healing and wholeness of life."

PREVENTION AND INTERVENTION

The response of the church to this significant problem of pastoral, professional misconduct that is creating a crisis of credibility in our churches should focus on prevention and intervention. Prevention involves development of clear policy on this issue, education at all levels of the church, and support for individual self-care for clergy and lay professionals. Intervention is what must be done when prevention fails.

Prevention

An ethics policy. A denomination needs to have a clear, unequivocal policy that states that clergy or lay professional sexual contact with parishioners, clients, and so on is unethical and unacceptable. The language needs to provide enough specifics to be clear about the parameters of the professional conduct. (Within most denominational materials, the only naming of misconduct is an offense defined as "an act or omission contrary to scriptures or the Constitution" or "conduct unbecoming the ministry." This lack of specificity allows for confusion and hesitancy to act. One Presbyterian pastor who had multiple complaints of professional misconduct involving sexual abuse filed against him said: "Where is it written that I cannot do these things?" It was a very effective defense.)

Education and training. Seminarians and all clergy need in-depth training in dealing with boundaries, dual relationships, sexuality, making appropriate referrals, stress, and so on. They also need mechanisms whereby they can seek regular, qualified consultation in the practice of the ministry.

Pastor/counselor self-care. All pastors/counselors need to regularly monitor their attention to self-care both personally and professionally. Guidance from the consultation process can be extremely helpful here.

Prevention can help many pastors minimize the risk they face of crossing the boundaries of the pastoral relationship. It can help prevent pastors from wandering unconsciously across boundaries, which can have devastating consequences. But prevention cannot stop the pastor who is a sexual predator. Only intervention is effective to remove the pastoral sexual predator and prevent others from being harmed.

Intervention

Procedures for effective response. When faced with a complaint of professional misconduct by a clergyperson or lay professional, the denomination must have a procedure in place through which to adjudicate the complaint and possibly take disciplinary action.

To be effective, these procedures must be easily available to church members. They must provide for due process in assessing the validity of the complaint; that is, the procedure must be clear, fair, and carefully followed.

If the complaint is found to be invalid, steps must be taken to restore the minister's credibility.

If the complaint is found to be valid, steps must be taken to

a. discipline the offending pastor;
b. protect and restore victims, including restitution where appropriate;
c. restore the integrity of the ministry;
d. restore the congregation in which the offense(s) occurred, including notification of the membership of the disciplinary action taken;
e. restore the offending pastor to professional health, if possible;

f. ensure that appropriate information regarding the offense(s) accompanies the movement of clergy to other churches.

CONCLUSION

In the face of the continuing revelations of serious cases of pedophilia committed by Roman Catholic priests in the United States and Canada, the resignation of an Evangelical Lutheran Church in America bishop faced with charges of pastoral misconduct involving sexual abuse of parishioners, the resignations of clergy at all levels in every denomination in the United States and Canada, and numerous complaints in every denomination, many ending in lawsuits, there can be no question that the church is in crisis. A secret long hidden has been disclosed and the church faces the challenge to respond in ways that can restore the integrity of the pastoral relationship. If it fails this challenge, its witness to a hurting world will be sorely compromised and it may never recover from this crisis.

PART II

Victims of
Professional Abuse

This section begins with first person accounts by three victims following a brief introduction by Jeanette Milgrom of Walk-In Counseling Center, who has worked with victims of professional abuse as long as anyone. The three first person accounts by Alex Acker, Laurel Lewis, and Melissa Roberts-Henry effectively convey the pain and damage wrought by professional abuse as well as the particular vulnerabilities inherent in receiving professional services. Laurel Lewis transformed her experience into contributions to professional literature. For Melissa Roberts-Henry, the transformation was into activist and lobbyist.

Estelle Disch and Janet Wohlberg discuss innovative responses in the Boston area, including support groups, advocacy, and attempts at legislative change. The organizations they helped start were generally run by and for victims of professional abuse. Despite their impressive efforts, the intransigence of the professional communities in which they reside remains considerable.

My personal reaction to the above contributions is complex. On the one hand, I am impressed at the transformation of pain into such productivity and creativity. On the other hand, I am saddened that it often falls to the victims of professional abuse to educate professionals about professional problems.

Peter Rutter, whose book *Sex in the Forbidden Zone* has been one of the most effective at reaching a broad audience on this topic, offers a meditation on victim experience. He weaves together, in a haunting manner, three figures from ancient, recent-past, and current history to illustrate the ramifications of abuse.

Two chapters, by Signe Nestingen and Walter Bera, focus on psychotherapy with female and male victims, respectively. These experienced psychotherapists make similar points. The treatment of those who have been abused by previous professionals cannot be business as usual. Issues of trust and vulnerability of the patient, maintenance of boundaries, and others not only make such treatment unusually complicated but often call into question the nature and meaning of psychotherapeutic services.

Finally, Ellen Luepker's chapter serves as a reminder to view the effects of professional abuse more systemically. The person directly abused is the most obvious victim. Families and loved ones are also victimized. Luepker offers a rare discussion of how to respond to these other victims, particularly in the context of the treatment of the primary or identified victim.

4

Victims' Experiences

AN INTRODUCTION

Jeanette Hofstee Milgrom

It was my privilege to introduce the victim/survivors and to moderate the panel at the Second International Conference on Sexual Misconduct by Clergy, Psychotherapists and Health Care Professionals. This followed more than 15 years of my working with many, many victims in an advocacy role, assisting them in making choices and connecting with resources within themselves and within the community. They collectively taught me most of what I know about what seemed to be an unthinkable phenomenon: sexual abuse of clients by counselors, therapists, and clergy.

In the past decade or two, much valuable knowledge has been developed by various experts addressing the psychological, legal, administrative, and ethical aspects of sexual misconduct by professionals. The victims/survivors have had a central role in all of this. Their first person accounts, despite certain similarities, are all different, and each experience is unique. This is why we have invited them to share their stories with you. You will find these accounts scattered throughout this volume.

In introducing the victims/survivors who contributed to these proceedings, it is worth noting that they, as well as the original panel members, have been willing and even eager to share their experiences with the general public, with other consumers/victims, and particularly with mental health and human service professionals. As professionals, we may be in the best position (and we have the clearest mandate) to do something about what after all is an iatrogenic injury: unnecessary and preventable harm.

Many victims have learned much in the process of becoming survivors. They have paid dearly, emotionally, financially, by losing years of their lives and in many other ways. Many have survived as stronger, wiser persons. Sharing their testimonials may be helpful to them as yet another step in the healing process. All their pain and struggle were not for naught if others, too, can learn from their experience and thus be in a better position to understand and respond to other victims.

We thank the contributing victims/survivors for their courage, insights, and willingness to help us get a clearer understanding of the common themes, patterns, and effects, as well as the distinct variables and consequences, in each person's experience. We sincerely hope that these individual stories will provide compelling reasons for you, the reader, to make a personal and professional commitment to work toward solutions.

5

Alex's Story

J. Alex Acker

When I was 4 years old, the monster in my life had a short, hairy body, long arms, one eye, and bad breath. It hid under my bed at night and waited to do horrible, terrible things to me. But this monster was imaginary. When I got scared, all I had to do was turn on the light and it was gone.

When I was 22, the monster in my life was 31 years older than I, was good-looking, had sparkling gray eyes, and used Listerine. This monster got into bed with me and did horrible, terrible things. Unlike my childhood imaginary monster, this new monster was very, very real. And no matter how many lights I turn on when I get scared, this monster never goes away.

In the aftermath of sexual exploitation there lies a path of broken dreams, shattered lives, and pain. It's my greatest hope that professional sexual misconduct can be stopped to allow victims and survivors, like me, the chance to recover from our horrible, terrible monsters.

AUTHOR'S NOTE: Alex is a female survivor of the sexual misconduct of a professional.

My own story of sexual exploitation occurred in 1979 in the Midwest, but I need to go back several years to explain how it happened. In 1975 I graduated from high school and went to college. Early into my freshman year I began losing weight, I couldn't sleep, and my grades were so poor I was put on academic probation. I had hoped that college would help me escape from being physically and sexually abused by my father, but my father was replaced by a male student who raped me four months into my freshman year. I went to the university's counseling center because my world was falling apart.

My first appointment turned into four years of therapy, yet, despite all those sessions, when I graduated from the university in 1979, my life was completely out of control. I believed that suicide was the only way I could end the pain of being sexually abused as a child, raped at the age of 18, and sexually exploited at 22.

The therapist who sexually abused me was a prominent figure at the university, had a doctorate in psychology, was the Counseling Center's associate director, and later became the university's associate dean of "student affairs." The therapist who sexually exploited me was also a woman.

Growing up I believed that women were caregivers and nurturers, while men—like my father—raped and abused. This mistaken belief only contributed to my fears and feelings of isolation, agony, and shame. I feared people would say that I led this therapist on and that I was responsible. But my biggest fear of all was that people would dismiss my pain and label the abuse a gay issue.

Although I've learned that sexual exploitation is not an issue of sexual preference, I still wonder sometimes if I could've prevented the abuse if I hadn't told Dr. Jeanne I was gay. She knew what my weaknesses were and where I was most vulnerable; she knew I had problems establishing boundaries and that I had difficulty saying no; but despite knowing about the abuse in my past, she turned around and abused me too!

This may be difficult for society to believe, but women do sexually exploit other women.

The first time Jeanne was intimate with me I was shocked, but then I never expected to be seduced by my female therapist. I was so confused and frightened. Though I had no other therapy to compare this with, I sensed I was in trouble. I wanted to flee, but how could I run away from my therapist, counselor, confidant, and friend? I trusted her and I believed she wouldn't hurt me.

During the four months that Jeanne was sexual with me, I was elated and depressed; I was emotionally pumped and physically drained; I loved her and hated myself; I saw her as the saint and saw myself as the sinner; I wanted it to continue and I prayed for it to stop.

When Jeanne abruptly ended our relationship and refused to see me, I was stunned. It was so devastating to think that the person who knew me the most suddenly didn't want me anymore. I felt so rejected and destroyed that I ran away from the world.

I had no dreams, I felt used, and I was severely depressed. With a college diploma in my hand and a hole in my heart, I moved back home and spent my days and nights locked in the safety of my room. My mother tried to find out what happened but I wouldn't talk about it. She encouraged me to see a psychiatrist but the thought made me retreat further into my despair. With so much pain, I simply wanted to die.

It took me several years before I found the courage to go back into therapy. In 1989, with the help of a wonderful therapist, I began working on the repercussions of being sexually exploited. Though the list of repercussions is a long one, I'd like to share a few of them with you.

It's been difficult for me to break the vow of silence regarding the abuse. Jeanne warned me not to tell anyone about our relationship. She said it would mean "professional suicide" for her. Like my father and the incest, Jeanne made me responsible for keeping the abuse a secret.

I'm working on self-esteem and self-confidence issues. The low opinion I have of myself is built on a foundation of incest, reinforced by the rape, and complicated by the sexual exploitation.

I live with the fear that my reluctance to take action against Jeanne has left other students open to similar abuse. I was not the only one sexually exploited by Jeanne. She sexually abused a female client the year before me.

I have a horrendous time with relationships because I fear I will be abused again. Consequently, I've had a trail of broken relationships, which has given people the impression that I'm anything but respectable. I am fortunate now, however, to have a devoted partner in my life who supports me in dealing with this horrible, terrible monster.

I also have a major issue when it comes to trusting people. In fact, this is probably the greatest issue I've had to deal with. It's so difficult for me to trust men and women in positions of authority. This lack of trust may be painful for caring, respectful professionals to hear about, but it's an unfortunate consequence of sexual misconduct.

In 1990 I filed a formal complaint with the Department of Regulation and Licensing in the state where the sexual exploitation occurred. Though I was told that my complaint warranted an investigation, the Licensing Board could not take action against Jeanne because she did not hold a license issued by the Psychology Board in that state. The response left me angry and doubtful that justice would prevail.

Several weeks after I received the board's letter, my college alumni newsletter arrived in the mail. A photo of Jeanne caught my attention and the accompanying headline announced, "Associate Dean's Career Focused on Students' Growth." Though I was relieved to learn that she had resigned from the university, I was also distressed to learn that Jeanne was doing volunteer work with sex offenders.

There's no greater plea I can make than to ask clergy, psychotherapists, and health care professionals to respect our rights and boundaries as clients. Clients, like me, come to your office looking for sanity, not sex. The threads of our lives are already mangled and crushed by the time we seek your help. Don't add to our already chaotic lives the devastation and destruction of sexual exploitation.

As a professional in your field, you can let your colleagues guilty of sexual misconduct know that their behavior is a horrible, terrible crime against us all. But more than anything, give your clients a safe place to grow and experience life without fear. And when the battle with our monsters is over, and we've succeeded, share in our joyful celebration— but leave the kiss of victory to our loved ones.

WHERE AM I NOW?

Thanks to the hard work of a therapist who adheres to professional ethics, I can stand up for myself and say, "I don't have to be a victim anymore." It's also been a boost in my recovery from sexual exploitation to have participated in the conference on which this chapter was based. I hope to do more work in preventing professional sexual misconduct, incest, and rape.

6

Growing Beyond Abuse

Laurel Lewis

The effects of sexual exploitation are worse than a middle ear infection that takes a very long time to heal and that leaves scar tissue that never heals. It is more difficult than having 30 shock treatments decreed by a Turkish intern when one is only 17 years and under the auspices of alcoholic and abusive parents. Recovery from sexual exploitation is harder than recovery from 17 years of substance abuse. Sexual exploitation is more painful than being the last person your friend talks to before she jumps off the Windsor Bridge. Those were just a few of the issues I took to the therapist/clergyman many years ago.

From the onset of therapy, my perpetrator convinced me that he would teach me God's love through a fatherly love. He would reparent me. He told me no one would ever hurt me, not over his dead body. After all, he was a master of therapeutic techniques. I felt as if life's joys and hopes were being presented to me on a silver platter. I was very grateful then for any help in my life, because I was lost and confused.

The abuse began when he thrust his groin into me while giving me a hug at the end of one of the first few sessions. Therapy moved to sitting on pillows on the floor. Next we were lying on the floor. The abuse progressed; he wrapped his leg around my body when he had an erection and began sexually nudging me while I told of my terror during childhood when my father beat my mother. The grand finale to all this abuse occurred when he tried to ram his hand up my vagina.

Why didn't I get out earlier? How did I get out? Where did I find the strength to escape this abuse? The answers are not so difficult today because I am growing beyond abuse. Growing beyond abuse means not focusing on why I did not leave this abusive man earlier. I did leave and I got away. I had a great deal of help. There was a wonderful Episcopal priest who fed me when I didn't want to eat any more. Five days before I left my home for good, she supported me by being a witness when I confronted my perpetrator about the abuse. This priest did more than I could ever repay. In my depressed state, she made me promise I would live three more years instead of killing myself. I moved to another state. She talked to me on the phone for months and months. During that time I was a recipient of welfare and in a transitional home for women. She was the only person I trusted in a world in which I was unable to function. I had lost the ability to trust my own self. I believed I was the cause of the abuse.

For almost two years, I had nightmares that prevented me from sleeping. I had a recurring dream where I found myself in a basement with three bins in front of me. Each bin was the size of an industrial trash collection bin and each contained plastic brackets with metal screws. The plastic pieces were to be attached to the other plastic pieces found in the remaining two bins. There was no one in my dream to tell me which way to put the pieces together or their purpose. All I knew was that I could not leave until the tens of thousands of brackets and screws were fitted together. I would cry, dreaming, until I awakened, and once I awoke I would cry for hours. One time I cried for 13 hours.

For more months than I can recall, there was no light at the end of this tunnel. No spiritual hope was inside. The levels of hopelessness and distrust I felt strangled my once resilient self. After I left the town with the Episcopal priest, there was one person who seemed to move into my tiny trust dot. She was a nurse from a crisis home program. She also saved my life. As I broke down emotionally, I began to believe that, because I was 33 years of age and Jesus was crucified then, there was some greater meaning to all of this. She told me that the records about Christ being 33 when crucified were wrong, that the actual chronological age was more like 38 years. I was so suggestible and I believed her. My reason for dying fell through the cracks. That nurse was a support

person for me for many months. She also told me not to let my perpetrator win by my suicide. Somehow I was able to hear this most
important data and take it into careful consideration.

In many ways this event and much distance from the perpetrator
helped me build the inner strength to try to prevent this perpetrator
from abusing anyone else. With great assistance from those at Walk-In
Counseling Center who acted as advocates, I wrote to licensure boards.
A very kind and ethical lawyer agreed to take my case pro bono. He and
another lawyer helped guide me to an out-of-court agreement that provided me with a few years of rest and therapy.

After many painful starts with other professionals, I began to work
with a professional psychologist. It took me at least 15 months to talk
about the abuse in some coherent way. I was so very brainwashed that
I could not see that the responsibility was not mine. Her patience is
remarkable. My eye contact with her is minimal. My perpetrator had
insisted I always look into his eyes. My therapist does not insist that I
look at her all the time. My therapist does not tell me that I am so special.
She is unlike the perpetrator. She does not tell me my fears are problems
with intimacy that can be overcome by having therapy on the floor. I
pay like everyone else and my rate does not change. She never tells me
that she will teach me God's love in a therapeutic session. I go to spiritual
direction with someone else. It is separate from therapy. I have healed
a great deal in this professional therapeutic relationship. Now after all
these years of recovering from sexual exploitation I am finally working
on the issues I first took to therapy.

For many months I was unable to find a survivor's perspective on
healing from the sexual exploitation of a therapist or clergy person. With
the moneys awarded I discovered that healing from childhood sexual
abuse and healing from sexual exploitation have many parallels. After
going to a group for incest survivors for additional support, I began to
write down some of these parallels in a set of meditations. Out of those
meditations, and with the help of my coauthor (and *not* my therapist),
a psychologist, Signe Nestingen, we created the workbook *Growing
Beyond Abuse: A Workbook for Survivors of Sexual Exploitation or Childhood
Sexual Abuse*. Writing this book and accepting support helped me to
explore the victim within and to transform myself into a survivor of
sexual exploitation. *Growing Beyond Abuse* is the place I stored those tools
from my journey through a darkness that seemed for a time to have no
end in sight. My story to heal both spiritually and emotionally is woven
into *Growing Beyond Abuse*.

7

Making the Leap

A PERSONAL STORY OF MOVING
FROM VICTIM/SURVIVOR TO "ACTIVITYIST"

Melissa Roberts-Henry

" This courtroom is a circus, I am the ringmaster and all I need is a whip to bring this lying bitch to order." This statement was made by defense attorney Alton Maddox in a New York court case (News Services, 1990), but it may as well have been said at mine. And what is the whip they use? The whip is the unbelievable detailed, humiliating, and irrelevant questions that a victim is asked about her sexual history in Colorado civil courts. These questions are not used to gather information that has anything to do with the case. These questions (on sexual history of a victim) are used to distract from the real issue at hand; that someone in a position of trust and power violated their professional ethics. These questions, I believe, are also used for terrorizing and intimidating victims. They are used to push victims over the edge; they are used to try to get victims to drop their suits. Because in Colorado civil courts, defendants are innocent till proven guilty, but victims are treated as guilty from the word go.

Those words formed the opening statement of my 1991 testimony to the Colorado State Legislature. They helped promote the passage of a "rape shield" bill to protect the sexual history of abuse victims in Colorado civil court cases, where the perpetrator was someone in a position of authority or trust. This was a bill that I initiated, cowrote, and lobbied for.

On a personal level, doing legislation, along with taping a PBS documentary ("My Doctor, My Lover"), marked, perhaps, an equally important passage—that of moving from viewing the issue of abuse by a therapist as "my trauma" to regarding it as a social and political issue.

Why did I select legislation as the vehicle to promote change? Despite a "victory" in civil court, I could not protect the public from my perpetrator. He was allowed to keep practicing. However, I decided this did not preclude me from doing something to protect the public in general. The media did not seem a consistent avenue for doing so; results were dependent on whether an individual reporter understood this issue or not. Furthermore, in speaking with the media, at times I was still subjected to falsehoods. In trial, the "defense" created a picture of my sexual history that was not true, but it became part of public record. Because I was so vocal, the defense continued to slander me to the media and even at a legislative hearing, long after the trial. An American Psychiatric Association publication (Robinowitz, 1992) slandered both my family and me this way and perpetrated lies. Thus the media does remain one avenue of change, and I continue to speak with them sporadically because it is sometimes positive and affirming, but at times it takes a heavy personal toll and impedes the healing process. Legislation seemed a less personal and equally far-reaching means of educating and protecting.

Why did I select a "rape shield" bill? Because few people report abuse by therapists, I didn't want to see those who did undergo further trauma. I was sick of seeing past sexual conduct used as a diversionary tactic to make this abuse look like a relationship. It is, as everyone well knows, *abuse.* Moreover, the perpetrators are the repeat offenders, not the victims. It made no sense that their backgrounds were protected while ours weren't.

At the beginning, I didn't know that I could do legislation. I was still suffering from fear of authority figures, had posttraumatic stress disorder, and, at times, couldn't leave my house. Also, I had never been in the state capitol! The thing is, I didn't know that I could do this—but I didn't know that I couldn't either. It felt important—so I just started—one step at a time.

But it took many steps and tools through the healing process to reach the point of doing legislation. So I'd like to backtrack and highlight my evolution from victim to "activityist." A brief story helps to illustrate one major tool that I drew upon.

Last April, to be stylish, I put on a black outfit and a big shaggy black coat. In a store mirror, at eye level, the outfit looked sophisticated; so I thought until I felt a tug on the bottom of my coat. That moment, I glimpsed down to hear a tiny little girl's voice ring out: "Mommy/ daddy, what kind of dog is this?"

The point of the story is that it all depends on the angle from which one sees things: perspective. Perspective, trying to see things from a different and better angle, this is one tool I used (still use) to move through the trauma of my abuse by a therapist. My passage from one phase of healing to another was marked by sharp shifts in perspective. I have constantly reevaluated and reached for a perspective to help me pull forward and move on to the next stage.

For me, there were four stages to healing. I labeled them (a) Staying Alive, (b) Starting to Value Life Again, (c) Getting a Life, and (d) Making Life Significant. Prior to Stage 1, my own abuse had included a tremendous amount of verbal manipulation and then sexual contact. It rendered me isolated from my support systems and solely dependent on my abuser. When I finally filed a lawsuit and reported him, it felt like an enormous loss. At that point, I was barely functional, afraid of people, scared to leave my house, and at times unable to move. So Stage 1 was very basic and was marked by taking one minute at a time. To get myself through, I made lists.

I made a list of bad things my abuser had done to me. Thus every time I felt like reconnecting with him or dropping the lawsuit, I could look at the list and see, for example, "that he had threatened my life." This quickly drew me back to the reality of the situation. Then I made a list of diversionary activities for those times when the emotional pain was so overwhelming that I couldn't stand it. My activities included mindless but busy-type things like vacuuming, watching videos; things where I could control my external stimuli.

Throughout Stage 1, my perspective was/had to be that it was not a waste of time to sit around and heal and that a lot of isolation was necessary to reestablish my boundaries.

With time, my perspective shifted to Stage 2, Learning That I Deserved to Be Alive and Starting to Value Life Again. Stage 2 involved moving out of isolation and being with other survivors. In Stage 2, I co-founded I.M.P.A.C.T. (In Motion—People Abused in Counselling and Therapy), a support network for victims/survivors. It was easy to listen to others and see that they didn't deserve their abuse. As I identified with them, I recognized that I didn't deserve the abuse either. I learned to translate my compassion for other survivors into compassion for and being gentle with myself. I also learned that it was OK to be angry at my abuser. I tried to combine anger with humor. I bought a mug with his name on it, my spit cup, and whenever I felt anger at him, I would spit in it.

Along with focusing on people throughout Stage 2, I developed a mental game to remove so much focus from my trauma and see that it was not all-significant in the scope of the universe (though it still felt that way). For instance, I would look at a tree, try to imagine myself in the day and life of that tree, and see that my trauma was nothing in the world of a tree. I thought of others who had had different traumas that I knew nothing of and tried to picture their stories. I started to tell mine. During Stage 2, I began to speak to the media anonymously and in a general way, as I was still in litigation.

The downside of Stage 2 was that all of my nonlitigation energy was devoted to I.M.P.A.C.T. and to speaking out. At this point, the perspective of Stage 3 evolved, thanks to Nita Benetin, a survivor/friend and now an attorney working on this issue. Nita used to call and shout into my answering machine, "Get a Life!" Therefore Stage 3, called Getting a Life, involved adding balance to my life, making a conscious effort to have some fun, and realizing that I could not continue to heal or work on this issue if it was the sum total of my life.

Finally, I was ready for Stage 4, Making Life Significant, doing something meaningful, positive, and lasting with the wisdom I gained through an awful experience. I chose to give up my paid job as a geologist and participate in the *Frontline* documentary "My Doctor, My Lover." I also ran and funded I.M.P.A.C.T. *And* I did the "rape shield" bill as a daily, unsalaried job. Many steps went into doing the legislation and many benefits accrued. Some of these were of a personal nature:

1. Doing legislation allowed me, in a very symbolic way, to separate myself from my abuser and those who do wrong, and to surround myself with people who are working to promote positive change.

2. I had some sense of control of the process, was delegated much responsibility, and was able to function as a professional working on the abuse
issue.
3. It helped me to overcome some of my trauma-induced fears, particularly
in that I was working with "authority figures" on a daily basis.
4. Ironically and unexpectedly, I got to stand up against the defense attorneys from my court case, as they showed up before a legislative panel to
testify against the bill I initiated. It put me on equal ground.

There are many more things I could add, but I will conclude with
something I wrote in July 1987:

Between Fear and Life

I am an emotional
basket case. A zombie.
I am paralyzed with fear.
Paralyzed totally. Immobile.
Unmoving. Lying in bed
days at a time.
Mentally dying. Emotionally atrophying.
Then I remember
if I can only act
I can be free. . . . I
can live again.

from Roberts-Henry, 1987

Victims need time to heal. But we can heal and go beyond that. One
way is by speaking out. I believe that if you are not paralyzed—and just
start doing—your achievements can exceed your greatest dreams. For
me, the "rape shield" bill is proof.

But why "speak out"? To protect other people, as much as you can.
To say it is not OK when someone harms you. To separate oneself from
those who abuse and do wrong. To build or find inner strengths. To
regain respect as a professional and to regain self-respect. An individual
who speaks out can make a difference and heal too. And so the point is
this: *Do speak out*. Speak out without expectations but with goals. Speak
out and say I may not succeed, but I am trying. Speak out and say I may
not succeed but then again I just might.

8

The Boston Experience

RESPONDING TO
SEXUAL ABUSE BY PROFESSIONALS

Estelle Disch

Janet W. Wohlberg

Our goal in this chapter is to describe the work of some of the many concerned and committed people in Massachusetts who provide clinical, legal, and support services for victims, who educate the public, who sensitize and train professionals, and who work on trying to deter abuse by professionals through legislative and legal action. We report on the work of BASTA! and TELL, two of the major players in the "Boston Experience." In doing so, we have shared our individual perspectives as founders and active participants in this movement. The first part is

AUTHORS' NOTE: We would like to thank Nancy Avery for helpful feedback on this chapter.

from the viewpoint of a professional (and was written by Estelle Disch);
the second part is from the viewpoint of a victim (and was written by
Janet Wohlberg).

BASTA! BOSTON ASSOCIATES
TO STOP TREATMENT ABUSE

In early 1984 I co-led the first Boston-area one-day workshop for
women survivors of sexual abuse by psychotherapists. For five years I
led or co-led one or two workshops a year and received about 20 inquiries
a year. During that time I was working at a feminist therapy center and
ran the workshops there. I also held a follow-up session following each
of the first three workshops, welcoming anyone who had attended any
prior workshop. At the second follow-up session, a group of survivors
decided to establish an unled, open support group. This group met
monthly for about a year and a half, starting in the winter of 1985. It
provided a place where survivors could talk about complaints they had
filed, share advice, mull over decisions about whether to file complaints, share information, and receive support. In addition to the initial
members and others I referred to the group, women found the group
by word of mouth. The support group ended after several people finished
their legal cases and decided to stop attending, leaving the group too
small to be viable (Disch, 1989d).

During those first five years, I was essentially working on my own
with helpful supervision and occasional input from other professionals.
I met Nanette Gartrell early on and learned about her research project
(Gartrell, Herman, Olarte, Feldstein, & Localio, 1986). Nanette and I
visited Minneapolis in 1985 and learned invaluable information from
Gary Schoener and Jeanette Milgrom at the Walk-In Counseling Center;
from Ellen Luepker, who was running groups for victims; and from
Barbara Sanderson, who had chaired the task force that successfully
established criminal and civil legislation in Minnesota. Clinicians in the
Boston area who were beginning to write about this issue were not
providing services to victims beyond individual treatment (Apfel &
Simon, 1986; Burgess & Hartman, 1986; Gartrell et al., 1986; Grunebaum,
1986), and it wasn't until 1988 that I learned of another clinician in the
Boston area, Nancy Avery, who was starting a group for victims.

In early 1989 a series of prominent newspaper articles about sexually
abusive psychotherapists and physicians in the Boston area permanently

changed how the Boston health community would treat this issue (see Bass, 1989; Bass & Foreman, 1989, among many articles). Hundreds of victims of sexually abusive treatment who had been suffering alone saw the names of courageous victims in the newspaper and began to realize that what happened to them was wrong, that there was help available, and that there were avenues of recourse. I began receiving dozens of calls each week from victims in need of validation, support, information, referrals, and legal advice. I also received frequent calls from journalists and concerned professionals.

After a few months of handling as many as a dozen phone calls a day, I met with Nancy Avery and we decided to form BASTA!, that is, Boston Associates to Stop Therapy Abuse. (The word *basta* means "no more!" or "enough!" in Spanish and Italian.) Since that time, Nancy Avery and I have had telephone contact with about 500 victims and have provided a range of services including one-day workshops (Disch, 1989d); 12-session groups based on a model developed by Ellen Luepker (Luepker, 1989b); advocacy and support for victims regarding complaint options and procedures; consultation to both male and female individual clients and groups of clients troubled by the same practitioner; consultation to professionals regarding questionable or unethical treatment; referrals to support groups, other victims, lawyers, and psychotherapists in many parts of the United States and Canada; psychotherapy; training for professionals; and publication of educational materials (Disch, 1989a, 1989b, 1989c, 1989d, 1991, 1992a, 1992b, 1992c). In 1991 we changed our name to Boston Associates to Stop Treatment Abuse to reflect the increasing number of complaints we were learning about from people who had been sexually exploited in medical treatment.

From the start, BASTA! has been committed to supporting victims to address their abusive experiences on three levels: self-awareness and education, group support, and taking some sort of action. We encourage clients to read about this issue and to talk about what happened to them, with the goal of understanding the full impact of the experience. We strongly encourage people to meet with others who have been through similar experiences as they are ready to do so, either via our groups and workshops or by attending TELL, the Boston support group for women victims described in the second part of this chapter. And we encourage victims to find some sense of empowerment in response to what has happened, by finding their voices (telling friends, confronting the offender, or going public via press, TV, radio), by taking action in response to the unethical treatment (via complaint procedures or legal avenues), or by getting publicly or politically involved by educating the public or lobbying for or against various pieces of legislation. We often meet with victims on a consultation basis, helping them to review their options, to choose the ones that feel right, and to pursue those options. We will take on an advocacy role if asked, coaching people to keep going when they get confused or lose energy for what they have chosen. From the beginning, BASTA! has been committed to providing afford- able services to participants in our workshops and groups. We also provide our educational materials free to those who cannot afford to pay for them.

We ourselves, when not working directly with victims, have taken our own advice to heart and gotten involved in this issue in various ways. We do supervision with each other to look at challenging clinical issues and to support each other in this painful, enraging work. We work with other professionals by providing in-service and other train- ing sessions, by participating in discussion groups, and by making presentations at conferences. We are politically involved with the leg- islative process in Massachusetts through active participation on a legislative task force and have signed various amicus briefs both in Massachusetts and in other states. And we have allowed our educa- tional pamphlets to be freely duplicated for use by victims and profes- sionals.

Because our workshop and group models have been described else- where, I will summarize and discuss here how we use two of our most helpful educational publications, *Is There Something Wrong or Question- able in Your Treatment?* and *Are You in Trouble With a Client?* I will then summarize briefly our other publications, whose use is self-explanatory.

Is There Something Wrong or Questionable in Your Treatment?

This checklist was designed to help clients figure out what went wrong in a prior treatment or what might be troubling them in a current one. Each item is either questionable or clearly unethical. Each is some- thing that one or more clients has defined as troublesome. The list has evolved as a result of feedback from both professionals and clients. Often we mail this to clients in advance of an initial consultation to help the client begin to think about a range of boundary issues and to help us to quickly get a sense of what went wrong.

If we believe the issues raised by the client are primarily related to transference, mild empathic failures, or misunderstandings, we suggest that the client attempt to talk things out with the therapist to see if they can reach a workable resolution and continue the treatment, in cases where the client would prefer to handle things on his or her own. If the client is very distressed and feels afraid to address the issues alone, we suggest a consultation with a third party (ourselves or someone else). If we believe the issues the client presents are reflective of major ethical breaches, we routinely suggest that the client either stop treatment immediately or initiate a termination process (e.g., in cases where sexual activity has begun). Occasionally we offer to consult to the therapist, if the client believes it would be useful, to help the therapist be more clear about boundaries for that particular client. We have consulted to many therapists who have inadvertently minimized the effects of a prior abusive treatment on the client.

The 158 items on the current version of the *Questionable* checklist are organized into the following 10 (somewhat overlapping) categories.

1. *Business practices.* This category includes such items as billing insurance for sessions that didn't occur; keeping the client waiting for long periods of time; seeing the client when no one else is around; taking phone calls during sessions; absence of a clear contract as to how long sessions will last; going out to eat during the session if the practitioner is hungry; and unclear fee arrangements, including buildup of large debts, vague barter arrangements, or abrupt, large increases in fees.

2. *Dependency, isolation, and goal derailment.* This category includes such items as encouraging the client's estrangement from family, partner, friends, and sources of support for no apparent reason or for reasons that don't seem legitimate; encouraging frequent contact with the practitioner, even when the client doesn't feel a need for such frequent contact; discouraging the client from pursuing career goals (e.g., to drop out of school, to not go to graduate school, to not take a wanted promotion); encouraging the client to follow the same spiritual or personal growth path that the practitioner has followed; telling the client how to dress or wear his or her hair; telling the client not to discuss the treatment with anyone; setting him- or herself up as the only person who really understands the client, the only one who really cares, and the only one who knows what is really good for the client.

3. *Social contact.* This category includes intentional social contact outside the treatment—parties, eating out, involvement with each other's families, using drugs or alcohol together, and so on, as well as inadvertent social contact that is not discussed as a treatment

issue (e.g., seeing each other at 12-step meetings, sports events, health spas, retreats, mutual friends' homes, conferences).

4. *Feeling special.* This category includes behavior by the practitioner that leads the client to believe that she or he is somehow better than other clients, such as telling the client about other clients, giving the client gifts, asserting how special the client is, and so on.

5. *Cult themes.* This category includes items that suggest that the therapist is part of a cult or cultlike community, of which clients are a part.

6. *Mind control.* This category includes such items as hypnotic processes in which the client hasn't consciously given consent, being programmed for suicide (e.g., practitioner suggested in one way or another that the client kill him- or herself), undermining client's strengths, and exploiting excessive dependency.

7. *Treatment process.* This is the most extensive category, covering issues such as role reversal; excessive self-disclosure for reasons unrelated to the client's growth; deciding what is best for the client without consulting the client; uncaring affect such as being cold, rigid, insulting, hostile, sadistic, excessively distant, or explosively angry; the practitioner's refusal to take responsibility for how his or her behavior might have affected the client (e.g., inappropriately interpreting everything as transference); inability to see the seriousness of prior abusive treatment; pushing his or her own agenda on the client; refusal to discuss the treatment process; refusal to discuss credentials or misrepresenting credentials or other qualifications; use of drugs or alcohol during sessions; encouraging clients with addiction histories to use drugs or alcohol; failure to offer the client a termination process; failure to offer a referral when appropriate; breach of confidentiality; and failure to explain the limits of confidentiality.

8. *Dual roles.* This category mentions various kinds of roles the practitioner might hold in addition to his or her role as a practitioner, such as teacher, lover, dissertation adviser, employer, supervisor, relative, friend, colleague, or clergy member.

9. *Sexual activity.* This category includes both overt physical sexual activity and sexualized verbal or physical behavior (e.g., seductive words or body language).

10. *Body work, health care, and so on involving physical contact.* This category includes physically hurtful or subtly sexualized touch, uncomfortable touch unrelated to the presenting problem, non-

negotiated touch that feels invasive to the client, treatment procedures that the practitioner has not discussed and carefully explained to the client, and leaving the client nude more than necessary.

Are You in Trouble With a Client?

This is another checklist, the purpose of which is to alert professionals to boundary issues that might be interfering with their ability to work effectively with clients. The current version has 52 items that address powerful feelings of the practitioner toward the client, overlapping social or professional networks, lack of boundaries around session structure and fees, role reversal, dual roles, and so on. The list has been published in a body work journal (Benjamin, 1992) and was distributed to all Massachusetts acupuncturists with their 1993 license renewal applications. It is especially helpful in supervision and training. We have found that the list easily stimulates discussion among professionals willing to address the complexity of boundary issues. Clients also find this list helpful when asked to imagine what might have been going on in the practitioner's mind.

After Sexual Malpractice: What Can You Do?

This is the title of a list of suggestions of what victims can do after a sexual or sexualized treatment relationship. It is also applicable to other forms of malpractice or unethical treatment. It includes a wide range of possible actions including reading, talking with trusted others, meeting with other victims, filing complaints and lawsuits, and going public in other ways. We send it to clients on request and usually ask new clients to read it before an initial consultation so that we don't have to spend time sharing information that the client can read on his or her own.

Client Rights and Therapist Obligations

This is a list of BASTA's ethical principles written in a comprehensible style. We address issues of boundaries, competence, confidentiality, and limits to confidentiality, including supervision. We name the organizations to which we belong that have ethics codes and grievance procedures. We also describe our philosophy of treatment, naming issues in the social order (sexism, elitism, racism, homophobia, and so on) that may affect our own and our clients' lives. We send or give this to new clients.

The Aftermath of Sexual Abuse
by a Health or Mental Health Professional

The article with this title defines sexual abuse by professionals and then presents the wide range of negative effects victims often experience, based on both the experience we have had with clients at BASTA! and on the experience of others in the field (Pope, 1988; Schoener & Milgrom, 1989). This article serves as an introduction to the issues and provides a short bibliography. This is mailed on request and frequently sent out before an initial consultation.

After Sexual Malpractice and When
There Seem to Be No Resources in Your Area

This leaflet makes suggestions regarding what people can do if they live in an area with no support groups and where they do not know any other victims. It includes suggestions for finding an alternative support group, for finding a therapist who might be willing to run a group, for starting one's own group, finding library resources, and so on.

If You Are Thinking of Providing These Services

Clinicians thinking of providing services like those offered by BASTA! can expect to encounter wonderful, courageous clients, many of whom are in deep pain. We recommend the following to anyone choosing to do this work:

1. Team up. Find one or more supportive colleagues with whom to work and do supervision, making sure the boundaries between and among you are as clean and clear as possible before embarking on this work. Line up backup supervision for those situations where your primary supervision is not viable (e.g., you discover that a colleague is treating your close friend's partner).
2. Prepare to learn a lot of painful and enraging information.
3. Learn the ethical and legal responsibilities that accompany what you learn from clients. In some states, various types of mandatory reporting laws affect situations in which you learn the name of the alleged offender. In some professional associations, there are ethical principles that require the reporting of unethical colleagues. The latter ethical principle is often in conflict with the principle of confidentiality so it is helpful to prepare yourself emotionally for

this conflict and begin to decide how you might handle it before you start this work. In my case, I learned early on (the hard way) that I needed to try to protect other clients from unethical or questionable therapists. At that point, I started telling clients that I didn't want to know the name of the therapist unless I could feel free to say to others something like, "I don't refer to that person," or "I have reason to believe that you should work with someone else." I protect client confidentiality in those cases by saying only that much, never giving details about what I know. I cannot emphasize strongly enough how stressful the burden of confidentiality can be in this work. At one point, after learning the names of a couple hundred therapists whom I believed had behaved either criminally or badly, I began to feel very burdened. Relief came, sadly enough, when I realized that the world is full of perpetrators and I just happen to know the names of a couple hundred of them.

4. Study the field, especially regarding treatment issues, complaint procedures, and legal issues before embarking on offering advice to clients. Attend trainings and conferences in order to network with concerned others. Learn the legal issues about which you might be ethically obliged to inform your clients—for example, statutes of limitations for filing civil or criminal charges or for filing other sorts of complaints and mandatory reporting laws.

5. Develop a list of ethical therapists for referrals. Consider asking them about their credentials and boundary philosophies; don't assume that everyone with a good reputation would agree with your definition of what is ethical. You can ask directly whether they have ever been sexually involved with a client or former client, among other things. And make sure that they understand this issue so that your clients don't have to educate them.

6. Decide whether you are available to provide expert testimony in court or as part of other complaint procedures, and let clients know where you stand on that issue.

7. Network with lawyers who handle malpractice cases so that you can make appropriate referrals for legal advice.

8. Be prepared to be honest about your mistakes and apologize. Although an honest apology and the taking of responsibility by the abusive therapist would ordinarily be most healing for the client, that seldom happens; offenders most often lie, deny, or minimize the effects of their errors or abuse. Short of a genuine apology from the offender, the next most healing thing for the clients we have seen is an honest subsequent therapist. Know that you are not perfect

and will make mistakes, and be ready to own them; turning them into "transference" will send your clients out the door. And then be ready to be patient as trust builds again; what might seem like minor errors to us are often perceived as major breaches by clients.

Nancy Avery and I greatly appreciate our work with the highly courageous clients who come to BASTA! They are courageous to walk through another therapist's door, and they are often using great courage to tell their stories, after in many cases having been told (or programmed) that they should never tell anyone, sometimes under threat of death by the perpetrator or programming for suicide. In the first few years of my work, the women attending my workshops had been abused an average of 10 years earlier and many had never told anyone. Now, thanks to informed media attention, victim support networks, and more sensitive clinical services, the time it takes people to come forward is much shorter because it is getting safer, and less stigmatizing, to "tell."

TELL: THE THERAPY
EXPLOITATION LINK LINE

Like most of the "Boston Experience," the coming together of TELL (the Therapy Exploitation Link Line) was truly serendipitous. Five women, whose winding roads to recovery ultimately crossed one another, began what has now grown into a support network of more than 400 women in the Greater Boston area who have been sexually exploited by therapists, clergy, and other health care professionals. To understand how this network came about, it is important to know something of each founder's story.

Diane's Story

Diane Aronson, whose professional and personal life has long been one of political activism, dates her "point of discovery" of the abuse to April 1987. Confused and frustrated, she spent many of the following months searching the library and other resources trying to locate material that might help her better understand what she was feeling about the exploitation she had suffered at the hands of Dr. Richard Ingrasci. "Most of all," she says, "I knew that if this had happened to me, it probably had happened to others, and I knew I had to meet other victims and do something about it."

That August, Diane's therapist was forced to terminate therapy with her. "I interviewed 17 therapists over the phone," she says, "and when I told them what had happened to me, most of them were vague in their responses. They said things like, 'Oh, yeah, I've heard of that happening' and 'I can help you through that,' but none of them seemed to be able to acknowledge the impact this experience had had on me. It wasn't until I got to Nancy Avery," Diane continues, "that I finally got an appropriate response. It's hard to explain," she says, "but Nancy let slip that what I was telling her made her angry and that it never should have happened."

Over the next months, Diane pushed Nancy Avery to help her find other victims. She even tried to gain access to other victims through contact with a reporter who had written a story about a Boston obstetrician, Dr. Robert Margulis, and his sexual exploitation of patients; but the reporter insisted that her sources were confidential and that she couldn't be of help.

Finally, through some aggressive networking, with Nancy contacting other therapists and asking them if they were treating victims who might like to meet others who had had similar experiences, and Diane continuing her tenacious efforts, the first group of victims came together in the summer of 1988. They met in two to three consecutive 12-week sessions, with some victims dropping out at the end of each 12-week period and new victims joining.

Concurrently, using a lawyer who had been recommended by Estelle Disch, whom she had located through a telephone conversation with Judith Herman (one of the authors of Gartrell et al., 1986), Diane sued Dr. Ingrasci. In February 1989 she settled the case and announced to her somewhat astonished lawyer that she was ready and wanted to go to the press. Diane managed to negotiate an agreement with the reporters to cover the story in depth, an agreement reporters and editors kept. Shortly thereafter, the first story of Dr. Ingrasci ran in the *Boston Globe*.

On August 3, 1989, the Massachusetts Board of Registration in Medicine, perhaps pushed by the publicity, allowed Dr. Ingrasci to voluntarily surrender his license to practice. As of this writing, it is believed he is practicing in Seattle.

Jean's Story

Author and educator Jean Gould had been put in touch with Nancy Avery by her subsequent treating therapist in spring 1989. Nancy Avery's

12-week group had just finished, and the next one wasn't due to begin for some time; but recognizing Jean's desperate need to meet other victims, Nancy accommodated her by holding a one-time meeting for her with women who had already been through the process. One of those present was Diane.

"Most of those in Nancy's groups were Ingrasci victims at that time," says Jean. "I wanted to meet some others, and I knew a one-time meeting wasn't going to be enough." Around the same time, her therapist gave her a letter from a western Massachusetts psychologist that had been published in the *Boston Globe*. In it, the psychologist had said she was interested in meeting and working with victims in group settings. Like Diane, Jean was an avid and determined networker who picked up the phone and called the psychologist. Within days, the psychologist had put Jean in touch with two other victims, Phyllis and Marlene, and had invited the three to attend a meeting in her home office at which time, she promised, they would also meet other victims. As it turned out, only the three of them showed up.

"It was strange," says Jean. "I had never met these other two women, and none of us knew what to expect from one another. But our experience was even stranger. We drove the hour's trip from Boston to her house together. Her office was in her garage, the entrance was a beaded curtain, and she had a one-way observation window. None of us could wait to get out of there, and on the way back, we laughed about what had happened. It was a kind of bonding experience. We realized that we needed something other than what this psychologist could offer us, and we also realized that we needed each other."

"That's when the idea for TELL was born," Jean adds. "Phyllis already had the name."

With the support of the women of TELL, and an outstanding subsequent therapist, Jean moved forward with her healing. She pursued a case against Dr. Stanley Kanter, which she ultimately settled, and although he has since given up his license, he continues to practice as a therapist in Massachusetts. In fall 1993, a television news reporter, wearing a hidden camera and posing as a patient, went to Stanley Kanter's office and the offices of two other psychiatrists, Drs. Sheldon Zigelbaum and Edward Daniels, who have also lost their licenses because of sexual misconduct. The resultant exposé, and Jean's forceful and eloquent statements, have further added to the public's understanding of the problem and its ramifications.

Phyllis's Story

Former advertising copy writer Phyllis Pagano has been TELL's most consistent and ardent supporter. She handles the telephone, keeps extensive archives of newspaper and magazine articles and videos of television programs, and is TELL's acronym expert. The TELL acronym was her idea. Phyllis has also been the most frustrated and thwarted in her attempts to ensure that her perpetrator be brought to justice. This may be due to the fact that she was exploited by a highly sexualized verbal invasion, and few in the therapeutic community understand that this kind of abuse can be just as devastating as sexual abuse involving intercourse, sometimes even more so.

In trying to make sense of what had happened to her, in January 1988 Phyllis sought consultation from the therapist who had referred her to her exploiter.

"Why don't you just feel flattered," he told me, "and let it go at that? From a three-hour consultation," Phyllis adds, "that was what he concluded. Then, when I got home, he called me and told me that he had found a file from when my perpetrator was in graduate school and that it included a note documenting similar seductive behavior from that time." Phyllis has tried since then to access that file, but even the efforts of lawyers have failed to surface the incriminating documentation, and every attempt to be heard has been thwarted. At one point, running into her perpetrator in the street, Phyllis confronted him with what she had been told. Later she learned that he had called the consultant and threatened him.

Phyllis, too, saw the letter to the *Boston Globe* from the psychologist. "What interested me," she says, "was that the letter was about problems with subsequent treaters. I felt just as abused by him [the consultant] as by the first therapist, so I called her."

"Within a couple of days, she called me back with two other names, and she put me in touch with Jean. As we talked on the way back that night," Phyllis adds, "it seemed logical to us to find other women who had had similar experiences, and I was interested in taking action. Both fit under the same concept."

Phyllis's perpetrator is still licensed and continues to practice in Newton, Massachusetts. The Massachusetts Psychological Association has refused to pursue the matter further.

Marlene's Story

Psychotherapist Marlene Selib Prince first became a patient of her abuser in 1975 as her marriage of more than 20 years was coming to an end. She continued to see him intermittently into 1989 when she began therapy with a subsequent treater because of extreme job stress.

"What had happened to me in the previous therapy came out during the history," she says. "When I told the new therapist about it, she pulled out a letter written by a psychologist to the *Boston Globe* and handed it to me. I slipped it into my handbag and forgot about it, but somehow that crumbled piece of paper went from the bottom of my bag to having a life of its own."

"A few days later, I called the author of the letter, and she put me in touch with Jean." It was then that Jean, Marlene, and Phyllis made plans for their trip to western Massachusetts.

"One of the reasons for going was to meet other victims. The fact that no one else showed up probably wasn't her fault," says Marlene of the psychologist. "It probably just speaks to how difficult it is for victims to come forward."

"I didn't even recognize the abuse as an issue at the time we went," Marlene notes. "I went because I was trying to work in therapy on why my life had been the way it was, why I had married two sick men, and why I had gone into a job that had some of the same stresses as my marriages. I just wasn't making the connection. It probably wasn't until about a year later that I took the issue with much seriousness." Still, it was in Marlene's living room, in summer and fall 1989, that the first TELL meetings took place.

Marlene attributes to the existence of TELL and its participants the strength and support she needed to get a lawyer and pursue a case against her abuser. She says that "the trust part was so bad that there were many times I didn't even trust the lawyers. In fact, Jean came with me to my first appointment with the lawyer." Ultimately, her case was settled.

"The women of TELL just kept saying that it wasn't my fault, that it was his responsibility. That helped," she says. "But I also didn't want to be identified as a victim, even though what had happened had taken a toll on almost two decades of my life." Today, Marlene recognizes the damage and acknowledges that meeting, at a TELL gathering, another woman who had been abused by the same therapist was a turning point. "Until then," she says, "I still held on to the belief that he really loved me."

In July 1993, Dr. Robert Ravven was allowed, by the Massachusetts Board of Registration in Medicine, to voluntarily surrender his license to practice medicine. It is rumored that he continues to practice elsewhere in Massachusetts.

My Story

I'm Jan Wohlberg, author, management consultant, and former college professor, and I too have had a role in the Boston Experience.

In early March 1989, I read the *Boston Globe*'s article on Richard Ingrasci. I was horrified, revolted, and also concerned—concerned that the paper's readership would dismiss Ingrasci as a nut and fringe practitioner of trendy holistic medicine. The psychiatrist who had sexually exploited me was mainstream—educated and trained at Harvard College and Medical School as well as holding a Harvard appointment. Three women exploited by Lionel A. Schwartz, including me, had told their stories to the Board of Registration in Medicine almost a year and a half earlier. Still, Lionel Schwartz had a license and was practicing. When asked why, the board's representative had replied glibly. "The Board is busy," I was told, "and besides, we don't consider him to be a menace to society." On April 3, 1989, Lionel A. Schwartz, then 66, was allowed by the Massachusetts Board of Registration in Medicine to resign his license, but not before the press had exposed the board's callous inaction. He continued to practice in Boston for approximately a year. He now lives in Los Angeles.

"Will you put your name on the story?" the reporters had asked me in response to my letter to them following the Ingrasci story. "Yes, unequivocally, yes." It became the first story to carry a victim's name, and my phone hasn't stopped ringing.

Of all the calls I received, it was the call from Phyllis, inviting me to attend a meeting at Marlene's, that most changed my life.

At the second meeting, our numbers had more than doubled. A dozen victims sat in Marlene's living room, sharing stories, cautious and fearful but also relieved to have found others who understood.

Within the next four months, attendance soared to more than 50 as the pent-up need for this kind of support system exploded, victims at last finding relief from the isolation that had so systematically been imposed on them by their exploiters. A number of victims of the same multiple abusers met one another in the safe setting of the group, breaking the last illusions of having been truly cared about, and allowing the weight of the ambivalence to shift toward anger and a recognition of betrayal. Attorney Linda Jorgenson and feminist therapist Judith Jordan attended as resources.

Rapid growth and a population of angry individuals whose ability to trust themselves and others was often limited created some rocky moments. Anger often flew about the room uncontrolled, falling where it would.

The five of us, as leaders, trying to do our own healing, were at best only marginally helpful at controlling the chaos. Fortunately, our diversity and different stages of healing allowed us to do enough to sustain the group through the stormy periods that hit the TELL network. Recognizing our own desperate needs for structure and safety, we developed meeting guidelines, wrote an informational brochure that made clear that TELL is not group therapy—although it is therapeutic—and developed opening and closing statements. Today, we also have a starter kit for victim groups that want to start up around the country. Thanks to Phyllis's determination and consistent dedication, we have a telephone line (617-964-TELL) that still gets answered five years after our inception.

TELL still holds monthly meetings, and the facilitator's role is rotated as we have learned to trust one another and share power. In alternate months, guest speakers are invited and meetings are open to the public. Currently, victim meetings are small, generally 10 or fewer, and the important work of TELL goes on largely over the vast telephone network that has developed. Victims are encouraged to be sure they have the name and telephone number of at least one other victim before leaving a meeting. For those who prefer not to attend meetings, victims are put in touch with other victims by telephone to encourage connections. Nancy Avery has said that "there is nothing any therapist can do for a victim that is anywhere near what other victims can do for a victim." That continues to be our experience, and the participants in TELL have been generous in support of one another.

As of this writing, media attention to the subject of sexual exploitation is limited. However, victims continue to be referred to us by friends and concerned subsequent treaters. Some still come, having clipped the stories that ran in 1989 and saved them, finally finding the courage and voice to call. In addition, TELL networks with individuals and support groups from around the country and Canada. TELL participants have appeared on television and as speakers at professional and lay conferences. The victim-to-victim network has served to support victims in their need to find voice, voice that makes clear that the abusers no longer control the lives of their victims.

In May 1992 the American Psychiatric Association awarded to TELL the Assembly Speakers Award for its contributions to the field of mental health. Jean, Marlene, and Phyllis were present at the Washington, DC, meeting to accept the award. In her short acceptance talk, Jean challenged the audience of psychiatrists "to be part of the solution by bringing this well-kept secret into a rational, open dialogue that can help all of us reclaim a sense of our own personal and professional value."

BPSI-TELL

Another key piece in the Boston Experience has been the coming together of a group of six psychoanalysts from the Boston Psychoanalytic Society and Institute with a group of seven TELL participants in an ongoing dialogue group that first formed in late 1990. Dr. Elizabeth Aub Reid, then president of the institute, and I conceived of the idea and moved ahead to make it happen. In monthly meetings, we found we shared a great deal, most notably our frustration and anger toward unethical practitioners. Our explorations have resulted in two presentations at meetings of the American Psychiatric Association, a number of presentations in other settings, and the development of a course on subsequent treatment. Although a second group met for about a year and then disbanded, the BPSI-TELL experiences of both groups have been, and continue to be, a healing force in the relationships between therapists and victims.

Legislation

Perhaps the most disappointing aspect of the Boston Experience has been the failure of a group of committed and active individuals—victims, therapists, clergy, attorneys, and interested citizens—to pass meaningful legislation in the Commonwealth of Massachusetts. Carefully and expertly drafted bills, including one dealing with the problem of unlicensed practitioners and another pushing for criminalization, have failed to make it out of committee. Weak political leadership and strong opposition from some politicians and many in the medical community thus have made it impossible to do what more than a dozen other states have succeeded in doing. In addition, and sadly, the governor recently signed a paternalistic bill that allows therapists to withhold their clinical notes from patients if they deem that reading those notes will be upsetting to the patient. Access is limited to subsequent treaters and attorneys, and the therapist is allowed to supply only summary notes. For patients who have been exploited, this makes taking action all the more difficult.

Despite the lack of political action and the waning interest of the press (which at times had been sustained by legislative activity), the victim's movement is continuing to gain strength. The public is slowly becoming educated about what happens in this kind of exploitation and how. Attendance at informational meetings for therapists and other health care practitioners at which TELL members have presented has increased dramatically. As this continues, and as more victims find one another, it will be increasingly difficult to ignore the need to protect consumers of health care services—which probably means everyone—from willful exploitation.

CONCLUSION

The Boston Experience has been a deepening 10-year evolutionary process involving hundreds of people rather than a transitory response to an often sensationalized problem. For this reason, we believe that the efforts of the many concerned therapists, attorneys, other professionals, clergy, and consumers will continue long after the media attention has waned. We hope that within the next few years the Massachusetts legislature will pass appropriate legislation to help stop this abuse.

9

Lot's Wife,
Sabina Spielrein, and Anita Hill

A JUNGIAN MEDITATION
ON SEXUAL BOUNDARY ABUSE
AND RECOVERY OF LOST VOICES

Peter Rutter

This chapter links the figures of Lot's Wife, Sabina Spielrein, and Anita Hill to the archetypal and historical struggle of our culture against sexual boundary abuse. I want to begin with Sabina Spielrein, who was a victim/survivor of one of the twentieth century's most horrific power abuses. In the first decade of this century, Sabina Spielrein became a patient of Jung's when he was in training at a hospital in Zurich. It is virtually certain that she had a sexual relationship with Jung, who ultimately referred her to Freud for both treatment and psychoanalytic training. In Vienna, she became a member of Freud's inner circle, a pioneering psychoanalyst in her own right who published several papers that are central to the early foundations of the psychoanalytic movement.

But there is more to Sabina Spielrein's story. She had originally come to Zurich from Russia. After the Bolshevik Revolution, she left Vienna, returning home to become one of the founders of psychoanalysis in the Soviet Union. But with the rise of Stalin, psychoanalysis was crushed. Until recently it was believed that Sabina Spielrein, who was Jewish, had been killed in the early 1930s as part of Stalin's infamous "Doctors Plot," a pall of darkness involving the murder of thousands of Jews and intellectuals. But since the fall of the Soviet Union, contact was established with a small, formerly underground, Jungian-oriented psychoanalytic community in Moscow. These survivors revealed a shocking new truth: Sabina Spielrein had in fact escaped the liquidation of the 1930s Doctors Plot only to be murdered, along with her children, when the Nazis invaded the Soviet Union in the early 1940s.

If we ever find ourselves underestimating, or forgetting, the connection between acts of power abuse at the intimate boundaries of relationships of trust, and those power abuses of mass murder and genocide, let us remember the life of Sabina Spielrein. It was she who witnessed, endured, and was finally claimed and silenced by both kinds of abuses. We must also remember that we can count in the millions the numbers of silenced victims of both intimate, and political, power abuses. Sabina Spielrein's voice was long silenced, her life rendered nonexistent. But now it is being remembered by our telling her story and in the publication of her diaries and papers.

In this meditation on voices lost and recovered, I now want to journey far back into our cultural and psychological history, to consider the story of Lot's Wife. As a Jungian, I have an interest in identifying deep unconscious patterns that exist, both in individuals and in cultures. These deep unconscious patterns are sometimes referred to as archetypal forces and are the least visible, but often the most powerful, shapers of day-to-day events. One way to identify archetypal patterns is to look at myth, especially at mythic stories that we still tell today. The story of Lot's Wife functions as a kind of origin myth for our culture, addressing, among other motifs, gender role stereotypes, dysfunctional defensive psychological patterns, and the dynamics of sexual exploitation.

In trying to "remember Lot's Wife," let us remember that she (who has no name) was, essentially, murdered because she looked. In psychological language, she would not suppress and split off the reality of the sexual shadow. She looked. We are enjoined to remember what happened to her as a cautionary tale about looking. We are never asked to consider the experience of this nameless woman, and the compassion she may have had for the suffering souls of the crushed cities that she looked back upon. Yet Lot's Wife did what women have been doing for thousands of years. The culture has assigned to them the task of carrying the knowledge and experience of rape and incest as part of a broad spectrum of sexual boundary violations.

One might wonder what else Lot's Wife saw, and why it is that she chose to look back on the suffering of Sodom and Gomorrah. But let us also consider what this story has to tell us about masculine psychology. Lot, in fact, goes on and never looks back. This establishes a model that I would term a *heroic form of dissociation,* and it is one style of functioning that to this day our culture greatly admires in men.

The story of Lot's Wife also tells us that, in their mother's absence, the now-motherless daughters of Lot plot to get their father drunk and commit incest with him. This myth is quite explicit in its evocation of strong psychological patterns of abuse that persist in our culture today. By its end, the mother is permanently silenced, and the daughters have become boundary-less sexual playthings—not just innocent sexual playthings but conniving, seductive women who use their sexual power to overwhelm the man. Lot allows himself to drink the wine they offer. In this way he can descend to his dissociated unconscious and engage in incest without putting up a fight against it, or suffering much consequence —our culture's archetypal model of so-called situational vulnerability.

What does it mean that, although the woman was not able, or chose not, to obey the entreaty not to look back at the sexual shadow, the man, Lot, successfully complied with this injunction? As a myth that represents an important building block in the evolution of our cultural psyche, the dissociative response it represents is as unchosen by men today as is women's carrying of the sexually abusive experience. In a sense, men are also being victimized to the degree that they continue not to look back. And although our culture has victimized men by purveying dysfunctional messages about what it means to be a man, men lose their innocence when they continue to reap the seeming rewards of the way this myth has structured their relationships with women.

Men of today did not create the cultural message that women are available to serve their needs, sexual and otherwise, but they bear responsibility for perpetuating it as long as they go along with it instead of fighting against it. Tragically, it has become easier for men to leave things the way they are, because the arrangement reflected in the story of Lot's Wife leaves them with power as well as support for the sexual opportunism that our culture so greatly admires.

Yet men still retain the capacity to feel, in the part of their psyches
that Jungians call the anima, the same legacy of Lot's-Wife-who-looked-
back that women bear more consciously. Unfortunately, unless men find
the pain this anima is feeling for them, such dissociated pain becomes
part of the dangerous dynamic that can lead to sexual boundary violations in relationships of trust. Because men have dissociated this pain
into the anima, they tend to experience it in projection onto the women
they get close to. In the helping professions, this means that women will
bring men their wounds, allowing the man to experience the real woman
as the projected embodiment of his own wounded feminine side. Because there is an unconscious drive toward wholeness by joining together the dissociated parts of oneself, men may mistakenly try to
recontact their wounded anima by touching the person of the woman
whose wound they are supposed to be containing and healing.

The resistance to having these Lot's wives, these Anita Hills, tell us
Another crucial part of the story of Lot's Wife that deserves our
attention is that women today are no longer obeying the silence pact.
They are speaking out. The heritage of Lot's Wife has passed to women
such as Anita Hill, who, on October 11, 1991, spoke out before all the
world, and in doing so defied the injunction not to look back on the pain
of modern-day women. Yet at this relatively early stage of breaking
silence, our culture is still trying to hold those who speak out to the
terms of the myth of Lot's Wife. It is these latter-day Lot's wives, these
Anita Hills, these women, now joined by some men, who continually
upset us by telling us about the sexual (and other) power abuses of our
once-respected colleagues and role models. But our first instinct as a
society is still to silence those who tell the secrets.

We silence them by attacking their credibility; by making them into
crazy women; by saying it never happened, that they made it up; by
attacking their motivation; by labeling them with "erotomania." We
silence them by saying that the sex did take place—but, because they
were the seducers, they agreed to it, or they "really wanted it." The story
of Lot's Wife did not create these feminine-demeaning, but culturally
acceptable, stereotypes. Rather, as an origin myth, it reflects the state of
the culture that has kept it alive and is a testimony to our culture's
deeply embedded attitudes toward those who carry knowledge and
experience of boundary violations.

The resistance to having these Lot's wives, these Anita Hills, tell us
their secrets can be seen at a political level as a refusal by men to give
up the power to define the interpersonal boundary. But men's resistance to having their secrets told also originates from the psychological
dynamic that every secret revealed chips away at the dissociation of

their pain. Every iota of pain, no longer held secretly by those who have experienced boundary-violating behavior, spills over back into the culture and especially into the male psyche, causing men to feel more of this pain. But in making these connections, in recovering from their own psychological legacy of traumatic dissociation, men begin to participate in a rebirth and renewal process that may help alleviate the way that we as a species inflict power abuse on one another, and may help us save the life of the planet as well as enhance the lives of many of the living things on it.

But we must stop murdering the messengers by degrading them with the time-honored accusation, "She really wanted it." This is repeated over and over whenever there is a boundary abuse. Men "know" what women want. They "know" by the way she was dressed, by how she looked at them, by her gratitude for listening to her pain for a few hours, by the fact that she didn't say no. These things that men "know" are, however, filtered through their fantasies, so that even when they fail to find any evidence based on how she dressed or looked or behaved, much of the time they *still* insist that they "know" it.

The very structure of the sentence, "She really wanted it," is a boundary violation—because a man has decided that he has authority over the inner reality of a woman. This attitude, in only slightly less direct language, has been institutionally adopted by certain circles of psychodynamic psychology, in the only-recently-challenged idea that, when women complained of sexual contact with their therapists, they were having psychotic transference fantasies. "Wish fulfillment" has been a crucial psychodynamic concept. But this is just the same old message, "She really wanted it," in modern-day psychological language.

This message still exists, either within individuals, or organizationally, where such attitudes are officially and ideologically sanctioned. After all, the image of the temptress, our culture's version of the archetype of the feminine seductress, appears just after the Creation. In the image of the seductress is the projection onto the woman of power over the sexual boundary that men actually maintain; it is a way of disowning that power and placing it in the woman. This disowning usually occurs when something goes wrong for the man—for instance, when his secret is told.

The real seductress certainly exists. Our dysfunctional culture has quite successfully produced many such women, driven them mad, in a sense, with their own sexuality objectified and turned against them. To see a seductress in a professional relationship is to see a woman who is either not in control of her own boundaries or one who is using her sexuality in a way that perpetuates her objectification and degradation. When a helping professional meets the seductress, because she is living out not just her *personal* wound but our *culture's* wound, we owe her the most diligent effort possible to maintain the standard of care, the ethical standard, the boundary between professional duty and sexual contact.

Most of us have personal knowledge of modern-day Lot's wives and Sabina Spielreins, those for whom the possibility of speaking out, and surviving, was denied. We must revivify and try as best as we can to recapture the lost voices and the experience of those who did not survive. But the hope lies in that we also have in our midst our own Anita Hills: This volume, among others, contains the stories of survivors of professional abuse. It is through those connecting voices, growing ever stronger in the network of recovery and advocacy groups, that the recognition of the numbed, silent, traumatic pain of boundary abuse, and the Voice that is its answer, will come. As was true for Lot's Wife, Sabina Spielrein, and Anita Hill, speaking out often comes at great risk; yet doing so carries hope of justice and renewal for our entire society.

10

Transforming Power

WOMEN WHO HAVE
BEEN EXPLOITED BY A PROFESSIONAL

Signe L. Nestingen

The ability of client to transform the (boundary) violation and infuse it with life affirming potential is a tribute to the healing power that resides with us all.

Peterson, 1992, p. 164

A woman who, when receiving medical, psychological, educational, or spiritual services, is exploited is often left with a distorted sense of her own power. What Jung called "a feeling of wholeness, a powerful and complete sense of the Self" (Henderson, 1964, p. 120) may be warped. Therapy, when it offers a place of containment and a trusting relationship that is steady and consistent, can offer a woman wounded in this manner an opportunity to transform the lethargy, pain, and despair of exploitation into the energy of well-being.

When working with a woman who has been exploited by a professional, it is important to understand the ramifications of exploitation and the subsequent presenting problems. It is essential to have significant understanding and insight into the needs the therapist might experience. Three therapeutic tasks—containment, relationship, and empowerment—that must be incorporated into the therapeutic process are discussed. These are integral to work with a woman who has been exploited, and are discussed in detail.

RAMIFICATIONS OF EXPLOITATION AND PRESENTING PROBLEMS

When a professional exploits a client, the client's sense of self is distorted, perhaps even nullified. Violations of professional conduct can leave individuals unable to center themselves in their own power or unable to identify their own instincts, thoughts, emotions, or ideas, which serve as guiding lines for life. A client coming to therapy after act(s) of exploitation may bring with her a number of presenting problems. The violations, due to the exploitation, that she may experience are countless and can leave a client stripped of all but minimum coping skills. She may present with one or more of the following problems:

- a current crisis or chronic crisis state(s)
- a decreased ability to make decisions
- a decreased ability to solve seemingly simple problems
- a decreased or limited capacity for employment
- an inability to articulate or describe the exploitation in an understandable and concise way
- a desire to minimize and/or deny the act(s) of exploitation
- the idea that act(s) of exploitation were due, in some manner, to her thought(s), feeling(s), or behavior(s)
- ambivalence about actions she can take as a result of the exploitation
- constriction of thoughts and emotions, including the mental, physical, and spiritual or religious processes

Posttraumatic stress disorder, depressive disorders, or anxiety and/or phobias may develop. The client may describe nightmares, an inability to sleep, or sleep disturbances. Physical problems may develop. These could range from mild physical problems such as headaches and nausea to ulcers, chronic fatigue, and the development of long-term physically debilitating physical problems.

Clients who have been exploited often find it difficult to trust another professional, and they may be wary and/or isolative. Boundaries in the therapeutic relationship may be severely tested over and over again.

The original reason(s) for seeking help may be greatly exacerbated. Previous therapy experiences must be considered. Although some previous professional relationships may have been destructive and painful, there may have been other prior relationships (psychiatric interviews, group therapy, spiritual guidance, and so on) that were beneficial in a constructive and affirmative manner. As therapy unfolds, this must be discussed and the impact on the current therapeutic relationship determined.

Other presenting problems, for a woman who has been exploited, might include decreased self-esteem and self-regard, and difficulty in intimate relationships including communication, blurred boundaries, identity of self, and sexual intimacy. There may be decreased interest in sexual interaction, difficulty with sexual arousal, or hypersexuality, difficulty with orgasm and penetration. There may also be an air of increased vulnerability with a corresponding lack of coping skills to deal with the increased vulnerability. A woman may experience myriad feelings including guilt, remorse, helplessness, rage, anger, fear, hopelessness, depression, grief, loss, or shame. There may be a strong desire to seek revenge. There may be increased risk for suicide (Pope, 1989a, p. 45).

For a woman who has been exploited, family and community are important players in the healing process. The client may not know how to walk through the maze of her needs and the needs of others. Because of the numerous variables in any given case of exploitation, a woman may experience a range of experiences in regard to her family and community; she may find a great deal of support, she may find that the discussion disturbs others so there is no discussion, or she may experience outright hostility. Family members and other close associates may see themselves as secondary victims. In addition to working with the woman who has been exploited, a therapist may find it necessary to provide assessment, referral, and information about resources to the secondary victims. There are numerous complex issues for the therapist to consider in regard to secondary victimization (Milgrom, 1989b, p. 237). Community members may feel they have been victimized. (For example, if a religious official exploits a woman, she, members of the religious community, and/or the larger community may feel victimized.) There also may be a variety of ramifications if the media are involved.

Apfel and Simon (1986, p. 149) address another therapeutic topic: Does the client prefer to work with a male or female therapist? Benowitz (1991, p. 101) addresses this issue when working with women who have been exploited by female therapists. The answer to this question may depend on several variables, including the sex of the offender, the violations that occurred, and the client's feelings in regard to her own sexual orientation and/or affectional preference.

Finally, a woman who has been exploited may have been previously victimized. She may have been raped or sexually harassed; she may have experienced prior act(s) of exploitation as a child or an adult; or she may be a survivor of incest. Van der Kolk (1987) asserts, and I agree, that those with a "prior history of traumatization are especially likely to develop long-term symptomatology in response to later trauma" (p. 12). Implications for treatment with women who have been so victimized include additional sensitivity in regard to several distinct areas. Increased shame, guilt, fear, and intense self-blame as well as increased fear of vulnerability may be demonstrated by the client. Difficulties with therapeutic containment may arise. Because there are myriad relationship wounds, this is very complex and multilayered work and the relationship between the therapist and the client is crucial. The therapist may need extra consultation and supervision for a case of this nature.

THE NEEDS OF THE THERAPIST

When working with women who have been exploited, supervision and/or peer consultation is advised. For those new to working with a client who has been exploited, consultation is imperative as the possibilities for revictimization are myriad (Pope & Gabbard, 1989, p. 89). Dealing with issues of power, boundaries, and maintaining emotional clarity can be areas of particular difficulty for therapists. Seeking consultation for the following matters is encouraged: (a) transference and countertransference matters, which can be both subtle and complex; (b) legal concerns (including the state statutes where the act[s] of exploitation occurred), mandated reporting laws for state and licensing agencies, and reporting information to supervisors and employers; and (c) issues in regard to any other ethical considerations that may arise.

Consultation, peer review, or supervision can help the therapist understand the ramifications of mandated reporting. When mandated reporting is not required, the client needs assistance so that she can determine if she wishes to file a complaint. Filing a complaint, in regard to the violation, "is always and only the patient's decision" (Pope & Gabbard, 1989, p. 96). When reporting is not required, there will still be ethical and perhaps some legal issues for a therapist to consider. Questions in regard to civil suits may arise and can also be brought to consultation, and appropriate referral places discussed. In regard to legal concerns, it is almost always true that the therapist is not the best individual to help the client with all the legal dynamics. Confusion, on the part of either the client or the therapist, may interfere in the developing relationship between the client and the therapist. An advocate, with some therapeutic skills, is often helpful to a client. While the legal system and licensing agencies frequently aid a client, with either of these systems, the potential for revictimization exists.

Some women who have been exploited are unable to complete therapy, seek several therapists over a period of time, or leave therapy and return at some later date. Therapists' expectations in regard to commitment can greatly influence clients. Therefore therapists need to examine their beliefs and values about commitment to therapy. Treading delicately and with skill when issues of commitment arise is advisable.

At times, financial difficulties are created for women when they are exploited. Sometimes financial stress is created as a result of the exploitation and sometimes women are deliberately exploited in regard to financial matters. It is essential that therapists have clarity in regard to the financial aspects of their practice. Countertransference issues about money do not need to become the client's problem.

The above mentioned are a beginning look at some of the issues that can arise when working with women who have been exploited. Because of the delicacy and complexities of cases of this nature, I urge those working with women who are exploited to have accessible, steady, reliable consultation, supervision, or peer review.

THERAPEUTIC TASKS

When working with a client who has been exploited, there are a number of tasks a therapist undertakes. Three central tasks are (a) to establish a contained and open space for the client; (b) to allow for and encourage the building of a relationship, founded on trust, so that a client can begin to take risks; and, as the first two tasks are under way, (c) to serve as witness to, and aid the client in, the development of a sense of empowerment and the emerging Self.

The Establishment of a Safe Container

Acts of exploitation create relationship distress and break relationship bonds. A client can transform the devastation and pain of exploitation and (re)develop a sense of self. For this to occur, a "free and sheltered space" (Kalff, 1988, p. 29) must be provided. This is the first task of the therapist. As a the client moves into and begins to trust the protected space, a relationship between the therapist and the client can be forged. As the Self emerges, the client is then free to examine whatever she desires.

A free and protected space is in part established with the setting of various kinds of boundaries. The therapist must establish boundaries that are consistent, respectful, reasonable, and honest, that do not create secrets or leave the client in untenable situations. Peterson (1992) deals with the basic underlying structure and the importance of clear boundaries. She clearly delineates four motifs that are present in every boundary violation: "role reversal, a secret, a double bind and the indulgence of professional privilege" (p. 76).

Boundaries are not simply rules for therapy, they are the basis for a relationship of honesty and integrity. The boundaries become the edges of the free and protected space, or the therapeutic container. It is within the therapy container that relational healing can occur—hence the critical nature of clearly established boundaries.

Laws create some boundaries; others are sanctioned by licensing agencies; and others are established by an individual therapist.

In some states, there are laws (boundaries) stating that it is illegal to engage in a sexual relationship with a client during or after the termination of the therapeutic relationship. In some instances, a governing body may authorize the release of confidential case notes when a complaint in regard to exploitation has occurred.

State boards and other licensing agencies often proscribe dual relationships with clients; an individual cannot provide a service for payment for a therapist (dentistry, for example) and also be a client of that same therapist. Many licensing agencies require cash payment, not barter, for counseling services. Some states and licensing agencies require the reporting of known or suspected cases of sexual exploitation on the part of a professional.

Individual therapists also establish physical or structural boundaries such as meeting times and places, fee structure and payment expectations, phone calls and therapist availability.

While it is extremely important that therapists be familiar with the limits of practice established by state mandates and licensing agencies, it is critical that therapists give considerable thought to *interpersonal therapeutic boundaries*. These are the boundaries that create trust and hope. These interpersonal boundaries (some of which may be the same as state or agency mandates), created in the spirit of the well-being of the client, provide an emotional and spiritual structure for a therapeutic relationship that is both free and protected. For women who have been exploited, trust and hope become the lifelines to transformation and empowerment.

Boundaries must create a space to provide containment for the client that is open to the client's experience. This means that the client is free to talk within the therapy relationship about anything she wishes and that she is free to talk about her therapeutic experience to anyone she chooses; no special friendships or relationships are created by the therapist, thus there is no need for a client to keep secrets about the therapeutic relationship. A protected space also means that the therapist refrains from excessive and/or inappropriate personal disclosure, thereby establishing an environment that is suitable to the client's exploration of her personal needs.

Creating a contained space for therapy also means a recognition of power. Power is conferred by mandates, by licensing agencies, by others in the community, by the therapist, and by the client herself. "Those who wear the cloak of professional authority and responsibility are expected to be ethical and trustworthy. Because of this, a person requesting professional services is especially vulnerable" (Nestingen & Lewis, 1991, p. v). When the cloak of power is worn unconsciously, it is dangerous for the client. A therapist has a moral, ethical, and spiritual obligation to understand the extent and limits of power.

Recognition of power brings a further obligation to establish boundaries that recognize this power. Basically this means (a) no dual relationships; (b) information from clients is confidential, it cannot be used for the therapist's personal gain (examples might be to achieve financial advantage, to find a new job); (c) clients cannot be placed in a position of protecting the interests of a therapist (i.e., asking a client to lie or steal, requesting a favor from a client, asking a client to break a law).

A therapist cannot create unnecessary tension for a client by violating the confidence of another or expecting a client to meet the emotional needs of the therapist.

For a client to rely on a therapist, a therapist must know her or his professional competencies. If the help a client requires falls outside the purview of the therapist's experience, consultation is advised and referral may be required.

As the boundaries are clarified, the client is able to explore the therapeutic container. As the therapeutic space is explored, and trust between the client and therapist begins to develop, the transformative process

of moving from the pain and despair of exploitation to the emergence
of the Self occurs.

Establishing Trust

Trust is not static. As in any relationship, levels of trust in a therapeutic relationship vary over time. Trust has its own strengths and fragilities. Building trust, and then allowing it to deepen, is central to the client's healing. As the client determines the limits of the sheltered space, and comes to rely on the freedom in the relationship, she can set about creating a relationship with herself.

A woman must be able to trust herself. As a result of exploitation, she may not be able to trust her inner judgment. Acts of exploitation establish a dangerous precedent. Directed by an inner need to seek help, the client was exploited by the person from whom she sought aid. When seeking help, in an effort to heal from the wounds of exploitation, violations of this nature may leave a client unable to trust herself. Can she trust her own inner prompting? Can she trust *her choice* of helper? Can she trust the container the helper creates? Can she trust the relationship that develops? These and other questions about trust are raised by women as a result of exploitative relationship(s).

Women who have been exploited may need to test, and test again, the trust levels in the therapeutic relationship. Without letting go of the protection of the therapeutic boundaries, the therapist must be willing to let the client have the freedom to test these limits. As a result, the therapeutic alliance can deepen. If the client is not reexploited, she probably becomes more vulnerable, reveals more of herself, and is presented with another double bind.

Wanting to heal from the wounds of exploitation, she must be vulnerable; yet while vulnerable, with a helping professional, she was harmed. A great leap of faith is required on the part of the client. At this point, it is critical for the therapist to maintain impeccable boundaries. The client will filter the therapeutic relationship through the screen of exploitation.

As the professional maintains steady, clear, and direct communication with the client and as the power of the relationship between the client and the therapist is acknowledged and examined, there is a greater likelihood that a client will allow deeper vulnerability to emerge.

This deeper vulnerability can lead to the client finding the strength within herself to experience the deeper feelings that the exploitative relationship engendered. These feelings may include rage and anger, fear, hurt, shame, guilt, and grief—grief for the loss of faith in herself and others.

This irretrievable loss of faith in the ability to trust her own judgments and rely on the aid and assistance of others is profound. When this faith is damaged or destroyed by act(s) of exploitation, it is not possible for the professional, acting as a healing agent, to restore trust. The client herself must come to terms with these losses and all the implications.

Recognizing power and its limits is crucial for therapists who wish to create an atmosphere of trust and openness for the client. Within this atmosphere, a client can begin to come to terms with the ramifications of exploitation and regain trust and faith in herself, her decisions, and her life. As this occurs, the Self emerges and the client recognizes her own strength and power.

The Client's Emerging Power

For a client to recognize her own strength and power, she must learn to rely on and trust her evolving instincts, emotions, thoughts, ideas, values, and beliefs. This task requires that any false sense of power with which a victimized woman has been imbued be examined.

There are times when a woman who has been exploited by a professional may have either felt powerful or been placed in positions of power as a result of an exploitative relationship. Sometimes women are seduced with promises of power. For example, a woman may have been told that she was very important; she may have been led to believe that she, above all others, had the ability to make the exploiting professional feel a certain way. A woman might have been given favors in return for exploitation. These are distortions of power. These and similar messages perpetuate the myth that power comes from outside a woman and not from her own internal sources.

Sometimes exploitation of women by professionals is obviously degrading and/or humiliating. A woman who is exploited in this way can be stripped of a sense of internal power and have little or no awareness of how she can reempower herself and/or have any effect on outer environments.

These egregious acts of exploitation, whether presented in a clearly degrading and humiliating manner or as something that *appears* to make a woman powerful, can leave a woman who is exploited without the ability to listen to or trust her internal self. Without these abilities, she is left struggling to make decisions or take action on her own behalf.

The shroud of silence, shame, and self-blame, which a woman who has been exploited often experiences, is transformed in the process of telling her story. As the threads of her story unfold, and she is encouraged to examine and explore from her own understanding each aspect of the exploitation, she can begin to let go of the oppression of exploitation and (re)experience the emergence of the Self and her true power. Discovering areas where she needs assistance (for example, housing, vocational aid, spiritual assistance), she can also discover areas of her strength (such as skills within a professional field, a curiosity about life). This storytelling weaves together various aspects of her life, bringing the personal, professional, social, and spiritual threads into a whole fabric.

The process of therapy does not erase the past, but as a woman heals she learns to rely more consistently on herself. As she no longer needs the therapist to set the parameters of freedom and safety, the client begins to pull away from the sheltered space of therapy. Her sense of Self is evolving; the inner core is growing stronger. The client's instincts, emotions, thoughts, and ideas are becoming her life guides. There is a sense of being alive and free. Movement through life becomes more easily accomplished. The wounds of exploitation have been transformed to a stance of strength, life, and empowerment.

SUMMARY

When working with women who have been exploited, therapists are confronted with any number of concerns. The myriad presenting problems clients bring with them after experiencing exploitation require a strong sense of self from the therapist as well as clear, solid boundaries, developed clinical skills, patience, and maturity. The ethical, moral, and legal labyrinths that exploitation leaves for both the victim and the therapist are best handled with the aid of consistent consultation.

For a woman who has experienced exploitation, and the subsequent loss or distortion of her own power and sense of self, the free and sheltered space of therapy is a critical link in the healing and regeneration process. There, in relationship with another, and herself, the client can prepare herself to (re)enter the world with her own power providing her with strength and vitality. This experience transforms both the therapist and the client.

11

Betrayal

CLERGY SEXUAL
ABUSE AND MALE SURVIVORS

Walter H. Bera

Over the last five years, I have treated nearly 60 male victims of clergy sexual abuse. The denominations involved were various. Most were members of a "cluster" of victims by a single offender. The largest cluster was a group of about 30 men who ranged in age from 19 through 48 who all had been abused by the same pastor during his 30-year perpetration career. Smaller numbers were seen in other clusters, but with similar dynamics.

Cluster sexual abuse is defined as the sexual abuse of multiple victims by an authority figure in an organization or church. At the onset of abuse, the victims are in their late childhood or early adolescence. They typically revealed or realized their abuse in late adolescence or adulthood.

AUTHOR'S NOTE: An earlier version of this chapter appeared under the same title in the *Dulwich Centre Newsletter* (1993, Issues 3-4, pp. 62-75, Adelaide, South Australia: Dulwich Centre Publications). Reprinted by permission.

The impact on a particular denomination and the number of people affected can be profound. Using the Catholic Church as an example, Berry (1992) states that, between 1983 and 1987, 200 priests or religious brothers were reported to the Vatican Embassy for sexually abusing youngsters, in most cases teenage boys. The vast majority had multiple victims. He reports that, by 1992, the church's financial costs reached an estimated $400 million in victim's settlements, legal expenses, and treatment of the clergy. M. Allen (1992) reports on the notorious Father Porter, who admits to abusing more than 100 youths while working as a priest. Many are now suing the church.

OVERVIEW OF CLUSTER
SEXUAL ABUSE CASES

While the treatment of male victims in cluster sexual abuse cases has special challenges, the therapy strategies can be successfully applied when there is only one victim as well. The offenders are technically called "ephebophiles" and are attracted to youngsters in puberty or just emerging, versus "pedophiles," who are attracted to prepubescent children.

A useful way of looking at why some people are victimized is that they were simply vulnerable and available to the offender. In clergy sexual abuse, vulnerabilities tend to occur in two basic patterns. The first pattern of victims includes youths who come from families who are very devout believers in their faith and their minister. These families encourage and willingly hand over their sons for mentoring, religious education, and counseling to the priest or minister, who is often charismatic, beloved, and thereby of high status within their church community. Their deep faith contributes to their vulnerability.

The other pattern of victims consists of those who come from "troubled" families who seek out the pastor for counsel on their difficulties with the adolescent. Families may be disorganized as a result of mental health, chemical health, financial, or other difficulties. Discipline and direction is requested for young males who at times are acting out or, conversely, sullen.

Whatever the causes of the young male's vulnerability and availability to the clergy perpetrator, the scenario is often the same: a conscious "grooming" of the family and the boy to completely trust the clergy person. The clergy person, in the course of youth counseling, social activities, and prayer, will talk in an increasingly sexualized manner on a variety of subjects and begin touching the boy in a more and more sexual way. This grooming can occur over years, and the victim can experience the contact as confusing but not "abnormal" because of the step-by-step behavioral shaping to accept the sexual behavior.

Secrecy is ensured in a variety of ways, such as promises to maintain "confidentiality" in the spiritual and pastoral counseling situation. The minister may threaten that others "won't understand," intimating that if the boy breaks the abuse secret it will result in blame of the victim and the minister. The minister engenders deep loyalty in the youth through being a significant nurturing and attentive adult prestige figure.

Although the numbers of religious cluster sex offenders that are available for study are small and it is clear that sex offenders in general are a heterogeneous population, there is one pattern often seen in the background of this group (Gonsiorek, Bera, & LeTourneau, 1994; Salter, 1988). In legal depositions and court-ordered psychological assessments, perpetrators often remark that their childhood was significantly neglectful and abusive. They may be gifted with intellectual or interpersonal skills. They had used these skills to cope with the adults in their households and might be called "parentified" children by observers. Psychologically rigid, needy, and vulnerable, they describe a sexual contact occurring in late childhood or early adolescence by an older male whose friendship they cherished. In this context, the sexual contact is experienced as positive. This experience of sexual arousal and orgasm with nurturing by their perpetrator is rationalized as "good"—a "good" they would grow to share with others in their late adolescence and early adulthood in divinity school, seminary, and church.

Partly out of the pain of his difficult childhood, the offender-to-be may turn to religion as a refuge and vocation, especially if the denomination has a rigid boundary against secular influence and cloisters the young religious student. This cloistering, added to the abuse effects, contributes to a developmental arrest often seen in such offenders (J. Gonsiorek, personal commuication, 1993). Some consciously and others unconsciously realize that this will also give them access to boys they may be able to molest.

They will throw themselves into their work as divinity students and later as pastors, often winning recognition for their devotion to their rigid religious ideals. Their gifts and talents can be used to develop successful church, youth, or sport programs. The "superminister" facade becomes so strong that the early reports of inappropriate contact are minimized or rationalized away because of the allegiance of those involved. Proof of the veracity of the pastor's vision can be the accumulation of power, money, and a large congregational following.

The more vulnerable churches are hierarchical or allow the centralization of a great deal of power and idealization of their religious leaders. The personal power of the charismatic minister becomes political, either by the nature of the organization or by changes in the organization as the pastor accumulates power over time. He can surround himself with the "true believers" in his vision and consolidate his power base.

A second scenario is observed among those denominations that have a significant commitment to retaining their clergy or priests (Berry, 1992). When hearing of some inappropriate or sexual misconduct occurring, they may chose a "geographic" solution and pull the pastor or priest out of one congregation and move him to another—at times across great distances. The offender may admit some small part of his behavior, and it will be rationalized as a "sin" that can be treated through mild remorse, prayer, and promises of "not doing it again."

With such dynamics and with the combination of factors such as victim selection and vulnerability, perpetrator history, and often unwitting organizational support, it becomes easier to see why such abuse can occur over decades before intervention. The final significant factors are the unique issues of male victims of sexual abuse that will be addressed in the next section.

MALE SURVIVORS OF SEXUAL ABUSE

There presently exist significant literature and awareness of female sexual abuse victims and therapy (e.g., Kamsler, 1990; Sgroi, 1989). Currently, a number of writers are demonstrating how male sexual abuse victims are underrecognized and misunderstood, and gender-sensitive therapeutic approaches are being presented (Bolton, Morris, & MacEachron, 1989; Gonsiorek et al., 1994; Pescosolido, 1989). The following sections address fundamental issues facing male sexual abuse victims in general and those in the church in particular. These issues are critical to understanding the therapy of male survivors of clergy sexual abuse.

Incidence of Male Sexual Abuse

A number of statistics point to the significant prevalence of male sexual abuse. As early as Landis's 1956 survey of 1,800 college students, evidence was found of a significant 30% of males reporting being victims as well as 35% of females (Landis, 1956). Finkelhor (1979) conducted a similar survey of 796 college students, which resulted in a sexual abuse victimization rate of 9% males and 19% females. Finkelhor et al. (1986) conducted a survey of research results across a wide variety of studies and found the range for males is from 3% to 31% and the range for females is from 6% to 62%. Finkelhor et al. concluded that there is a general prevalence of two to three female victims to each male victim. Based on my own experience, child and adolescent victims of religious authorities reflect this gender ratio as well.

Barriers to Identification
of Male Victims of Sexual Abuse

There are a number of barriers that keep boys and men from reporting a sexual abuse history. Primary is the socialization of boys and men toward stereotypical masculine roles. As noted by McLean (1992) and M. White (1992), society and its institutions train males to be strong and to deny hurt or significant emotional distress. Competition leads to a "go it alone" way of dealing with others and their feelings—a need to feel invulnerable and always in control or the aggressor rather than admitting being the victim or loser. Finally, these strong socialization features lead to shame about admitting being a victim, or even a psychological repression and denial of that position. Literally, boys cannot see themselves as being a victim, especially of sexual abuse.

Studies report that about two thirds of sexual abuse against boys is committed by a male (Bolton et al., 1989). Homophobia prevents the acknowledgment of the abuse having occurred. Boys often feel that they "must have led him on" when targeted by a male religious figure, or that the offending cleric picked up some sexual confusion or ambivalence that is construed as gay. Finally, because boys can experience an erection and even ejaculation during abuse, enormous confusion occurs as to why any pleasure was experienced in the course of a manipulated abuse event. Overwhelmed with confusion, ambivalence, and homophobia, the male victim of clergy sexual abuse constructs a defense of denial and repression.

It is also important to note that, when the sexual abuse is perpetrated by a female, such as a baby-sitter, aunt, or female teacher or counselor, it is frequently done in a seductive or romanticized manner that belies the manipulative quality and powerlessness that the victim experiences

(C. Allen, 1991). Society frames such encounters as "luck" coming to the male by having a female freely seek sexual contact with the male. The boy did not have to "chase the female" as the image is portrayed in the culture.

Some of the above issues point to the considerable confusion around sexuality for males. The "sexual act" can appear the same from the outside but can be experienced in a number of ways. It can be seen as a way to prove manliness, to be nurtured, as a drug for escape, to accommodate in order to get through a difficulty, to express love, to conceive, and so on. Given this significant confusion about sexuality in society, it is not unusual that males would have trouble identifying when they are forced, tricked, or manipulated into a sexual act by a trusted religious figure who used his position of intimacy or authority.

Once boys realize that they may have had something happen to them that was confusing or not right—something that involved touch or sex— there are no clear resources for clarifying this confusion. Rape crisis centers and other victim services are generally staffed and identified as for children or girls and women. The focus of the advertisements, literature, and atmosphere of the organization can prevent the male victim from ever coming forward.

Therapists, psychologists, psychiatrists, and others who provide counseling and services suffer from the lack of awareness of the extent and nature of male victimization. As a result, they fail to ask questions in a way that would allow males to recognize that what occurred was sexually abusive and possibly of some consequence. There is a significant lack of research and theory addressing the issues of male victims of sexual abuse.

Finally, society and the arts in general fail to identify male victimization in the context in which it actually occurs or even depict it as a positive or wonderful experience. For example, in Barbra Streisand's 1991 film *Prince of Tides*, a female psychiatrist becomes sexually involved with a male collateral client (her primary client was his suicidal sister). This sexual liaison is somehow mutually "curative"! Few protested and the film won Academy nominations. Another case in point is the film *Teacher's Pet*, which portrays a female high school teacher being sexual with one of her students. Such films keep male victims from having models with whom they can identify in an empowering way and thereby keep them alienated.

Male Sexual Abuse Myths
That Lead to Underreporting

Primarily as a result of culture-based sexual stereotyping, erotophobia, and homophobia, there exist a number of myths concerning male sexual abuse. These myths lead to a lack of recognition and therefore under-reporting by both victims and helping professionals. The following is a list of 10 common myths (Dimock, 1988).

1. *Males cannot have sex against their will.* For children and adolescent males, just as with young females, the vast majority of sexual abuse is perpetrated by family members, relatives, or friends. The sexual abuse is brought about by tricks or manipulation by someone they trust, and the experience most often results in an initial feeling of confusion. This is the form taken by most clergy sexual abuse. With older teens and adults, sexual abuse can occur with force involved. The victim may be vulnerable as a result of being in a residential, correctional, or armed services setting and threatened by a person or group who has coercive power and authority in that setting.

2. *If a male has an erection and ejaculates, there was consent.* Male children and adolescents can experience erections in a variety of situations and, with stimulation, ejaculate. This, of course, is confusing for the male as well as for those who hear his report. Again, trickery or manipulation of the victim, whereby he "goes along" with a situation, in no way implies consent. Like many female victims, male victims of clergy abuse may go along to "get it over with" and survive or to maintain an important relationship.

3. *Sexual abuse of boys by males is done by homosexuals.* A number of research studies show that the vast majority of sexual abuse against boys is perpetrated by heterosexual males or females (C. Allen, 1991). Again, this is an equation of "sexual abuse" with "sexuality" —something that is no longer tolerated with regard to female sexual abuse victims but continues to be applied to males. The majority of offending ministers are heterosexual. In denominations that allow married ministers, they are also married with children.

4. *If abused by a male, it was because the victim was gay or acted gay.* This particular myth causes considerable anguish and confusion for boys. Often targeted by pedophiles or ephebophiles whose abuse focus is on the androgynous qualities of male children or young

adolescents, the victim can pick up this focus. The clergy offender may comment, "How smooth your skin is" or "How good you look," which leads to considerable misattribution of blame and responsibility on the victim. Finally, for adolescents who are experiencing some sexual identity conflict or are at the beginning of a coming out process, this adds considerable burden to a healthy gay or bisexual identity.

5. *If abused by a male, the victim will become gay.* Some correlational research reports that male victims of sexual abuse are almost twice as likely to identify themselves as gay in adulthood (Gonsiorek et al., 1994). It must be emphasized that this is a "correlational study," and there is no direct causal factor determined at this time. One rationale may be that a young male who is in the coming out process may have been "read as such" by the ephebophile. Again, this is taking advantage of the special vulnerability of a child or adolescent in a homophobic society or religious denomination.

6. *If forced or tricked by a female into being sexual, the victim should consider himself lucky.* This myth is perpetuated by a number of teen sexploitation films that show older or adult females being sexual with adolescent boys. The reality is that the male victims feel forced or tricked through the manipulation of a power relationship, and can be left as hurt and confused as any female victim would be in a corresponding situation.

7. *If sexually abused, the victim will become an offender.* Sometimes called the "vampire syndrome," which asserts that once abused the victim will become an abuser, this myth is frequently used as an explanation for the reason people become sex offenders. Research finds that only a minority of adolescent sex offenders in an outpatient treatment program report being victims of sexual abuse (O'Brien, 1989), and figures are not much different with adult offenders in an outpatient population (C. Allen, 1991). Unfortunately, this myth is readily perpetrated on male victims of religious figures who, on revealing their abuse, are often asked, "Have you sexually abused anyone?" Few immediately ask or assume that a female victim will become a perpetrator and this again reflects gender stereotyping.

8. *Boys are less hurt by sexual abuse than girls.* Again, stereotyping boys as stronger, tougher, and not as emotionally vulnerable as girls implies that, if they are abused, it won't bother them as much. This is clearly not true based on a review of the literature (Bolton

et al., 1989). Unfortunately, this sexual stereotyping can lead to emotional repression and denial that can make the abuse more insidious and invisible versus its symptomatic consequences (Pescosolido, 1989).

9. *Boys can protect themselves from sexual abuse.* This seems to present sexual abuse as a correlate to physical assault whereby "tough boys" are supposed to be able to physically defend themselves. This reflects the stereotyping that if a boy is physically taunted by a bully he should fight to protect himself and his manhood. The same is expected of sexual assault. This results from the lack of awareness that most male sexual abuse, especially by ministers, is brought about by tricks and manipulation. Force is rarely used.

10. *Males are initiators of sex or, if abused, they got what they were looking for.* Sex role stereotyping implies that males are the initiators and aggressors of every sexual encounter. The truth is that they are as vulnerable to manipulation and seduction as many females, especially by a charismatic religious authority.

CONGREGATIONAL DYNAMICS AND INTERVENTION STRATEGIES

Some authors have noted the incest metaphor as a useful perspective in viewing clergy sexual abuse of minors (Fortune, 1991; W. White, 1986). The congregation in which the sexual abuse occurs shows many of the dynamics observed in incest families in which the father has sexually abused his children. Table 11.1 shows the range of responses for a congregation suffering from such organizational incest.

The first group includes those who "Don't Believe." They typically constitute those who have been emotionally and spiritually closest to the offending pastor and are caught up by his "goodness" and all the positive work that has occurred in developing the congregation. As a consequence, they believe it couldn't happen in such a superb congregation and therefore must be a conspiracy of grand proportions.

The "Confused" group is typically less devoted to the minister but cannot reconcile how someone who was so good or so successful could have perpetrated sexual abuse, especially if multiple victims are reported. They appear stunned and confused.

The "Easy Grace" group entertains the possibility that "something" inappropriate may have happened but minimizes the gravity of the

TABLE 11.1 The Range of Responses for a Congregation

Don't Believe	Confused	Easy Grace	Believe—But Don't Understand	Anger	Rage
Couldn't happen here	How could it be?	We're all sinners	Dynamics of sexual abuse	At offender	At offender
Conspiracy	She or he was so good or successful	Not that bad	Offenders or victim dynamics	Organization	At scapegoat
		Just a mistake Not that serious Forgive and forget		Others	At God

circumstance with a variety of justifications. They rationalize that all people are sinners and thereby worthy of forgiveness, and they want to forgive and forget that such an uncomfortable and unfortunate behavior has occurred. They discount the seriousness of the abuse and forgive the pastor for having made a "mistake." The people from this group are frequently active in discussions and try to be peacemakers in a divided church.

The "Believe But Don't Understand" group thinks that the sexual abuse was serious and yet struggle to understand the dynamics of how it happened. They are trying to understand how the abuse could have gone on for so many years and yet was reported only recently by the victims. This group tries to understand how someone can present the face of a moral and righteous person and then have a secret life of pedophilia and/or ephebophilia.

The "Anger" group is often made up of victims' parents or others close to them. They are angry at the offender for his abuse and at the organization for having not intervened earlier or not responded more appropriately. They are angry at those in the congregation who are minimizing, denying, or even defending the abusing minister. This group most often constitutes the change agents within the congregation. They are often those who have risen to a leadership position on the issue because of a perceived or real failure of leadership by the church board, congregational supervisors, or bishops. It is common for a victim or an angry parent to become the "internal investigator" within the congregation, seeking to know the extent of the abuse by questioning others and checking on the pastor's background.

The "Rage" group are the small number of congregation members who may have had past run-ins with the offender or have previous abusive experiences in their own histories. They may have been personally violated as the result of the abuse within their families, and their anger has risen to the level of pure rage and hatred. This group can be explosive toward the offender, toward those who appear in any way to support the offender, and often also toward God for having allowed this to happen. Suicide, setting fire to the church, and risk of homicide to the offender can exist in members of this group.

Intervention on organizational incest dynamics must occur at the system level. Such interventions are important in creating more "space" for therapeutic change to occur for the identified clients (Imber-Black, 1987; Waldegrave, 1990). Sometimes called "congregational healing," this involves leading a workshop with a one- or two-session format in front of the entire congregation on understanding, healing, and recovering from sexual abuse. Ideally, the workshop should take place immediately after the removal of the offending pastor, when the congregation is in ongoing crisis and division.

Using two or more leaders preferably of both genders, the workshop uses visual materials and goes through an educational model of the fundamental issues involved in cluster sexual abuse. The goal of the workshop is to engage and empower the congregation in a therapeutic conversation about the abuse by providing knowledge and awareness of the reality, seriousness, and dynamics of sexual abuse. The workshop ultimately increases victim sensitivity and compassion.

It is clarified in the workshop (remembering that the audience can include open and secret victims, their families, and friends) that a sex offender can be anyone who is known to the victim and family who abuses his or her position of authority, trust, and intimacy. Table 11.1 is presented to help people define where they are in their divisions. Emphasis is placed on how people can respond to a victim by listening, believing, and affirming him. Also stressed is the importance of helping an offender by not minimizing or denying the abuse but supporting the person to be honest and to get help to change. Healing processes are presented, such as talking to those you can trust, learning as much as you can on the topic, and breaking secrets in the process of sharing and processing the abuse. Therapeutic and pastoral resources are provided both within and outside the church.

In the course of presenting such an overview of sexual abuse and healing, questions and dialogue occur between the congregation and leaders. They share their indigenous knowledge and mobilize for change. At times, victims and parents of victims have stood up to share or detail the seriousness of the abuse acts that occurred. Faced with new and unwanted information in this dramatic setting, there have been people who chose to walk out, feeling that their once beloved offender was being "crucified."

In the process, information about language, concepts, and dynamics of sexual abuse in an organizational setting encourages ongoing conversation and movement from a narrative of division and disempowerment to that of greater unity and empowerment. On one hand, the congregation becomes significantly more victim sensitive, while, on the other, those who cannot separate themselves from their enmeshment with the offender may leave to join another congregation.

INDIVIDUAL AND FAMILY THERAPY ISSUES
FOR MALE VICTIMS OF CLERGY SEXUAL ABUSE

Significant context issues present themselves for therapy of male victims of cluster clergy sexual abuse. Most continue to hold strong religious values. Just as it is important that the therapist be sensitive to race, ethnicity, sexual orientation, class, and educational diversity, it is also important that the therapist be sensitive to the religious and family values of the client.

The betrayal of the religious trust will create significant theological dilemmas: Was the baptism of my child holy? Was my confirmation holy? Was the marriage with my wife holy if conducted by the clergy perpetrator? Why did God let this happen? Why did God let it go on for so long? These issues are beyond the training of secular therapists and are most appropriately addressed by empowering and victim-sensitive pastoral counselors (Fortune, 1991).

It is also important that the therapist ally with the victim's parents, spouse, or significant other to mobilize as much support and resources as possible. Therefore a family systems perspective is most useful, and one can deal early on with the common myths on perpetration and victimization of males that spouse and parents can hold.

There are significant legal limitations and issues of which the therapist should be aware. For example, it is important to warn your clients on the limits of confidentiality before they provide information on their issues. It is typical ethical practice to inform the client that everything discussed will remain confidential except unreported child abuse or neglect or danger of harm to self and others. This "standard" warning is not enough. Such clients should also be informed that the chart information can be used for and against them in a court of law.

Mandated reporting of child abuse and "duty to warn" are common in U.S. practice as well as in other countries, but what is often forgotten is that the charts for victims can and will be subpoenaed should they decide to pursue a criminal or civil action against the offender. In a civil context in which money damages are awarded based on psychological damages, all past psychological data are considered germane to the court proceedings. When taking notes, it is prudent for the therapist to be aware of the potential and future readers and to abide by appropriate standards of charting.

Sexual abuse survivors' groups have long been a modality of choice in the treatment of sexual abuse (Salter, 1988). Unfortunately, group therapy is often not an option, especially putting victims of the same perpetrator in the same group. If the client is potentially or presently involved in a legal proceeding, a common defense used against his testimony is that his abuse history was the result of what he heard others say and does not come out of his own experience. This "commingling" of information significantly contributed in undermining the well-known, alleged cluster sexual abuse McMartin Preschool trial in California in which therapists had child victims talk about their abuse with each other in a group setting (Eberle & Eberle, 1992). While group therapy has a significant history of being beneficial for abuse victims, it can also have this very unfortunate consequence. In cluster sexual abuse, group therapy should occur later in the therapy process after depositions and interrogatories have been completed or when the client clearly will not pursue a legal action.

So too is it inappropriate to use hypnosis or trance because the product or results of such hypnosis are not admissible in U.S. and other court settings. This is because the suggestibility of a person in trance may confound the information generated.

In the United States, there has emerged a group called the False Memory Syndrome Foundation. They have taken the position that a significant minority of adult victims reporting childhood abuse do so as the result of conscious or unconscious manipulation and coaching by therapists (Freyd, 1993). This group has received some significant support from established researchers, hypnotists, psychologists, and psychiatrists (Loftus, 1993). They especially attack some therapists' use of sodium amytal, guided imagery, dream interpretation, body massages, as well as hypnosis, survivors groups, and grandly generalizing self-help books in the recovery of repressed abuse memories. These are the same techniques easily critiqued by defense attorneys. It is prudent for all therapists working with sexual abuse to be aware of such criticism, and this further argues for a therapy of curiosity and empowerment that seeks the indigenous knowledge of the client rather than the imposition of "expert" knowledge.

THE THERAPEUTIC PERSPECTIVE
OF EMPOWERMENT AND CURIOSITY

The therapeutic perspective one uses is critical in successfully empowering survivors of clergy sexual abuse. Amundson, Stewart, and Valentine (1993) searched for guiding principles out of which to conduct such therapy. They contrast what they call therapies of "certainty and power" to therapies of "curiosity and empowerment." They summarize the directions in which the narrative approach of Epston and White (1989) and the solution-focused approaches of O'Hanlon and Wilks (1989), as well as others, have been developing.

Therapies of certainty demand structure and clarity, insist on a diagnosis, rely on problem-saturated descriptions of client behavior, can see clients as having "resistance" that must be broken through, are concerned about teaching and explaining their "expert knowledge," and discount or overlook the resources of the client.

Amundson et al. (1993) further state that therapies of power are more hierarchical, can act as agents of social control, demand client responses to therapy, "rescue" the client, may foster dependence, may use jargon to sell "expert knowledge," may consider the client to be uncooperative or unaware, and under larger system pressures may unilaterally "set goals" for the client.

Unfortunately, this therapeutic approach can recapitulate the style and structure of the clergy sexual abuse in which the therapist, like the offending minister, sees the client in a one-down, controlled position of "a patient needing help that only the expert can provide."

Survivors of clergy sexual abuse respond well to a therapy of curiosity, which tolerates confusion and ambiguity, moves slowly in defining the problem, takes care to discover exceptions to the problem behavior's symptoms, considers that if clients "don't get it" it is because the therapist hasn't asked the right kind of questions, asks circular questions and examines the effects of the problem, considers observations from many system levels, always considers the therapist-client interactions and system, looks for special indigenous knowledge of the client, and takes special care to discover the strengths that are present in the client's behavior and responses.

Amundson et al. (1993) state that a therapy of empowerment will be more cooperative; considers consequences of control; focuses the therapy to respond to the client; calls for special knowledge and competencies of the client; fosters independence, competence, and self-confidence in the client; avoids jargon and uses the client's language and metaphors; frames the client as restrained or oppressed; creates a context of discovery; when frustrated, improvises therapeutically; and exercises coconstructed definitions of solution.

Durrant and Kowalski (1990) have presented a similar contrast of therapeutic approaches specifically in regard to sexual abuse (see Table 11.2). The reader will recognize the respectful principles of curiosity and empowerment in their model.

TABLE 11.2 Therapeutic Approaches

Promotes "Victim" Identity *(Problem-Saturated)*	*Promotes "Competent" Identity* *(Solution-Focused)*
1. Therapist is expert—has special knowledge regarding sexual abuse to which the client needs to submit.	1. Client is expert in her or his life—has ability to determine what is best for her or him. Therapist respects this.
2. Client is viewed as damaged or broken by the abuse.	2. Client is viewed as oppressed by and struggling with the effects of the abuse.
3. Deficit model seeks to "fix" client.	3. Resource model seeks to build on strengths and resources of the client.
4. Insight into dynamics of the abuse is the key goal of treatment.	4. Goal of treatment is client viewing him- or herself as competent and as in control of the influence of the effects of the abuse.
5. A cathartic or corrective experience is necessary to produce change.	5. Best "corrective experience" is client getting on with his or her life in his or her own way. Change promoted by experiencing "possibilities."

SOURCE: From Durrant and Kowalski (1990); Walter H. Bera Workshop copyright © 1993.

At first, survivors can feel confused by the atmosphere of deferential respect provided by such a style of empowerment and curiosity, because it is so different than their past relations with authorities. They quickly respond to such respect and even begin to demand it from others. The therapist is well served to be conscious of maintaining this approach with the survivor's family and congregation as well.

Finally, as Greenberg (1992) emphasizes, there is a significant difference between the role of the therapist and the role of the forensic evaluator. The therapist works for the client and maintains a supportive, accepting, client-centered position to assist the individual in therapeutic change. The forensic evaluator works for the lawyer, and alternatively the court, to benefit the legal process. To try to play both roles is fraught with conflict and ethical concerns.

NARRATIVE THERAPY

Michael White and David Epston have developed a theory and therapy over the last several years that focuses on the narrative epistemology or dominant story that makes sense of our lived experiences. People organize these experiences into a dominant story that may be empowering and generative or disempowering and oppressive (White & Epston, 1990). Therapy becomes the process of storying and restorying the lives and experiences of sexual abuse survivors. Durrant and White (1990) have edited a volume on the use of these concepts for the therapy of sexual abuse.

Externalization of the abuse and other problems helps survivors in identification and separation from unitary knowledges and restraining beliefs that are oppressing them. Developing an alternative story seeks past and present examples that are exceptions to the dominant story. This alternative story can then be circulated to family and significant others in the person's life.

Examples of externalizing questions found useful in clergy sexual abuse work are as follows:

What was going on that seemed to make you vulnerable to the minister's manipulations?
How did he set you up or "groom" you into the sexual contact?
What did he try to get you to believe about yourself?
What did you do to survive the sexual abuse?
How did the abuse he perpetrated affect your beliefs about yourself?
How does the abuse he perpetrated affect your relationship with others?
How did you get the courage to speak up? To come forward? To stand up to the offender?

To develop the alternative story, ask questions about "times you did not act from the imposed 'victim' identity and rather noticed you acted out a 'survivor' identity" or "times you noticed you moved from a 'reactor' position to an 'actor' position." See the aforementioned volume edited by Durrant and White (1990) for many other examples.

IDENTIFICATION
AND ASSESSMENT ISSUES

The clinician should be aware that male victims rarely present with sexual abuse as the primary issue. A confusing or troubling past relationship with a religious figure is often secondary to other concerns. If inappropriate contact is recalled, it is often minimized. Male victims of clergy most often present as a result of being motivated to deal with some psychological, behavioral, or relational problem. It is through awareness, information, and therapeutic trust and safety that the full extent of the abuse history and effects can be clarified.

Symptoms that have been associated with male sexual victimization include sexual compulsivity, intimacy impairment, homophobia, depression, hypermasculinity, workaholism, chemical abuse, self-defeating behaviors, and conduct disorders, among others (Bolton et al., 1989; Pescosolido, 1989). If someone presents with such a symptom, *it does not positively indicate that it is the result of sexual abuse.* Many traumas and difficulties can bring about sexual, relationship, and psychological difficulties in men (Gonsiorek et al., 1994). Rather, it is suggested that questions about the symptoms' connections to a sexual abuse history be explored.

MALE SEXUAL ABUSE ASSESSMENT STRATEGIES

To do an assessment for sexual abuse, the following points may be useful. A sexual and relationship history may provide the therapist with sets and settings in which sexual victimization may have occurred. Ask specific and frank questions that allow frank answers by the adolescent or adult male. The history should include any commission or experiencing of sexual contact either through vaginal or anal intercourse, oral sex, fondling, and so on.

Review any noncontact sexual behaviors that may have occurred, such as exposing, obscene phone calling, window peeping, fetish burglary, or pornographic photography. Be aware of sexually intrusive behaviors that the male may have experienced, such as unusual sexual questions, sexual punishments, enemas, unnecessary physical examinations, and so on.

Finally, review inappropriate relationships such as having been a "special friend" to an adult or parent whereby "covert incest" may be a factor. Be aware of situations relating to sleeping with a parent, authority figure, or special confidant. It is in these contexts that sexual abuse of males often occurs.

SUGGESTED STAGES OF THERAPY FOR MALE VICTIMS OF SEXUAL ABUSE

The stages that follow are offered to help structure the therapy for male victims of clergy sexual abuse. The actual therapy must be appropriate to the survivor's unique circumstance and such stages should never be imposed in the course of a cocreated therapy.

The first stage is the reassessment (restorying) and therapy of the presenting problem in the political context of the sexual abuse. Providing information about myths and issues of sexuality and male sexual abuse and victimization behavior can be useful. This provides language and concepts to clarify confusing experiences he may have had. Such information can also elicit defensiveness and strong reactions as a result of past indoctrination by the offender. Difficult dreams or other symptoms may emerge because of discomfort with the emerging realizations. Processing these alternative narratives can lead to freedom to admit that, indeed, there had been some sexually confusing or abusive behavior that contextualizes current concerns.

With an admission of sexual abuse, the next stage is set in which the abuse story is developed and elaborated. With men this can be facilitated through therapeutic dialogue or at times the use of books on sexual abuse or the writing of an abuse biography. One of the few books that covers both genders in a succinct and useful way is Bear and Dimock's (1988) *Adults Molested as Children: A Survivor's Manual for Women and Men.*

With increased awareness that sexual abuse occurred and an elaboration of the details, numerous contexts and alternate narratives can then be developed for the presenting problems. Processing of the facts and feelings, and the development of empowering alternate narratives, often leads to significant symptom remission. For example, men presenting as angry and oppositional can move toward a grief and expression of hurt for the betrayal of the abuse.

In processing the facts and feelings resulting from sexual abuse, it is important that any misattributions of blame or responsibility be overcome. This often leads to a confrontation of sexual stereotyping and roles because of the difficulty males have in accepting the "victimization."

Additional solutions become possible as the survivor sees other ways to deal with his hurt and anger. One way is to have him write a letter to the offender or dictate an audiotape in which he details the full story of the abuse and puts the blame squarely back on the offender.

On occasion, it is possible to use that letter to the offender as a means to set up a face-to-face confrontation/clarification session with the offending clergy (Bera, 1990). At other times, when face-to-face processing is not possible, the letter to the offender can be sent through the mail if deemed appropriate by the victim.

As therapy draws to an end, a recapitulation about what has been learned in the course of therapy and how to prevent reabuse in the future, of self or others, sexual or not, is helpful. At this point, the therapy often closes. Occasionally, a referral may be made for collateral personal, religious, or vocational issues.

CONCLUSION

With the increase of public awareness regarding clergy sexual abuse, more and more male survivors are coming forward to deal with their victimization. Therapists and victims alike must overcome social and organizational barriers in recognizing the confounding dynamics of this abuse and deal not only with the trauma to the individual but with its effect on the victim's family of origin and his "spiritual family" as well.

Recognizing the incestlike dynamics of the congregation and assisting in intervention workshops creates a catalyst for "congregational healing" and provides a forum for increased victim sensitivity, open discussion, and mobilization for change.

A gender-sensitive therapy is fundamental in identification, assessment, and treatment strategies for male survivors of clergy sexual abuse. It is also essential to incorporate the issues of theological dilemmas brought on by the betrayal of religious trust.

Specific legal limitations over and above common U.S. practice must be brought to the client's attention and subscribed to by the therapist to prevent jeopardizing any potential and current legal proceedings.

Therapies of curiosity and empowerment are most beneficial in the treatment of male survivors of sexual abuse. They may be incorporated through "storying" the experiences of sexual abuse survivors, externalization of the abuse to help the victim clearly delineate his needs from the needs of others, overcoming misattributions of blame, and "re-storying" to encourage agency and empowering behavior.

While this chapter focused on cases of multiple male victims of clergy in cluster sexual abuse cases, the dynamics are similar to sexual abuse of young males by many types of leaders: teacher, coach, theater director, therapist. Those who sexualize their counseling, advice, and direction blind the recipient by their presentation of the sexualized touch under the guise of caring, help, religion, or even politics of sexual liberation.

Offenders range throughout the whole spectrum of political, philosophical, and religious as well as gender and sexual orientation. Sadly the old truism, "If power corrupts, then absolute power corrupts absolutely," seems to hold. People invest themselves and their loved ones through the highest sense of devotion and ideals in spiritual, artistic, or therapeutic guides. This investment carries a degree of power and trust that, when abused, can cause the deepest and most lasting of wounds. It is the ultimate betrayal.

12

Helping Direct and Associate Victims to Restore Connections After Practitioner Sexual Misconduct

Ellen Thompson Luepker

The focus of practitioners trying to repair the damage to clients from traumatic sexual exploitation by previous practitioners typically is limited to treating the direct victims. These victims, however, are members of families—women are daughters, sisters, wives, mothers, and partners; men are sons, brothers, husbands, fathers, and partners—in deeply meaningful relationships, and the disturbing effects of the traumas induced by practitioner misconduct inevitably spill over into their relationships. Hence the members of the families and the partners of direct victims become associate victims. In this chapter, the effects of practitioner sexual misconduct on a group of direct and associate victims are examined and the roles of the latter victims in their own and the direct victims' healing processes are described.

The term *associate victim* seems preferable to *secondary victim*. *Secondary* may be interpreted as indicating a lesser status. More important, it does not accurately or realistically indicate the painful reactions of family members to the trauma suffered by the direct victim. Furthermore, *associate victim* provides a broader treatment focus in dealing with the aftereffects of practitioner misconduct. It is a recognition that the direct victim's pain and suffering have spread like a virus among the persons who are close to her (or him).

THE DIRECT VICTIMS

The major reason that most direct victims first sought help from practitioners is relationship problems. When these practitioners engage in exploitative sexual behavior, however, the initial problems are neglected or, worse, exacerbated. It seems to make no difference to exploitative practitioners whether a client is married, in a committed relationship, or single. Thus the goal of therapy subsequent to the exploitation is to help victims to obtain relief from problems stemming from the traumatic experiences so as to assist them to return to and to readdress those problems for which the victims had originally sought help (see Luepker, 1989a). This goal provides rewarding growth opportunities when the traumatic events can be integrated and understood within the context of other life experiences. A significant task in the treatment of direct victims is to carefully evaluate each client's need for including persons close to her (or him) in the treatment process and the best time for the inclusion.

At least 30% of the victims of practitioner sexual misconduct have described "predator-type" practitioners who stalk them relentlessly, never leave them alone, and use derogatory comments and other brainwashing techniques to confuse them and undermine their trust in their own judgment and reality and to isolate them from others (Luepker, 1989a). Further isolation occurs because some direct victims require psychiatric hospitalization at some time after the occurrence of the exploitation. The high prevalence of such hospitalizations reported in Luepker (1989a) appears to be a constant.

Generally, practitioner exploitation leaves direct victims with the posttraumatic stress disorder (PTSD) symptoms of hyperarousal, intrusion, and constriction (see Herman, 1992). Many also describe traumatic events that are similar to those experienced by, for example, victims of captivity (Herman, 1992). However, the effects of PTSD on the families of the direct victims of practitioner sexual exploitation have not been examined heretofore. We know what the effects of PTSD do to the families of veterans, however, and can see the parallels with our populations.

The report of findings from the National Vietnam Veterans Readjustment Study devoted one chapter to a family perspective on PTSD among the veterans. The investigators concluded,

> Posttraumatic stress disorder not only affects the veteran, it also impacts on the lives of his or her loved ones. Families of PTSD victims may have a father, mother, wife, or husband who wakes up in the middle of the night screaming, who is distant, unable to show emotion or affection, who becomes intensely angry over little things or becomes violent, who is nervous and restless, or who drinks heavily or uses drugs. . . .
>
> . . . the information offered suggests that the toll of PTSD goes beyond that paid by the veteran—perhaps even into the next generation. (Kulka et al., 1990, p. 236, all italics in original)

In the aftermath of practitioner sexual misconduct, as with effects of other types of trauma described by Herman (1992), there is an exquisite interplay between the loss of self and the need for others and, at the same time, a self-protective distancing from others. Herman (1992), in her chapter on disconnections, described trauma victims as

> spontaneously seek[ing] their first source of comfort and protection. . . . Wounded soldiers and raped women cry out for their mothers, or for God. When this cry is not answered, the sense of basic trust shattered, traumatized people feel that they belong more to the dead than to living. (p. 52)

The trauma induced by practitioner sexual exploitation is the source of the direct victims' estrangement from partners and family members. The estrangement, in turn, creates various disturbing effects in the associate victims.

ASSOCIATE VICTIMS

It is startling to learn how much pain associate victims are suffering, especially when they do not know or understand what has happened to cause the changes they see in the direct victim.

Yet associate victims, for the most part, continue to be hidden from the public eye. Typical media reports usually are limited to descriptions of direct victims, charges, and/or sanctions. Even the most recent professional literature continues to focus primarily on the characteristics of direct victims and the more narrow context of the victim/practitioner relationship. Unfortunately, many practitioners have grown so accustomed to working in insular ways with clients who suffer from practitioner misconduct that they tend to ignore what is going on among the people in the client's life outside the consulting room.

DISCONNECTIONS: CAUSES AND EFFECTS

To understand the relationship between damage to the self and the isolating disconnections from important others, the relational attachments in the direct victims' lives must be examined. The attachments may range from that to the practitioner who exploited the victim sexually to the victim's partner, children, family of origin, and even friends.

Common indications of disconnection seen in the direct victim are estrangement (unexplained distancing) from individuals, mood swings, irritability and/or outbursts of anger, school/career problems, and psychiatric hospitalizations. Other problems, some severe, that are specific to the relationship, follow.

The break with the exploitative counselor may be, in itself, painful for the victim. The "traumatic disillusionment" with the often idealized practitioner, for example, is described in Luepker (1989a). Also discussed there is the primary victims' resulting distrust of help from subsequent practitioners.

Unable to tell the reasons for breaking off the sessions with the counselor, the victim's act may be attributed to her "illness" by anxious family members; they may make strong efforts to get her back into the consulting room with the same practitioner or with another. The victim, however, at this point probably distrusts all practitioners. Thus the victim suffers doubly—the effects of the exploitation and the well-meaning efforts of her family—and her symptoms may be exacerbated.

Severing the consultation relationship—however exploitative it may be—with a clerical counselor tends to be more complicated than doing so with a lay practitioner and tends to extend to community loyalties. Some victims who have been involved in church affairs and activities may, along with the family members, have developed personal relationships with the counselor's family. Staying away from the counselor's influence may mean breaking the friendships, leaving the church, and, if the counselor is accused publicly, incurring the wrath of the congregation. Almost invariably, whatever the evidence, the church community sides with the counselor and blames the victim. Additional pain and misunderstandings may be aroused when the victim's partner and children are deprived, for reasons they do not understand, of participation in church activities and friendships within the congregation.

Effects on Partner

What partners see. The generic term *partner* describes either a spouse in a marriage or a participant in a committed relationship. Partners of direct victims may see the following chaotic, unpredictable evidence of PTSD as well as the common ones listed above.

The victims may disconnect emotionally from both partner and children. They often become sexually dysfunctional—unable to experience sexual pleasure or to function sexually. Even when they succumb to their partners' requests for sex, they may have no pleasure. They are more likely to avoid the partners physically without being able to discuss the reason.

They may make sudden unexplained requests for divorce without a reason. These requests may occur when the victimized partners suffer feelings of intense shame for "permitting" themselves to have been used by the exploitative practitioner, betraying their domestic partners, and violating their personal morality.

Double betrayals. In some relationships, both partners have been counseled by the same practitioner so the husband also becomes a direct victim. In one case, the practitioner was sexually exploiting the wife but the husband was kept ignorant of the misconduct. When the wife started showing distress owing to the exploitation, the husband sought understanding and help from the counselor for the new relational problems. The practitioner labeled the wife "crazy," told the husband he couldn't "expect improvement right now," and instructed him to distance himself by not asking for sex. The consequence? The abuse of the wife remained a secret and was perpetuated, and the husband was victimized by the violation of his trust in the counselor.

Other forms of partner betrayal also may occur. In another case, when both husband and wife were being counseled by the same practitioner and the latter was exploiting the wife sexually, the practitioner, in response to the husband's concern with the changes in his wife's behavior, instructed the husband to give the wife extraordinary sums of money. It did not take long for the husband to deplete his business assets and to run up unprecedented debts.

Relationship Problems After Disclosure

When partners learn of the sexual exploitation by practitioners, they feel estranged—emotionally cut off—from the victims.

Anger. Partners struggle with feelings of anger toward the victim and the abuser. They want to be supportive of their partners, but they also want to understand the partners' vulnerability and why they were unable to refrain from consenting to the exploitation, yet they have difficulties.

Some partners say, "It would have been a lot easier to understand and accept if my wife had been raped by a stranger or even a neighbor; then I would know who is to blame" (see Luepker & O'Brien, 1989, and the discussion of support groups for spouses).

Controlling anger is difficult for some partners. In two cases, for example, when husbands learned that practitioners had sexually exploited their wives, they went to the homes of the practitioners and physically assaulted them. The husbands were charged by the police. Some men wanted to disrupt the practitioner's family life just as theirs had been disrupted. When they saw the practitioners and/or his family members in cars, the husbands reacted impulsively. One started to jump out of his truck at a stop light. Surprised by his impulsiveness, he said, "The only thing that held me back was the seat belt."

Loss of feeling of safety. Partners do not know if the other member of the dyad is in good professional hands when the direct victim begins to look worse during the course of treatment. This is the period when the trauma is surfacing. Another period when partners become fearful for the victims is when the primary victim opts for a particular kind of compensatory action, such as the institution of litigation proceedings. Will public exposure make her worse?

Impatience. Partners wonder: Will the victim ever be the same? Will things ever get back to normal? In the hurry to close out the whole episode and return home life to normal, some partners push the victims to initiate lawsuits before they have been able to sort through their options for action or feel ready to take any action.

Loss of sleep. Partners describe the inability either to fall asleep or to stay asleep. Many are wakened in the middle of the night to help the victims manage nightmares, and many partners suffer from nightmares themselves.

Loss of work. Many partners describe difficulties in concentrating and thus difficulty in functioning optimally at work.

Loss of money. Partners may suffer financially owing either to the loss of the ability to work or to their efforts to subsidize the victims' treatment expenses. Other expenses are incurred by paying for counseling for themselves and/or children.

Increased responsibility. Often partners must take over the household. When the direct victims are hospitalized, the partners must assume the entire responsibility for the care of the home, including, in many cases, young children.

Horror. While direct victims have difficulty writing narratives of their traumatic experiences, partners have difficulty reading the descriptions of events. Spouses who were counseled by the same practitioners who exploited their wives speak of feeling a horror for which they can find no words. They also struggle to write their narratives, sometimes as part of recovery in treatment or as part of their separate causes of action. Increasing numbers of spouses have discovered that they have their own causes of action and choose litigation in which to confront the practitioner to regain some psychological and financial control.

Disorders. Many partners of victims also suffer from PTSD and some meet sufficient criteria for diagnoses of "major depressive disorder." They may require counseling help and need psychiatric consultation on the necessity for psychotropic medications.

The Effects of Mothers' Behaviors on Children

Few direct victims with children are able to tell them about the sexual exploitation. The children, even young ones, become aware that something is wrong, however. They see a growing deterioration in the mother's behaviors and her gradual alienation from them and their needs. The children react to what they see and sense in the household.

Mothers' excessive sleep. Many direct victims withdraw from the family to spend more and more time in their bedrooms, where they are known to cry or to sleep. A mother who had been victimized by her pastor developed a major depressive disorder that caused her to sleep for long hours during the day; she described waking one day to see her pre-school son playing quietly with his toys on the floor next to the bed—a way of staying close to her. She mourned the loss of active engagement with him during this period of his life.

Role reversals. In some cases, children feel or actually are called upon to reverse roles and to parent their mothers, who are unable to care for themselves. The reversal has taken many forms: carrying their mothers around, feeding them, and even protecting them. The children take the calls from the practitioners who caused the problems and refuse to let them speak with the mothers. They avoid telling their mothers of the gossip they hear about them.

Struggle for control. Children see their mothers struggling to maintain control. For example, in their efforts to regain control over their sense of "dirtiness" and feelings of shame, many direct victims engage in excessive ritualistic cleaning. They may berate their children for making "messes" that are normal for their ages. They reenact their own traumas within the relationships with the children. For example, many feel extreme anxiety about the children's being hurt in some way by practitioners. When the exploiter has been a clergy member, many mothers cannot allow their young children to participate in church activities (e.g., first communion training). Those who have been exploited when the children were young try to make up for the lost time and become anxious about the children's growing older. After describing instances of his mother's extreme anxiety, one 16-year-old son said, wistfully, "While my mother's trying to recapture my childhood, I'm just trying to hold on to my teenage years!"

Unpredictability. Children may experience their victimized mothers to be just as the mothers feel—unpredictable. In a case of the sexual exploitation of a widowed mother, the counselor had taken over the role of father. He promised the children trips and other things that never materialized. One son said, "I would repeat to my friends his announcement that we would be moving out of state, and then it never would happen. My friends lost trust in me and I lost trust in my mother—things never happened the way she would say they would."

Separations. Some mothers leave their children to travel with the practitioners who are exploiting them. They have asked the children, before
the trips, to keep their whereabouts secret. Hence the direct victims may
unwittingly engage the children in the perpetuation of the exploitation.
This behavior becomes an issue in subsequent treatment. During the
recovery period, mothers also may have to leave the children if they are
hospitalized for psychiatric reasons.

Parental conflict. When the partners learn of the practitioner exploitation, some children are forced to witness uncharacteristic scenes of parental conflict despite parental efforts to hide their conflict. Sometimes
violence occurs; one mother, for example, was thrown down the stairs.
In other households, children see one or the other parent leaving home
after a loud fight. Some children are witnesses to unexpected discussions
of divorce.

Losses. In cases of clergy abuse, the parents suddenly may leave the
church and remove the children from Sunday school and the many friends
they had there. Some children lose their favorite baby-sitters—the
children of the offending clergy.

Taunting. In small towns, children actually have been taunted by members of the community. Hawthorne's plot in *The Scarlet Letter* is still
acted out today. One 11-year-old boy came home and told his mother
that a neighbor had told him his mother was a "whore." The mother was
unable at that time to answer his questions.

Leaving. An added mystery, for children, is seeing parents going off
every week for subsequent counseling appointments without knowing
where they are going or why.

CHILDREN'S REACTIONS

While parents try to manage the traumatic aftermath of the sexual
exploitation by practitioners, their children react with strong emotions
of their own. They include confusion, fear, helplessness, and loss of safety.

Overburdening. Children feel overburdened by the turmoil of their once
peaceful, supportive homes. They are especially weighed down when
they have been forced into role reversals or when the parents' trauma

has been reenacted with anxiety about the child's own separation-individuation tasks.

Loneliness. The secretive nature of the family's problems isolates the child and keeps him or her feeling alone both within and outside the family of origin. Loneliness is particularly a problem in communities in which the members lack understanding and avoid members of the family.

Differences. When one mother was in the psychiatric hospital, a father brought their 7-year-old daughter to see me. The daughter reported that she felt "different." When asked what made her feel so, she said, "Most kids don't have moms who are sexually abused by their pastors." Her feeling reflects what we know children feel about experiences that are not yet understood or discussed in society, just as divorce used to be.

Relations With Families of Origin

Less understood are the disconnections and need for the restoration of connections in relationships with the victim's family of origin when the victim tries to keep the past exploitation hidden from them. Many victims say they wish they could have help from these families but, unfortunately, few are able to talk about the abuse they experienced. To do so, they may need some encouragement and, in many cases, professional help. Many victims also fear that the knowledge will "hurt" their mothers. Indeed, some insist that their parents could not understand. Certainly, there are some parents who are unable to look beyond themselves to their children's separate reality; nevertheless, many parents are able to understand and to provide welcome support.

Because they are unable to tell the members of their families of origin or are unable to talk about their feelings and needs if they do tell, direct victims remain isolated and disconnected from people who are important to them. Because the wounds they suffer are invisible to others, this invisibility seems to exacerbate the direct victims' own self-doubts about the reality of their pain.

What the family of origin sees. Before a direct victim discloses her trauma to her family, the members may have a sense of chaos. Whenever they visit the victim, they see signs of trouble but, typically, do not know the reason for them. Many parents and siblings of clients say they have tried to organize the sense of chaos by making up explanations, yet the aura of illusion and feeling of chaos persist.

Caring families of origin may show confused reactions toward the changes that occur in the direct victim because of the hidden victimization. These reactions may not be evident, however, in the members of those families in which (a) there is a considerable emotional distance to begin with or (b) the parents are unable to look beyond themselves to notice changes in their children's moods or circumstances.

The typical signs of trouble noted by family of origin members are the common indications of disconnection listed previously. But the family may see and worry about other signs of trouble as well.

Estrangement of the victim may be the most troublesome. A loving daughter or sister suddenly avoids the family members using flimsy, untrue excuses or has nothing to say.

Lack of knowledge about the cause of the trouble can be confusing. Even when they have been told that the direct victim has been exploited by a practitioner, family of origin members may not understand the dynamics of the problems; therefore they remain confused.

Lack of role or script can introduce distance. Learning about the practitioner abuse does not tell how to help the victim or what the family's role should be. Some caring and well-meaning parents reach for suggestions (e.g., "OK. Now maybe you can try to put it behind you.") out of the desire to show care and support for the victim. The latter, however, does not see these parents as such. The trouble is that the victimization is probably outside the parents' experience and they do not know how to react to the revelation or what to say or do, yet they do not want to appear rejecting.

Fear is an offshoot of lack of knowledge.

Loss of safety. Family members have reported that the world no longer seemed safe. Even when they did not know about the practitioner misconduct, they feared they might lose the direct victim.

Need to blame someone. Parental lack of knowledge about the dynamics of practitioner misconduct causes some parents to take sides, that is, to blame the direct victim or the partner, depending upon the relationship.

Helplessness. The combined weight of the preceding feelings makes family members feel helpless.

Treatment Strategies

Telling. Whether or not the direct victim needs professional help to talk with family members or the partner alone, assistance may be sought in order to consider who may be safe to tell and/or to clarify the goals and agenda of the discussions. In suggesting what to say, the therapist can stress that sentences beginning with the phrases, *I feel* and *I need* have a better chance of being "heard" by others. Furthermore, a direct victim may need help to limit her or his expectations so that disappointments will be minimized.

Sometimes the focus of the discussion agenda will be to inform family members or others about the practitioner abuse. Sometimes it may be couple counseling for relationship difficulties that is needed. Counseling of partners or family members either separately or together with the direct victims may be an essential adjunct to the individual or group treatments for the direct victims.

Sometimes the children of victims may need supportive counseling. In such instances, the victim's and his or her partner's needs should first be clarified, and then the children's. Initial family sessions should, whenever possible, be timed so that all family members can be present so as to prevent further fragmentation of information and experience. Later, decisions are needed on whether children should be seen alone, with the parents, or a combination of the two.

Indications for Inclusion
of Family Members or Partners

In discussions with victimized male and female clients on whether the time has come to include family members and/or partners in the treatment process, three key factors must be considered: (a) the victim's *readiness* to tell, (b) the *relevance* of such discussions to the victim's healing process, and (c) the *indications for professional help* in family/ partner discussions.

Readiness. Is the victim strong enough? Physically and emotionally? Sufficiently stable biologically to get enough sleep? To eat regularly? Does the victim feel sufficient safety to engage others in the helping process? Is the victim able to organize the process sufficiently to articulate it to her- or himself in order to describe it to others? In a committed relationship, has there been sufficient opportunity for the direct victim to discuss the specifics of the practitioner abuse and aftermath with the partner so that both direct victim and partner are adequately comfortable with the topic, the agenda, and the method of telling so as to bring the children into the discussion?

Relevance. Is the inclusion of family member(s) or partner relevant to the direct victim's healing process? Will talking with family member(s) or the partner reduce the direct victim's fear, anxiety, isolation?

Indications for professional help. Is it needed? Is the direct victim able to talk with family members or partner alone or is professional participation needed to facilitate the discussions?

Goals for the Inclusion
of Family Members or Partners

Sessions in which family members and/or partners participate provide opportunities (a) to help them to talk about what they have observed; (b) to provide an overview of the general dynamics of practitioner power abuse as a prelude to the specific dynamics of the trauma suffered by the direct victim; (c) to help family members to understand the symptoms that have been seen; (d) to encourage them to talk together about how they feel about the situation, past and present; and (e) to clarify roles. It is also essential to help partners and family members to look ahead to what they can anticipate in terms of future issues: How long can the victim's problems be expected to last? What are the reasons for litigation or other complaint action, if the victim opts for it? What occurrences may be associated with the complaint action? What may be the community's potential reactions?

Putting words to the actual happenings and possible eventualities helps family members and partners to piece together the confusing events and conditions they have been living with, sometimes over a period of several years.

Meeting the helpers. It is also advantageous for family members and/or partners to meet with the counselor so that he or she is no longer a mysterious person. Parents, whatever their ages, who have been concerned with their children's safety want to be certain that the children are working with a safe person. Also, the victim's children benefit from, first, seeing the actual place where their parents go for counseling and, second, having the opportunity to ask questions.

A 4-year-old at one session asked a counselor if she ate at McDonald's "like I do."

Her 8-year-old brother asked if the counselor had been sexually abused. The counselor said, "No, but that's a good question. Why did you ask?" He said he had wondered how she had learned to help people who had been so abused. "From listening to people like your parents," the counselor responded. "Your mother and father taught me a great deal about how they felt and what they needed when they talked about their experiences."

The 9-year-old daughter's question: "Is it only ministers who sexually abuse people?" The counselor explained that anyone can harm anyone. All people at times have urges to hurt others, either physically or with words. But there is a difference between such feelings and a person's actual behaviors.

Discussions with children frequently include techniques for staying "in control" of one's own behavior, handling threatening events with others, and people's right to expect that if they go for counseling or other professional help they will not be hurt. These, of course, are topics children must deal with themselves on a daily basis—in their neighborhoods and on school playgrounds. In this way, the "good-guy/bad-guy" dichotomies that are neither realistic nor helpful are avoided.

Clarifying needs and goals. Direct victims, often for the first time since the exploitation occurred and, more important, perhaps for the first time in their lives, have help in stating their needs and the kind of support they require from family members. In couple sessions, partners have the opportunity to express their respective concerns and to negotiate differences.

The sessions also are opportunities for the counselor to clarify whether family members or partners may need individual counseling. If some individuals do need independent counseling in addition to the family work in the context of the direct victim's treatment, referral to a colleague is essential.

Children who have been taking on parenting roles and caring for their parents learn that, although the parents still may be acting upset, they are getting help from the counselor to increase their ability to take care of themselves. Thus the counselor clarifies that it is the role of the counselor and not the children to care for troubled parents.

Mastery. Finding strategies for mastery is the final goal. The first step is to obtain knowledge about one's own and other victims' experiences and feelings, and then having help to articulate these feelings and to so organize events that one feels less at their mercy. By making the traumatic events and their effects visible and understandable, direct and associate victims are able to piece together the chaotic fragments of the histories. Just as direct victims feel better knowing what the intrusive symptoms are and why they happen, so do associate victims feel more in control of their lives by understanding the direct victims' reactions to the traumatic events and their own reactions to their own disturbances.

One teenager was asked how he had felt when he heard that his mother had been sexually abused by their pastor. He replied, "It was very important for me to know. If I hadn't learned the reason she was acting so anxious with me I would've been out of here a long time ago."

Direct and associate victims participating in family sessions can learn how to identify what are reactions to the direct victim's traumatic experiences, and to voice their concerns in a way that is helpful to themselves and to others. For example, many concerned parents have difficulty talking about sex with their teenagers. For direct victims, this anxiety is compounded. Thus mothers need to be helped to clarify their specific worries about teenagers' sexuality. Another important aspect of mastery is achieved if the mothers can find ways to state these worries without becoming overwhelmed by and imposing their own personal traumatic histories. In the same way, direct victims who avoid their partners' sexual advances can be helped to speak out about their problems and what they need from the partners.

Daughters sometimes use the family sessions to ask their mothers how they can avoid sexual abuse. All children need to explore the phenomenon of power imbalance: people in positions of greater power abusing their positions. The children can be encouraged to talk about related topics that they deal with at school and socially on a daily basis, for example, to "tell" persons in charge when they or others are being scapegoated or even when they themselves are participating in scapegoating. They learn during the family sessions how their parents are standing up for themselves and "telling" people in charge that they have been hurt.

The children learn about sanctions: One 3½-year-old asked, "Will the minister get a second chance?" At her developmental stage, "second chances" are part of daily life. To answer the question, the parents explained that the minister already had been given a second chance, but because his behavior was still out of control, the people in charge of the church decided he had to take "time out" from his work so he wouldn't hurt others. By picking up on and using children's own concepts and words, they can be helped to gain more understanding.

Partners feel less anxious about the litigation or complaint process when they have an opportunity to express their fears, obtain information, and learn ways to talk with their own parents about what they are going through. The older parents can learn what they can do to help:

sometimes to "just listen and be there," and sometimes, when the direct victim is overwhelmed by traumatic memories, to provide child care.

Finally, young children see their own parents as valuable role models; they observe the parents identifying problems and seeking help for them. At a time when society is concerned with the problem of teen suicide, and we know that suicides usually are precipitated by a sense of hopelessness and the perception that there are no alternatives, the children benefit greatly from watching their parents seek help when they need it.

SUMMARY

By clarifying their respective histories and needs, direct and associate victims expand their understandings of themselves and of each other. They become better able to move together into a shared future.

While the direct victim learns to trust him- or herself by gaining biological equilibrium and safety and exploring the meaning of the traumatic events within the context of her or his own life experience, the involvement of others (e.g., partners, family members, friends) helps to restore the connection to oneself as well as to others. Direct victims' fears, isolation, estrangement, anxiety, confusion, and powerlessness can be reduced through planned discussions with family members and/or partners as part of the process of healing the wounds of the practitioner-induced trauma.

In the same way, family members and partners can be helped to dispel their parallel isolation, estrangement, anxiety, confusion, and powerlessness through planned involvement in the direct victim's healing process. Whether family members and partners are included in professionally facilitated sessions together with the primary victims or seek counseling separately or need no counseling, they are empowered through the clarification of previously fragmented, chaotic events and their personal roles and scripts.

It was not too long ago that physical disabilities—even those suffered in war—and divorce and rape, for example, were regarded as social stigmas and hidden behind veils of secrecy—out of sight, out of mind. Communities have benefited from doing away with these blind prejudices. Destroying the veils has encouraged the integration of people with disabilities into the community and encouraged them to use their talents for the community's benefit. Divorce has become better understood. The victims of rapists are no longer blamed for the victimization;

many community organizations now assist them to return to their rightful places in society.

Today's communities and people benefit from open discussions of sexual abuse, whether it occurs in the home, on the street, or in professional/pastoral offices. For example, four years after he had learned in a family counseling session that his mother's psychiatric hospitalizations had been precipitated by their pastor's sexual exploitation of her, a teenage son told his mother that he had chosen this family topic for a high school class speech assignment. It meant a great deal to him, regardless of his classmates' potential responses, to share what he and his family had gone through so his classmates "would know this kind of thing can happen." His teacher reported that his classmates had respected and appreciated his speech. Thus his family's shared experience created a broader ripple effect; perhaps it helped others to prevent or intervene more appropriately in similar crises.

PART III

Perpetrators

While some in recent years have grabbed headlines with hasty pronouncements about perpetrators of professional abuse, others have been patiently logging innumerable hours observing, assessing, and ordering their observations about those who engage in professional abuse. Glen Gabbard of the Menninger Clinic is perhaps the most painstaking of such individuals. A chapter describing his incisive observations from decades of work with perpetrators of professional abuse opens this section.

Working independently until recently, a group in Minneapolis has been similarly collecting information. We developed understandings of professional abuse perpetrators, similar in many respects to Gabbard's. I describe this model, and from a forensic psychological perspective, outline the challenges of evaluation and assessment for rehabilitation of professional perpetrators. Recent controversies about perpetrators are also discussed.

Years before it was permissible to speak of professionals who transgressed sexually, one area of professional impropriety or impairment was the first to be recognized: substance abuse. It is not surprising therefore that some working from an addiction-ology perspective have evolved into working in the area of sexual abuse by professionals. Richard Irons describes a sophisticated in-patient assessment model for professional perpetrators of sexual impropriety. While this model may have originally derived from an addictionology perspective, much more is brought to bear on this assessment process.

A comforting but false assumption often made about profes-sional abuse perpetrators is that they represent a few "rotten apples" in the health care and clerical professions. These three contributions will, I hope, dispel this simplistic idea and give an appreciation for the diversity of perpetrators. William White's contribution goes further. He takes a systemic view of profes-sional abuse and describes the organizational systems that can be as much a part of professional abuse as the improprieties them-selves. Bill White has been writing about the dynamics of sick organizations for decades. Mental health professionals are espe-cially prone to see problems as mere individual psychopathol-ogy; they in particular are directed to his chapter.

It was noted earlier that, too often, it is the victims of profes-sional abuse who educate professionals about their respon-sibilities. Similarly, it often has been graduate students who educate their mentors about the seriousness of this problem. Dissertations by Linda D'Addario (1977) some years ago and more recently by James Robinson (1993) are important ex-amples. The chapters by Laura Lyn and Mindy Benowitz are two examples in this volume. Laura Lyn's graduate research ad-dressed the social and sexual interactions between gay, lesbian, and bisexual therapists and their clients. Mindy Benowitz's dis-sertation intensively studied women exploited by therapists of both genders. Another chapter of mine completes this part with a discussion of particular boundary challenges in gay male communities.

Most professional abuse, about 80%, consists of male professionals abusing female clients. The next most common is female professionals and female clients, about 11%. About 6% are male professionals abusing male clients and about 3% female professionals abusing male clients. These are not exact figures but are based on the nonrandom samples observed by our group in Minneapolis.

The various health care professions and many clerical denominations are almost all skewed in their gender distribution. For example, psychiatry remains predominantly male; psychology was so, but is rapidly approaching gender parity and may develop a female majority; and social work has been predominantly female. Religious denominations have been exclusively male except for those in recent decades that have admitted women. Recently, in some denominations, extraordinary numbers of women have been entering the clergy. One cannot separate the distribution of different kinds of perpetration dyads from the gender disparities in the professions measured. We are a long way away from knowing the "true" gender distributions of professional abuse.

There is little doubt that most professional abuse is perpetrated by men upon women. It is a bit surprising that the next most common dyad are women professionals and women clients. Many have speculated that male victims of professionals of either gender are underrepresented across the board because of particular male characteristics inhibiting both recognition and reporting (see Gonsiorek, Bera, & LeTourneau, 1994).

The three chapters in this part describing patterns other than male perpetrator and female client are not meant to suggest that this latter pattern is not the most common. Rather, they attempt to remedy the silence about other variations of professional abuse. If we are to truly understand professional abuse, we must understand it in all its diversity, not only in its most common form.

13

Psychotherapists Who Transgress
Sexual Boundaries With Patients

Glen O. Gabbard

With sexual misconduct rapidly becoming the number one liability concern for the mental health professions, the field has been struggling to understand the phenomenon (Apfel & Simon, 1985; Gabbard, 1989; Gartrell, Herman, Olarte, Feldstein, & Localio, 1986; Pope & Bouhoutsos, 1986; Schoener, Milgrom, Gonsiorek, Luepker, & Conroe, 1989). Among these efforts have been several attempts to develop typologies of therapists who transgress sexual boundaries with patients (Averill et al., 1989; Gonsiorek, 1989a; Olarte, 1991; Pope & Bouhoutsos, 1986; Twemblow & Gabbard, 1989). A psychodynamic understanding of these therapists and what forces lead them to resort to such highly self-destructive behavior is more difficult to ascertain.

Part of the difficulty has been a tendency in recent years to politicize therapist-patient sex in such a way as to discourage systematic

AUTHOR'S NOTE: Reprinted with permission from the *Bulletin of the Menninger Clinic*, Vol. 58, No. 1, pp. 124-135, Copyright © 1994, The Menninger Foundation.

psychodynamic understanding. The "politically correct" view of the phenomenon in some venues is that thoroughly evil male therapists prey on helpless female patients (Gutheil & Gabbard, 1992). In this model the problem can be solved simply by eradicating the "bad apples" from the profession. This reductionistic view has the appeal of reassuring therapists that those who engage in sexual misconduct are vastly different than they are. They are a group of "impaired professionals" who can be differentiated from everyone else by their utterly corrupt superegos and their morally reprehensible behavior.

Another aspect of this narrow view of therapist-patient sex is that it lends itself to sexual stereotypes in the culture (Gutheil & Gabbard, 1992). Men are the seducers, and women are the seduced. In one study of sexual transgressions, when female therapists were involved with male patients, the male patients were regarded as responsible and blameworthy for the behavior, and the female therapists were viewed as their victims (Averill et al., 1989). While most studies suggest that males are the perpetrators in the vast majority of cases, substantial evidence now demonstrates that females also are involved in sexual misconduct. Moreover, same-sex pairings represent a significant problem even though they are less frequently reported than opposite-sex pairings (Benowitz, 1991; Gonsiorek, 1989a; Gutheil & Gabbard, 1992; Lyn, 1990).

The fact that sexual misconduct is a complex problem involving a variety of different scenarios becomes apparent to anyone who studies a sufficient number of cases. Systematic examination of data often yields results that do not conform to politically correct formulas. At the Menninger Clinic, where therapists who have transgressed sexual boundaries with patients have been evaluated and treated for many years, this diversity of psychodynamic themes has emerged in the work with these individuals. In this chapter, I would like to report on a series of pastoral counselors, social workers, psychiatrists, and psychologists whom I have seen in psychoanalysis, psychotherapy, hospital treatment, or consultation, in addition to other cases in which I have been indirectly involved as supervisor or consultant to other clinicians.

In trying to explicate the psychodynamic themes in these therapists, I have encountered a problem related to confidentiality that others in the field have shared. Because I am discussing the psychology of colleagues who may be recognizable to readers of this chapter, I am not at liberty to describe the details of individual cases. Instead, I am forced for ethical reasons to talk about the psychodynamic themes I have observed in broad brush strokes that paint a general picture but leave out the idiosyncratic and specific details of any one therapist.

A PSYCHODYNAMIC
CLASSIFICATION

It is heuristically useful to group these therapists in rubrics that are psychodynamically based rather than limited to specific diagnostic categories. The vast majority of therapists who become sexually involved with patients will fall into one of the following four groups: (a) psychotic disorders, (b) predatory psychopathy and paraphilias, (c) lovesickness, and (d) masochistic surrender.

The first category, psychotic disorders, is definitely the smallest group of the four and consists of therapists who suffer from such disorders as bipolar affective disorder, paranoid psychoses, schizophrenia, and psychotic organic brain syndromes. They generally require extensive treatment that includes pharmacotherapy and vocational counseling so they do not continue in the career of psychotherapist.

Because the other three categories are more common and more complex from a dynamic perspective, I will consider each of them in substantially more detail.

PREDATORY PSYCHOPATHY
AND PARAPHILIAS

Within this rubric I am including not only antisocial personality disorders but also severe narcissistic personality disorders with prominent antisocial features. Although all persons suffering from paraphilias are certainly not psychopathic predators, those who act on their paraphilic impulses with patients they are treating generally have severely compromised superegos and character pathology on the narcissistic to antisocial continuum.

These therapists are generally male, but female practitioners have been reported to fit this category also. Benowitz (1991) reported two female therapists who engaged in violent behavior during sex with clients, such as urging a patient to perform violent acts with sharp objects on herself. Another female therapist asked a patient to perform the same behaviors that had been degrading to her in past sexually abusive relationships, a common form of sadistic humiliation in this category of therapists. Male offenders in this group tend to have been involved with a long string of clients and are notoriously refractory to rehabilitation of any kind. When caught, they may pretend to be remorseful and claim that they were in love with the patient. They may be masters at manipulating the legal system as well, so often they escape any severe legal or ethical sanctions.

For therapists in this category, patients are merely regarded as objects to be used for the therapists' own sexual gratification. Because the therapists lack empathy or concern for the victim, they are incapable of feeling remorse or guilt about any harm they might have done to the patient. This massive failure of superego development appears to be related to profound impairment of internalization during childhood development. The only form of object relatedness they appear to know is the sadistic bonding with others through the exercise of destructiveness and power (Meloy, 1988). Some of these therapists have childhood histories of profound neglect or abuse, and some clinicians have understood their exploitation of others as an effort to achieve active mastery of passively experienced trauma (Schwartz, 1992).

One particular variant operating in same-sex dyads involves split-off homoerotic feelings. Therapists who may ordinarily regard themselves as heterosexual may split off and projectively disavow both their own self-loathing and their sexual feelings toward persons of the same sex (Gonsiorek, 1989a). They then act out such feelings secretly with their patients, often with cruel and sadistic methods, as a way of compartmentalizing ego-dystonic homosexual feelings.

LOVESICKNESS

Most therapists who become sexually involved with patients are either predatory or lovesick. In one survey of psychiatrists (Gartrell et al., 1986), 65% of those who had been in a sexual relationship with a patient described themselves as in love with the patient. Lovesick therapists may be associated with a variety of different diagnostic categories (Gabbard, 1991a; Twemblow & Gabbard, 1989). In some cases, they suffer from less severe forms of narcissistic personality disorder that lack the antisocial features typical of the predatory group. The narcissistic themes in these therapists involve a desperate need for validation by their patients, a hunger to be loved and idealized, and a tendency to use the patient to regulate their own self-esteem. Some lovesick therapists may have borderline personality disorder that leads them to quickly idealize patients and impulsively act on their feelings of infatuation. Still others have neurotic problems, and some therapists in this category are essentially normal, from a diagnostic standpoint, but are in the midst of a life crisis.

The most common scenario is that of a middle-aged male therapist who falls in love with a much younger female patient while he is experiencing divorce, separation, disillusionment with his own marriage, or the loss of a significant person in his life (Gabbard, 1991a; Twemblow & Gabbard, 1989). He may begin to share his own problems with his patient and present himself in psychotherapy sessions as needy and vulnerable. This role reversal is a common precursor to sexual transgressions.

One way of viewing this development in a psychotherapy process is to describe the countertransference as having become erotized in the same way that certain incest victims and borderline patients develop erotized *transference* (Blum, 1973; Gabbard, 1991a). The ability to distinguish a countertransference wish from the reality of the situation is compromised, so that the loving feelings toward the patient lose the "as if" quality characteristic of milder forms of transference. The therapist can no longer appreciate that something from the past is being repeated and that feelings for significant persons from the therapist's past are displaced onto the patient. In light of this loss of insight, a form of "nonpsychotic loss of reality testing" can be observed (Twemblow & Gabbard, 1989). Outside the particular *folie à deux* that involves the therapist-patient dyad, the therapist's reality testing appears to be intact. Within the dyad, however, a loss of judgment and reality testing makes it difficult for the therapist to see how self-destructive and harmful the relationship has become. Indeed, many lovesick therapists, when confronted, will insist that the relationship transcends any considerations of transference and countertransference.

A variety of psychodynamic themes can be identified in cases of lovesickness. In any single case, one or several of the following issues may figure prominently in the therapist's transgression.

Unconscious Reenactment of Incestuous Longings

There can be little doubt that therapist-patient sex is symbolically incestuous to both therapist and patient. Each member of the dyad is a forbidden object to the other. For the therapist, the psychological proscription is intensified by ethical and legal prohibitions. One way of viewing the development of a sexual relationship in the context of psychotherapy is that it is a re-creation of an earlier incestuous situation for both persons. As Kluft (1989) has noted, incest victims tend to put themselves in situations where they become revictimized and therefore are "sitting ducks" for therapist-patient sex. Freud observed in 1905: "The finding of an object is in fact a refinding of it" (Freud, 1905/1953, p. 222). Both therapist and patient are refinding forbidden objects from the past, and the therapist colludes in an enactment rather than interpreting the unconscious wish to repeat past trauma, all under the guise of "true love."

A Wish for Maternal Nurturance
Is Misperceived as a Sexual Overture

With incest victims in particular, receiving care may be inextricably bound up with sexuality. They may explicitly demand some form of physical contact to be reassured that they are cared for and valued. The professional boundaries of the relationship may be regarded with contempt, and the longing to be loved and held may be repeated again and again until the therapist acquiesces (Gabbard & Wilkinson, 1994). Therapists often misconstrue the patient's wish for maternal nurturance as a sexual overture and act accordingly. A pregenital need is misunderstood as a demand for genital sexual activity.

Interlocking Enactments
of Rescue Fantasies

Apfel and Simon (1986) have noted that the patient's tendency to repeat his or her past may, in fact, be mirrored by the therapist's need to repeat. A female patient may have harbored a childhood fantasy that she was somehow ministering to a father who was despairing over his marriage. Similarly, a male therapist may be unconsciously rescuing his depressed mother. Hence the therapist-patient dyad is involved in interlocking rescue enactments.

Patient Viewed as an
Idealized Version of the Self

Lovesick therapists with narcissistic problems may project aspects of themselves onto the patient. This projected ego ideal or idealized self-representation may then obscure the patient's real qualities. Just as Narcissus fell in love with his own image in the water, these therapists are infatuated with an idealized reflection of themselves.

Confusion of Therapist's
Needs With Patient's Needs

Harry Stack Sullivan (1954) once noted that psychotherapy is a truly unique profession because practitioners must put aside their own needs in the interest of addressing the needs of the patient. An occupational hazard for all therapists is to inadvertently or unconsciously gratify their own needs while they think they are meeting the patients' needs. In cases of sexual misconduct, this dynamic is particularly problematic. Because many therapists grew up in homes where they felt unloved, they may attempt to elicit from their patients the love they did not receive from their parents (Gabbard, in press; Sussman, 1992). Longings to be loved are defended against by giving to others. Many lovesick therapists genuinely feel they are giving something wonderful to their patients, even though they are involved in an ethical transgression. In this manner, they defend against acknowledging their own dependency longings and their use of the patient for their own gratification.

Fantasy That Love in
and of Itself Is Curative

This theme is also closely related to conscious or unconscious childhood fantasies that persist in adult therapists. They may feel a deep conviction that they would have been much happier as adults if they had been loved as children. Similarly, therapists who transgress sexual boundaries with patients often harbor a belief that they can love the patient better than the patient's own parents did. Many films that feature sexual relationships between therapists and patients suggest that love itself is much more curative than any technique acquired through professional training. In Barbra Streisand's 1991 film *Prince of Tides*, for example, the audience is left with the impression that Tom's improvement is primarily related to his love affair with his therapist rather than to insight or understanding related to the therapist's professional expertise.

Repression or Disavowal of Rage at
Patient's Persistent Thwarting of Therapeutic Efforts

For some therapists, the patient's improvement is essential for the therapist's self-esteem. When certain patients continue to deteriorate despite the therapist's most zealous efforts, some therapists may resort to sexual relationships out of despair at the frustration of their omnipotent strivings to heal (Searles, 1979). The rage at the patient for failing to respond is buried beneath professions of love and caring.

Anger at Organization, Institute, or Training Analyst

When therapists work in institutional settings, they may develop bitterness and resentment over the years based on their perception that the institution has mistreated them. Investigations of therapist-patient sex in such settings commonly reveal that anger has been acted out at the organization through the ethical transgression. In cases of pastoral counselors, resentment toward the church or a particular church official may form a fertile field for sexual misconduct. When an analyst is the transgressor, anger at the training analyst or institute is often involved. Such behavior may also represent an unconscious fantasy of revenge against one's parents.

Manic Defense Against Mourning and Grief at Termination

In every psychotherapy relationship, there is an inevitable loss. A paradox of the process is that, if treatment goes well, the relationship must end. Neither therapist nor patient looks forward to dealing with the feelings of grief and mourning at the time of termination. One defensive way to avoid such feelings is to deny the ending by beginning a new, personal relationship (Gabbard, 1990). Indeed, many cases of therapist-patient sex begin as the therapy is ending.

The Exception Fantasy

Some lovesick therapists convince themselves that their sexual relationship with a patient is somehow an exception to accepted ethical guidelines. Often these therapists will view the love between them as having transcended transference or countertransference. They may view themselves and their patients as "soul mates," who were destined to find each other and just happened to have done so in the context of a psychotherapy relationship. The love is regarded as so extraordinary that mundane ethical codes are irrelevant.

Insecurity Regarding Masculine Identity

Male therapists who engage in sex with patients are often insecure about their maleness. Some may be seeking affirmation and validation for themselves as men because they feel they did not receive that sort of affirmation from their mother or father while growing up. The sexual gratification in such cases is secondary to a validation of their gender identity.

Patient as Transformational Object

While drawing parallels between the forbidden aspects of the oedipal situation in childhood and the boundary violations between therapist and patient as adults is tempting, clinical work with such therapists suggests that primitive preoedipal themes are prominent (Twemblow & Gabbard, 1989). One is the wish to be transformed by the patient. Bollas (1987) noted that the mother is initially experienced not so much as a separate person but as a process of transformation: "In adult life, the quest is not to possess the object; rather the object is pursued in order to surrender to it as a medium that alters the self" (p. 14). Hence, at the most fundamental level, the therapist may harbor the fantasy that the patient will be a love object that serves as an agent of magical change.

Settling Down the "Rowdy" Man

Although the majority of the literature on the dynamics of therapist-patient sex has been focused on a male therapist involved with a female patient, female therapists are also prone to become involved in misguided efforts to rescue male patients. In such scenarios, the patient tends to be a young man with a personality disorder diagnosis characterized by impulsivity, action orientation, and substance abuse (Gabbard, 1991a). Despite these characterological symptoms, however, the young man usually possesses considerable interpersonal charm and may have a knack for engaging females in a treatment capacity. A female clinician often will be drawn to such a man with an unconscious fantasy that her love and attention will some how influence this essentially decent young man to give up his wayward tendencies and "straighten up" (Gabbard, 1991b).

Within American literature and film, a pervasive cultural myth is that a "rowdy" young man simply needs a "good woman" to settle him down. In the beginning of Clint Eastwood's 1992 *Unforgiven*, for example, the protagonist repeatedly comments on how he was a cold-blooded murderer and a drunk until the right woman transformed him into a decent husband, father, and breadwinner. Another theme in these female therapist-male patient dyads relates to the woman's vicarious enjoyment of the danger and risk typified by her male patient's lifestyle.

Conflicts Around Sexual Orientation

In same-sex dyads, some therapists will use a relationship with a patient as a way of acting out conflicts around their own sexual orientation. In the Benowitz (1991) study of 15 female therapist-female patient liaisons, 20% of the therapists identified themselves to patients as heterosexual, 20% as bisexual, and only 40% as clearly lesbian; 20% said they had not been sexually involved with a woman before, and 33.3% demonstrated internal conflict around their sexual orientation or sexual behavior with women. Gonsiorek (1989a) has noted a similar pattern in male therapist-male patient dyads.

MASOCHISTIC SURRENDER

The last category involves certain therapists with fundamentally masochistic and self-destructive tendencies who allow themselves to be intimidated and controlled by a patient even though they know the deleterious consequences of their actions. I am not using *masochistic* here in the Freudian sense of deriving pleasure from pain. Rather, I am describing a relational mode in which the therapist allows himself to be tormented by the patient. In the typical scenario, these therapists, who are usually male, feel badgered into increasingly escalating boundary violations as a way of preventing suicide (Eyman & Gabbard, 1991). The patient, often an incest victim, may suffer from syndromes such as post-traumatic stress disorder, dissociative disorder, or borderline personality disorder. As a result, the patient may demand some concrete demonstration of love such that the therapist extends hours, holds the patient during the session, accepts frequent late-night phone calls, and even gives free therapy. Therapists who fit this category attempt to accommodate these demands even though they know better. They often feel they have no choice. The therapist soon learns that the patient's demands are bottomless and endless and begins to feel tormented. Demands to be held escalate to demands for sexual contacts that the therapist feels compelled to oblige.

These therapists characteristically have problems dealing with their own aggression. Setting limits on the patient feels as though it is sadistic. As the patient's demands escalate, the therapist uses reaction formation to defend against the growing resentment and hatred of the patient. Just at the point when the therapist's resentment is reaching monumental proportions, the patient may accuse the therapist of not caring. In such confrontations, therapists often feel that their negative feelings have been exposed. The ensuing guilt feelings lead them to accede to the patient's demands, so that aggression in either member of the dyad is kept at bay.

Clinical work with such therapists commonly reveals an overidentification of the therapist with the patient. In many cases, both have childhood histories of abuse. Because of this overidentification, these therapists try to gratify the patient's entitlement to be compensated for suffering as a child. Like lovesick therapists, masochistic therapists may be reenacting their own childhood abuse in addition to the patient's. Unlike lovesick therapists, however, they are not in love with the patient and often feel they are being "dragged down" by the patient. Some therapists who have masochistically surrendered in this manner describe dissociation or depersonalization during the sexual episode. They feel as though they are going through the motions of sex or are in an altered state of consciousness.

Many of these therapists recognize the unethical nature of the sexual activity after it has happened, and they will attempt to seek help for themselves and stop the therapy. They may masochistically turn themselves in to licensing boards or ethics committees in the hope of getting help with their problems. When litigation enters the picture, they often fare far worse than the psychopathic predators because they are much less manipulative and they deal with the proceedings in a straightforward and honest manner.

CONCLUSIONS

These categories and the psychodynamic themes that accompany them should be considered tentative hypotheses that require further confirmation. There may well be other sexually exploitative therapists who "fall through the cracks" and who require new categories to describe them. In addition to the heuristic value of attempting to classify such therapists, these groupings are useful in identifying which of the sexually transgressing therapists are likely to benefit from treatment and rehabilitation.

The psychopathic predators are almost always refractory to treatment in that they either deny the patient's allegations or do not view them as problematic and requiring treatment. These therapists clearly should not continue in the mental health field. While *some* persons suffering from paraphilias may be treatable in *some* settings, they, too, should not work in a field in which intense and highly intimate relationships are part of the daily practice.

Certain lovesick therapists are also unlikely to be treatable when they are in the throes of infatuation with a patient. They may be puzzled that anybody would suggest treatment for such an ecstatic mutual experience. Because they regard their love as unrelated to transference or countertransference issues, psychotherapy is viewed as having no purpose. However, when the infatuation dissipates, many of the lovesick therapists then have greater insight into their folly and may be amenable to psychotherapy or psychoanalysis as a way of helping them understand what intrapsychic issues made them vulnerable to such unethical transgression. Those therapists who have been involved in a masochistic surrender scenario generally are filled with remorse and are eager to receive treatment so that they do not repeat such self-destructive behavior.

Even with successful treatment, therapists who have acted on sexual feelings with patients should consider themselves at high risk for repeating the transgression. In most cases, they should probably avoid psychotherapeutic practice and confine their work to less intense forms of clinical practice.

14

Assessment for Rehabilitation of Exploitative Health Care Professionals and Clergy

John C. Gonsiorek

Since the mid-1970s, the group of us at Walk-In Counseling Center in Minneapolis have collectively seen over 3,500 cases of therapist, health care professional, and clergy abuse. We have seen these from all perspectives: sometimes working with the victims; sometimes the perpetrator; sometimes the employer; sometimes a licensing board, ethics committee, or organizational board; sometimes the attorneys for any of the above; sometimes for a spouse or significant other of the victim; and sometimes with colleagues or coworkers of the perpetrator. Our experience is akin to Akira Kurosawa's movie *Rashomon* (1951).

In this film, two individuals come upon a crime scene in which an assailant has murdered and raped a woman and assaulted a man. The authorities conduct an inquiry; in the film, all characters speak directly into the camera; the viewer is effectively the "authority." The action goes back in time as all characters, the two witnesses who came upon the scene, the surviving male assault victim, the male perpetrator, and the deceased female victim represented through a medium, each tell their stories. Each party tells an internally consistent, entirely plausible, and persuasive story. Each is significantly different in important details. The movie ends with the narrator despairing, because reality cannot be understood.

The perspective of our group is similar to that in this movie, without the despair of the narrator. We have found the multiple perspectives enriching. Our diverse experience has taught us that our initial assumptions are not always accurate and that any individual in the system is capable of falsification, conscious or unconscious, faulty memory, or distortion. We have nevertheless learned from our experiences that exploitation by clergy and health care professionals is not uncommon but is real, damaging, and complex. We do not perceive, in particular, that simple black-and-white distinctions about perpetrators are useful.

Our work has not been research in an empirical sense but the ordered observation and description that precedes focused research. The samples we see are biased, particularly those of perpetrators. Given our work in developing legislative and professional remedies and giving testimony, we are not neutral figures. Many of the most troubled perpetrators are not likely to seek assistance from us. We are more likely to see those who are remorseful and genuinely seeking assistance.

Another important feature is that our work is primarily assessment. We occasionally provide individual therapy; however, as most evaluations are from other states and provinces, we cannot provide ongoing services; many need a multicomponent program that our group is to small to provide; and, in the role of evaluator, it is generally ill-advised to function in the same cases as therapist. Finally, the role of evaluator and forensic psychologist creates demands that make a large therapy caseload impractical.

We have generally taken the position that we usually cannot assess rehabilitation potential unless the person being assessed has admitted serious wrongdoing. Without such admission, there is little rationale for an assessment: One assesses to evaluate a problem and suggest remedies. If a person claims that no problem exists, assessment focus is usually unclear. We sometimes assess cases in which there are two (or more) incompatible versions of factual events. We then configure the results of psychological testing and interviewing with different fact situations, and let the adjudicating body make a determination about which version is taken as fact—and therefore which formulation and set of recommendations will be adopted. It is inappropriate for a forensic evaluator to serve as a finder of fact.

Given these constraints, our samples are clearly nonrandom. We have the greatest information about particular kinds of perpetrators, generally those with a better prognosis. However, we have considerable experience hearing about other perpetrator types through the perspectives of their victims and employers, and also have seen enough varieties of perpetrators over the years directly, so that we can with some confidence offer the model below.

This model is a work in progress and should not be viewed as complete or unchangeable. It contains approximate descriptions covering most but not all cases we have observed. Some individuals appear to share characteristics of different types. We have no ability with our database to make a determination about the percentages of perpetrators in the different types. Sampling biases are considerable, and any estimation of percentages would be premature. We are not supportive of attempts to reify this typology into a set classification system, particularly based on theory. We offer the following only as a tentative summary of orderly observation on skewed samples.

A TENTATIVE TYPOLOGY
OF PROFESSIONAL PERPETRATORS

We have observed the following types and have described them elsewhere (Gonsiorek, 1987, 1989c; Gonsiorek & Schoener, 1987; Schoener & Gonsiorek, 1989).

1. Naive. It can be difficult for someone trained and licensed in a mental health profession to find plausible the concept that a provider may be so naive as to not recognize that sexual contact with a patient is unethical. However, many mental health services are provided by those not trained in mental health, such as family practice physicians, substance abuse counselors, clergy, and others. Some of these groups may simply not know (or have such simplistic understandings that they might as well not know) about sexual impropriety with patients, particularly in responding to sexual involvement immediately following counseling.

For example, some nonpsychiatric physicians have believed that, as long as sexual contact does not occur while the patient is actually treated in the office, then the person is not technically a patient. Further, many mental health professionals are inadequately trained in ethics and professional conduct in their training programs. In particular, they are most poorly trained in negotiating gray areas in boundary management.

Many individuals in this category do not literally believe it is permissible to have sex with a patient. Typically, they are naive about ethical gray areas that, once transgressed, often eventuate in increasingly inappropriate and boundaryless behavior that may result in sexual misconduct. They are naive about the trajectory of their behavior and start down the "slippery slope."

The prognosis in this naive group is variable. Some individuals are simply untrained, inexperienced, or ill-prepared; these factors can usually be remedied. Some, however, are characterologically naive, that is, too intrapsychically and interpersonally "dense" to effectively negotiate the boundary dilemmas required by mental health practice, and so are not rehabilitatable.

2. *Normal and/or mildly neurotic.* We use this admittedly obsolete *DSM-II* term to communicate an important concept. These individuals potentially constitute all health care professionals and clergy.

The typical individual in this group is a reasonably well-trained, responsible professional who, at a bad spot in his or her life, is often socially isolated, depressed, and lacking in adequate support, often after the end of a primary relationship. A client who fits his or her countertransference like lock and key enters the caseload. The professional begins a slow and gradual process of developing a romantic attachment to the client, often by inappropriate self-disclosure, moving to social interaction, and sometimes, but not always, proceeding to romantic and sexual interaction. Such individuals literally fall in love with their patients. Gabbard (Chapter 13, this volume) calls these "lovesick."

Such individuals are often their attorney's worst nightmare; they can become remorseful and guilt-ridden about their behavior and confess to authorities, licensing boards, media, ethics committees, and the like and/or withhold information that may help their defense because they are still in love with the patient and do not want to hurt the patient. Almost without exception, these perpetrators have one and only one victim.

Their prognosis for rehabilitation is generally good. They have a clear awareness of the unethical nature of their conduct, often terminate or try to circumscribe the inappropriate behavior on their own, typically have situational stressors that seem to have precipitated the behavior, and often become highly anxious and depressed once the impropriety is disclosed.

It is our impression that the number of these perpetrators is not small. It is one of the most common groups that we have assessed. The key concept here is that any professional, at a bad spot in his or her life, is capable of becoming this type of perpetrator to some degree. *To some degree* is the operative phrase here. Not every professional in distress is capable of sexual exploitation; rather, all professionals, when at their worst, are capable of engaging in a greater degree of boundary violation than they otherwise might imagine.

In the description above, the professional's behavior was unethical and improper even before overtly sexual contact occurred. Transforming the relationship to meet the therapist's needs is the core exploitative quality. Sex is merely one possible exploitative outcome, noteworthy because more noticed.

That it is perceived by the therapist as well intentioned is irrelevant. One is reminded of Hanna Arendt's phrase about the "banality of evil"; in other words, professionals in this category begin taking small steps down a slippery slope of boundary erosion and end up much further down the road than they could imagine in their worst nightmares. Such therapists generally genuinely intend no harm. Unfortunately, for all involved, intent is irrelevant. There is no clear and necessary relationship between the motivation and intent of the therapist and the harm rendered. With all the types discussed here, a full range of damages to the victim can occur, from mild to severe. The therapist's pathology and motivation do not result in a simple prediction regarding damage to the client.

3. *Severely neurotic and/or socially isolated.* This group looks like the normal or mildly neurotic group except that their problems are long-standing and more significant. They often have ongoing depression, feelings of inadequacy, low self-esteem, and social isolation. Work tends to be the center of their lives and most of their personal needs are met in the work setting. Their inappropriate romantic and sexual involvement with clients appears on the surface to be like the romanticized situations of the healthy or mildly neurotic group; however, it is repetitive in the sense that every few years, or even every decade or so, the situation recurs.

Inappropriate boundaries develop as in the healthy/neurotic group. While situational variables may precipitate the specific inappropriate events, the impropriety is more clearly rooted in long-standing problems of the therapist. These therapists may experience guilt and remorse, yet are less able to terminate their inappropriate behavior than members of the preceding category. Their guilt leads to self-punitive behavior rather than change. They tend to have more highly elaborated rationalizations about the inappropriate behavior and are more cognitively resistant about understanding the nature of their impropriety. For example, they may rationalize that, because they truly love a client, the behavior is not inappropriate; because they were vulnerable or open, they had equalized the relationship; and so on. They may vacillate between self-revelation, remorse, defensiveness, and self-justification.

An impediment to bringing this category of therapists to accountability is that they chronically tend to "go the extra mile" for clients and as such are often highly regarded among other professionals as particularly giving, skilled, dedicated, and hardworking professionals. This is often true; but they often do not have sufficient lives of their own and are driven to be "superprofessionals." They may in fact have a track record of being extraordinarily helpful to difficult people whom others have given up on. However, the same factors that predispose them to this dedicated behavior also predispose them to periodic, repetitive, severe boundary violations with a small number of their clients.

Simply stated, such therapists need to get a life and keep a life outside of work—but they rarely do. Often underneath are feelings of inferiority or worthlessness and a sense that they are only worthwhile as human beings to the extent that they produce. In spite of their overall "neurotic" picture, there may be more subtle narcissistic elements involving grandiosity: Because of their "dedication," they are allowed special compensation, that is, inappropriate behavior.

Rehabilitation may or may not be feasible with this group. Their prognosis is mixed and guarded because of the long-standing and repetitive nature of their problems and the significant cognitive distortions they present. They gravitate toward therapeutic modes that lend themselves to bending boundaries and therefore often require a major overhaul in therapeutic style and skills before they can be considered truly rehabilitated.

4. Impulsive character disorders. These professionals have chronic problems with impulse control, usually with legal or interpersonal difficulties in their histories. Their problem behaviors are not limited to boundary violations but may include insurance fraud, sexual harassment of staff or trainees, poorly controlled sexual behavior in their personal lives, tax fraud, and a wide variety of inappropriate or criminal activity. Some repetitive, compulsive sex offenders are found in this category.

Colleagues often do not believe that someone whose behavior is so seriously out of control is in their midst. They lack planfulness and cunning, do not cover their tracks, and so are often easily caught once investigated. They can amass multiple, sometimes many, victims because of their dramatic behavioral disinhibition.

When they receive consequences, they may often appear to experience guilt, remorse, and depression and in fact can pose a suicide risk. However, they rarely have a true appreciation of the effects of their behavior on victims. They simultaneously admit some improprieties while denying others. They are often troublesome for their legal counsel, as they may impulsively confess to cases other than the ones being investigated or to other areas of criminal activity, or display other strikingly poor judgment when apprehended. In the evaluation process, they are often demanding yet dependent and engage in more poor judgment, such as offering bribes. These individuals are unrehabilitatable. The best response is to remove them from positions of public trust.

5. Sociopathic or narcissistic character disorders. Like the impulsive group, these individuals have a long history of problems with impulse and behavior controls; however, the history is often less obvious because they tend to be far more deliberate and planful. Typically they are cool, calculating, and detached and often carefully select clients who are vulnerable and/or lacking in credibility should they complain. They may be respected professionally for their skills. They are cunning enough to maintain appropriate boundaries in some situations, particularly ones in which they have public exposure, so that it is hard to believe that they would be exploitative.

This group is adept at manipulating colleagues. Often, these individuals situate themselves at the center of lucrative financial or referral networks, making other professionals beholden and loyal to them. They have no compunctions about using these connections to fight allegations against them. When caught, they mimic the healthy/neurotic therapist who is remorseful. They "confess" only to inappropriate behaviors they believe others already know about. However, when their attempts to manipulate are not persuasive, they often become hostile and engage in counterattack. They do not hesitate to damage others to avoid consequences and are adept at outmaneuvering others.

Occasionally, some might voluntarily seek therapy and appear to be deeply involved in a rehabilitation effort; however, they are adept at manipulating their way through programs, particularly structured programs that can be "figured out." Simply stated, they are more skilled at manipulation than non-character disordered individuals are. These individuals are not rehabilitatable and should be removed from situations of professional trust.

6. Psychotics. This is a diverse group categorized together for convenience. They have in common impaired reality testing and significant functional impairment. They demonstrate great variability in their understanding of the effects of their behavior upon victims and in their ability to feel remorse. In terms of dealing with the legal system and authorities, their behavior is also unpredictable. This group is generally not rehabilitatable because their chronic impairments are so significant that the risk of future inappropriate behavior is essentially unpredictable.

7. "Classic" sex offenders. This group generally consists of chronic repetitive pedophiles and also physically aggressive sex offenders regardless of the age of victim. We include this group not because it is a discrete type; many pedophiles may, in addition, have other features such as impulsivity and narcissism. Rather, the focus of the pedophile or the aggressive nature of the inappropriate behavior is so distinctive that we classify them separately even though there may be other dynamics operating.

Our view is that these individuals are not rehabilitatable and should not be allowed back into health care or ministerial professions. The data on treatment success with sex offenders are controversial and represent a different situation than that for health care professions and clergy. Criteria for treatment success in nonprofessional sex offenders are generally that they no longer offend in the larger community and learn to avoid situations that may trigger reoffense. However, health care professionals and clergy are, by definition, in environments in which individuals with vulnerabilities are under their care; they have enhanced opportunities for inappropriate behavior as a result. In other words, clergy and health care professionals who are classic sex offenders work in environments that are maximally likely to elicit their problematic behavior.

While one can debate whether or not classic sex offenders as a group are rehabilitatable to function in general society, they are not rehabilitatable to function in these specific professions that present such opportunities to reoffend. Such a work activity is the type of eliciting environment that competent sex offender programs typically counsel nonprofessional sex offenders to avoid permanently.

8. Medically disabled. These are individuals who, because of a medical condition, engage in inappropriate behavior with clients. Their history suggests they are otherwise not problematic. The two largest groups in this category are individuals who are neurologically impaired and who have true bipolar mood disorder.

In the former, a well-respected health care professional or clergy member may, after a medical problem with neurological involvement, begin to display impaired judgment, problems with behavior control, and so on. Inappropriate sexual contact or other impropriety results. An impediment to responding to such individuals is that they are often older, established, and well regarded. Colleagues therefore may not give them critical feedback when their behavior or judgment begins to show subtle improprieties. Their behavior becomes increasingly inappropriate and eventually seriously so.

In the latter category, professionals, during the course of a manic episode, engage in a variety of out-of-control behaviors that may include boundary violations and impropriety, including sexual contact with clients. If this is truly a case of bipolar disorder, the contact is often abrupt, unplanned, and out of character. For example, they may engage in sexual contact with clients contrary to their typical sexual orientation. It is important to assess bipolar illness by history to make certain other groups do not mimic this category.

The prognosis for this group is quite mixed, ranging from very poor to very positive, depending on the medical situation involved. For example, some individuals who have sustained brain damage or neurological impairment may not be rehabilitatable, simply because there is no known remediation of their neurological impairment. In lesser neurological impairments, such as a mild stroke, varying degrees of rehabilitation may be possible. Some with true bipolar illness who are well managed on lithium may be very rehabilitatable. This group represents a situation in which the seriousness of their inappropriate behavior is essentially a random match with their rehabilitation potential. This is unlike most other perpetrator groups, where the number of victims and quality of the inappropriate behavior provide some degree of prediction of rehabilitation potential.

9. Masochistic/self-defeating individuals. For some years, our group noted perpetrators who appeared to present a peculiar mix of both neurotic and character disordered features. We were often puzzled about these cases. Gabbard (Chapter 13, this volume) has astutely conceptualized another category, which we endorse. These masochistic or self-defeating individuals often appear on the surface to be overworking therapists like the more severely neurotic/socially isolated type. However, in response to certain severely disturbed, often Axis-II clients, they are unable to manage and resist the increasingly boundaryless demands of the clients, because of their internal conflicts about setting limits.

Gabbard notes dynamics in which they are resentful of the demands such clients place upon them but do not set limits or recognize their anger, and so increasingly give way to the client's inappropriate demands. Typically, with borderline personality or similarly disturbed patients, their otherwise reasonable clinical practice deteriorates. They become seriously impaired and boundaryless, at times with behavior involving romantic and sexual contact.

It is typical in this group to find other examples of masochistic and self-defeating behavior, for example, not collecting fees, not taking adequate care of themselves in personal and financial areas of life—generally being long-suffering and self-defeating in multiple areas. The prognosis for rehabilitation in this group is guarded. Their problems run deep; the demands of psychotherapy practice may simply be a bad fit for their characterological weaknesses.

SPECIAL FEATURES OF ABUSE BY CLERGY

This model was primarily developed on health care professionals; there are some differences with clergy. First, much of the characterization in our typology depends on knowing the factual basis of the complaints. In other words, accurately knowing the number of victims and the way the perpetrator interacted with victims is very important. Health care professionals are, as a rule, licensed. Usually, when investigation occurs, staff working for the licensing boards independently investigate complaints. Boards then often arrive at a finding of fact, that is, a set of presumptions that the board will take as assumed in adjudicating the case.

This rarely occurs in clergy situations. Religious denominations generally have no mechanism or authority to reproduce an administrative law investigation that can be helpful in determining basic facts as in health care professionals' cases. As a result, obtaining a clear factual basis on clergy cases is often more difficult.

Second, clergy roles are inherently more complex and fraught with boundary strains. The role of a typical clergy member involves liturgical activities, spiritual direction, pastoral and other counseling, fundraising, group leadership, and social activities, all with the same group of individuals. Health care professionals generally have much more circumscribed roles. In fact, some health care professions, such as psychology, consider such a complex role to be inherently unethical, because of dual relationships. In effect, some health care professions have determined that the extraordinary diversity of roles that clergy routinely play are simply impossible to manage appropriately, because of boundary strains.

It becomes difficult, then, to evaluate rehabilitation potential for clergy, when some of their required and standard roles involve such serious boundary challenges. Simply suggesting that clergy become like health care professionals is often not a viable solution, as there is a long tradition of clergy playing these multiple roles. Such a change might well require a radical redefinition of clergy activity. A clergy member might be rehabilitatable then, but under circumstances and in a redefined and circumscribed role that the denomination may not be able to accommodate or even perceive as a clerical role. One can recommend a mental health professional be limited to medication management, chart review, case management, psychological testing, and so on only as part of a rehabilitation plan, and that professional still has a viable professional role, with genuine employment possibilities. Recommending a clergy member perform "liturgy only," as part of a rehabilitation plan, may be nonsensical in terms of role, employment realities, or denominational tradition.

THE ASSESSMENT FOR
REHABILITATION PROCESS

We have outlined in detail (Gonsiorek & Schoener, 1987; Schoener & Gonsiorek, 1988, 1989) specific aspects of our assessment process, which is essentially a forensic assessment. Forensic assessments are different than standard psychological assessments on a number of levels. First, the assessment question tends to be clearly focused while the methods of assessment tend to be broad ranging. This is in contrast to standard psychological assessment in which the assessment questions may be very broad (e.g., What are the person's psychodynamics and how do they affect therapy goals?) but the methods tend to be very limited such as interviews and psychological testing. Forensic evaluations in contrast usually use investigative materials, police reports, corroborative interviews, and generally more data sources than standard psychological assessments (see Melton, Petrilla, Poythress, & Slobogin, 1987; Shapiro, 1991, for details on forensic evaluations).

An implicit point is worth making explicit regarding forensic evaluations. Forensic evaluations do not attempt to uncover "truth"; rather they attempt to generate a hypothesis and set of derived recommendations that are most consistent with the data available. In other words, forensic assessments determine coherence and consistency given a particular set of assumed facts. What this means is that, if facts change, everything else that derives from them may also warrant substantial revision.

It is crucial that those doing forensic evaluations disabuse themselves of the notion that they are engaged in truth finding. Such a function is properly the goal of the legal system. Engaging in fact finding or truth finding in the context of a forensic evaluation is an abuse of mental health evaluation techniques and corrosive to the legal system. If in fact mental health forensic evaluations could determine truth or fact, the court and jury systems could be eliminated—to the detriment, I believe, of the general public and the mental health professions. Forensic evaluations or any mental health evaluations simply do not have the ability to make factual determinations.

The first aspect of our assessment process is that there is an admission that some inappropriate behavior has occurred before an evaluation to determine rehabilitation potential. If a professional steadfastly maintains that no impropriety occurred, there is no legitimate reason for an evaluation. A mental health forensic evaluation cannot prove innocence, nor can it prove that someone is psychologically healthy. "Proving" psychological health is equivalent in research design to proving the null hypothesis; that is, it simply cannot be done. If a professional maintains innocence, he or she can best be served by legal counsel, not an evaluation. An evaluation for rehabilitation potential must assume that a problem exists that requires rehabilitation; otherwise, the evaluation is nonsensical.

An exception is a situation in which there is an acknowledged frank disagreement about facts. Both parties agree that an evaluation will occur in which the psychological forensic data will be configured with both versions of events. Essentially two sets of recommendations and hypotheses will be offered and it is then up to the referring body to make a determination about which set of facts is persuasive. Such distinctions are not splitting hairs but recognize that forensic psychological evaluations can play an important function—within their limitations.

The overall purpose of the assessment is a thorough understanding about what led to the improprieties and what, if anything, can be done to remediate the possibility of recurrence. All aspects of the professional's situation are possible sources of relevant information. The professional's individual dynamics; situational factors; features of the clients involved; organizational factors; practice style; problems with training, role modeling, mentoring, and supervision; medical history; relationship problems; and others are potential factors that may be weighed in a formulation. The assessment attempts to examine any factors that may have a bearing on the why the improprieties occurred.

Depending on the specifics of the case, a variety of corroborative information may be used. Interviews with spouses, colleagues, past supervisors, family members, current and past therapists, and others may or may not be relevant in a particular case. Investigative and police reports, relevant depositions, and others are also important. It is important to obtain a description of the impropriety from the victim's perspective; this is best accomplished via investigative reports and statements gathered by the referring institution. Extensive psychological testing is an important component of any evaluation, as it gives independent information with relatively well-understood limitations.

A formulation of why and how improprieties occurred is the goal; it is essentially a working hypothesis. If no such a hypothesis can be derived—that is, if there is no clear understanding of the impropriety— then no determination of rehabilitation potential or rehabilitation plan can be offered. This can be a frustrating situation for all involved, but occasionally no clarity results from the evaluation. If so, it is important the available data not be distorted to manufacture a plausible hypothesis.

When a hypothesis is developed, an estimate is usually made about rehabilitation potential, and specific rehabilitation goals and procedures are outlined. These are outlined in terms of concrete goals and suggested methods for reaching them, as opposed to specific programs or providers to render the service. Specific goals vary in every case. The usual vehicles for reaching these goals may involve psychotherapy, marital therapy, group therapy, structured treatment programs, supervision, retraining, practice restrictions, and others.

Another body, usually a licensing or ecclesiastical board, then determines the acceptability and feasibility of the evaluation. The professional must also determine whether he or she is willing to undergo the suggested rehabilitation.

If agreement is reached about rehabilitation, it is crucial that a mechanism be in place to monitor the rehabilitation plan. The plan can best be construed as the best guess at one point in time about rehabilitation. As the plan is implemented, all parties involved in rendering the plan should report back to the monitoring body with progress reports and impres-

sions about whether the rehabilitation strategy is on target. It is norma-
tive for there to be "fine tuning" in rehabilitation plans as they are
rendered. Occasionally, rehabilitation plans, even when carefully made,
are found to be insufficient or inaccurate and may require substantial
revision. When an agreed-on rehabilitation plan has been rendered in
its entirety and appropriately modified as information derived during
the rehabilitation process surfaces, rehabilitation for professional practice can be considered to have happened.

Licensing boards and ecclesiastical authorities are encouraged to
make a careful distinction between rehabilitation and punishment. The
primary task of a licensing board is protection of the public, not rein-
statement of troubled professionals. They may decide that the offending therapist's behavior, regardless of rehabilitation potential, requires,
for the best interest of the public, revocation of license. This is a licensing
board's prerogative and in some circumstances may be their obligation,
as their statutory requirement is protection of the public. It is important,
however, that the licensing authority not distort information about
rehabilitation to justify its decision about punishment. Similarly,
evaluators must not distort evaluations in anticipation of a decision of
the licensing board.

Decisions about rehabilitation and punishment are separate. The
evaluator's job is to estimate if rehabilitation potential exists and the
specifics of a rehabilitation plan. The job of the licensing body is to
protect the public. These are very different functions and should be so.
It is important that a licensing body not modify a rehabilitation plan to
punish a professional. Doing so contaminates the rehabilitation plan.
Licensing boards have the authority to fine, suspend, and revoke licenses; it is recommended that, if they wish to punish, they use these
mechanisms.

Licensing and ecclesiastical boards do, however, have the right and
the obligation to critically scrutinize proposed rehabilitation plans.
Modifications should attempt to develop the most effective plan. Punishment should be separate from decisions about rehabilitation.

It is recommended that boards and evaluators be cautious of rehabilitation plans that rely heavily on long-term or unwieldy practice restrictions. Certain kinds of practice restrictions are ultimately unfeasible.
For example, requiring that a professional always have a colleague in
the room when rendering services is impractical. The economic problems with that arrangement appear insurmountable; further, if a professional is so untrustworthy or behaviorally disinhibited that the physical
presence of a colleague is required, then the professional should be

deemed unrehabilitatable. Restrictions about seeing certain diagnostic groups, presenting problems, or patient types assume the professional has the ability to discern these features. Unless the professional works in a setting where this can be reliably and independently arranged, such restrictions may not be viable. Practice limitations more appropriately involve concrete measurable restrictions that can be easily monitored, for example, limiting a psychiatrist to medication evaluations or diagnostic workups, or limiting a psychologist to assessment or chart review.

ISSUES AND CONTROVERSIES IN
REHABILITATION OF PROFESSIONAL OFFENDERS

It is important that evaluators understand and accept that anyone in the evaluation process can lie or distort. An evaluation is only as good as the data on which it is based. Alleged perpetrators, alleged victims, colleagues, spouses, licensing boards, and ecclesiastical officials all periodically lie or distort, at times entirely in good faith. Understanding that an evaluation only produces the best hypothesis about congruence of available facts, and not "truth," is central.

Evidentiary rules and reasonable legal strategy create slippage between what is sound psychological practice and what is good law. Alleged perpetrators and victims often have motivations for lying; spouses, advocates, attorneys, and colleagues of both have reasons to lie. An evaluator who believes that he or she must determine truth will find him- or herself in an impossible bind.

Recidivism has emerged as a controversy in rehabilitation of professional offenders. Simply stated, there is absolutely no data on recidivism with health care professionals and clergy who have been involved in sexual impropriety with their clients.

Recidivism means (a) allegations have been made and adjudicated as fact; (b) there is agreement about facts sufficient for evaluation to occur; (c) a rehabilitation evaluation occurs; (d) it comes up with a workable hypothesis and suggested rehabilitation plan; (e) the case is adjudicated and the rehabilitation plan is accepted by the licensing or ecclesiastical authority and the professional; (f) the plan is fully implemented, monitored over its course, and modified as necessary; (g) a determination is made that rehabilitation is adequate; (h) the professional is reinstated to an appropriate role; (i) and the person is then followed up until death or retirement. The goal of rehabilitation is simple: 0% incidence of repeated professional impropriety until death or retirement.

Pope (1989b, 1991), however, has claimed an 80% recidivism rate for sexually inappropriate professionals. The justification for this conclusion is as follows. Holroyd and Brodsky (1977) examined 21 psychologists who admitted sexual contact with patients: 80% of these psychologists admitted to contact with more than one patient, that is, 80% were repetitive offenders. Pope interpreted this 80% repetitiveness as an 80% recidivism. Repetitiveness and recidivism are not equivalent.

Further, this 80% repetitiveness is higher than that found in other studies. For example, in a more recent study by Gartrell, Herman, Olarte, Feldstein, and Localio (1987) looking at psychiatrists, only about a third of psychiatrists who admitted sexual contact with patients had contact with more than one patient. Another source cited by Pope as evidence of an 80% recidivism rate is a pamphlet put out by the California Department of Consumer Affairs (n.d.), which asserts "that 80% of sexually exploiting therapists have exploited more than one client" (p. 14). This pamphlet cites no source for this, although presumably it is Holroyd and Brodsky. Pope equates this statement about repetitiveness as equivalent to recidivism.

Another source cited by Pope is the article by Borys and Pope (1989) that discusses cites Borys's (1988) dissertation research. In this questionnaire study, Borys asked respondents a number of questions, including whether there was sexual contact with patients. The options were "no, few, some or many"; one instance of sexual contact with patients was not a possible response in the research design. "Few" might represent a combination of single and multiple offense cases. In addition, no differentiation was made between situations after termination versus during therapy. This research, then, appears unable to accurately address repetitiveness, much less recidivism.

Finally, a source from the American Psychological Insurance Trust was cited as evidence of an 80% recidivism rate. When our group questioned the Insurance Trust, we were told this is inaccurate. What they actually noted was that, when offending therapists attempt rehabilitation without an independent evaluation, clear treatment plan, and follow-up, it was their impression that rehabilitation was ineffective. We entirely agree with this and, in fact, would predict that outcome.

It appears then, that, despite the oft-quoted assertion of an 80% recidivism rate for professional offenders, there is no basis for that conclusion.

An important professional practice problem is embedded in this recidivism debate. Even if the recidivism rate were known (which it is not and probably will not be for some decades as the required research requires long-term follow-up), knowing a reasonably accurate recidivism rate would not, in itself, provide a basis for predicting recidivism in an individual case.

An analogy can be helpful here. If a physician knows that a particular cardiac medication is effective 80% of the time, ineffective but harmless 15% of the time, and damaging or fatal 5% of the time, it is not an adequate standard of care for that physician to say that, because the medication is effective 80% of the time, it is appropriate for all cardiac patients. At the core of professional responsibility is a requirement that recommendations and treatment plans on an individual be based on a specific and individualized assessment of that person.

Even if recidivism is high, it is not *clinically* justifiable to view every professional perpetrator as unrehabilitatable on this basis alone. Rather, the clinically appropriate response is to understand and research which professionals are rehabilitatable and which are not, and make a determination about the individual in question, if possible. Recidivism data, when available, will be an important component, but not the sole factor, in clinical determinations in individual cases. Future recidivism data will be genuinely useful to the extent they can help differentiate which offenders, with what characteristics, have different outcomes; that is, data must involve specific, not generic, prediction of outcome.

The argument offered by Pope is essentially that of an insurance actuary: If most cases fit a pattern, then one can act as if all cases fit that pattern. While such reasoning may be acceptable for insurance companies, sole reliance on actuarial data, particularly when the group in question is likely heterogeneous, is an inadequate standard of care in the essentially clinical, not actuarial, process of evaluation for rehabilitation potential in individual cases.

SUMMARY

At this point in time, the understanding of health care professionals and clergy who sexually exploit is operating in a context of discovery, not the context of justification. A context of justification will eventually be required, but its rendering will be expensive, difficult, and long in coming. Until then, the typology and theory base developed by us and others such as Gabbard (Chapter 13, this volume) are based on a reasonable extrapolation about what is known from other knowledge. It would frankly be surprising if current incidence estimates, typological descriptions, and other current ideas are found to be precise once the context of justification and research is engaged. Our group believes, however, that our approach provides a useful mechanism for the orderly accumulation of further data and is a clinically reasonable compromise during this early stage of understanding professional impropriety.

At this point in time, indiscriminately removing all professional perpetrators is not responsible public policy based on a reasonable degree of scientific certainty. Rather, it is as irresponsible and negligent as denial of exploitation by professionals and clergy, which was the norm and prevailing wisdom only a very short time ago.

15

Inpatient Assessment of the
Sexually Exploitative Professional

Richard R. Irons

A buse of power and position for control and personal gain can occur in the professional-patient or professional-client relationship and has been recognized since ancient times, as documented by warnings, admonitions, and codes of conduct that can be found in virtually all major cultures and professional traditions.

Professional sexual misconduct and offense are emerging from secrecy as compelling issues that threaten public welfare and safety while eroding trust in our important relationships with professionals. For the purpose of our discussion, let us define *professional sexual misconduct* as the overt or covert expression of erotic or romantic thoughts, feelings, or gestures toward the client that are sexual or may be reasonably construed *by the client* as sexual. And let us define *professional sexual offense* as a non-therapeutic, nondiagnostic attempt by the professional to touch, or having actual contact with, any of the anatomical areas of the client's body commonly considered reproductive or sexual. Offense may also involve forcing, coercing, or manipulating the client to touch the professional in these anatomical areas. The relationship between the professional and the person served is considered protected, bounded, and fiduciary in all professions. Those served may be called by various labels such as *patient, client, parishioner, counselee,* or *analysand.* For simplicity, we will refer to them in this discussion as *clients.* Others involved or potentially exploited include employees, coworkers, students, and peers. When individuals feel that a professional has engaged in potential professional sexual misconduct or offense and have mustered the courage to report victimization, we will refer to them as *complainants.* It is beyond the scope of this chapter to discuss the incidence and prevalence of professional sexual misconduct and sexual offense in this society or the dynamics of and effects that sexual violation has upon its victims. Readers are referred to other chapters in this volume for these topics.

These issues take on direct and immediate importance when events occurring between a client and a professional lead to an allegation or formal complaint against a professional. In our Professional Assessment Program, we have completed formal assessments on more than 150 clergy, lawyers, and licensed health professionals who have been accused of sexual misconduct or sexual offense. Our experience with these men and women is the basis upon which this approach to assessment has evolved. The Professional Assessment Program is a short-term (usually five-day) inpatient or day hospital process that provides multidisciplinary assessment for possible impairment associated with such allegations.

This program was developed in response to the needs expressed by licensure boards, regulatory agencies, and professional societies to have an objective forum in which allegations of sexual harassment, sexual misconduct, and sexual offense could be explored and considered independent of treatment, therapy, administrative due process, civil suits, and criminal legal process. It is not intended to be a substitute for the finding of facts and the judgment of a legal proceeding but is an alternative or supplementary means by which the accused professional may come to consider the possible personal vulnerabilities and errors in judgment that may have contributed to the complaint(s) or allegation(s) that have been brought forward. This is a more comprehensive and expensive option than independent evaluation by a psychologist and/or psychiatrist. In straightforward cases where the professional acknowledges most if not all of the sexual impropriety alleged, an outpatient evaluation by one or two professionals may well be sufficient. Schoener and Gonsiorek have pioneered this approach and have written and lectured extensively on this type of evaluation. The development of our process has relied greatly upon their sound and practical guidelines, derived from their experience in private practice and at the Walk-In Counseling Center in Minneapolis, Minnesota; and the reader is referred to their work, including Chapter 14 in this volume.

It has been our experience that there are many situations in which the allegations and/or formal complaints made against a professional are either categorically denied by the professional or substantially disputed. In other cases, the allegations are imprecise or lack sufficient corroboration to initiate legal proceedings, yet need to be addressed. Many boards and professional organizations wish to give the professional one more opportunity to explore the reasons the complaint(s) have arisen before advancing further into formal due process, in the hope that the trauma and expense of this course of action can be averted and an informal settlement negotiated.

GOALS OF ASSESSMENT

We believe that in a formal assessment the team should carefully review the course of events leading to this evaluation as described by complainant(s) and as presented in investigatory materials available from concerned parties. We then provide the program participant with an opportunity to discuss with each team member his or her theories and opinions on why the complaints have arisen. The amount of information from the complainants and concerned parties that can be shared with the professional varies from case to case.

We have found that most professionals referred to us have already been confronted with sufficient detailed information on the scope of allegations during the intervention process to allow the team to proceed without the need for additional disclosures from regulatory agency investigatory materials. Collateral information is crucial to challenge the program participant's defenses, such as rationalization, minimization, intellectualization, and blaming of the complainants.

The *goals of assessment* are presented in Table 15.1. The professional entering the assessment becomes a patient (program participant) and is requested to set aside his or her professional role and its attendant defensive armor. The crucial objective in assessment is to establish a causal hypothesis that helps explain the reasons for the complaint(s) and the behavior of the program participant. The ability to formulate such a hypothesis requires exploration of the middle ground between the complainants, coworkers, and/or peers and the program participant's versions of events leading to the formal complaint(s). The degree

TABLE 15.1 Professional Assessment Program Goals

1. To construct a reasonable summary of events leading to assessment
2. To review past corrective actions, previous evaluations, and treatment
3. To compare the patient's version of past actions with collateral sources of information
4. To assist the patient in making appropriate self-diagnosis
5. To break through defenses that prevent the patient from recognizing the nature of his or her problems and the need for change
6. To establish a causal hypothesis that helps to explain past actions
7. To provide diagnostic conclusions and recommendations for the future
8. To encourage the patient to formulate and implement a plan following discharge

to which this hypothesis can reconcile disparities in multiple accounts of the events determines to a large measure the value, acceptance, and utility of the assessment conclusions and recommendations. It is important to reiterate that the assessment is not a trial, and the team members are not being asked to sit as judges or a jury. When the disparity between the complainant's and professional patient's versions of events remains too great, then the assessment team should not feel obligated to advance a causal hypothesis, may report the assessment as inconclusive, and will often recommend that the matter be forwarded into formal legal process.

THE FORMAL ASSESSMENT

Over the past three years, we have refined the assessment process. We are able to complete formal multidisciplinary assessments on program participants within five working days, and provide concerned parties with objective, useful conclusions with specific, practical recommended courses of action in over 95% of cases. Prior to admission, we request from concerned parties and referral sources all available information on the professional, including the allegations, rumors, and complaints that are known. Our policy is that we are unwilling to proceed with an assessment unless we have a reliable statement from complainant(s) that expresses in detail their version of the events that constitute the alleged professional misconduct or offense. We have chosen not to contact or interview the complainant(s) or the professional's clients directly so as to remain independent from current or future legal proceedings. Types of additional information obtained from collateral sources before and during assessment are outlined in Figure 15.1.

Information From Collateral Sources

Family, friends, colleagues
Education and training references
Professional work reports
Summary of problems, events, or complaints leading to assessment
Records from previous disciplinary action, corrective action, or legal actions if any

Professional Evaluations

Records from previous evaluations or treatment
Component evaluations by assessment team members
— Psychiatrist
— Psychologist
— Addiction medicine
— Internal medicine
— Case manager

Patient Contribution

History of events leading to assessment
Personal history
Family history
Psychosocial history
Self-evaluation for symptoms and signs of addictive disease

Figure 15.1. The Assessment Process: Data Accumulated Prior to Assessment Team Staffing

Collateral information is available for review by any assessment team members but is never provided directly to the professional patient unless we are specifically authorized to do so and believe that it would be of clinical benefit. Assessment team members are chosen from a pool of experienced professionals based on the nature of the case. Each evaluator works with the client separately and individually, completing his or her evaluation prior to team staffing. The professional patient is required to describe his or her version of events and background history to every team member. Team evaluators use an array of interview techniques, self-evaluation tests, written assignments, formal medical examination procedures, and psychological tests that are eventually incorporated into written reports completed by each team member. Additional consultations from other specialists are requested on an as-needed basis. Data from each evaluation and consultation are brought to the assessment team staffing.

The purpose of team staffing is to present information obtained from collateral sources, the component evaluations by each team member, and data from consultants. Then the assessment team collectively works to construct a dynamic causal hypothesis that reasonably explains why and how the events transpired that led to the complaint(s). This leads directly to a determination of whether *professional impairment* is currently present, to diagnostic conclusions using *DSM-III-R* criteria, and to recommended courses of action. Staffings are lively and interactive. The team works to achieve consensus (rather than complete agreement) on these matters. The strength and effectiveness of this program comes from this team effort. Joint conclusions and recommendations carry much more weight and are more easily defended than those of an individual.

The results of the team staffing are presented to the professional patient and, if appropriate, patient advocates. As outlined in Figure 15.2, this sets the stage for the second phase of the assessment process, in which the assessment team observes the patient's responses and level of acceptance of the assessment results. The patient remains in the program long enough to receive feedback from the individual evaluations by team members and to develop an action plan to be implemented upon discharge from the assessment program.

During this second phase in the assessment process, it is important to carefully follow the patient. The conclusions of the team staffing are first presented to the patient in a formal session that is usually conducted by the team director and the case manager. When the patient is expected to react to this information adversely, or when it is anticipated

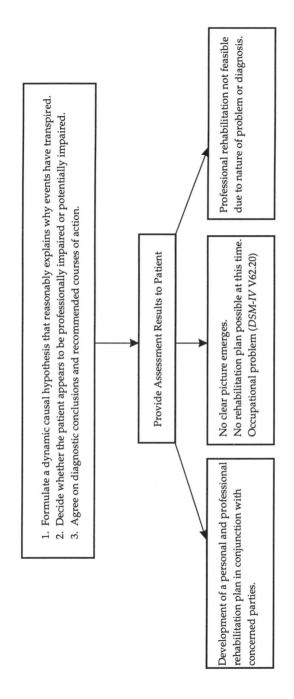

1. Formulate a dynamic causal hypothesis that reasonably explains why events have transpired.
2. Decide whether the patient appears to be professionally impaired or potentially impaired.
3. Agree on diagnostic conclusions and recommended courses of action.

Provide Assessment Results to Patient

Professional rehabilitation not feasible due to nature of problem or diagnosis.

No clear picture emerges. No rehabilitation plan possible at this time. Occupational problem (*DSM-IV* V62.20)

Development of a personal and professional rehabilitation plan in conjunction with concerned parties.

Figure 15.2. The Assessment Process: Assessment Team Staffing Goals

that this session will constitute another intervention on the patient, the attending psychiatrist will be asked to participate as well. The case manager records the information given to the patient as the medical director presents the material. Conference calls with the patient's advocates are often helpful. We have noted that many of our professional patients may have difficulty hearing and assimilating some, or at times all, of the information presented. Repetition of this material is assured through the forthcoming summary sessions with assessment team members over the next 24 hours, to facilitate effective communication of this essential information and to watch the program participant's responses evolve.

It is the responsibility of the patient's attending psychiatrist to meet with the patient after team staffing and prior to discharge to reevaluate the patient. Although uncommon in our experience, some patients will have difficulty during this phase. Clinical depression and situational stress may become more severe. Careful inquiry and behavioral observation are helpful to assure that the patient is able to proceed with a reasonable and safe plan of action following discharge. Suicidal or homicidal intentions or significant probability of engaging in self-destructive or self-defeating behavior must be ruled out to the greatest extent possible prior to release from the program and must be documented in clinical records.

DUTIES AND ROLES OF
ASSESSMENT TEAM MEMBERS

Each team member has important and defined roles in the assessment process. It is the collective effort of the team that provides the depth, perspective, balance, and expertise necessary to achieve the goals set forth and provide conclusions and recommendations that are fair, objective, reasonable, and able to be defended and challenged. Individual duties for each team member include the following.

Team Director

- Determines appropriate patients for assessment
- Defines specific questions to be addressed by the team
- Supervises selection of appropriate team members
- Reviews all collateral materials
- Completes own evaluation of patient

- Moderates clinical staffing
- Communicates results of staffing to patient and patient advocates as well as concerned parties
- Writes assessment summary report
- Represents the team in continued contact with the patient after discharge and in meetings with concerned parties, depositions, and formal hearings

Attending Psychiatrist

- Is the physician of record and manager of patient care
- Completes psychiatric intake and evaluation of patient
- Orders additional consultations when needed
- Determines patient suitability for discharge
- Assures precision and accuracy of diagnostic conclusions, in accordance with *DSM* criteria

Consulting Psychologist

- Reviews past psychological testing
- Decides upon appropriate psychological tests for this evaluation if departure from the standard testing battery is warranted
- Looks for cognitive impairment and recommends additional neuropsychological testing when appropriate
- Conducts clinical interviews
- Administers interactive and projective tests
- Scores and interprets personality tests (usually MMPI-II and MCMI-II)
- Provides results of psychological tests and psychological evaluation to patient
- Completes a formal evaluation report

Internal Medicine Consultant

- Takes a comprehensive medical history
- Completes physical examination
- Documents signs and symptoms of addictive disease
- Orders appropriate diagnostic tests with the approval of the attending psychiatrist
- Provides results of evaluation and test results to patient
- Completes a formal evaluation report

Case Manager

- Introduces the program to the patient
- Obtains necessary releases of information
- Serves as primary team liaison with the patient and with unit nursing staff
- Makes appropriate calls to collateral sources and family members with patient's written consent
- Administers self-evaluation instruments
- Completes biopsychosocial history and family genogram with patient
- Takes a comprehensive family, vocational, and sexual history from patient
- Helps patient in development of an action plan following presentation of assessment results
- Completes a formal case management report

Assessment Unit Hospital Staff

- Completes admission process and nursing intake
- Observes patient behavior before and after sessions with assessment team members
- Notes how patient treats unit staff
- Documents attitudes and behavior while completing written assignments and during time between sessions with assessment team members
- Advises team of any significant observations or concerns
- Obtains unannounced random urine drug screen under chain of custody provisions
- Conducts belongings search for questionable articles brought to the hospital by program participants

COMPLETION OF ASSESSMENT

Following patient discharge, each team member completes his or her *formal evaluation report*. These are reviewed by the team director, who then prepares the final summary report that pulls together these component evaluations and documents the opinions, diagnostic conclusions, and recommended courses of action agreed upon in team staffing. The program participant's responses to the recommendations and conclusions, and progress in developing a plan of action, are also documented.

This formal summary report is provided to the patient, patient advocates, and concerned parties under the dictates of state and federal confidentiality laws. Figure 15.3 shows how assessment results may be used as part of the database upon which responsible parties may make appropriate decisions concerning the professional patient. A carefully written summary report that clearly and directly conveys this information in nontechnical language can be of great value and may help soften the personal reactions and biases that concerned parties may bring to proceedings in which such complaints are presented and important decisions are made.

A formal assessment as described herein is a labor-intensive undertaking on the part of team members and the professional patient. It is expensive and time consuming and may not be needed in all cases. The value of this approach will be appreciated over the weeks and months that follow the hospitalization. As a result of participation in the program, patients may be able to better see themselves as other people see them. They may come to recognize how their words and actions were interpreted by the complainants. Many come to believe that they have exploited power and position and are then prepared to take responsibility for their actions and commit to a program of personal and professional rehabilitation.

When professionals are confronted with allegations of sexual misconduct or sexual offense, their careers are in jeopardy. They deserve a fair, thorough, and comprehensive assessment to *determine whether rehabilitation is possible* or necessary before punishment and sanctions are administered unless there is immediate *danger to personal or public health and safety.* In approximately 5% of our formal assessment cases, complaints have been found to be either substantially exaggerated or false. If professionals see no hope for healing, they are forced to admit guilt, plea bargain, or take the matter to formal hearing or trial, where they will be found either guilty or innocent. Due process can take many months, and professionals may be permitted to continue to practice without treatment, therapy, or adequate supervision while waiting for the matter to be adjudicated.

The assessment process and its results have often averted the need for formal due process and legal proceedings, saving many thousands of dollars in legal fees, investigations, and administrative costs. Careers and families have been salvaged, although major life and vocational transitions are often required. Even when a professional has engaged in professional sexual offense and is believed to have rehabilitation potential, it has been our experience that usually 12 to 24 months of treatment are required before professional reentry in a structured, monitored setting can be recommended.

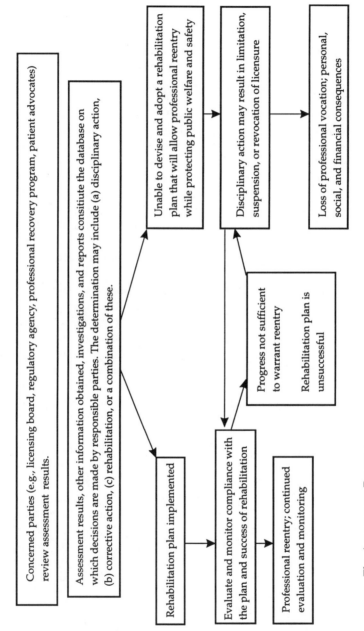

The boxes in the flowchart contain the following text:

Concerned parties (e.g., licensing board, regulatory agency, professional recovery program, patient advocates) review assessment results.

Assessment results, other information obtained, investigations, and reports constitute the database on which decisions are made by responsible parties. The determination may include (a) disciplinary action, (b) corrective action, (c) rehabilitation, or a combination of these.

Unable to devise and adopt a rehabilitation plan that will allow professional reentry while protecting public welfare and safety

Disciplinary action may result in limitation, suspension, or revocation of licensure

Loss of professional vocation; personal, social, and financial consequences

Progress not sufficient to warrant reentry

Rehabilitation plan is unsuccessful

Rehabilitation plan implemented

Evaluate and monitor compliance with the plan and success of rehabilitation

Professional reentry; continued evaluation and monitoring

Figure 15.3. The Assessment Process

SOURCE: Adapted from Schoener and Gonsiorek (1987).

The approach presented offers an initial step toward immediate corrective action. When sexual misconduct has occurred, it potentially represents an opportunity for atonement, treatment, reconciliation, and verification to victims to help heal violence and abuse of power at its origin. We have found that over 80% of the participants in our program have physical, emotional, and/or sexual abuse in their history. Many have progressed from victims to victimizers as a misguided effort to maintain control and obtain gratification in their lives. In our experience, approximately half of our participants are candidates for professional reentry over the ensuing two years, but more than 90% could benefit from treatment, thereby reducing the incidence of reoffense.

If we are to disrupt the cycles of violence that grip our society, we must offer hope, treatment, and opportunity for healing whenever possible. Regression into fear, retaliation, shame, secrecy, and denial is an ineffective and unfortunate alternative for both offenders and victims. Through collective action, we can establish guidelines and then standards for assessment and treatment of sexual misconduct and offense that are responsible and effective while protecting public welfare and safety. Disciplinary action and even incarceration should be used when justified and necessary. Further research and long-term studies will provide the data upon which we will be better able to determine optimal management of sexually exploitative professionals. We will then be able to better determine how effectively some can be rehabilitated through appropriate therapy, monitoring, supervision, and career transition, in which sexually exploitative professionals should not be given the opportunity for professional reentry.

16

A Systems Perspective on Sexual
Exploitation of Clients by Professional Helpers

William L. White

The personal perspective I wish to contribute to the understanding of the sexual exploitation of clients by professional helpers comes primarily out of my work as an organizational consultant—a role I assumed after years working as a clinician and clinical supervisor in mental health and addiction treatment agencies. In my organizational research and consultation, I have specialized in exploring how to restore physical and psychological safety within organizations that have been plagued by enduring abuses of power including multiple incidents of sexual harassment of workers and/or sexual exploitation of service consumers.

This chapter will

a. outline seven models of conceptualizing the etiology of sexual harassment and the intervention strategies that flow from each model,

b. define key propositions within a systems perspective on the sexual exploitation of clients by professional helpers, and

c. outline an ecological framework for understanding sexual exploitation that identifies multilayered prevention and intervention strategies.

I will attempt to broaden the traditional focus on the victim-perpetrator dyad and define an ecology of sexual exploitation that opens up a broad array of prevention and intervention strategies.

SEXUAL EXPLOITATION: MODELS FOR PROBLEM DEFINITION AND STRATEGY DEVELOPMENT

In my involvement in professional organizations over the past 25 years, I have observed six reductionist models that have explicitly or implicitly guided attempts to prevent or intervene in episodes of sexual harassment of clients by professional helpers.

In the *Perpetrator Morality Model*, the etiology of sexual exploitation is viewed as emerging from the evilness of the perpetrating professional helper. It is assumed that only a person totally lacking superego controls—in short, a psychopathic predator—could so exploit the fiduciary nature of the helping process. Our task is to screen out evil workers whose predatory proclivities are masked by the images of good citizen and good worker. Our further task is to find such persons who fooled us and got into the workplace and extrude them from our agencies and our professional fields.

The model has general appeal because such persons can occasionally be found, and treating all exploiters as sexual psychopaths magnifies the distance between ourselves and the perpetrator. It allows us to believe as professional helpers, for example, that, because we see no such exploitative tendencies in ourselves, we are not vulnerable to sexual involvements with clients—a belief that probably increases our chances of being involved in just such a relationship. It also allows organizations to believe that they have addressed the problem of harassment or exploitation solely by extruding an identified sexual predator.

The second model is closely related to the first but defines the source of evilness not within the alleged perpetrator but within the alleged victim. The *Victim Morality Model* denies the reality of harassing and exploiting events and casts the problem within the maliciousness of the complainant's character. The complainant misinterpreted the intentions or actions of the accused or is retaliating with false allegations against the accused out of personal animosity. Another version of this model portrays the client, through his or her seductive and manipulative wiles, overwhelming the otherwise ethical helping professional.

Organizations in which this belief permeates are notorious for scapegoating complainants. Even when such organizations have clear policies and grievance procedures related to sexual exploitation, hearings are often turned into a systematic indictment of the complainant. The procedures for redress, in short, become vehicles for revictimization. Like children breaking silence about sexual abuse or the survivors of rape on the witness stand, the dangers of revictimization are great. The scapegoating and revictimization of persons who have broken silence on exploitation deepen the silence of other victims and protect exploiters from experiencing the consequences of their actions.

In the *Clinical Model*, the etiology of sexual harassment or sexual exploitation is defined in terms of psychopathology. Harassing or exploitative behaviors are viewed as transient aberrations in judgment emerging from chronic or transient emotional disturbance. This model is exemplified in political, religious, business, or service leaders—when efforts to escape harassment or exploitation charges fail—running off to alcoholism or psychiatric treatment centers with the implicit explanation that their abuses of power resulted from their drinking or transient emotional crises.

The Clinical Model dictates one of two responses to the identified perpetrator. Where such emotional disturbance is validated by clinical assessment and is adjudged to preclude the person's ability to perform his or her prior role, the person is extruded from the organization or field through such actions as revocation of professional license. In other cases, when one's impairment is not so severe or enduring as to preclude professional performance, one is restricted to only particular types of professional activity and is mandated to continued participation in some form of treatment activities. The Clinical Model applied to the helping professions posits that such professions must screen out persons whose emotional instability precludes their ability to work with vulnerable persons. It also posits that effective programs of early intervention, such as employee assistance programs, must be in place to intervene at an early stage in the deterioration of a helping professional before such deterioration has threatened the health and safety of the clients with whom that professional is involved. There is also an assumption that some exploiters can be treated and returned to practice roles with minimal risks of future exploitative incidents. This model, like some of the others, may contain elements of the true story of sexual exploitation but fails to capture the whole story.

There is a variation of the Clinical Model that defines the problem in terms of the client's psychopathology. The client's allegation of sexual misconduct is interpreted as delusion, as fantasy, as a transference problem, or as retribution for "imagined slights by the borderline personality." In some complaints, the initial presentation of the allegation is framed more as a clinical case study of the client than an administrative hearing to determine fact regarding an allegation of professional misconduct. One problem in this regard is that the most insidious sexual predator is going to select precisely those clients who have the greatest vulnerability and whose allegations would be most easily discounted.

The fourth reductionist model of sexual exploitation is the *Anomie Model*. This model, which is often found in new, emerging disciplines and organizations (or those going through turbulent change), defines the etiology of sexual exploitation as the absence of a clear body of ethical standards defining appropriate and inappropriate conduct in worker-client relationships. The source of the problem according to this model is the lack of definition of standards of etiquette and appropriateness governing service relationships. With this model, our task is to generate codes of conduct that define appropriate and inappropriate behavior within these relationships. All but the most extreme harassing and exploiting behaviors may be excused in these systems on the grounds that no standards have been defined or communicated in these areas.

When organizations have created standards and continue to have problems with sexual harassment and sexual exploitation, it is time to redefine the problem. *The Training Model* defines the etiology of sexual harassment and sexual exploitation in terms of the knowledge and skill deficiency of the worker—it is a problem of inadequate professional socialization. The solution as defined in this model for helping professionals is to provide preparatory and ongoing training in ethical standards and ethical decision making for all workers and targeted training designed to rehabilitate practitioners who have been involved in poor boundary maintenance in their relationships with clients.

The sixth reductionist model, *The Environmental Model*, defines the etiology of sexual exploitation as an isolated aberration of chemistry between the exploiter and his or her environment at a particular point in time. The model argues that, because this event was idiosyncratic and unlikely ever to occur again in a different context, the best strategy is to relocate the exploiting practitioner to another role, department, or geographic location. The same logic could justify transferring the exploited client to another treatment resource. While the church has been visibly criticized for moving pedophile priests from parish to parish, many large, complex organizations have responded to problems of sexual exploitation through geographic relocation of perpetrators.

Reductionist models of explanation and intervention, which predominate in the early stages of exploration of any problem, must eventually give way to models that can encompass complexity and diversity. All of the models described above tend to define the problem of sexual exploitation in ways that narrow our view of etiology and restrict our vision of prevention and intervention strategies. Some are based on errors of fact. Others describe an element of the problem but do not encompass the problem. Our task is to integrate the best within these models into a coherent whole. The goal of the systems model outlined below is to provide a framework through which such wholeness can be sought and achieved.

SYSTEMS PERSPECTIVES

The systems model begins by defining the problem of sexual harassment or sexual exploitation as a breakdown in a relationship. It is a breakdown in the fiduciary relationship that exists between the helping person/institution and the service recipient. This breakdown occurs when certain elements essential to the success of this relationship get lost and certain new elements get injected. What gets lost in the helper-client relationship is respect and integrity; what gets injected into the relationship is the manipulation and abuse of power. The factors and conditions that lead to the depletion of the former and presence of the latter are multiple and synergistic in their interaction.

Prevention and intervention strategies must understand and target these multiple influences. A systems model provides a conceptual map within which the existing data and viewpoints can be linked together and within which understandings of new complexities can be integrated.

Four propositions can help introduce this systems perspective.

Proposition 1: Sexual harassment or sexual exploitation can best be viewed as a process rather than an event. Sexually exploiting behaviors often exist on a continuum of disrespectful, demeaning, and/or discriminatory behaviors. Sexual exploitation is often the last stage of what has been a progressive violation of intimacy barriers in the helper-client relationship. Allegations of sexual exploitation are often a breaking into light of what has been a progressive deterioration in the integrity of the helper-client relationship. The helping relationship could be displayed on a continuum of intimacy. At one end of this continuum is complete physical and emotional disengagement; at the other is a high level of emotional and physical intimacy. Somewhere in the middle, depending on the nature of our organization, our role, and the nature of our clients, a zone of appropriateness will mark the boundaries of appropriate intimacy. (See Chapter 13 in this volume.)

This concept can help us first develop a deeper understanding of the experience of victimization that results from sexual harassment and sexual exploitation. The trauma from sexual exploitation results from the entire continuum of boundary violations, not just the overt sexual acts. Where boundary violations have been sustained and accelerating, but stop short of sexual acts, the client may be traumatized but lack the ability to clearly label his or her exploitation. In family and therapeutic relationships, this is sometimes described as emotional incest. The concept of continuum also suggests that violations can occur at the other end that may also be traumagenic. Many case studies of exploitation, in fact, involve violation at both ends of the continuum—sexual exploitation followed by precipitous termination and abandonment of the client. Therapists should be held as accountable for the latter as for the former.

The understanding of this proposition is also critical to effective strategy development. Interventions are doomed to failure that seek to address the sexually exploiting behavior in isolation from this broader continuum. The fact that sexual exploitation is often preceded by a progression of other boundary violations provides a window of opportunity to both identify boundary problems at an early stage and potentially prevent more severe transgressions in the helping relationship. Sexual exploitation of clients cannot be dealt with in isolation but must be addressed within the broader context of abuses of power that occur at both ends of the intimacy continuum.

Proposition 2: The process of sexual exploitation and the sexual exploitation event that emerges from this process are ecologically nested within professional, organizational, community, and cultural environments. These elements of influence can serve to promote or inhibit boundary violations in the helping relationship. There are two major implications of this proposition. The first is that the identification of forces at all levels of this ecosystem that promote or fail to inhibit sexual harassment and exploitation must be identified. The second implication is that our prevention and remediation strategies must target multiple sites within this person-environment ecosystem. The layers of this ecosystem will be described shortly.

Proposition 3: Strategies and programs to address sexual exploitation must reflect an in-depth understanding of dynamics through which organizations resist and experience change over time. Organizations tend to respond to crisis and demands for change with responses that minimize real change. If boundary problems with clients, and sexual exploitation in particular, become an issue generated internally or through the fiat of some external regulatory or contracting body, the organization's first efforts are likely to be superficial and mechanistic. An individual worker is extruded. An appendage is added—a policy, a person, a training seminar—none of which is intended or is likely by itself to alter the nature of the organizational culture. In the case of abuses of power such as sexual harassment or sexual exploitation, the agency acquires another agency's sexual harassment/exploitation policy, replaces their name, and, with minimal involvement from anyone, sticks it in the five-inch thick policy and procedures manual. The complaint procedure and mechanism is quickly manufactured in a similar manner and an outside trainer is brought in to do one-shot training for all supervisors. The agency feels it has responded to the problem of sexual harassment/exploitation. This is not how an organization changes; this is how an organization avoids change.

This inherent resistance to change in most human systems suggests that efforts to address serious problems often result in superficial rather than systemic change. Our response is to take some singular action or add some appendage to the system rather than change the culture *within* the system. It is easier to focus on one sexual exploitation incident than to focus on widespread boundary problems in helper-client relationships that are pervasive within an agency. It is much easier to extrude one sexual predator than to confront an entire organizational culture that has lost its service focus or has become toxic and abusive.

Proposition 4: A change in one part of a system produces accommodating changes in all other parts of the system, raising the potential for unforeseen problems created by any attempt at problem resolution. This proposition demands that organizations take extreme care in avoiding strategies that, while designed to protect clients, end up revictimizing or otherwise harming clients. In a similar manner, we must avoid policies or procedures that in protecting clients fail to also protect the procedural rights of professional helpers.

THE ECOLOGY OF SEXUAL EXPLOITATION

System perspectives can aid in strategy development by helping identify the multiple etiological roots of a problem, by targeting desirable targets of intervention, and by elucidating the potential interaction of strategies simultaneously or sequentially implemented at multiple levels within a dynamic system. The problem of sexual exploitation can, for example, be placed within an ecological framework. An exploiting event involving a single exploiter and single person being exploited is viewed as occurring within an environment that is itself nested within a large environment and so forth. This model places the interaction of these two individuals at the center of this ecological onion. There may be things at each layer that contributed to the unfolding of this event and resources and strategies at each layer that may contribute to problem resolution.

The center of this model is ontogeny—the unique developmental histories of the exploiter(s) and the person(s) being exploited that brought them to this exact point in time. The systems model seeks to identify any characteristics or circumstances that contribute to either role. The purpose of such inquiry is not to psychologically excuse the exploiter or blame the victim for his or her own victimization. Knowledge of the characteristics of the exploiter and the exploited and situational cues related to when, where, and how the exploitation occurred may help develop policies and structures that decrease the likelihood of such behavior. Exploiter profiles may help exclude persons with predatory proclivities from being hired or may tell us the circumstances under which otherwise ethical practitioners may be at high risk for intimacy violations in their service relationships. A better understanding of persons targeted for harassment could lead to the discovery of strategies to reduce client vulnerability. If, for example, it is discovered that the lack of knowledge of what is and is not appropriate within a helping relationship contributes to client vulnerability, programs of client orientation to such issues become a potential prevention strategy. If it is discovered that particular types of clients are being targeted, special systems of prevention, intervention, protection, and support could be designed and implemented.

In addition to examining what each individual brings to the exploitative helper-client relationship, the presence of any special chemistry in the client-helper relationship that seems unique to the exploitative event can also be explored. It seems that some therapists are vulnerable to boundary violations with only a particular type of client. A greater understanding of such chemistry could help reduce client and therapist vulnerability by influencing how therapists are assigned to work with particular clients. It would also reveal particular types of therapist-client combinations that might be worthy of much more frequent and rigorous clinical supervision.

The exploiting event occurs within a physical, professional, and social environment. This second layer of our ecological onion is the microsystem—the smallest unit of the organization that surrounds each worker. The microsystem is a shift, a physical plant, a work team, a supervisor, a job description. The point of inquiry in the microsystem is an examination of forces or conditions in this environment that influence positively or negatively the incidence of sexual exploitation. Conducting this kind of force field analysis can generate a series of microsystem intervention strategies. The strategies seek to reduce those promoting forces identified and strengthen the identified inhibiting forces. Microsystem strategies include such areas as client education about boundary issues in the service relationship, client access to grievance/complaint procedures, worker and supervisory training programs on ethical and boundary issues, worker access to clinical consultation, supervisory access to technical consultation, access to internal resources of employee support (employee assistance program), and access of the exploited client to external resources of support, such as advocacy services, personal/legal consultation, counseling, and support groups. Microsystem strategies also target the alleviation of role stressors that may have contributed to the deterioration in boundary appropriateness, such as role overload, role-person mismatch, and role ambiguity.

Each microsystem is ecologically nested with the mesosystem—the total organization that embraces and links all of the organizational units and defines their relationships with one another and the outside world. At the mesosystem level, one can examine how broad organizational processes and structures either enhance or inhibit sexual harassment and exploitation of workers. Mesosystem issues include things ranging from the existence, clarity, accessibility, and enforcement of policies and standards governing worker-client relationships to the attitudes, values, and behaviors modeled by organizational leaders. Mesosystem strategies to address sexual exploitation are encompassed within ethics committees, quality improvement committees, and planning processes that seek to consciously shape the service culture of the organization. Below, two particular mesosystem issues will be explored in detail—the sexual culture of the organization and the propensity for abuse within closed organizational systems.

The examination of microsystem and mesosystem influences on sexual exploitation recognizes that there is a dynamic relationship between what the individual worker and the individual client bring to the organization and what the organization brings to these relationships. In the chemistry of this interaction, the propensity to exploit and the vulnerability to be exploited can be either decreased or increased. This step neither blames the organization nor exculpates the exploiter from responsibility for his or her actions. It does acknowledge that organizations can play a contributing role by promoting or tolerating conditions that nurture exploitation or by failing to serve as an active restraining agent to sexual exploitation.

Each organization (its microsystems and its workers) is nested within a broader geographic, social, political, and economic environment (exosystem). There is a complex and continuing relationship between the organization and this immediate environment that influences the internal values and behavior within the organization. It is important for an organization to have some understanding of the degree to which the values, attitudes, and entrenched behaviors within this exosystem will serve to enhance or inhibit sexual exploitation within the workplace. Where enhancing factors exist in great strength, the organization may choose to link itself with other organizations in a campaign of community education designed to weaken such forces or, having an awareness of such external factors, intensify its internal programs to prevent sexual exploitation. Through its political voice and through its trade associations, the organization may also contribute to weakening such enhancing factors in the broader culture (macrosystem).

The chapters in this volume discuss detailed strategies targeting various layers of this ecosystem. The issue is not which one of these strategies is preferable. The issue is how these strategies can be integrated with existing resources into a coordinated program that targets these multiple levels of intervention.

With this broad overview in place, I will focus on three mesosystem and microsystem problems that have been a focus of my consultations with organizations:

- Shaping nonexploitative organizational sexual cultures
- Creating an organizational Code of Professional Practice as the centerpiece of a value-driven, service-oriented organizational culture
- Addressing the special problem of sexual exploitation of clients within closed organizational systems

ORGANIZATIONAL CULTURE: BOUNDARIES CONTROLLING THE EXPRESSION OF POWER, AGGRESSION, SEXUALITY

One dimension of the microsystem and mesosystem environment that influences sexual exploitation is the culture of the organization and its work units. Every organization can be said to have a culture. Each organization's culture can be described in terms of its history, traditions, heroes and heroines, values, symbols, slogans, rituals, and taboos. Some can be described in terms of particular customs related to dress, food, leisure, music, and art. In a similar manner, it can also be said that each organization has a sexual culture. The sexual culture defines the customs and etiquette that will guide professional and personal relationships between organizational members and between members and their service constituents. The sexual culture of an organization shapes a climate of respect or disrespect that can serve either to inhibit or to nurture exploitative behavior. Strategies to discourage abusive behavior in the workplace can examine how worker values and behaviors are shaped by such cultural elements as the following:

- **Language,** such as customary use of disrespectful, profane, or derogatory language; racial epithets; demeaning humor; labels that objectify and depersonalize; or verbal threats and intimidation
- **Artifacts and symbols,** such as paintings, sculptures, books, magazines, posters, articles of clothing, or other objects in the work environment that may contribute to a climate of disrespect
- **Ethics and values,** such as the absence or lack of clarity in values defining proper and improper behavior in worker-client relationships and work practices that devalue particular groups of workers such as gender inequity in salaries, work assignments, or promotions
- **Modeling of relationships,** such as the values and behavior modeled by organizational leaders in worker-worker and worker-client relationships in both formal and informal settings

In many organizations, the struggle is to bring the implicit and real culture into compliance with the culture defined aspirationally in policy. Incongruencies between aspirational and real values within the organizational culture provide a breeding ground for abuse. Well-written sexual exploitation/harassment policies and procedures are rendered meaningless in an environment where organizational leaders are practicing or openly condoning the exact behaviors tabooed in the policy statements.

What many of the recommended strategies presented in this text do is define and transmit organizational values and standards that define appropriate and inappropriate behavior. These strategies define the organizational etiquette governing relationships between workers and clients. They define the behaviors and values to which organizational members are to aspire, and they define behaviors that are tabooed within the organizational family. Through the conscious examination of our organizational cultures, we can seek to remove abuse-condoning elements and replace them with elements more conducive to client health, worker health, and organizational health.

SHAPING MESOSYSTEM
AND MICROSYSTEM VALUES

The centerpiece of any response to sexual exploitation of clients by professional helpers is the clear definition and monitoring of the boundaries of appropriateness and inappropriateness within the helping relationship. Both our ability to prevent abuses of power in helping relationships and our response to persons who commit such abuses are contingent upon the clear articulation of these boundaries.

A growing number of organizations are using the vehicle of an organizational Code of Professional Practice (CPP) as a primary means of shaping organizational values and organizational culture. The CPP encompasses and extends traditional personnel codes and codes of ethics. The CPP includes standards ("Thou shalt not . . ."), aspirational values, procedural directives, folk wisdom ("It has been our experience that . . ."), and other explicit articulations of organizational norms. The CPP also covers all organizational members rather than a single discipline or direct service workers. Most of the codes have articulated such boundaries of appropriateness and inappropriateness in broad categories as personal conduct, professional conduct, conduct in business practices, conduct in relationships with service consumers, conduct in professional peer relationships (internal and external), and conduct involving threats to public safety.

The process of developing the CPP is a highly participatory process involving all full- and part-time staff, core volunteers, organizational members, board members, and the organization's primary external constituency groups. It takes the organization through a process of defining those standards and values to which all members of the organization shall be held accountable. Because of its importance, the process is consciously slow and deliberate, often taking 12 to 18 months from inception to implementation of the code.

Such codes not only articulate values and standards that address sexual harassment and sexual exploitation of clients but also address standards governing the whole continuum of boundary violations and abuses of power that often predate and set the stage for harassment and exploitation. A core value that is often embedded in the CPP is the presumptive vulnerability and innocence of the client. The codes of many agencies declare unequivocally that setting boundaries in helping relationships is always the responsibility of that person with the greater ascribed power—the professional helper. The client's interest in, initiation of, or compliance with sexual intimacy has no relevance and in no way diminishes the helper's *total* responsibility for maintaining boundaries of appropriate conduct in the helping relationship. Such responsibility is the very essence of the fiduciary relationship—the special duty and obligation taken on by the professional helper to protect the interests and well-being of the client.

Developing a CPP provides a framework through which each service setting and each supervisory process can define as concretely as possible the zones of effectiveness, zones of abuse, and zones of marginality (periods of increasing intimacy or disengagement that may be clinically appropriate but reflect a heightened level of vulnerability and decreased safety for both the client and helper) in worker-client relationships. By defining these areas, all activities within the zone of marginality can be structured in a manner to reduce the vulnerability and potential threats to the physical/psychological safety of all parties, such as a shift from single practitioner to team service delivery, increased supervision, external consultation, and use of external advocate/monitor for clients whose capacity for self-protection is compromised. Developing a CPP and operating with a highly visible CPP are powerful tools for shaping and monitoring service practitioner values within a strong client-centered organizational culture. Such codes articulate clear standards and a body of aspiration values that can serve as inhibiting influences to boundary violations and abusive behavior.

ORGANIZATIONAL TURBULENCE
AND CLIENT-HELPER VULNERABILITY

I have often been asked whether there are any types of organizations or particular stages in the life of an organization that generate a greater incidence of sexual exploitation problems. There are two such circumstances that I have noted from my consulting experience. The first is an increased incidence of harassment and exploitation in organizations going through periods of turbulence and rapid change. The second is the great potential for the abuse of power—including sexual harassment and sexual exploitation—in what I have described as closed, incestuous systems. In both contexts, helper-client boundary violations—including sexual exploitation—can be elicited from and be symptomatic of aberrations in group process and organizational health.

Rapid change within an organization disrupts the psychological homeostasis of all workers. Workers at all levels who have lost their sense of personal and professional value may seek a variety of channels through which to reassert and affirm their value and potency. The increased incidence of voluntary sexual intimacy between workers, incidence of sexual harassment, and incidence of sexual exploitation of clients during such periods probably have little to do with sex but are means of seeking fulfillment for other needs. Attempted sexual contact in worker-worker and worker-client relationships during such turbulent periods may have more to do with power, anger, aggression, physical depletion, loneliness, or desperate needs for self-affirmation than with sexual attraction.

During periods of organizational turbulence, there is a weakening of organizational culture and values. The organization loses its power to shape, monitor, and self-correct boundary problems within worker-client relationships. Weak organizational cultures lose the capacity to define boundaries of appropriateness in service relationships. Weak organizational cultures exert little influence or control on individual practitioners. Rapid staff turnover or growth opens up the possibility of new workers and emergent subcultures that deviate from an organization's historical values. Turbulence within organizational systems, just as in family systems, marks a period of great vulnerability for role boundary violations. Strategies to address boundary violations amid such turbulence must include the active management of change and the strengthening of the organizational culture and the values guiding helper-client relationships.

INCESTUOUS SYSTEMS

In the mid-1970s I began publishing articles and monographs on the propensity for abuse within a particular kind of organizational setting and process. Applying family systems theory to organizations, I described the extreme disruption of personal and organizational health associated with sustained organizational "closure." An incestuous dynamic was described that resulted from this closure—a stage in the life of an organization marked by increasing numbers of staff meeting most, if not all, of their personal, professional, social, and sexual needs inside the boundary of the organization. The progressive closure of such organizations over a number of years was marked by such predictable elements as the following:

- Emergence of organizational dogma—a rigid and unchallengeable belief system
- Centralization of power and preference for charismatic styles of leadership (the emergence of high priests/priestesses)
- Progressive isolation of the organization and its members from the outside professional and social world
- Homogenization of the workforce by age, race, sex, religion, or values via a tendency to isolate and expel that which was different
- Excessive demands for time and emotional energy of workers
- Development of a work-dominated social network by organizational members
- Intense focusing on the personal and interpersonal problems of staff
- Disruption of team functioning from problems arising in worker-worker social and sexual relationships
- Projection of organizational problems on an outside enemy or scapegoating and extrusion of individual workers
- Escalation of interpersonal and intergroup conflict to include staff plots, conspiracies, or coups against organizational leadership
- Emergence of a punitive, abusive organizational culture
- Fall of the "high priest/priestess" and a contagion of staff turnover (breakup of the system)

Sustained closure of organizational systems (or subsystems) both disrupts the health of workers and undermines the health and survivability of the organization. It is my experience that closed organizational systems have a high incidence of sexual harassment and sexual exploitation and that the intensity and duration of abuse incidents tends to be greater and more debilitating to victims than in incidents in more open systems. The potential for abuses of power in closed systems and the intensity of abuses in such organizations is magnified by the following:

- The violation of the boundary and balance between one's work life and one's personal life
- The loss of outside sources of personal, professional, social, and sexual replenishment
- The progressive depletion (physical and emotional exhaustion) of personal and group health resulting from excessive demands on worker time and emotional energy
- The distortion of organizational values resulting from the loss of external feedback and external mechanisms for reality testing with the outside social and professional community

At its worst, sexual exploitation can be institutionalized as an element of the culture of a closed system. In such circumstances, the abusive episodes are large in number, occur over extended periods of time, and involve large numbers of perpetrators and exploited clients. Sexual harassment of workers and sexual exploitation of workers often emerge out of the same abuses of power within such organizations. The high level of unmet needs and the distortion of values within the closed system make anyone interacting with this system at high risk for exploitation.

In such circumstances, issues of sexual exploitation of clients are inseparable from broader issues of organizational health. Clients or staff cannot be protected without intervention into basic problems of structure and process within closed systems. Intervening in such systems requires action targeted at multiple layers of the ecosystem.

THE BROADER VIEW

In summary, when we speak of sexual exploitation of clients by professional helpers, we are speaking of the abuse of power. We must eventually link our internal organizational efforts with broader movements seeking to confront the whole spectrum of abuses of power, in general, and the institutionalized violence against disempowered persons, in particular. If we see sexual exploitation only in terms of psychopathology or skill deficiency of the individual exploiter, we miss the broader social milieu that incites or fails to inhibit such behavior. Sexual exploitation of clients is part of a broader continuum of aggression and violence toward the culturally disempowered, particularly women and children. As we understand sexual exploitation within these broader frameworks, we can link ourselves to parallel resources and movements seeking to enhance the health of our clients, our organizations, our communities, and our culture.

17

Lesbian, Gay, and Bisexual Therapists' Social and Sexual Interactions With Clients

Laura Lyn

DUAL RELATIONSHIPS
AND ETHICAL GUIDANCE

The boundaries of therapy can be challenged by out-of-session social interactions between therapists and their clients. In addition, sexual interactions between therapists and their clients radically alter the boundaries of the therapeutic relationship. Both social and sexual interactions between therapists and clients raise a continuum of ethical boundary dilemmas. In the ethics literature, these boundary dilemmas have generally been discussed under the heading "dual relationships."

A number of theoretical pieces have been written on therapist-client dual relationships. Several of these pieces recommend against the creation and/or maintenance of such relationships (Burton, 1972; Corey,

AUTHOR'S NOTE: I would like to thank my thesis chair and academic adviser, Barbara J. Yanico, and my mentor, Laura S. Brown, for their guidance and support with my thesis, the research project on which this presentation was based.

Corey, & Callanan, 1984; Keith-Spiegel & Koocher, 1985). Authors have opposed extratherapy relationships, both during and after therapy, contending that therapy does not leave its participants free to be friends. The results for therapists of trying to create and/or maintain "nonprofessional" relationships with clients, social or sexual, have been reported to include loss of objectivity, lack of or decrease in confrontation and challenging skills, and danger of exploitation. Over the years, several ethical guides have been written that have, in part, tried to address the dilemmas arising from therapist-client dual relationships. The most well known of these guides is the American Psychological Association's *Ethical Principles of Psychologists and Code of Conduct* (1992b). Another major ethical guide, the *Feminist Therapy Ethical Code*, was published by the Feminist Therapy Institute (FTI, 1987). Both of these ethical guides give a brief description of the issue of dual roles between therapists and clients and attempt to provide some direction in dealing with such dilemmas.

Direction in the area of dual relationships of a sexual nature with clients appears to be relatively straightforward. Both the American Psychological Association (APA) and the FTI guides clearly oppose sexual relationships with clients. The interpretation of what constitutes a client, however, has been controversial in the APA. That is, does a client mean a current client, former client, or both? The FTI code specifies that sexual relationships with both current and former clients are unethical. The former version of the APA principles (1990a) opposed sexual relationships with clients but did not specify current or former. The current APA principles (1992b) clearly oppose sexual relationships with current clients (Ethical Standard 4.05, Sexual Intimacies With Current Patients or Clients). They also proscribe sexual contact with former clients for at least two years after the termination of therapy (Ethical Standard 4.07a, Sexual Intimacies With Former Therapy Patients). If a sexual relationship begins after the two years, it should occur only in the most unusual circumstances. It is also incumbent on the psychologist to defend the appropriateness of such a relationship, demonstrating that there has been no exploitation in light of seven relevant factors listed in the standard (Ethical Standard 4.07b, Sexual Intimacies With Former Therapy Patients).

The current APA principles are the result of several years of revisions. The revisions were undertaken, in part, to achieve clarification of APA's stand on sexual relationships with former clients. During the revision process, several drafts of new principles were published in the *APA Monitor* (June, 1990b; June, 1991; May, 1992a) for perusal and comment by the membership. A heated controversy fueled by a wide range of views on the ethics of sexual contact with former clients arose during the process. The current document is a product of the whole organization's input but likely does not please its entire membership.

Ethical counsel in the area of nonsexual, or social, relationships with clients (current or former) is less clear in the APA principles and the FTI code. The APA principles espouse the tactic of avoiding any dual relationships if at all possible. For the first time, the 1992 principles acknowledge that this is not always possible for psychologists who work in certain communities and situations. The FTI code encourages ongoing therapist-client negotiation of the dual roles in which therapists and clients may find themselves. In addition, therapists are urged to take responsibility for management of the power differential and effective use of personal power within the therapist-client relationship.

As mentioned above, avoiding any nonsexual dual relationships with clients may be quite impossible for some therapists. Roll and Millen (1981) pointed out that violating ethical mandates to avoid nonsexual dual relationships is nearly guaranteed in small communities due to their small size and structure. Keith-Spiegel and Koocher (1985) recognized that in such communities members ultimately have the same limited public space and there is thus an increased likelihood of contact among all community members (i.e., the "small world" phenomenon). They concluded that it is nearly impossible to create clear ethical guidelines regarding dual relationship boundary dilemmas because community variables necessitate that each dilemma be viewed within its own context. Overall, they maintained that strict ethical guidelines on nonsexual therapist-client relationships do not work and the best that can be done is to sensitize therapists to the potential problems inherent in dual role relationships.

Lesbian, gay, and bisexual communities are good examples of small communities and have been referred to as "sociological and psychological small towns" (Brown, 1988b). In addition to their small size, these communities are quite therapy oriented, where being in therapy is a norm, not an exception. According to the National Lesbian Health Care Survey done by Bradford and Ryan in 1987, nearly three fourths of their sample of 1,917 lesbian respondents reported having been in therapy at some point in their lives. Although such information is not available for gay men and bisexual individuals, it could be surmised that the use percentage might be similar given the similar life stresses they experience in society.

In any community where the therapy use rate is high and the community space is small, it is critical that therapists ethically examine their social interactions with clients to ensure appropriate boundary maintenance. Such maintenance may be difficult as social interactions may be plentiful and unavoidable. Interactions may also seem attractive to the lonely, isolated, or distressed therapist. It is, however, the therapist's responsibility to be aware of and manage these interactions as they can affect ongoing client treatment issues and/or serve as precursors to sexual involvement with clients.

THE PRESENT STUDY: METHOD
AND DEMOGRAPHIC INFORMATION

The majority of the research and literature on extratherapy interactions between therapists and clients has focused on sexual interactions (Applebaum, 1987; Bates & Brodsky, 1989; Bouhoutsos, Holroyd, Lerman, Forer, & Greenberg, 1983; Brown, 1989; Edelwich & Brodsky, 1991; Peterson, 1992; Pope & Bouhoutsos, 1986; Pope & Vasquez, 1991; Rigby, 1986; Schoener, Milgrom, Gonsiorek, Luepker, & Conroe, 1989). In contrast, little research has been done in the general area of social interactions between therapists and clients, including both social relationships and social encounters. The majority of work on social relationships comprises clinical writing, most of which remains unpublished. The few actual studies that have been published frequently confound social and sexual relationships (Gross, 1986; Sell, Gottlieb, & Schoenfeld, 1986; Temerlin & Temerlin, 1982) or fail to distinguish consistently between interactions with current or former clients (Pope, Tabachnik, & Keith-Spiegel, 1987). Social encounters between therapists and clients have been the least studied area to date (Borys, 1988; Borys & Pope, 1989; Brown, 1984; Moss, 1987; Tallman, 1981).

I conducted a study of lesbian, gay, and bisexual therapists' social and sexual interactions with current and former clients. This chapter primarily describes and discusses that portion of the above data that focused on sexual interactions. However, some of the data on social interactions have also been included to help describe lesbian, gay, and bisexual communities and the lesbian, gay, and bisexual therapists who work and may live within them. It is important to look at the social interaction data also as they can provide clues to the precursors of sexual interactions with clients.

TABLE 17.1 To How Many Clients and Colleagues the Therapists Were "Out"

	Clients		Colleagues	
Scale Point	Frequency	N	Frequency	N
"None"	9.4%	22	0.4%	1
"A few"	23.5%	55	11.1%	26
"Some"	20.1%	47	11.1%	26
"Most but not all"	35.0%	82	36.3%	85
"All"	11.5%	27	40.6%	95
Blank	0.4%	1	0.4%	1

The complete study was a mail survey of the 738 individuals on the nonconfidential mailing list for APA's Division 44 (i.e., Society for the Psychological Study of Lesbian and Gay Issues) during late spring 1990. A description of social and sexual interactions between therapists and their current and former clients, and the impact of such interactions on therapists' professional and personal lives, was obtained using the Social Interaction Questionnaire (SIQ), a 10-page, primarily open-ended questionnaire that I developed. The survey was designed for any mental health practitioner who identified her- or himself as lesbian, gay, or bisexual and whose professional activities included, to any degree, the practice of counseling or psychotherapy with clients.

A total of 239 questionnaires were returned. A return rate of 27.2% ($n = 201$) was achieved when counting only Division 44 members (some respondents passed the questionnaires on to colleagues). There were 234 surveys that were usable for data analyses.

Of the total sample of 234 respondents, 49.6% ($n = 116$) were women and 50.4% ($n = 118$) were men. Of the female respondents, 88.8% ($n = 103$) identified as lesbian and 11.2% ($n = 13$) identified as bisexual. Of the male respondents, 93.2% ($n = 110$) identified as gay and 6.8% ($n = 8$) identified as bisexual. Table 17.1 shows to what degree respondents were "out" about their sexual orientation with clients and colleagues. The sample was 91.5% ($n = 214$) white, 3% ($n = 7$) African American, 4.3% ($n = 10$) Hispanic, 0.4% ($n = 1$) Native American, and 0.4% ($n = 1$) Asian. The majority were partnered (70.9%, $n = 166$) and lived in communities populated by over 1 million people (47.9%, $n = 112$). The mean age of respondents was 43.1 years ($SD = 8.0$, range = 25-71).

The majority of the respondents held a Ph.D. (79.1%, $n = 185$) and worked in private practice (79.5%, $n = 186$). Their average experience (number of years seeing clients) was 13 years (SD = 6.9). Respondents'

degrees were mostly in either clinical psychology (50.9%, n = 119) or
counseling psychology (26.1%, n = 61), and the model theoretical orientation they identified with was dynamic/analytic (36.3%, n = 85). A
separate question asking respondents if they would call themselves
feminist therapists elicited 161 (68.8%) affirmative answers (95 female
therapists and 66 male therapists).

RESULTS AND DISCUSSION

The data on therapist-client interactions from the survey are reported
in descriptive statistical terms. However, open-ended responses and
additional comments on questionnaires added a richness to the data
that could not have been achieved by numbers alone. Written responses
were encouraged and were numerous. They have been woven into the
results for elaborative purposes. The data on social encounters, social
relationships, and personal and professional problems encountered by
therapists are all reported first. These data will help paint a picture of
the unique situations that lesbian, gay, and bisexual therapists must
deal with when working and interacting in lesbian, gay, and bisexual
communities. The data on sexual interactions are reported last.

Social Encounters

Of the 234 therapist respondents, 89.7% (n = 210, 106 women and 104
men) had ever encountered current clients and 94.9% (n = 222, 110
women and 112 men) had ever encountered former clients. In general,
the numbers are higher for former clients. Female therapists reported
encountering mostly lesbian clients (88.8%, n = 103) and male therapists
reported encountering mostly gay male clients (84.7%, n = 100). The
most commonly identified reason therapists generated for encountering
their "most encountered client" was due to sharing the same community with the client. These numbers are important because they reveal
just how small lesbian, gay, and bisexual communities are and how common social encounters within them can be.

Within their communities, respondent therapists described commonly
encountering clients in public places, at public social events, at private
social events, and at work or professional events (paid or volunteer).
Public places included restaurants, synagogues, churches, hairdressers',
baths, movies, stores, pools, streets, rest rooms, bookstores, theaters, parks,
symphonies, beaches, and health clubs. Public social events included

TABLE 17.2 Respondents' Estimation of the Degree to Which Therapist-Client Social Encounters Were an Ethical Dilemma for Them in Their Professional Practice and for Their Colleagues in the Community in Which They Practiced

Scale Point	For Respondents Frequency	N	For Their Colleagues Frequency	N
"Not at all"	38.9%	91	13.2%	31
"Slightly"	38.9%	91	36.3%	85
"Moderately"	13.2%	31	29.9%	70
"Very much so"	7.7%	18	12.4%	29
"Constantly"	0.9%	2	1.7%	4
Blank	0.4%	1	0.4%	1

sporting events, AIDS charities, concerts, community events, 12-step meetings, parades, clubs, and organizations. Private social events included funerals, parties, meals, birthdays, holy unions, weddings, and other client special events. Work situations included conferences, workshops, presentations (either attending or giving), board meetings, and community organization work.

The frequency of therapist-client social encounters in lesbian, gay, and bisexual communities is quite high, as revealed by this study. Again, the social encounter data help to document the reality of how small such communities are and thus why avoiding social encounters is unrealistic and sometimes impossible. The data also reveal a type of community in which therapist-client boundaries have the potential to frequently become blurred due to extratherapy contact. This heightens the need for ongoing examination and monitoring of boundaries by therapists working within such communities.

Many therapists in this study found social encounters with clients to present some degree of an ethical dilemma either for themselves or for their colleagues (Table 17.2). A *dilemma* was defined as "a situation in which a clear course of action is not evident." Most believed it was a more salient issue for their colleagues than themselves, and more female than male respondents indicated that it was a dilemma on some level for them.

Therapists who are not clear with themselves and their clients about therapeutic boundaries may find themselves slipping down the continuum of ethical behavior due to the continuous challenges of out-of-session contact. Some types of extratherapy contact are more intimate than others but any type that occurs frequently can lead to boundary blurring and potential violation if not clearly and ethically managed.

For instance, some therapist respondents in this study reported encountering clients in contexts that were sexualized (e.g., porno bookstores, bathhouses, bars) or involved nudity (e.g., health club showers, pools/lakes, women's music festivals). Several were concerned about how their presence in such situations would be interpreted by clients. One managed these situations in the following way:

> I do not go to explicitly sexually oriented events (i.e., jack off clubs, adult bookstores, public cruising areas) for a variety of reasons, including my desire to avoid situations where I might encounter a client in a sexually ambiguous context.

Social Relationships

Beginning with the percentage of respondents, 12.4% (n = 29, 15 women and 14 men) had ever engaged in an ongoing social relationship with a current client, while 41.9% (n = 98, 48 women and 50 men) had ever done so with a former client. As with social encounters, the numbers are higher for former clients. Considerably fewer social relationships with clients than social encounters were reported. In other words, almost all therapists in this study encountered their clients in social contexts but most also did not develop social relationships with their clients. If they did develop a social relationship with a client, it was much more likely to be with a former than a current client.

Therapists generated many situations in which their social relationships with clients began. Some of the general categories that emerged included (a) contact through mutual friends, (b) client inviting therapist out, (c) therapist inviting client out, (d) social relationship predated therapy, (e) contact due to work environment, (f) contact due to public social events and small community, and (g) both client and therapist chose the social relationship. One therapist shared how ongoing social contact with a client can emerge:

> It is very difficult for a gay therapist to remain either politically, professionally, or socially active in the gay community without encountering current/former clients. It is actually easier to control casual social encounters than it is to avoid ongoing interaction when serving on committees, and remaining active in organizations.

Respondents were also asked the degree to which they considered social relationships between therapists and clients to present an ethical

TABLE 17.3 Respondents' Estimation of the Degree to Which Therapist-Client Social Relationships Were an Ethical Dilemma for Them in Their Professional Practice and for Their Colleagues in the Community in Which They Practiced

Scale Point	For Respondents		For Their Colleagues	
	Frequency	N	Frequency	N
"Not at all"	38.9%	91	11.5%	27
"Slightly"	38.9%	91	29.5%	69
"Moderately"	13.7%	32	33.8%	79
"Very much so"	6.8%	16	17.9%	42
"Constantly"	0.4%	1	1.7%	4
Blank	1.3%	3	5.5%	13

TABLE 17.4 Respondents' Estimates of the Degree to Which Social Relationships Between Therapists and Clients Are Ethical With Current Clients and With Former Clients

Scale Point	Current Clients		Former Clients	
	Frequency	N	Frequency	N
"Never ethical"	53%	124	10.3%	24
"Ethical under rare conditions"	28.6%	67	35.9%	84
"Ethical under some conditions"	13.2%	31	38.5%	90
"Ethical under many conditions"	1.7%	4	11.5%	27
"Always ethical"	0%	0	0.4%	1
Blank	3.4%	8	3.4%	8

dilemma (Table 17.3). As with social encounters, most respondents believed social relationships to present a more significant ethical dilemma for their colleagues than for themselves, and male respondents considered them to be less of a dilemma than did their female counterparts.

Respondents were also asked the degree to which they considered social relationships between therapists and clients to be ethical (Table 17.4). Most respondents judged such relationships with current clients to be "never ethical" (53%, $n = 124$, 67 women and 57 men). Respondents took a less conservative stance on relationships with former clients and judged them to be either "ethical under some conditions" (38.5%, $n = 90$, 41 women and 49 men) or "ethical under rare conditions" (35.9%, $n = 84$, 50 women and 34 men). Overall, women judged social relationships with current and former clients to be less ethical than did men.

There was a range of thought on the issue of therapist-client social relationships. Four therapists wrote comments from the more conservative perspective:

> In my opinion the relationship between a therapist and a client/former client can never be equalized and is always a hotbed for difficulties.

> I think a lot depends on the nature of the therapy and the importance of the transference dynamic in the therapy. The ultimate yardstick has to be what serves the best interests of the client.

> Depends on a) amount of time that has elapsed since termination of treatment, b) that it is understood that social contact precludes the possibility of a renewed therapeutic relationship, c) the level of intactness of the client, e.g., that social contact will not undo therapeutic gains.

> I think that social relationships with clients are probably ethical most of the time, but I also feel that they are unprofessional most of the time.

However, there were also dissenting views that advocated not only for social relationships with clients but for ongoing interaction in clients' lives in general. For example, one respondent commented:

> In order to be an effective helper, it is essential to garner accurate and reliable information. I make it a practice to visit my clients' homes and places of work, to talk with their friends and lovers to get a "real" picture of them. We all know the accuracy of self-report and this is a way to get at that issue.

Therapist social relationships with clients represent a different point on the ethical continuum of appropriate behavior than do social encounters. Most of the therapists in this study did not believe that engaging in such relationships reflected ethical behavior on the part of the therapist. However, all therapists were certainly not of the same opinion. It is imperative, though, that whether a therapist chooses to engage in such relationships or not, she or he must recognize that such relationships can significantly alter the boundaries of therapy, paving the way for serious boundary violations such as sexual activity. The next section on results focuses on how therapists recognized and managed extratherapy interactions with clients by discussing them with clients and colleagues and spending personal time thinking about them.

Impact on Professional Lives

Most therapists (64.1%, n = 150, 81 women and 69 men) reported discussing guidelines for social interaction with their clients and generated several types of guidelines they discussed with clients. These included (a) little personal interaction when social interaction occurs, (b) no discussion of treatment outside of session, (c) negotiating introductions, (d) letting the client initiate contact first and then deciding on acknowledging, (e) therapist maintaining confidentiality and acting ethically, (f) discussing social interaction in next session, (g) establishing a waiting period after treatment ends before socializing, (h) no social interaction during treatment, (i) no social interaction after treatment, and (j) no sexual interaction during or after treatment. Overall, women therapists appeared to be more active than men in discussing social interaction issues with their clients.

Respondents were also asked if they ever discussed therapist-client social interaction issues with their colleagues. Again, most (71.4%, n = 167, 88 women and 79 men) did discuss these issues with colleagues. In fact, more therapists reported talking with colleagues than with clients. Again, overall, women therapists appeared to be more active than men in discussing social interaction issues with their colleagues.

Finally, respondents reported whether they personally thought about therapist-client social interaction issues. The majority (82.1%, n = 192, 96 women and 96 men) did. More therapists personally thought about the issues than discussed them with either colleagues or clients. Reasons generated for thinking about social interactions included (a) that clients were interpersonally attractive, (b) to protect clients (ethical boundary maintenance), (c) to protect oneself, (d) to avoid social interaction, (e) because it was an ongoing issue, and (f) because it limited one's social interactions. Unlike discussing social interaction issues with clients and colleagues, an equal number of female and male therapist respondents appeared to personally think about social interaction issues. Two respondents added comments on why it was important for them to personally think through social interaction issues:

> I've met a number of really terrific people (no character pathology, etc.) who would probably make terrific friends, but I feel this is an "occupational hazard" of being a therapist. I've learned that I must go to other wells for my water.

> I sometimes feel awkward and "in a fishbowl" when I am somewhere where current/former clients may be. Sometimes I choose not to go places because of concerns about showing/not showing appropriate "boundary behavior."

Finally, respondents were asked to describe any professional problems or issues they had been faced with when socially interacting with their current or former clients. Some of the issues respondents generated included (a) boundary issues, (b) negotiating social encounters, (c) redefining the relationship with a client after treatment, and (d) personal discomfort when socially interacting with clients. Again, it is imperative that therapists are clear about the boundaries between therapeutic and personal relationships as clients may not be so clear and may intentionally or unintentionally challenge those boundaries. Two therapists elaborated on finding themselves in situations where clients wanted to change the boundaries of therapy to accommodate an intimate or sexual relationship:

> Patient wanting to prematurely terminate therapy in order to pursue personal relationship with me.

> On more than one occasion I have been cruised to the point of inappropriate touching by a client (e.g., attempts to kiss or leaning against me in bars), expressions of sexual interest. These were all with former clients who believed, despite my having explained my position, that we could have such a relationship now that therapy had concluded.

Impact on Personal Lives

The final results of the social interaction data report the impact of therapist-client social interaction issues on therapists' personal lives. The majority (76.5%, $n = 179$, 98 women and 81 men) of respondents indicated that social interactions with current and/or former clients (or the potential for such interactions) had at some point had an impact on decisions they had made about their own social lives and interactions. Many indicated that it had made them both more conscious of social interaction issues (57.3%, $n = 134$, 74 women and 60 men) and inhibited them in their social lives and interactions (61.1%, $n = 143$, 81 women and 62 men). Female therapists reported more impact of therapist-client social interaction on their lives than did their male counterparts. Additional comments highlighted the issues both genders discussed:

> At times I have not referred a client to particular social settings or events—usually lesbian and gay—because I wished to attend and relate not as a therapist to persons encountered there.

[I] take more initiative to meet people in non-clinical settings—[I] live where I do not work so I can just be myself when I'm not "in role."

I have always felt uncomfortable cruising when clients were at the bars—I always make sure I conduct myself with dignity in public. [I am] aware that I am a model in the community.

I feel like I can't let loose in a social situation if I see my clients there. It inhibits my spontaneity—I don't want to feel this way but I worry about any ramifications of my behavior. It feels like a burden at times. Other times I'm OK with it—just focus on my right to socialize, stay with friends—avoid clients.

That these therapists felt more conscious of social interaction issues seems positive in that they were more aware that their interactions outside of therapy with clients were meaningful to clients. They were watched by clients, seen as role models, and acted accordingly. They made complex decisions about how and in what contexts it was appropriate to interact with their clients. That these therapists also feel inhibited is not surprising but is potentially dangerous. The isolation and frustration expressed by some respondents could lead them down the continuum of ethical and appropriate contact with clients. As a result, intentional or unintentional boundary violations and exploitation may occur as they try to meet their own personal social and sexual needs.

The isolation and frustration for therapists in trying to meet their own personal needs was reported by both partnered and nonpartnered respondents in this study. Single therapists are often seeking partners in the same community from which their clients come. Two respondents noted:

When I was single [therapist-client social interaction issues were] a real bummer! But since I became partnered it's been easier. However, my lover had just moved here from out of town. I often wonder if we would have met in this way had she lived here long enough to try to see me for therapy, since I was the only therapist in town then.

As a gay therapist, and one of a handful in the city, there is always the possibility of running into a client or of having someone that one once flirted with come on to appear for an initial interview. . . . I wonder how often gay/lesbian therapists are embarrassed by someone whom they have danced with or even slept with (in a casual encounter) showing up for therapy and being surprised!

An interesting side note is that 11.1% (n = 26, 16 women and 10 men) of the respondent therapists were also partnered with other therapists. These partnered therapists' social worlds appeared to be even more restricted than their unpartnered or non-therapist-partnered colleagues due to the existence of two client/ex-client caseloads around which to manage boundaries and extratherapy interactions. One therapist expressed her despair in the following comment:

> My partner is also a psychologist—between the two of us I swear we have treated, at some time or another, every lesbian and/or her partner or ex(es) in this area. As a couple we are much impacted. We are isolated and avoid social situations, support groups, etc. that would be good for us individually and as a couple. We are very much out as lesbians but we have no lesbian friends.

Sexual Activity

The final portion of the questionnaire addressed sexual activity between therapists and clients. Sexual activity was defined as any type of sexual behavior between therapist and client that occurred either during or outside of therapy time, either once or multiple times.

Beginning with the numbers of respondents involved, eight therapists (3.4%, 3 women and 5 men) had *ever* engaged in sexual activity with a current client, while 29 (12.4%, 13 women and 16 men) had *ever* done so with a former client. Only one respondent (0.4%, male) was *presently* engaging in sexual activity with a current client, while six respondents (2.6%, 5 women and 1 man) were *presently* doing so with former clients. Overall, the numbers are higher for former clients and lower for present activity.

These results fall, for the most part, into the range of occurrence rates generally found in the literature where samples are identified only by gender and not by sexual orientation (Bouhoutsos et al., 1983; Holroyd & Brodsky, 1977; Pope, Keith-Spiegel, & Tabachnik, 1986; Pope, Levenson, & Schover, 1979). The occurrence rate for ever having engaged in sexual activity between male therapists and their former clients (13.6%, n = 16) was somewhat higher than what has been reported in the literature. Occurrence rates for (a) ever having engaged in sexual activity between female therapists and current clients (2.6%, n = 3), (b) presently engaging in sexual activity between female therapists and their current (0%, n = 0) or former clients (4.3%, n = 5), and (c) presently engaging in sexual

TABLE 17.5   Respondents' Estimation of the Degree to Which Therapist-Client Sexual Activity Was an Ethical Dilemma for Them in Their Professional Practice and for Their Colleagues in the Community in Which They Practiced

Scale point	For Respondents Frequency	N	For Their Colleagues Frequency	N
"Not at all"	86.8%	203	33.3%	78
"Slightly"	7.3%	17	24.4%	57
"Moderately"	1.7%	4	22.6%	53
"Very much so"	2.1%	5	9%	21
"Constantly"	1.3%	3	1.3%	3
Blank	0.8%	2	9.4%	22

activity between male therapists and their former clients (0.8%, $n = 1$) were all lower than those established in the literature.

Using the same five-point Likert scale as for social interactions (ranging from "not at all" to "constantly"), respondents were asked to indicate the degree to which they perceived therapist-client sexual activity to present an ethical dilemma (Table 17.5). For themselves, most reported that it was "not at all" (86.8%, $n = 203$, 105 women and 98 men) a dilemma. For their colleagues, however, respondents were divided between believing it to be "not at all" (33.3%, $n = 78$, 34 women and 44 men), "slightly" (24.4%, $n = 57$, 31 women and 26 men), or "moderately" (22.6%, $n = 53$, 26 women and 27 men) a dilemma.

Finally, using the five-point Likert scale (ranging from "never ethical" to "always ethical") that was used for social relationships, respondents were asked the degree to which they considered sexual activity between therapists and clients to be ethical (Table 17.6). With current clients, most respondents judged such activity to be "never ethical" (98.7%, $n = 231$, 114 women and 117 men). With former clients, respondents were less conservative overall, with men being less conservative than women. The majority still judged such activity to be "never ethical" (54.3%, $n = 127$, 74 women and 53 men) but 29.9% ($n = 70$, 31 women and 39 men) judged it to be "ethical under rare conditions" and 12% ($n = 28$, 6 women and 22 men) judged it to be "ethical under some conditions."

There were many additional comments in this section that added dimension to the numbers. Two therapists wrote about their own experiences with attraction to clients and/or engaging in sexual activity with them:

TABLE 17.6 Respondents' Estimates of the Degree to Which Sexual Activity Between Therapists and Clients Is Ethical With Current Clients and With Former Clients

| | Current Clients | | Former Clients | |
Scale Point	Frequency	N	Frequency	N
"Never ethical"	98.7%	231	54.3%	127
"Ethical under rare conditions"	0.9%	2	29.9%	70
"Ethical under some conditions"	0.0%	0	12.0%	28
"Ethical under many conditions"	0.0%	0	1.3%	3
"Always ethical"	0.0%	0	0.4%	1
Blank	0.4%	1	2.1%	5

My partner came to see me 3 times for counseling five years ago. I realized I was attracted to her and referred her to another therapist and had that therapist help us to terminate our counseling relationship. We have been in a permanent relationship since. I consider my action to be unethical and I agonized over the choice I made. I am also happy and my life is rich because of my relationship. My partner was as attracted to me and considers we made a mutual choice. I have never had this kind of struggle before or since.

Experience was a painful teacher. I immediately terminated our treatment relationship, yet the damage to the client and myself was irreversible. I deeply regret allowing this interaction to occur and can only blame my inexperience, and the emotional pain I was undergoing. In addition, this client was extremely skilled at sexual seduction but that information is not offered as any kind of excuse for my impulsive and poorly conceived behavior. I was "young" in my profession and too frightened to seek advice.

These comments elucidate how the therapists got into sexual interactions with their clients and how they dealt with their situations. Neither considered their actions to be particularly ethical although they made different choices about how to handle the situations.

Other therapists disagreed with some of the more conservative thinking on therapist-client sexual activity either in the views they expressed or by the interactions they engaged in:

Sexual activity to me belongs in a relationship. . . . I do not believe that the therapist/client bond is for life. I do believe in love and in special affinities.

And I believe that our notions of "boundaries" are male-based and that we as yet do not know what is appropriate, given the chance to rethink and restructure the world from a woman's perspective.

While I have wanted to bed many of my pretty clients, I do not think it is good for them, and I get them into the gay world instead. I have been the first sex for several young men I have talked with on the phone about being gay, at their request.

I had one (nonpaying) client referred to me by another therapist to see if he liked gay sex. He did, got into the gay community, but never again into my bed.

Several therapists, however, expressed questions and confusion. They could envision sexual activity with former clients, but only under qualified circumstances:

Again, I think it depends on the nature of the therapeutic relationship. If you have a significant transference relationship, I doubt that it is ever ethical to later become sexually involved. If you met once to do a screening for a group that the client didn't attend, and then met socially 5 years later, is it unethical to become romantically involved? I don't know.

With former clients it may be ethical if the therapy was not long term and did not involve regression on the part of the client. For all dynamic therapies I think it is unethical if the treatment has been longer than a brief crisis intervention.

Finally, the data from this study indicate that most therapists were clearly opposed to sexual activity especially with current but also with former clients. There were many additional comments supporting this position:

Some people seem to think that developing a sexual relationship with a former client or current client is excusable because of the difficulty in finding a partner within the minority (gay) community . . . I feel this is an ethical violation fueled by distorted beliefs about the size of the gay population or the therapist's reluctance to build their practice through legitimate means.

Again, once a therapist, always a therapist as far as I am concerned. I do not believe that the professional relationship can be truly redefined after therapy and having sex during therapy is similar to rape.

My policy is an "open door" one with former clients. The possibility of the return of a client for a crisis session, or to deal with an old problem in a different way, or a new one, disallows for any sexual activity on my part. Although I strive for an egalitarian situation in therapy my role as therapist is often interpreted as having power. To use this sense of power granted me would be completely unethical.

At the conclusion of the entire questionnaire, there was one last additional comment block. Three themes ran throughout the additional comments from the entire questionnaire: acknowledging the power inherent in the role of therapist; boundaries as a treatment issue in lesbian, gay, and bisexual communities; and balancing personal and professional roles as a therapist. The following three long comments summed up these general themes:

> [This is] an important area of ethics for us all that has been terribly muddied by trying to be feminist and non-elitist, the touchy-feely therapy we've all been exposed to in the 1970s, our own developmental dilemmas, and the lack of training in our educational programs. . . . I think we've underestimated the power of therapy and the therapist role because we've often been uncomfortable with being too powerful. The disservice to the client is not to recognize and acknowledge the power differential and behave ethically therein. I'm as angry about the therapists who sleep with clients using this ambivalent atmosphere as an excuse as I am at incesters and I believe we all have to clean up our act in order to stop enabling this extreme behavior.

> This is a difficult topic area—even in such a large metropolitan area, it's almost impossible to be completely separate from current and former clients. I believe boundaries (or lack of) is one of the most important treatment issues for lesbians and gay men—and that includes therapists. It takes time and energy to keep myself and my clients' relationships protected from "contamination"—and then I still have to "do regular therapy" and enjoy a personal life.

> I feel very clear about the boundary issues for the type of work I do. I also have friends/colleagues who run the gambit [sic] from holding similar views to discrepant views. Clearly the gay/lesbian community must contend with the fact that we are a minority, and that service providers within our community live and socialize among the people we serve; and, this is as it should be. Nevertheless, I have never met a therapist (gay or straight) who I believe successfully and ethically balances the roles of activist/socialite/therapist, all in the same community, and I fear that exploitation of clients occurs where this attempt is made. Regretfully, this pull to be all these things is particularly strong for lesbians and gay men who work professionally, politically, and

personally to overcome the oppression we experience and which we perpetuate in a myriad of ways. Lesbians and gay men who are therapists tend to
have the knowledge, the insight, and the skill to facilitate healthy social functioning in the community, to promote progressive political and legal changes, to
live full and inspiring lives ourselves, and to aid in the recovery of injured
and troubled clients. When these processes are not in concert, I believe the
first responsibility goes to our clients when our own lives are in order; otherwise
to ourselves first.

CONCLUSION

The research results presented in this chapter document and describe
the experiences of lesbian, gay, and bisexual psychotherapists who
practice within their communities and must negotiate the effects of the
"small world" phenomenon on their personal and professional lives.
Overall, data from this research study show that social encounters with
clients occur very frequently and that social relationships also occur but
less frequently. Sexual activity between therapists and clients was also
documented but occurs much less frequently than does any type of
social interaction with clients. All kinds of therapist-client interactions
occurred more frequently with former rather than current clients.

The data also show that the therapist respondents encountered myriad problems, both professional and personal, in negotiating social
interactions with their clients. Some of these problems (e.g., isolation
and resentment) put them at higher risk for sexual activity or other
boundary violations with clients. Of particular importance in resolving,
negotiating, and/or preventing potentially harmful or unwise boundary situations are a therapist's perception of the dilemma in the first
place and her or his judgment about how to proceed with the matter in
an ethical manner.

In this study, it was clear that all respondents felt that the social and/
or sexual interactions they were faced with were not as much of a dilemma
(again, "a situation in which a clear course of action is not evident") for
themselves as for their colleagues. Male respondents followed this trend
to an even greater degree than did their female counterparts. In addition, men were less conservative than women in judging how ethical
they believed engaging in either social relationships or sexual activity
with clients to be.

It is unclear how to interpret these results. Is it that the respondents
(particularly males) in this survey were more attuned to and trained for

ethical dilemmas of these natures and thus experienced them as less of a dilemma for themselves than for their colleagues? Or is it perhaps that these respondents (particularly males) were more harsh in perceiving the behavior of their colleagues and/or possibly more in denial about their own behavior? If the former is true, then these respondents appear to have been trained well and it is their colleagues who need more work. If the latter is true, then there is twice as much work to be done. It is, of course, possible that there are other explanations for these trends in the ethical dilemma ratings. However, as long as therapist denial of a problem or potential problem is a possible explanation for these trends, then the danger of client exploitation is still a significant concern in need of serious attention.

In addition, the fact that men in this study were more liberal than women in judging how ethical it is to engage in either social relationships or sexual activity with clients is not easy to interpret. Is it that the male therapists in this study really believed such types of interactions with clients to be more permissible than did women? Or could it be that the female therapists in this study were more aware of the negative consequences of such interactions and judged them more harshly? Research indicating that more male than female therapists engage in sexual activity with their clients would support the first conclusion (Bouhoutsos et al., 1983; Holroyd & Brodsky, 1977; Pope et al., 1986). The fact that a significant amount of the initial clinical writing and discussion about therapist-client boundary issues (particularly in lesbian and gay communities) came from the feminist therapy community would support the second conclusion. Thus both conclusions are valid to some degree and other interpretations may also apply.

Discussion of the findings of this research study and related others is important to help establish clearer guidelines for the ethical practice of therapy, especially for those therapists whose experiences are not wholly taken into account by present ethical guidelines. This type of research can be a springboard for generating complex thinking on strategies for effectively dealing with the therapist-client interaction dilemmas that emanate from lesbian, gay, and bisexual communities. Such strategies are crucial in preventing therapists from sliding down the ethical continuum toward behaviors that place both client and therapist in jeopardy. Sexual activity with current clients is the extreme end of the ethical continuum, representing a complete breakdown of therapeutic boundaries and personal and professional judgment.

18

Comparing the Experiences of Women Clients Sexually Exploited by Female Versus Male Psychotherapists

Mindy Benowitz

In reviewing the research on sexual exploitation of clients by therapists, one finds that it is focused almost exclusively on male psychotherapists' abuse of female clients. Female therapist-female client sexual exploitation has only been addressed in a limited number of anecdotal reports (Applebaum, 1987; Brown, 1985, 1987a, 1987b, 1988b, 1989; Gartrell & Sanderson, 1994; Gonsiorek, 1989b; Rigby, 1986; Sonne, Meyer, Borys, & Marshall, 1985). There has been no systematic, empirical research on the impact and dynamics of women psychotherapists' sexual abuse of their female clients.

Research is needed to explore common characteristics shared by clients who are sexually exploited by female therapists, determine whether the process of exploitation and its impact differ according to the therapist's gender, and assess which variables affect the emotional impact of the exploitation. A systematic comparison of female and male exploitative therapists, as well as clients and therapists of different sexual orientations, could also shed light on the impact or process of the exploitation. This chapter reports on a study of these issues (Benowitz, 1991).

The reported prevalence of female therapist-female client sexual contact varies from 1% to 12% of female therapists. Averaging survey results on female therapists' self-report of sexual contact with female clients (Gartrell, Herman, Olarte, Feldstein, & Localio, 1986; Holroyd & Brodsky, 1977; Lyn, 1990) yields an average of 4%. When one averages the studies that include female clients' reports of sexual contact with their female therapists (Friedeman, 1981; Russell, 1984; Schoener, Milgrom, & Gonsiorek, 1984), the average is increased to 7%.

In comparison, 4% to 14% of male psychotherapists surveyed report sexual contact with either male or female clients, with most studies yielding figures over 7% (Akamatsu, 1988; Derosis, Hamilton, Morrison, & Strauss, 1987; Gartrell et al., 1986; Holroyd & Brodsky, 1977; Kardener, Fuller, & Mensh, 1973; Pope & Bouhoutsos, 1986; Pope, Levenson, & Schover, 1979).

The purpose of the current study was to examine the experiences of women who had verbal or physical sexual contact with a female psychotherapist or counselor. Major topics examined included characteristics of the participants and of the therapists, characteristics of the sexualized therapy relationships, the impact on the participants, and comparisons with women who had sexual contact with male therapists. (The study also examined participants' use of redress procedures, which are not summarized in this chapter.)

Fifteen women were interviewed. During the interview, the participants also completed three Symptoms Check Lists (SCLs) pertaining to the few weeks after the relationship ended, a baseline time prior to the relationship, and the time of the interview. The interviews and the SCLs were based in part on Vinson's (1984) research, which allows comparisons with her data on women exploited by male psychotherapists. (Vinson's 22 female participants included one woman whose exploitative therapist was female. Data from this participant were deleted from analyses when possible.) The results and their implications are discussed in each section.

CLIENT CHARACTERISTICS

This study explored potential commonalities of the participants, such as history of physical and sexual abuse, sexual orientation, and general demographic factors. The participants were Caucasian and averaged 36 years of age. Of the 15 women, 13 had at least 16 years of formal education, and 7 had graduate degrees. Of interest, one third ($n = 5$) were in training to be or were practicing mental health professionals at the time of the exploitative therapy. The high level of education and the number of mental health professionals among the participants support the notion that simply being in the client role is inherently vulnerable. Although there was a wide range in the participants' level of daily functioning, the data clearly show that education and competence do not necessarily protect clients from harm by therapists. The data support current ethical and legal guidelines that client consent is not an adequate defense for sexual contact with clients.

One might speculate that survivors of childhood abuse are more vulnerable to later exploitation by a therapist. In this sample, 80% of the participants ($n = 12$) reported childhood sexual abuse and 80% reported childhood physical abuse. However, because a history of childhood abuse is quite high among clients in general, and there are exploited clients who have not been previously abused, it is premature to conclude that childhood victimization predisposes clients to further sexual exploitation.

One factor that may have increased the participants' vulnerability to exploitation by a female therapist was the participants' need to discuss sexual orientation issues. Many of them were in the process of questioning and reidentifying their sexual orientation. For seven—almost half—this was their first sexual relationship with a woman. It appears that the stage of exploring a bisexual or lesbian identity and openly discussing it in therapy may be risky for clients whose therapists are prone to abuse.

THERAPIST CHARACTERISTICS

Therapists from all backgrounds and types of training have been reported to be sexual with clients. Research (Borys & Pope, 1989) has shown relatively proportional rates of sexual contact with clients among social workers, psychiatrists, and psychologists. The female therapists in this study included psychologists ($n = 6$), social workers ($n = 2$), pastoral counselors ($n = 3$), marriage and family therapists ($n = 1$), and those with nontraditional or unknown training ($n = 3$). Two worked in sexual assault programs.

Most of the therapists ($n = 10$) in this study were older than the participants, by an average of 11 years. This is similar to male therapists who sexually exploit clients (Butler, 1975; Callan, 1987; Dahlberg, 1970), although it holds true for therapy in general (Friedeman, 1981). The therapists averaged five years in practice at the time of the sexualized therapy. Two had Ph.D.s, ten had M.A.s, and three had B.A.s.

The data clearly dispute the notion that sexual contact between female therapists and female clients is a one-time, harmless case of two women who just happened to fall in love. Over half (n = 8, 53%) of the participants had heard that the therapist had also been overtly sexually involved with another client at some point. This number reflects only those cases the participants knew of (often from therapist disclosure) and therefore probably underestimates the actual number of repeat offenders among these therapists. The percentage of multiple-victim offenders reported in this study is lower than in some reports of primarily male therapists and female clients (Butler, 1975: 70%; Holroyd & Brodsky, 1977: 80%) and higher than other reports (Gartrell et al., 1986: 33%).

Regarding sexual orientation, one fifth of the therapists were reportedly heterosexual, one fifth bisexual, two fifths lesbian, and one fifth reportedly said nothing to the participants about their sexual orientation. One third of the therapists were married to men during the participants' therapy. Both the covert and the overt categories of sexual relationships included therapists who identified as heterosexual, bisexual, and lesbian. The diversity of sexual orientations among the therapists validates anecdotal reports (Brown, 1988b; Gonsiorek, 1989b; Rigby & Sophie, 1990) that a heterosexual orientation or being in a committed relationship with a man are not clear predictors that female therapists will refrain from sexual contact with female clients.

The data also support the anecdotal literature (Brown, 1985; Gartrell & Sanderson, 1994) indicating that therapists who are not comfortable with their feelings of same-sex attraction may be at higher risk for acting inappropriately with their clients. Over one third of the therapists were described as demonstrating conflict about their sexual behavior with women, and 20% of the therapists (n = 3) told the participant that this was their first same-sex involvement.

The descriptions of the therapists' shame due to heterosexism are based on the clients' observations and memories of therapists' comments, and the incidence of shame might be higher if one were able to study the therapists directly. One sharp example of internalized oppression was one of the pastoral counselors, who demonstrated enormous conflict about being sexual with a woman. The participant reported that, the last time they had sexual contact, the counselor "said she was praying for God to kill us" (Benowitz, 1991, p. 75). This participant also cited examples to support her belief that the counselor encouraged her to kill herself. Discomfort with same-sex attractions was not a universal theme, however. Several of the therapists were open about being lesbian and did not appear to the participants to feel uncomfortable with their sexual orientation.

To prevent sexual abuse of female clients, all female therapists must become comfortable with whatever same-sex attractions they feel. This could decrease the therapists' sexual experimentation with clients, with whom sex may seem safer and more hidden than with peers. It would also increase the likelihood of using supervision more effectively for cases in which one is vulnerable to acting on sexual feelings toward clients. This would be important for counselors in any type of professional setting or counseling role.

The literature on sexual exploitation by male therapists indicates that experiencing high stress in their personal lives, such as ending a relationship, may increase therapists' vulnerability to sexual acting out with clients (Butler & Zelen, 1977). Slightly over half of the therapists ($n = 8$) in this study reportedly experienced a major change in their relationship status (mostly breakups) during the sexualized therapy. Some of the therapists may have sought reassurance of their attractiveness and self-worth from their clients.

CHARACTERISTICS OF THE EXPLOITATIVE RELATIONSHIPS

Sexual exploitation exists on a continuum that begins with poor judgment, proceeds to covert exploitation, and ends with overt sexual exploitation. The 11 overtly sexual dyads in this study all included breast and/or genital contact. Covert sexual contact in this study consisted of flirting, sexualized talk, and physical contact without touching of obviously sexual parts of either body. Four of the therapists were categorized as covertly sexually exploitative and had behaviors such as flirting and types of touch commonly shared by lovers (e.g., kissing; very long, full hugs). One of the covertly exploited participants described how, over the course of their therapy, the counselor joked about the two of them running away to get married, had lain on the floor at the end of a session and made "flirtatious" or "coy" comments to the participant, held the participant's hand during sessions and played with her jewelry, stroked her hair, mentioned watching pornographic movies the previous night and feeling aroused by them, and stood and talked while hugging at the end of sessions with her face very close to the participant's.

Due to the absence of overtly sexual touch, the participant doubled her own perceptions. When she attempted to discuss the sexual dynamics, the therapist reportedly denied her own role and would only focus on the participant's sexual attraction to the therapist. A second woman described frequently receiving full, long hugs from the therapist, sometimes with accompanying back rubs. After the participant asked to be held by the therapist, the therapist was described as having pulled the client to her while on the couch and "crushed [the client] into her" (Benowitz, 1991, p. 82). This therapist also told the participant details of her sex life, such as describing a female friend's genitals and telling the client about advice she received to improve her own sex life.

The dynamics of the overt and covert relationships were similar in most respects. The participants in each group described the same types and same intensities of feelings. Both groups commonly expressed feeling in love with the therapist, feeling that this was a very important relationship to them, and feeling betrayed and used later on. However, those who experienced covert and no overt sexual contact from their therapists had much more difficulty identifying the exploitation. The occurrence of nonsexual boundary violations helped them take their discomfort about the sexual dynamics more seriously.

There were several themes in the exploitative relationships. The relationships tended to be of a secretive, affair nature. In 8 of the 11 overtly sexual dyads, the therapist and/or the client were also involved with someone else. Socializing with the client was common for the overtly sexual therapists. Seven of these eleven dyads kept the sexual nature of the relationship hidden, pretending to just be friends. Three of the overtly sexual therapists were violent with the clients—two were sexually violent and one was physically abusive. The covertly sexual therapists in this study did not socialize with the participants outside of sessions.

Physical touch was common in the therapy itself, but not universal. The therapists tended to initiate the touch and did so under the pretext of comforting the clients. This tended to progress to more intense, covertly sexual touch and then to overt sexual contact. Although all but one of the relationships were described as important love relationships, only one fit the pattern described by Rigby (1986) of committed, primary relationships in which the couple intended to or did live together.

Sexual exploitation involves a series of decisions and behaviors that show a pattern of poor boundaries on the therapist's part. To identify precursors to sexual exploitation, the participants were asked if, in retrospect, they could identify hints that the therapy would become sexual. Almost all of the participants (n = 13) could identify hints.

Common hints involved the therapist's body language (n = 13, 87%). Examples included touching the client's legs or hands, the therapist sitting in a way that revealed sexual parts of her body, affectionate touching that felt sexual to the client, much holding of the client in sessions, hugs that felt like "a lover hug and not a friend hug." The second most frequent precursors were comments made by the therapists (n = 9, 60%). Being told that she was a favorite or "special" client was often cited as a retrospective hint.

Another hint involved the blurring of therapeutic boundaries such as the choice of setting for therapy and socializing with the client (n = 8, 53%). Examples included the therapist asking the participant out to dinner, talking about therapy issues in informal settings, using the therapist's bedroom as an office with the client seated on the bed, and disclosing their own problems to the client. When asked specifically about self-disclosure, 14 of the 15 participants said that the therapists discussed their personal problems in ways that seemed very inappropriate. This began prior to the sexual contact in all but two cases.

Exploitative therapists also exhibited seductive behavior (n = 6, 40%), such as flirting or offering the client a hug and then giving her a five-minute back rub along with the hug.

In comparing the precursor data to Vinson's data on male therapist-female client sexual exploitation, similar percentages of participants could retrospectively identify hints that the therapy would become sexual and similar types of hints were cited.

In an attempt to learn how exploitative therapists justify their sexual behavior with clients, the participants were asked if the therapist ever commented about mixing sex and therapy. Nearly half (n = 7, 47%) never commented on the matter. Of those who did comment, the most common justification was that the sexual contact would help the participants; this was reported by eight (53%) women. Explicit messages that the therapist was reparenting the participant were recounted by four (27%) women, and another five (33%) said that similar messages were given with a less specific framework. One participant's statement is typical of several responses: "She said that all my past relationships have been so harmful, and she wanted to teach me how to have a healthy relationship, how to get close to people" (Benowitz, 1991, p. 91). Other ways the therapists said they were helping the clients were by modeling talking openly about sexual matters and by being a guide in the coming out process.

Four therapists (27%) said it was permissible to be sexual with the client because they were not in a counselor role, either due to terminating therapy or to having a grassroots orientation such as working in a sexual assault program. In the four cases in which the therapist cited the termination justification, the participants described a clear sexual dynamic during therapy, and three of the four discussed sexual attraction and desires for a relationship while conducting the therapy. A final type of comment about mixing sex and therapy involved admitting that it was wrong to be sexual with the client but doing it anyway.

The results on precursors and types of justifications imply a need to educate therapists about the ongoing nature of transference and about responsibilities therapists continue to hold after termination. They also imply a need for all types of counselors to acknowledge being in a counselor role with people they help in any organized, systematic way. The therapists' justifications show a great deal of denial about power dynamics and their own sexual dynamics in therapy and point to the need for all therapists to learn more about their own sexual dynamics that could lead to sexualizing clients. The data also underscore the need to educate mental health professionals about the harm caused by sexualizing the therapy relationship.

Comparing the male and female psychotherapists on the dynamics and process of sexual exploitation yields several interesting observations. The female therapists' justifications are quite similar to the beliefs of sexually exploitative male therapists, who have a tendency to believe that sexual contact is less harmful and more beneficial to the client than do therapists who do not have sexual contact with clients (Derosis et al., 1987; Gartrell et al., 1986; Twemblow & Gabbard, 1989). However, the majority of (mostly male) offenders in these studies knew it was harmful to the clients and did it anyway.

The common scenario in sexual exploitation of female clients is that the therapist initiates the sexual contact. This is even more pronounced among the female therapists in the present study than among the male therapists in Vinson's study: 93% of the female therapists were described as having initiated the sexual contact, compared with 72% of the male therapists. Furthermore, the female therapists began the sexual contact earlier in the therapy relationship than did the male therapists in Vinson's study (averages of 6.5 months versus 9 months). This contradicts the stereotype of more mutual participation and equal power in female therapist-female client sexual contact.

Heterosexism and the belief that women in general are not abusive led many women to discount their perceptions of sexual dynamics. For example, one woman stated, "I was curious about whether this was OK or not. If this were a man, I would have gotten it after the second session. It didn't fit my belief system regarding women. So [I'd like] more information that women can also be perpetrators, can be inappropriate too" (Benowitz, 1991, p. 112).

Many participants in the current study described fear that others would not believe them and also received comments that discounted the impact and the exploitative nature of the relationship. Fear of others' heterosexist judgments also increased the clients' isolation and impeded them from seeking redress. A participant stated, "I wish, if I could change anything [about resources available to help them cope], it would be that people would accept lesbianism as OK, because that's what compounded what went on. It was why I had to keep so much secret. It was one more added thing to deal with" (Benowitz, 1991, p. 112). Heterosexism may have led some therapists to confuse nurturing feelings with sexual feelings, or to mislabel their own behaviors with clients.

The results illustrate the importance of eliminating heterosexism on individual and societal levels. Eradicating heterosexism would decrease exploited clients' shame and isolation, allowing them to recognize the exploitation sooner, making them more likely to get help and to seek redress more often. This in turn would increase accountability and consequences for exploitative therapists.

A final difference in the dynamics of the exploitative relationships was that the female dyads tended to socialize more openly than the male-female dyads. In Vinson's study, the male-female dyads never blended their social lives. However, in the present study, 10 of the 11 dyads who socialized together did so with the therapist's friends or family, although they often hid the sexual nature of the relationship. It may be that the heterosexist assumption that sex occurs only between males and females allowed the female dyads to "get away with" being social in public. When men and women socialize together, a sexual relationship is more often suspected. It is also possible that community norms permitted social relationships between female therapists and female clients.

IMPACT ON CLIENTS

Nearly all of the women in this study described varying degrees of harmful impact from the sexual contact and concomitant boundary violations. The most painful period occurred immediately after the relationship ended. Posttraumatic stress disorder (PTSD) (American Psychiatric Association, 1987) was very common after the therapy or relationship ended, experienced by three fourths of the participants ($n = 11$). Fourteen of the fifteen women (93%) said that the relationship worsened the problems for which they originally sought help, by intensifying the issues, by postponing attending to them, and/or by creating new issues in addition to the original ones.

The negative impact was quite long lasting for many participants. The average length of time elapsed since the sexualized therapy was seven years. As a group, the participants had fewer symptoms at the time of the interview than they described having at the end of the exploitative relationship. However, two thirds of the women said they were worse off—endorsed more symptoms on the SCL—an average of seven years after the sexualized therapy than at a baseline time before the therapy began. Four women (27%) still had PTSD.

The women also described various ways that the relationship continued to affect their lives. Over half described experiencing intense anger and betrayal feelings ($n = 10$, 67%), decreased trust in people in general ($n = 11$, 73%), and depression and feelings of abandonment ($n = 9$, 60%). Two thirds said the relationship hurt their view of themselves as sexual partners and increased their feelings of inadequacy and their fears of being vulnerable. Forty percent ($n = 6$) reported still struggling with guilt and shame about positive feelings about the relationship and/or self-blame for the relationship.

The relationship's impact on the participants' feelings about their sexual orientation were quite varied and almost evenly divided among four themes: (a) The relationship had little or no effect on the women's feelings about their sexual orientation; (b) the relationship helped them to acknowledge or validate a lesbian or bisexual identity (two of these four women felt regret and conflict that this occurred with their therapist as opposed to someone else); (c) the relationship led participants to feel less trusting of women in general, and therefore made them less comfortable with their lesbian or bisexual identity; (d) the relationship increased their feelings of confusion regarding their previously held sexual orientation, both heterosexual and lesbian.

The sexualized relationship also increased the clients' mistrust and cynicism about therapy and therapists for 12 (80%) of the participants. Almost half of the group indicated that subsequent therapy helped them to regain their trust of some therapists. For those who sought further psychotherapy, the sexualized therapy appeared to influence the participants' choice of the gender and/or sexual orientation of subsequent therapists, although who they felt safe with varied greatly among the participants. It is interesting that some participants believed that seeking a heterosexually identified female therapist would provide them with automatic protection from future sexual exploitation. The results of this study challenge this assumption.

Positive effects coexisted with negative effects for nine participants, including feeling more attractive (20%) and learning more about boundary/power issues, which subsequently helped them in their personal and work lives (33%). Positive feelings toward the therapist and/or the sexual contact contributed to later guilt feelings for many participants.

This study provides some preliminary data on factors that may affect the impact on the client of sexual exploitation by a female therapist. Due to the small sample size, the results of these analyses must be viewed as trends that need further validation but provide interesting information for present consideration and future research.

First, the vast majority of participants experienced similarly high levels of symptoms after the relationships ended, and varied more in the types and degrees of symptoms at the time of the interview. This indicates that specific variables may have a greater effect on the long-term rather than the short-term impact of the relationships.

Second, the results suggest that covert sexual relationships have the same degree of harm as overt sexual relationships. There were no significant differences statistically or qualitatively between participants whose therapists were covertly versus overtly sexual on any of the impact variables tested (the number of symptoms when the relationship ended, current feelings about therapists and therapy in general, impact on the participants' original problems, and whether they ever considered filing a complaint). Covert sexual exploitation is probably much more common than overt and deserves more attention in future research.

Third, the results suggest that shorter, less intense therapeutic relationships without ongoing and pervasive sexual dynamics during the course of therapy may contribute to a less negative impact. For example, analyses indicated trends such that more therapy sessions before the sexual contact began were related to more symptoms when the relationship ended ($r(14) = .425, p = .11$) and at the time of the interview ($r(14) = .40, p = .14$). Also, the longer therapy continued after the sexual contact began, the more symptoms participants reported experiencing after the relationship ended ($r(15) = .59, p = .11$) and at the time of the interview ($r(15) = .64, p < .05$). This suggests that continuing the therapy after the initiation of sexual contact increases the negative impact of the experience. Terminating the therapy did not prevent negative consequences, however.

The impact of the exploitative relationships on the participants in this study was remarkably similar to the women in Vinson's (1984) study who were sexually exploited by male therapists. The percentages were nearly identical for the two groups of participants on the following variables: the number of participants experiencing each SCL symptom; the incidence of PTSD in the few weeks after the relationship ended (this study: 67%; Vinson: 64%); the negative impact on the participants' feelings about therapists and therapy in general (this study: 80%; Vinson: 86%); the negative impact on their original problems (this study: 68%; Vinson: 87%); and their "very negative" evaluation rating of the relationship (this study: 60%; Vinson: 59%); impaired personal relationships, difficulty trusting people, and discomfort with sex (this study: 60%; Vinson: 59%); and feelings of guilt and shame (each study: 40%). Furthermore, Vinson's data also indicated that, for women exploited by male therapists, a brief sexual involvement was necessary but not sufficient to avoid PTSD after the relationship ended.

CONCLUSION

The results of this study show that sexual exploitation of female clients usually produces lasting harm to clients. Female therapists from all counseling disciplines and sexual orientations sexually exploit their female clients. Recognizing the existence and impact of the problem is an important first step in preventing future abuse.

19

Boundary Challenges When Both Therapist and Client Are Gay Males

John C. Gonsiorek

Gay male counselors and therapists, working and living in their own communities, experience frequent and at times abrupt challenges to personal and professional boundaries. Generally, these challenges are a variant of the "small town" problem; that is, any therapist who lives and works in a small ("small" can be literal or not) community faces comparable challenges. Rural mental health providers, racial and ethnic minority providers working in their own communities, and sexual minorities working in their own communities share these similarities. When both therapist and client are gay males, maleness and same-sex orientation powerfully shape challenges, dilemmas, and responses (see Robinson, 1993, pp. 13-23).

Robinson (1993) describes in detail the experience of, and reactions to, abuse by male therapists of gay male clients. His research is highly recommended.

PREVALENCE OF SEXUAL EXPLOITATION
OF MALE CLIENTS BY MALE THERAPISTS

The data suggest that male-male dyads are rare. Early data from Walk-In Counseling Center suggest that 4% to 5% of cases consist of a male therapist and male client (Gonsiorek, 1989c; Schoener, Milgrom, & Gonsiorek, 1984). Gartrell, Herman, Olarte, Feldstein, and Localio (1986) found 7.6% male-male dyads. For further discussion of this literature, see Gonsiorek (1989c) and Robinson (1993, especially pp. 7-13).

While there has been considerable and articulate discussion of boundaries between client and therapist in lesbian communities (Brown, 1985, 1988a, 1994; Gartrell & Sanderson, 1994; see also Benowitz as well as Lyn in this volume for reviews of this literature and original research), there has been considerably less discussion among gay male mental health provider communities.

It is difficult to tell if the seemingly low rate of victimization of males in the psychotherapy relationship is true or partially an artifact. Although there appears to be little doubt from the literature that men sexually exploit more than women in both the health care context and others (see introduction to Part III), it is difficult to determine "true" data on gender breakdown of victims and perpetrators. This is an ongoing controversy in many areas of the sexual abuse field (see Gonsiorek, Bera, & LeTourneau, 1994, chap. 3).

EFFECTS OF SEXUAL EXPLOITATION
BY PROFESSIONALS ON MALES

The general effects of sexual exploitation by psychotherapists (see Luepker & Retsch-Bogart, 1980; Pope & Bouhoutsos, 1986; Schoener, 1989b; Schoener et al., 1984) include client guilt, shame, grief, anger, depression, loss of self-esteem, ambivalence, confusion, fear, and distrust. Both male and female victims appear to display such characteristics. However, it is my observation that male victims also manifest some unique reactions.

As a group, male victims have a difficult time perceiving they have been victimized. I hypothesize that this is related to male sex role socialization. It is congruent for a woman socialized in our society to perceive herself as victimized. However, the same socialization encourages males to assume that any power dynamic operates in their favor; they therefore often have a higher level of rationalization and denial about their own victimization. In other words, males, over and above the general tendencies of victims to deny the reality of victimization, tend to have even stronger denial. To admit victimization is not only frightening, as it is for female victims, but is also perceived as a threat to one's essential maleness, in a way that has no comparison for female victims.

In addition, the psychological consequences of sexual victimization are often especially difficult for male victims to comprehend. Recognizing and acknowledging the existence of sexual abuse sequelae are often also perceived as threats to maleness.

Men often stereotypically view sexual expression as a male prerogative. Sexual experience is seen as something they have chosen or created rather than something in which they have been manipulated, tricked, or forced to participate. It is striking how many male victims—even in the face of evidence that their psychotherapists were exploitative or manipulative—retain the belief that sexual interactions were freely chosen. This is especially true when the therapist is female and the client is a younger heterosexual male. My observation is that the responses of gay male victims of male psychotherapists tend to fall between those of female victims of male therapists and male victims of female therapists. I hypothesize that this represents a complex interaction between gender and sexual orientation.

While most gay and bisexual men are socialized in typically male ways and generally make the prototypically male assumptions described above, many often have in their later developmental experience some information that would allow greater recognition about both the reality and the effects of victimization. Many gay males, in the process of coming out, experience sexual manipulation, at least initially, by other males, and in the coming out process may learn to identify and avoid it. This experience is not typical of most heterosexual males. In other words, the experience of being the object of male sexual desire mitigates for some gay and bisexual men, first, the stereotypically male barriers against recognition of the reality of victimization and, second, recognition of the effects of victimization.

Should victimization occur to a male client by a male therapist, complex interactions on the basis of gender and sexual orientation may eventuate. If a male client is heterosexual and certain of that, such clients are apt to view the experience of sexual contact with a male therapist as highly dystonic. This may have two different paradoxical effects. On the one hand, because it is perceived as dystonic, the individual may quickly recognize and report that abuse. On the other hand, because of societal homophobia, individuals may consciously or unconsciously fear that, if they report the abuse, they also will be perceived as homosexual and so may be less likely to report the abuse. Given irrational societal reactions to homosexuality, this fear is not unwarranted in some contexts.

If a client is homosexual and certain of that, he may experience sexual contact with a male therapist in a similar variety of paradoxical ways. Some gay males may view any sexual behavior as their prerogative and perceive the situation as merely another sexual contact. In other words, the "supermale" mentality in some parts of the gay community may block recognition of the exploitative nature of the situation. Other individuals who recognize the exploitative nature of the situation, perhaps as their male socialization is altered in the coming out process, may nevertheless find it difficult to complain about such a therapist, even though they recognize the experience as abusive. They may fear being regarded as being disloyal to their own community if the therapist is an openly gay male. Their perception of the exploitative therapist as a member of their own oppressed minority group can create mixed feelings about filing a complaint.

There sometimes are realistic external fears: In complaining about an exploitative therapist, the client's sexual orientation may become public and he may then become victimized by societal homophobia. While this concern may sometimes stem from the clients' own internalized homophobia (i.e., self-hatred for being gay; see Gonsiorek & Rudolph, 1991; Malyon, 1982), the process of complaining does represent a realistically greater risk for gay male clients. They may well experience discrimination if their sexual orientation becomes public.

The experience of being exploited by an individual of the same sex may increase internalized homophobia of gay male clients if it encourages a belief that same-sex relationships are untrustworthy, damaging, or improper. Exploitation by a gay male therapist can often play into fears that other gay men and hence oneself are inherently damaged. Thus the internalized homophobia may be deepened and the client's therapeutic progress toward resolving such issues interrupted.

EXPLOITATIVE THERAPISTS
IN SAME-SEX MALE SITUATIONS

Therapists who perpetrate sexual abuse on clients have been described elsewhere (Gonsiorek, 1987, 1989c; Gonsiorek & Schoener, 1987; Schoener & Gonsiorek, 1989; and, in this volume, Gabbard; Gonsiorek;

Irons). Male therapists who sexually exploit male clients are not substantially different than these descriptions. The descriptions that follow are not meant to substitute for these typologies but to elaborate on them.

Male psychotherapists in the process of working through their own coming out issues can be especially vulnerable to boundary violations, including sexual exploitation. As such therapists are processing their own sexual identities, their conflicts may be acted out, projected, or in other ways foisted upon clients. Such therapists might be consciously or unconsciously needy to clients, particularly if the psychotherapist fears taking risks by disclosing sexual orientation to others. Alternatively, they may encourage clients to take risks that they themselves are fearful of taking in a way not appropriate for the clients. In these situations, the therapist's objectivity can become impaired and the situation can become exploitative, although not necessarily sexually, if the client's needs are not placed first.

Another risky situation can occur when a gay male therapist whose sexual orientation is stable becomes socially isolated. The situation may arise out of poor social skills, depression, stress, disappointments in his personal life, or other factors characterological or situational. Such a psychotherapist may be tempted to view gay male clients as peers or a support system, particularly if such a psychotherapist perceives himself to be powerless, fearful, or unsuccessful in social situations with other gay men. He may socialize with gay male clients to provide an environment in which he can feel respected, successful, and powerful. This situation may or may not lead to sexual exploitation per se, but it is exploitative nevertheless because the therapist's needs are placed before the client's. While such problems are not unique to sexual minority psychotherapists, such therapists may have fewer actual opportunities to reduce isolation than others.

Some minority groups, including gay and lesbian communities, often tolerate less well trained and credentialed professionals. Given the disparagement such communities have endured from "established" mental health professionals until recently, this tolerance is not surprising. Such communities are more likely to attract mental health "practitioners" with no or minimal training and credentials, some with little understanding of professional boundaries and ethics concerns. Others who are adequately trained may see professional standards as "establishment" and therefore oppressive or irrelevant. Both groups can thereby be at higher risk for boundary violations.

Boundary violations that are not primarily or at all sexual can nevertheless be problematic. Gay male therapists active in community organizations may develop complicated and overlapping ties within their own communities. If care is not taken to maintain professional boundaries, the therapists may blur distinctions among different organizational, social, and therapeutic roles. More typically, this confusion can eventuate in confidentiality problems, conflicts of interest, and occasionally sexual impropriety, impaired objectivity, or dual relationships.

A final variant I have noted involves psychotherapists who are deeply ambivalent and profoundly conflicted about their same-sex feelings. They are often intensely homophobic; their same-sex feelings are unintegrated. Such individuals may act out sexually with clients of the same sex and treat the situation as "a dirty little secret." They often project their intense ambivalence and self-hatred onto clients and overtly or covertly blame clients for the sexual interactions. The clients may be blamed as sick and perverted, and told that the involvements are their fault. Such psychotherapists are frequently highly disparaging toward gay communities and label openly gay individuals as pathological. They may deny that the sexual contact with the client is a same-sex sexual experience; instead, it may be termed a *special friendship* or something similar. The effects upon the client are often profoundly damaging because, in addition to the "usual" sequelae of sexual exploitation, there is considerable mobilization of internalized homophobia. This variant is often seen in pastoral counseling situations, particularly when the denomination is homophobic.

SPECIAL BARRIERS TO FILING
COMPLAINTS IN SAME-SEX SITUATIONS

If an exploited gay male client wishes to file a complaint, he may not be believed, particularly if the exploitative psychotherapist is heterosexually married or alleges to be heterosexual. The client's sexual orientation may be pathologized and his credibility thereby diminished. A purportedly heterosexual therapist who is a "pillar of the community" but who sexually exploits clients of the same sex is an extreme example of this. It should be remembered that same-sex behavior does not necessarily indicate gay identity in any party.

Gay male clients are often conflicted over issues of loyalty to their minority community in filing complaints. There may be a realistic component to this conflict, in locales where psychotherapists who exploit clients of the same sex and/or are believed to be gay are, in fact, treated more harshly than heterosexual offenders by licensing bodies, courts, ethics committees, the media, and the public. Gay clients may be faced with the untenable choice of either not taking action to stand up for themselves or initiating a process that may result in yet more discrimination against members of their own community.

When boundary problems occur within minority communities, stakes are often higher. Bigots are apt to focus on failings within minority communities and use such situations to discredit them. In turn, a defensive "siege mentality" may develop in minority communities, engendering unproductive responses, such as labeling a legitimate complaint as "homophobic."

At the same time, gay therapists may be at greater risk for false or exaggerated accusations. Many oppressed communities have within them a certain number of "walking wounded," persons who for a variety of reasons have absorbed a greater than average share of self-hatred for being a minority member. The concept of internalized homophobia is its variant among gay men (for a general discussion, see Allport, 1954; see references above for specific information on internalized homophobia). Open and successful gay professionals can be prime targets for such individuals, who may attempt to reduce their internal discomfort by attacking that which they fear: open, successful gay men.

More generally, for gay clients who are socially isolated and "closeted," an openly gay male therapist may be the most prestigious gay male he knows and so will be a lightning rod for the client's complex emotional responses to his own homosexuality. If the client is also seriously troubled or intensely homophobic, his transference can become quite negative. This volatile situation can be exacerbated when inexperienced, untrained, or naive gay male therapists view all members of their own communities as simply a politically oppressed minority group. They underestimate the deep roots such oppression can lay and how it can interact with other preexisting problems. They also neglect to understand that within gay male communities, as in the general population, there are some seriously disturbed individuals, whose disturbance is not mitigated by being of the same community as the therapist.

STRATEGIES FOR BOUNDARY MAINTENANCE

The challenges of being a gay male therapist working and living in a gay male community can be more pointed if the therapist is single and/or extroverted. Particularly after one has worked for years in the same community, normal socializing can become transformed into an exercise of thinking quickly on one's feet regarding boundary challenges. It can become virtually impossible, for example, to go to a social event without running into a few clients, many ex-clients, and all their partners, ex-partners, and friends. For all these people, the therapist is not a neutral figure; and it is the therapist, not the client, who has the professional, ethical, and legal responsibility to manage situations that may arise. Confidentiality challenges are the most frequent, but many boundary challenges are possible.

Many gay male therapists must eventually come to accept that the price of being therapists in their own communities is acceptance of a degree of social limitation. While certain strategies can be helpful (see below), ultimately there remains a higher background level of potential hazard. For therapists with a well-developed friendship network, who are in relationships, or who are not extroverted, this can be a minor inconvenience. For therapists whose affiliation needs are high, who may be single and wishing to find a partner, or who may not have a well-developed friendship network, the situation can pose a repeated dilemma: restriction of social life versus risk of professional impropriety.

Some strategies can help:

1. Regular opportunities for case consultation regarding such dilemmas with professionals who have a realistic appraisal of the boundary challenges, yet are not too supportive to the extent of minimizing early stages of weakening boundaries, are highly recommended. Confidentiality concerns may arise here and must also be professionally managed. Gay male therapists should remember that other minority professionals practicing in their own communities and/or rural mental health providers may also be logical choices for colleagues with shared dilemmas and experiences.

2. Maintaining a personal support system, an identity separate from one's profession, and a meaningful and varied life can be some of the best insurance against therapist vulnerability to boundary problems. Simply stated, get a life and keep a life. Therapists who treat their work as an identity, not a job, are likely to have increased vulnerability to boundary problems.

3. Monitor one's life stresses, and alter practice style and client mix to keep out of harm's way, during periods of personal problems. Coming out is an obvious example; gay therapists are advised to wait an extended period (one to two years) between their personal

coming out and working with gay clients. Social isolation, relationship difficulties, loss of loved ones to HIV, and others might warrant a review of whether current professional activities should be altered, at least temporarily, to accommodate such stresses.

4. Seeking consultation when there are prolonged countertransference reactions, especially if erotic or if one's typical practice style begins to change, is advised. Therapists are encouraged to acknowledge and monitor "reasonable" idiosyncracies in their personal practice style (e.g., preferring not to see patients on weekends or at a certain times of the day; not wanting to see more than a certain number of patients with a particular problem or diagnosis per day or week). Deviations or plans to deviate from one's typical practice habits can be useful to flag cases where a review of professional boundaries is advised.

5. Develop and maintain at least one other area of professional competence separate from sexual orientation concerns and gay clients. This not only provides "shelter" when working with one's own community becomes too stressful, but the ability to view one's work within the gay community from a different vantage can enhance creativity, assist problem solving, reduce stress, and increase longevity in working with gay communities.

PART IV

Responses

I first direct the reader to note what is not in this response section: more chapters on therapy for victims of professional abuse. Many victims want and can benefit from these services; the chapters by Bera as well as Nestingen in Part II of this volume offer an introduction. But therapy is often not the best response; it is certainly not the only response.

The development of legislation, legal theory, and case law in the area of professional abuse has probably been the most explosive of any variety of response. Linda Jorgenson's two chapters, while written from a legal perspective, are accessible to nonattorneys. Her chapter describing legal developments on sexual contacts in professional relationships adeptly guides the reader through otherwise arcane legal concepts. Similarly, her discussion of the legal implications of employee and supervisor liability provides a thorough education, for attorney and nonattorney alike. I hope readers derive from these two chapters an appreciation of the seriousness with which the U.S. legal system is beginning to view this problem.

The contribution by Gary Schoener on employee and supervisor liability approaches this topic from a different angle, namely, that of an administrator in a health care organization. Walk-In Counseling Center, under the direction of Gary Schoener, has been a leader for many decades in such preventive work. His contribution is filled with pragmatic suggestions.

A dramatic development in the past decade has been the criminalization of sexual exploitation by professionals. More than 10 states are experimenting with this response, and the number seems to grow every legislative session. Andrew Kane, a psychologist, and Melissa Roberts-Henry, a victim/activist, were key figures in such legislation in the states of Wisconsin and Colorado, respectively. Andrew Kane provides some initial data on the effects of criminalization. Melissa Roberts-Henry provides a riveting account of the legislative process and its initial effects in Colorado.

The next two chapters focus on responses to clergy abuse. Contributions by Rev. Margo Maris and Rev. Kevin McDonough describe, respectively, how the Episcopal Church handles victim complaints and how the Roman Catholic Church responds to the clergy named in such complaints, both in Minnesota. Both of these religious leaders have extensive experience in handling complaints. Those affiliated with religious institutions will find their contributions worthwhile; those in nonreligious institutions will likely draw many parallels. Don Houts, a psychologist and minister, discusses an innovative program in the Midwest to prevent sexual misconduct by clergy and provides the readers with a variety of resources in this area.

Completing this part is a chapter by Nancy Biele and Elizabeth Barnhill, both of whom have many years of experience in advocacy. They provide a determined yet level-headed description of the advocacy process.

20

Sexual Contact in Fiduciary Relationships

LEGAL PERSPECTIVES

Linda Mabus Jorgenson

Professionals, including therapists,[1] physicians other than therapists,[2] and lawyers,[3] engage in sexual relationships with their patients and clients. Self-report surveys show that as many as 12% of therapists acknowledge that they have engaged in sexual contact with their patients.[4] Estimates based on patients' reports place the percentage as high as 20%.[5] A 1976 survey of five physician specialties found that obstetrician-gynecologists were the most likely to report having engaged in some kind of erotic behavior with patients (18%), followed by general practitioners (13%), and internists (12%).[6] Psychiatrists and surgeons were the least likely to report engaging in such contact with patients.[7]

AUTHOR'S NOTE: I acknowledge Pamela K. Sutherland, partner at Spero & Jorgenson, P.C., Nancy Flynn Barvick, associate at Spero & Jorgenson, P.C., and Edith Pacillo, law clerk at Spero & Jorgenson, P.C., for their invaluable assistance. The materials and information contained in this chapter are current as of February 15, 1994.

A more recent study of the same specialty groups confirmed these data.[8] A 1992 study of attorney-client sexual contact revealed that 6% of attorneys self-reported having engaged in sexual contact with clients.[9]

Therapists, physicians, and attorneys are all professionals who share the distinction of being fiduciaries with respect to their clients. *Fiduciary* is a legal term applied to professionals in whom patients or clients must repose trust. In recognition of the powerful position fiduciaries hold relative to their clients, fiduciaries are held to higher standards of behavior than nonfiduciaries and are required to act only in their patients' or clients' best interests.

Sexual contact with a patient or client is a breach of the professional's fiduciary duty to that client. Studies document that the majority of patients/clients who become sexually involved with a professional acting in a fiduciary capacity are harmed. One of the earliest studies of therapist-patient sexual contact found that 90% of patients who had become sexually involved with their therapists had been harmed by the contact,[10] and later data support this figure.[11] Therapist-patient sexual contact may cause posttraumatic stress disorder,[12] exacerbation of an existing disorder,[13] problems in marital or family relationships, difficulty trusting professionals, and increased hospitalizations due to emotional breakdowns.[14]

Less is known about the impact of sexual contact between nontherapist physicians and their patients. Two Canadian studies concluded that in-office sexual contact between a physician and a patient may harm the patient.[15] Similarly, a 1992 study by Gartrell found that 63% of physicians responding believed that patients were harmed by sexual contact with their physicians.[16] In contrast, a Dutch study of physicians who admitted to having sexual contact with patients found that only 42% of male gynecologists felt that the sexual contact was harmful; none of the male ear, nose, and throat physicians believed that such contact caused harm.[17]

These studies did not distinguish between sexual assaults and other types of sexual contact, leaving it unclear whether the physicians perceived the harm to have been caused by an assault or to have resulted from the power imbalance inherent in the fiduciary relationship. An early study by Feldman-Summers and Jones, which also did not distinguish sexual assaults from other sexual contact,[18] found no significant differences when comparing the psychological impact of sexual abuse by therapists with abuse by other health care providers. The authors theorized that no significant differences resulted because all health care practitioners breached their positions of trust. Upon realization of this breach, the impact on the patient was the same regardless of whether the abuser was a therapist or another health care provider.

Lawyers have been slower to investigate the prevalence of sexual misconduct in the legal profession. Upon review of the sparse case law on attorney-client sexual contact, Jorgenson and Sutherland found that the types of injuries caused by attorneys who engaged in sex with their clients were similar to those documented in therapist-patient sexual contact cases. These injuries include mental anguish, suicidal ideation, an inability to trust others, nightmares and flashbacks, depression, and hospitalizations.[19] The similarities in harm may be attributable to the similarities between the attorney-client fiduciary relationship and the physician-patient fiduciary relationship, both of which contain elements of power imbalance and trust.[20]

All major mental health professional organizations prohibit sexual relationships between therapists and their patients.[21] In 1989 the American Medical Association (AMA) declared physician-patient sex that takes place during the course of the professional relationship to be unethical.[22] The AMA did not distinguish between psychiatrists and other physicians in its proscription. In 1992 the American Bar Association (ABA) issued an opinion advising that a sexual relationship between lawyer and client may represent an unfair exploitation of the lawyer's fiduciary position.[23]

Courts have held professionals who sexually exploit their patients or clients legally liable for the resulting damages. Lawsuits against therapists for sexual misconduct have become increasingly prevalent; patients' and clients' legal actions against nonpsychiatric physicians and attorneys are less common but are increasing in number. Fiduciary theory provides one basis for recovery in these lawsuits against professionals who have engaged in sexual contact with their patients/clients. Other legal theories have also been applied in lawsuits involving professional-client sex. This chapter presents an overview of the legal issues that may arise when fiduciaries engage in sexual contact with their patients or clients.

FIDUCIARY RELATIONSHIPS

A fiduciary relationship exists when one person justifiably places confidence, faith, and reliance in another whose aid, advice, or protection is sought in some matter. It is "the relation existing when good conscience requires one to act at all times for the sole benefit and interests of another."[24] Inherent in the relationship is a power differential in favor of the fiduciary—the therapist, physician, or lawyer—who is entrusted with the power to take actions, give advice, and otherwise act in the best interests of the patient or client.

Most people seeking help from a therapist, physician, or lawyer do so in an admitted position of vulnerability, coping with a physical or psychological problem, a threatening legal matter, or perhaps simply the vulnerability intrinsic to lack of knowledge. The patient or client asks the professional for help with a stressful problem and is typically required to disclose confidential information, thereby increasing his or her vulnerability and reliance on the loyalty of the professional.

The patient or client often endows the professional with a near magical power not only to solve the problem at hand but to make *everything* come out right. Transference, a psychological phenomenon by which a patient or client transfers experiences and expectations from the past onto the professional, may also develop.[25] As a result, the patient or client may come to view the professional as a powerful and benevolent parent figure.

The potential for professionals to abuse and overreach in fiduciary relationships is apparent. Accordingly, the law affords protections and privileges to the less powerful party. Fiduciaries owe special duties to their patients/clients, including loyalty and good faith, due care, and full disclosure of all material facts. They are obligated to take no action that is adverse to the patient's or client's interests. Special privileges, such as the attorney-client privilege and the therapist-patient privilege, prohibit the fiduciary from revealing information gained during the course of the fiduciary relationship.

These fiduciary duties now extend to fiduciaries' personal relationships with patients and clients. Courts are beginning to enforce strict sanctions against professionals who overstep the bounds of the original common purpose of the relationship—whether legal advice, mental health therapy, or physical healing—to unduly influence the trusting party to engage in potentially harmful conduct. The task of setting boundaries for fiduciary relationships, however, is circumscribed by the existence of countervailing legal considerations, including the constitutional rights to privacy and freedom of association. The balance between protecting patients and clients from professionals who overstep their bounds and respecting individuals' constitutional rights must be accomplished by the least restrictive alternative. Nonetheless, various theories of recovery are available to clients and patients against professionals who overstep the bounds of the fiduciary relationship.

Negligent Breach
of Fiduciary Duty by Therapists

In one of the first recorded decisions holding a psychiatrist liable for sexual misconduct, the court based its conclusion on the theory of negligent breach of fiduciary duty. In the 1975 case of *Roy v. Hartogs*,[26] Dr. Hartogs engaged in sexual relations with his psychiatric patient, Julie Roy. Dr. Hartogs induced Roy to have sex with him by telling her that sexual relations were a necessary part of her treatment. As a result of Dr. Hartogs' "treatment," Roy's mental illness was aggravated and she was twice confined in a mental institution.[27]

The court found that Roy had stated a proper cause of action by alleging "coercion by a person in a position of overwhelming influence and trust,"[28] noting that "there is a public policy to protect a patient from the deliberate and malicious abuse of power and breach of trust by a psychiatrist when that patient entrusts to him her body and mind in the hope that he will use his best efforts to effect a cure."[29] Subsequently, fiduciary theory has been applied in several psychotherapist malpractice cases.[30]

Negligent Breach of Fiduciary
Duty by Nontherapist Physicians

Courts have held nonpsychiatric physicians who engage in sexual relations with clients liable for damages. In *Norberg v. Wynrib*,[31] the patient became addicted to a prescription painkiller following the extraction of an abscessed tooth. Her doctor, Dr. Wynrib, offered to supply her with the drug in exchange for sex. After a period of time under her doctor's "care," Norberg entered a treatment center on her own and sued Dr. Wynrib for his coercive sexual abuse.[32]

In deciding the case, two of the five justices on the Supreme Court of Canada relied on fiduciary theory to sustain Norberg's claims.[33] The court acknowledged that Norberg's relationship with Dr. Wynrib was based on unequal bargaining power and that, as a result, Norberg could not give valid consent to sexual relations.[34] The court quoted, with approval, the findings of a Canadian task force on the inherent inequality in the physician-patient relationship:

Patients seek the help of doctors when they are in a vulnerable state—when they are sick, when they are needy, when they are uncertain about what needs to be done. . . . The unequal distribution of power in the physician-patient relationship makes opportunities for sexual exploitation more possible than in other relationships. This vulnerability gives physicians the power to exact sexual compliance. Physical force or weapons are not necessary because the physician's power comes from having the knowledge and being trusted by patients.[35]

Noting that its aim is to protect trusting parties from those in "special positions of power," the Court awarded Norberg general damages for her suffering and loss during the time she was addicted to drugs due to the doctor's negligence as well as punitive damages for sexual exploitation.[36]

Negligent Breach of Fiduciary Duty by Lawyers

Courts have applied fiduciary theory to establish liability in cases of attorney-client sexual contact as well. In *Barbara A. v. John G.*,[37] Barbara A. retained John G. to represent her in a postdivorce proceeding.[38] During the course of the legal representation, John G. and Barbara A. had sexual intercourse. When Barbara A. asked that the lawyer use a contraceptive, John G. refused, telling her that he could not "possibly get anyone pregnant."[39]

Barbara A. did become pregnant, however, and was forced to undergo lifesaving surgery because of complications; her fallopian tube was removed, and she was rendered sterile.[40] When she sued John G. for her damages, the court held that she had a valid cause of action and provided an advisory opinion on the subject of fiduciary relationships.

The essence of a fiduciary relationship, according to the *Barbara A.* court, is "that the parties do not deal on equal terms, because the person in whom trust and confidence is reposed and who accepts that trust and confidence is in a superior position to exert unique influence over the dependent party."[41] Therefore, owing to the client's vulnerable position, the court stated that members of the State Bar should not under any circumstances attempt to deceive another person.[42] The court found no reason to restrict this principle to clients' financial claims and extended it to actions alleging physical damages resulting from attorneys' breach of fiduciary duty.[43] Accordingly, the court noted that it might be appropriate to presume that the lawyer exerted undue influence over his client, shifting to the lawyer the burden of proving that the client fully and freely consented to sexual relations with him.[44]

THERAPIST-PATIENT SEXUAL MISCONDUCT

Patients who have been sexually exploited by their therapists may choose to pursue legal remedies other than those based solely on the fiduciary nature of the relationship. These include filing complaints with the therapist's licensing board, common law causes of action for money damages, and criminal or civil statutory actions. A patient may generally pursue any combination of these options, as they are not mutually exclusive.

Common Law Causes of Action: Civil Suits

A patient may hire a lawyer to pursue a civil lawsuit, for money damages, against the therapist. A civil suit differs from a criminal proceeding. In a criminal proceeding, the patient files a complaint with the state, and the state's lawyer (a district attorney, prosecutor, or attorney general) pursues the case against the therapist. Compensation for the patient's injuries is generally not available in criminal proceedings.

Civil suits may be based either on the common law or on a specific statute. The common law derives from written court opinions deciding the cases brought before the courts for resolution. Legal principles develop through analogies between settled cases and new cases as they arise. Generally, patients' claims for breach of fiduciary duty are based on the common law.

Negligence

Plaintiffs may assert claims based upon negligence in cases against sexually abusive therapists. To prevail under a negligence theory, the complaining party, or plaintiff, must establish that (a) the defendant owed a duty of proper care to the plaintiff, (b) the defendant breached that duty, (c) the breach caused the harm, and (d) the plaintiff was damaged because of it.[45] To establish the existence of a duty, the plaintiff must prove the existence of a therapist-patient relationship. To prove the breach of the duty, the plaintiff must establish that the therapist acted in violation of his or her duty. A breach of the duty owed is the act that is understood to be negligent: for example, the sexual contact or wrongful termination of the therapeutic relationship. The causation element requires that the plaintiff prove that the therapist's wrongful act caused the plaintiff to suffer the injuries for which compensation is sought. To prove damage or injury, the plaintiff must show that she suffered physical or psychological injury as a result of the therapist's negligent conduct.

1. *Malpractice.* Malpractice, the legal name given to professional negligence, is the most commonly alleged theory of negligence in therapist-patient lawsuits. Courts have held that the patient's consent to sexual contact is not a valid defense to a claim of malpractice or professional negligence because "malpractice involves the breach of a professional duty; where the duty itself is to refrain from sexual contact, consent would not excuse the breach."[46]

Under a malpractice theory, a psychiatrist is required to treat his or her patient with the same or similar care as that which would be exercised by an average, qualified psychiatrist.[47] The specific elements and standards for proving malpractice vary from state to state.[48]

Zipkin v. Freeman[49] was the first reported U.S. case to hold that sexually abusive behavior by a therapist constituted malpractice. Mrs. Zipkin was referred to Dr. Freeman for psychiatric counseling in connection with headaches and other physical ailments she had been experiencing. After two and a half months of treatment, her ailments abated, but Dr. Freeman insisted that she continue treatment. He persuaded Mrs. Zipkin to move away from her husband into quarters she rented from the doctor, to purchase a farm for him and work on it as a manual laborer, and to steal her husband's suits for his use. Mrs. Zipkin accompanied her doctor on social outings, overnight trips, and nude swimming parties; they also had sexual relations. Dr. Freeman completely controlled her life. Mrs. Zipkin successfully proved that the doctor's sexual relations with her constituted malpractice stemming from the doctor's improper handling of his patient's transference.

In discussing Dr. Freeman's departures from recognized professional standards, the court stressed that the transference phenomenon is a common reaction in psychotherapy and must be handled with the utmost care.[50] The court did not distinguish between the doctor's engaging in sexual intercourse with his patient and his other professional boundary violations. In fact, the court concluded that "the damage would have been done to Mrs. Zipkin . . . even if there had been ballroom dancing instead of sexual relations."[51]

The court found that Mrs. Zipkin had succumbed to her psychiatrist's exploitation because of the particular dynamics of the psychiatrist-patient relationship. During the course of the relationship, Mrs. Zipkin came to believe that she was in love with Dr. Freeman. She trusted him completely, so when he told her she needed to divorce her husband to get completely well, she did so.[52] The court recognized that Mrs. Zipkin had a positive transference toward Dr. Freeman and that his negligent mishandling of her transference departed from the accepted standard of practice and caused her injuries. Since *Zipkin,* other plaintiffs have also successfully argued the malpractice claim of "negligent mishandling of transference."[53]

A therapist may breach the proper standard of care in other ways. These breaches include the following: (a) misusing drugs in the treatment process; (b) isolating the patient, which unduly increases his or her dependence on the therapist; (c) permitting therapist and patient to reverse their respective roles; (d) breaching patient confidentiality; (e) failing to treat the patient appropriately; (f) practicing therapeutic techniques beyond the scope of the therapist's competence; (g) practicing while intoxicated or under another disability; (h) terminating the patient's therapy without appropriate follow-up or referral; (i) failing to inform a patient that his treatment harmed her; (j) failing to obtain appropriate consultation and referral; and (k) engaging in inappropriate social contacts other than sexual intercourse, such as involving patients in business relationships or asking them to perform personal tasks for the therapist.[54] Additional theories of liability may be identified as courts continue to respond to the unique nature of the therapeutic relationship.

2. Negligent infliction of emotional distress. Plaintiffs alleging sexual abuse by their therapists have also proceeded under a theory of negligent infliction of emotional distress, a relatively new cause of action. Originally, this cause of action applied in cases in which individuals suffered physical harm as a result of witnessing catastrophic injuries to family members. The plaintiff had to be a "bystander" to the negligence as a threshold matter and had to suffer physical harm as a result. The plaintiff also had to prove, as is required in all negligence actions, that the actor was negligent with regard to that plaintiff. The plaintiff had to show that the actor breached a duty that was owed to the plaintiff.[55]

Some jurisdictions have relaxed the threshold "bystander" element. For example, in *Marlene F. v. Affiliated Psychiatric Medical Clinic, Inc.,*[56] a California court held that the mother of children who were sexually assaulted by a therapist had stated a sufficient cause of action for negligent infliction of emotional distress, even though she did not witness the assault.[57] The court noted that the therapist owed a duty directly to the mother as well as the children because they were involved in family therapy.[58] In another California case, *Richard H. v. Larry D.*,[59] the court found that a patient had a cause of action for negligent infliction of emotional distress against a therapist who had engaged in sexual relations with the patient's spouse.[60] The patient recovered damages for the injuries he suffered upon learning of the affair.[61]

Other courts have relaxed the requirement that the plaintiff suffer actual physical harm as the result of witnessing the injury to another, holding that symptoms such as headaches, sleeplessness, and inability to concentrate may constitute sufficient physical harm.[62] As a result, negligent infliction of emotional distress may be a means of redress for family members of patients sexually abused by their therapists.

Intentional Wrongs

Plaintiffs may also be able to proceed against sexually abusive therapists on the theory that the therapist intentionally, rather than negligently, committed a wrongful act. Theories such as battery, assault, intentional infliction of emotional distress, or fraudulent misrepresentation are of limited use to plaintiffs in sexual misconduct actions, however, because many professional liability insurers exclude coverage for intentional wrongs from professional liability policies.[63] Therefore the plaintiff's ability to obtain compensation is limited.

1. *Battery.* Battery is the unprivileged, unconsented to, harmful, or offensive touching of another.[64] Battery is not a commonly pursued civil cause of action against a therapist for sexual contact with a patient, unless the therapist has personal assets sufficient to satisfy a judgment.

2. *Intentional infliction of emotional distress.* A cause of action for *intentional* infliction of emotional distress typically requires that the plaintiff prove that the defendant's conduct was (a) intentional or reckless, (b) extreme and outrageous, and (c) caused (d) severe emotional harm to the plaintiff.[65] In a lawsuit brought by a patient alleging intentional infliction of emotional distress, the therapist may argue as a defense that the patient consented to the activity.

As with negligent infliction of emotional distress, this cause of action is most often asserted by patients whose spouses have been sexually abused by a therapist. For instance, in *Figueiredo-Torres v. Nickel*,[66] the husband and wife were both patients of the defendant. The couple entered marriage counseling with the therapist, who then encouraged the wife to have sexual relations with him and to leave her husband. The husband was successful in his suit against the therapist on the legal theory of intentional infliction of emotional distress.[67]

Nonpatient spouses have also used intentional infliction of emotional distress in suits against sexually abusive therapists. In *Spiess v. Johnson*,[68] a husband successfully sued his wife's therapist under theories including intentional infliction of severe emotional distress.[69] The court found that the therapist had sexual relations with Mrs. Spiess with the intention of causing Mr. Spiess severe emotional harm.

3. Fraudulent misrepresentation. To recover under a claim for fraudulent misrepresentation, the plaintiff must show that (a) the therapist knowingly made a false representation (b) with the purpose of defrauding the patient, (c) who justifiably relied on the misrepresentation; (d) the patient would not have allowed the injurious act had the misrepresentation not been made, and (e) the misrepresentation caused the plaintiff injury.[70]

In *DiLeo v. Nugent*,[71] a therapist administered illicit drugs to his patient and had sexual intercourse with her. When the patient questioned his techniques, the doctor reassured her that the sex was part of the therapy, and the therapy continued. The patient alleged that she had been sexually abused as a result of the therapists's fraudulent misrepresentation. The jury agreed and found that Dr. DiLeo had fraudulently misrepresented the reasons for his unusual treatment, and the plaintiff prevailed.[72]

Breach of Contract and Breach of Warranty

Some courts have held therapists liable for sexual misconduct under the theory that the therapists breached their contracts with the patients. Although many jurisdictions have declared it contrary to public policy to hold a physician liable for a promise worded generally to "cure" a patient, other courts have recognized that physicians do have contractual obligations to their patients.[73] In *Anclote Manor Foundation v. Wilkinson*,[74] for example, the husband of a patient who had committed suicide after her therapist's sexual contact with her sued the therapist for breach of contract. The husband prevailed on this theory but recovered as damages only the amount of money he had paid in fees to the therapist.[75]

When a therapist breaches an express, rather than implied, promise, however, he or she may be held liable. In *Spiess v. Johnson*,[76] Mrs. Spiess and Dr. Johnson became intimate after she sought psychiatric treatment from him for marital difficulties. The court found that Dr. Johnson had promised Mr. Spiess that he would treat Mrs. Spiess but breached the promise when he failed to provide therapy. The doctor's "treatment" of Mrs. Spiess included following Mr. and Mrs. Spiess on family vacations to California and Hawaii and encouraging Mrs. Spiess to divorce her husband. Although the court found that the psychiatrist owed Mr. Spiess no fiduciary duty to abstain from sexual intercourse with Mrs. Spiess, it did find that he had breached his contractual obligations to Mr. Spiess.

Claims against therapists based on the theory of breach of implied warranty have not generally been favored by the courts. In *Dennis v. Allison*,[77] for example, the court held that, because so many possible theories of liability could be applied to a therapist sexual abuse case, it would be unnecessary to proceed against the therapist on a breach of implied warranty theory.

Posttermination Liability

Sexual relations with a patient after the professional relationship has ended may also be actionable. The case of *Noto v. St. Vincent Hospital and Medical Center*[78] addressed the issue of common law posttermination liability.[79] In *Noto*, the patient entered the hospital for treatment of substance abuse and "seductive behavior." Three weeks after her discharge from the hospital, the therapist who had treated her there commenced a sexual relationship with her and encouraged her to start using drugs again. The court held that the discharge from the hospital and technical termination of treatment did not necessarily insulate the therapist from liability.[80]

Spouses' Causes of Action

As noted earlier, the spouse of a sexually abused patient may also seek damages from the treating professional. In some states, a spouse may also assert a claim for damages resulting from loss of consortium, alleging that, as a result of the therapist's malpractice or abuse of the patient, the spouse was deprived of the patient's love, companionship, and services.[81] This right to compensation for loss of consortium is independent of the patient's spouse's claim for negligence because it constitutes a separate deprivation of rights. In other states, spouses can proceed on theories of alienation of affection or criminal conversation. In Utah, for example, the court recently upheld a husband's suit for alienation of affections when his wife left him and their children after she engaged in sexual relations with her therapist.[82] Many states, however, have abolished these causes of actions because they rest upon the outmoded premise that the integrity of a woman's body is a property right owned by the woman's parents or husband.[83]

Nonpatient spouses, generally, have been unsuccessful in pursuing malpractice actions against therapists who have become sexually involved with their patient spouses.[84] Courts have been reluctant to extend professional duties owed the patient to third parties, such as the patient's spouse, even when the third party can demonstrate harm. For example, in *Homer v. Long*,[85] it was held that, absent special circumstances, a psychiatrist has no professional duty to a patient's spouse even though the spouse initially employed the therapist and pays the therapist's fees.[86]

As previously discussed, when a therapist engages in sexual contact with the patient's spouse, the patient has a claim for malpractice in most states. In *Mazza v. Huffaker*,[87] the court upheld a patient's claim against a therapist for professional negligence resulting from the therapist's sexual involvement with the patient's spouse. The court opined that a psychiatrist has a strict duty not to breach the trust necessary for an effective therapeutic relationship and that becoming sexually involved with a relative of a patient is a failure to exercise "the requisite amount of skill, learning, and ability that a psychiatrist in any community in the United States ought to exercise."[88]

More recently, in *Figueiredo-Torres v. Nickel*,[89] a therapist who was providing counseling to a husband and wife engaged in sexual relations with the wife.[90] The court sustained the husband's lawsuit on the theories of professional negligence and intentional infliction of emotional distress.[91] The court noted that the nature of the trusting relationship between therapist and patient distinguished it from one in which the seducer was "the milkman, the mailman or the guy next door."[92] The court noted that the gravamen, or essence, of the claim for intentional infliction of emotional distress was not merely the sexual act or the alienation of his wife's affections but "the entire course of conduct engaged in by his therapist, with whom he enjoyed a *special relationship*."[93]

Statutory Causes of Action

The foregoing cases represent common law remedies for the harm done to patients by their therapists. Statutory law provides another important means of regulating professional conduct. Changes in statutory law may be more dramatic than the evolutionary progress of the common law, thus statutes regulating sexual conduct by therapists may provide a greater range of remedies for plaintiffs.

Statutory Civil Causes of Action

Recently enacted statutory laws have been drafted specifically to provide a remedy for patients who have been sexually exploited by their therapists. Theoretically, these laws have addressed and corrected problems in application of the common law to therapist-patient sexual misconduct lawsuits.

States, including Minnesota,[94] Illinois,[95] Texas,[96] California,[97] and Wisconsin,[98] have enacted statutes creating civil causes of action for psychotherapeutic exploitation. Each of these statutes provides that a patient who proves that sexual relations with the therapist occurred in a therapeutic relationship need not prove that the therapist was negligent in initiating the sexual relationship. In other words, the second element of negligence, breach of the duty of care, is established once the plaintiff proves that the sex took place. Accordingly, the plaintiff must then prove only that harm occurred as a result of the sexual contact.[99]

The Minnesota, Illinois, and Texas statutes are substantially similar and create a cause of action for sexual exploitation against a psychotherapist if the exploitation occurred during or after the period that the patient was receiving psychotherapy, the patient was "emotionally dependent" on the psychotherapist, or the sexual contact occurred by means of "therapeutic deception." Under these statutes, a therapist may not assert the defense that the "sexual contact . . . occurred outside a therapy or treatment session or that it occurred off the premises regularly used by the psychotherapist for therapy or treatment sessions."[100]

Statutes in California, Wisconsin, and Texas permit a former patient to recover damages without proving emotional dependence on the psychotherapist.[101] Additionally, the Wisconsin statute permits recovery for "purely" emotional injuries as well as for all physical and psychological damages resulting from the sexual contact, including aggravation of a preexisting condition. Like the Minnesota and Illinois statutes, a therapist may be liable for damages for sexual contact occurring in or out of treatment. In Wisconsin, the therapist may raise the defense of consent only if the sexual contact with the patient occurred more than six months after the termination of treatment.[102] Colorado board regulations prohibit sexual relations between a therapist and a former patient for a period of six months after termination; Illinois prohibits such relations for one year; California, for two years; Minnesota, for up to two years if the former patient can prove emotional dependency; and Texas, for two years and beyond if the former patient can prove emotional dependency.[103]

The Wisconsin, Minnesota, Illinois, and Texas statutes define *psychotherapist* broadly to cover nearly all counselors, both licensed and unlicensed, vastly enlarging the class of potential defendants. A plaintiff could otherwise encounter great difficulty in establishing a duty of care for clergy malpractice or "New Age" counseling. These statutes hold unlicensed therapists who are otherwise unaccountable to licensing or other disciplinary procedures responsible in the same way as licensed, board-certified therapists. By including unlicensed psychotherapists, the statutes effectively eliminate many common law loopholes.

Though the class of defendants has been enlarged by the statutes, the type of sexual conduct prohibited is typically quite specific. For example, although the Minnesota statute has a broader definition of "sexual contact" than the other statutes, it is actually very specific:

> "Sexual contact" means any of the following, whether or not occurring with the *consent* of the patient or former patient:
>
> (1) sexual intercourse, cunnilingus, fellatio, anal intercourse or any intrusion, however slight, into the genital or anal openings of the patient's or former patient's body by any part of the psychotherapist's body or by any object used by the psychotherapist for this purpose, or any intrusion, however slight, into the genital or anal openings of the psychotherapist's body by any part of the patient's or former patient's body or by any object used by the patient or former patient for this purpose, if agreed to by the psychotherapist;
>
> (2) kissing of, or the intentional touching by the psychotherapist of the patient's or former patient's genital area, groin, inner thigh, buttocks, or breast or of the clothing covering any of these body parts;
>
> (3) kissing of, or the intentional touching by the patient or former patient of the psychotherapist's genital area, groin, inner thigh, buttocks, or breast or of the clothing covering any of these body parts if the psychotherapist agrees to the kissing or intentional touching.
>
> "Sexual contact" includes *requests* by the psychotherapist for conduct described in clauses (1) to (3).
>
> "Sexual contact" does not include conduct described in clause (1) or (2) that is a part of standard medical treatment of a patient.[104]

While such definitions may satisfy the need for clarity, they may also fail to allow for an infinite variety of sexual contact.

Criminal Statutes

Fourteen states have criminalized psychotherapist-patient sexual contact.[105] Criminal actions differ from civil actions in three respects. First, after the patient files a complaint with the appropriate authorities, the patient becomes merely a witness in the state's prosecution of the therapist. Second, the attorney who prosecutes the therapist in a criminal action (the district attorney, prosecuting attorney, or attorney general) represents the state, not the patient. Third, criminal sanctions against the therapist include imprisonment and other penalties but generally not monetary compensation to the victim. The severity of the sanctions available depends upon whether the crime is classified as a felony or a misdemeanor.

Five states define sexual contact, under the pretext of medical treatment in general, as rape, thus potentially including this behavior by psychiatrists in the interpretation.[106] Prior to specifically including psychotherapy in its criminal statute, for example, New Hampshire applied its sexual assault statute to a psychologist who assaulted his patient during counseling.[107] Sexual contact resulting from a physician's misrepresentation is criminalized in Alabama and Michigan.[108] Wyoming criminalizes sexual contact that results from coercion by a person in a position of authority over the victim.[109]

Thirteen out of the fourteen states classify therapist sexual misconduct as a felony,[110] thirteen punish both sexual intercourse and sexual contact,[111] and twelve have statutes that apply to both licensed and unlicensed practitioners.[112] Most of these statutes also eliminate the patient's consent as a defense to prosecution.[113] Seven out of the fourteen criminalize a therapist's sexual contact with a former patient.[114]

Statutes criminalizing sexually abusive conduct provide a clear statement of society's policy against such conduct and may offer some measure of deterrence. Additionally, criminal prosecution can empower the patient through participation in the action and aid in the patient's recovery from the abuse. Criminal penalties may, finally, satisfy the patient's wish for retribution, if not restitution.

Victim Shield Provisions

"Victim shield" provisions are included in many civil and criminal sexual abuse statutes. Victim shield provisions are written into statutes to protect victims from publicity and from other hazards such as the well-known defense tactic of putting the plaintiff on trial by opening up his or her sexual history for the court or jury.[115] Victim shield provisions protect the victim from attempts by the defendant to humiliate or embarrass the victim by admitting his or her sexual history. The statutes recognize that a plaintiff's sexual history or "consent" is largely irrelevant to the question of liability because the therapist has the duty and responsibility of avoiding sexual involvement with patients.

Reporting Abusive Therapists

Some statutes contain provisions concerning mandatory reporting by other therapists and anonymous reporting by the patient. Mandatory reporting statutes require therapists to report known cases of therapist sexual misconduct. Anonymous reporting allows a therapist, or the patient, to report such abuse without subjecting the victim to publicity and scrutiny.[116] Anonymity provisions encourage patients to come forward and identify abusive therapists, thereby providing regulatory authorities with the information needed to curtail the activities of abusive practitioners. Texas has the strictest reporting statute, requiring mental health workers who suspect that a patient has been sexually exploited by another mental health worker to report the alleged conduct to both the prosecuting attorney and the appropriate state licensing boards.[117] The patient is entitled to request anonymity.

Regulating Abusive Therapists

Colorado has enacted an innovative licensing statute permitting its courts to prevent both licensed and unlicensed psychotherapists from continuing in practice if they present a risk to their patients.[118] When the continuing practice by abusive therapists poses an unnecessary risk of harm to other patients, the therapists may be stopped from practicing. The statute permits an injunction to be issued that prohibits therapists from continuing to practice psychotherapy.

Wisconsin has also enacted another innovative statute to address the concern about abusive therapists who remain hidden from licensing bodies. A 1991 law declares void

any provision in a contract or agreement relating to the settlement of any claim by a patient against a therapist that limits or eliminates the right of the patient to disclose sexual contact by the therapist to a subsequent therapist, the department of regulation and licensing, the department of health and social services, the patients compensation fund peer review council or a district attorney.[119]

This law curbs the common practice of therapists and their lawyers to offer to settle cases in exchange for the patient's agreement not to report the abusive conduct (also known as "silent agreements" or "gag agreements").

Statute of Limitations

Every state has a time period within which a lawsuit must be filed. These statutes of limitation reflect a balancing between the plaintiff's right to seek compensation for mental or physical injury and the defendant's right to be notified promptly of a claim while events are fresh in people's minds and records documenting a claim are still in existence.[120] Statutes of limitations may range from a strict period of one year following the act that gave rise to the lawsuit, to that of many years after the act. A plaintiff who files a claim after the relevant statute of limitations has expired may be *barred* from bringing the claim.

State legislatures and courts have recognized exceptions to the application of statutes of limitations when the plaintiff is under a legal disability sufficient to excuse him or her from filing suit within the required time. Examples of legal disabilities include repressed memories of the abuse and the patient's inability to connect the past abuse by the therapist with his or her current psychological injuries.[121]

Discovery Rule

When a plaintiff has a legal disability, strict application of the statute of limitations may inequitably restrict his or her access to court.[122] To remedy such inequity, some jurisdictions have applied a discovery rule in interpreting their statute of limitations, holding that the limitation on bringing suit "will not mature until plaintiffs discover or should discover that they have been harmed as the result of the defendant's conduct."[123] This rule is often applied in situations involving a fiduciary relationship because courts recognize that the trust reposed in the fiduciary by victims "may blind them to the wrongdoing because of undue influence."[124]

Riley v. Presnell[125] illustrates Massachusetts's use of a discovery rule to accommodate a patient's need for time to recover from sexual abuse before filing suit. In 1975 Riley was referred to Dr. Presnell for treatment for emotional difficulties. Dr. Presnell used marijuana and alcohol in therapy sessions and had sexual relations with his patient. The doctor also prescribed Valium for Riley, who eventually became addicted to it. During the course of therapy, Riley came to believe that Dr. Presnell "might be God."[126] The doctor told Riley not to tell anyone about the nature of the therapy because "it was special and the world would neither understand nor approve."[127]

In 1979 Dr. Presnell abruptly terminated Riley's therapy, without referring him to another therapist. Riley developed severe emotional and psychological problems and began to drink heavily.[128] In 1980 Riley began therapy with another psychiatrist, who helped Riley overcome his addiction to Valium and put him in touch with another former patient of Dr. Presnell who claimed to have been similarly abused by Dr. Presnell. Riley asserted that it was not until he met this other patient that he realized that there was a link between his condition and the treatment he received from Dr. Presnell.[129]

Riley filed suit against Dr. Presnell over five years after the termination of his therapy. Under the Massachusetts statute of limitations governing Riley's case, the cause of action accrued when an ordinary and reasonable person knew or would have reason to know that he or she had been harmed by the defendant's conduct.[130] The court recognized, however, that Dr. Presnell's wrongful conduct may have prevented Riley from realizing that he had been injured. Therefore the court applied a two-part test to determine whether Riley had "(1) knowledge or sufficient notice that [he] was harmed and (2) knowledge or sufficient notice of what the cause of harm was."[131] The court ruled that this determination was a question of fact to be decided by the jury, taking into account the possibility of mental injury caused by the defendant.[132]

In essence, the Massachusetts court created a "reasonable victim" standard to use in psychotherapist sexual misconduct cases:

> If the defendant's conduct would, in an ordinary reasonable person, cause an injury which by its very nature prevents the discovery of its cause, the cause of action cannot be said to have accrued. Accrual of the cause of action occurs when *the ordinary reasonable person who had been subject to the experience would have discovered that the injury was caused by that experience.*[133]

The court's ruling in *Riley v. Presnell* essentially opened the courtroom door in Massachusetts to patients whose abuse took place many years in the past but who did not immediately realize the nature or cause of the harm.

Equitable Estoppel

A plaintiff may also be able to file a lawsuit after the statute of limitations has expired by using the theory of equitable estoppel. The doctrine of equitable estoppel prevents a defendant from asserting the running of the statute of limitations as a defense to a claim if the defendant's actions hinder the plaintiff's recognition of the harm. The result is the same as under the discovery rule: The plaintiff's case proceeds. Equitable estoppel theory, however, focuses on the way in which the defendant's conduct may have contributed to the plaintiff's inability to assert his or her legal rights within the statute of limitations period.

In *Coopersmith v. Gold*,[134] the plaintiff's psychiatrist engaged in sexual relations with her. The following day, she asked the doctor whether the sex had occurred as a result of her positive transference toward him. Her doctor told her that it had not and continued to have sexual relations with her during ensuing therapy sessions. The psychiatrist stopped billing her and stopped scheduling appointments with her in 1981. The sexual encounters, however, continued for another three years.[135] When the plaintiff filed suit in 1986, the doctor claimed that the statute of limitations had expired in 1983, two years after he had officially stopped "treating" her in therapy. The court held that the plaintiff had presented sufficient evidence to justify a jury trial as to whether the defendant ought to be prevented, or estopped, from asserting the statute of limitations as a defense to her claim. The court justified this holding by finding that her doctor had falsely advised her that no transference had existed in order to sexually exploit her, this misrepresentation hindered her realization of the harm, and she was, due to the delay in realizing her harm, unable to file her claim within the statute of limitations period.[136] The court also found that this course of conduct had persisted for three years.

Fraudulent Concealment

The theory of fraudulent concealment may also toll (i.e., suspend) the running of the statute of limitations. Fraudulent concealment is similar to the discovery rule because it focuses on what the patient knew or should have known about his or her possible legal actions. A therapist who fails to inform a patient of the likely effects of improper treatment, and thus conceals a possible cause of action, breaches his or her fiduciary duty to the patient. Accordingly, the statute of limitations does not begin to run until the patient knows or has reason to know of the therapist's wrongdoing and the damage it may have caused. The court applied the fraudulent concealment theory in *Riley v. Presnell*,[137] noting that it puts the plaintiff on the same footing as in application of the discovery rule.[138]

Contributory Negligence

Therapists sometimes raise the defense of contributory negligence in sexual abuse cases. A minority of jurisdictions completely bar plaintiffs from making negligence claims if the plaintiff contributed to the injury by failing to exercise ordinary care for his or her own safety.[139] In sexual misconduct cases, however, courts rarely recognize contributory negligence as a defense.

In *DiLeo v. Nugent*,[140] for example, Dr. DiLeo contended at trial that, because his patient, Nugent, was herself a mental health professional, she contributed to her own injuries by following his questionable professional advice. This advice included the use of illicit drugs and the act of engaging in sexual relations with the doctor. Criticizing this defense as "specious," the court held that, even though patients may have suspicions about the recommended treatment, they are entitled to rely on their doctor's advice.[141] The court also discussed whether Nugent should have been held to a higher standard of watchfulness than the average person because she had expertise in the mental health field. The court decided, however, that the jury could find that Nugent did not actually know that her treatment was harming her, in which case the court would not impose on her a duty to evaluate her treatment from her professional perspective in a situation in which she had given herself over to another professional for treatment.[142] The court based its holding on the nature of the trusting relationship that exists between doctor and patient that encourages the patient to defer to the doctor's "expert" judgment. This decision implicitly recognized the coercive power inherent in fiduciary relationships.

Thus, unless a patient has actual knowledge that a course of treatment is injurious and submits to it anyway, generally the court will not find that the patient has contributed to her injuries. Courts impose no duty on the patient to investigate or second-guess the doctor when that patient has already implicitly admitted the need to consult a professional for help with handling a medical or mental problem.

Malpractice Insurance Issues

Plaintiffs in sexual abuse cases seeking to recover damages will often find that the therapist's professional malpractice insurance is the best, or only, source of compensation for their injuries. Some courts have determined that professional liability policies covering risks associated with "professional services rendered" cover claims brought against therapists for engaging in sexual relations with their patients. Liability is typically premised upon the therapist's negligent mishandling of transference. Insurers' attempts to avoid liability on contractual or public policy grounds generally have been unsuccessful.[143]

Zipkin v. Freeman,[144] discussed earlier, is one of the leading cases holding that a therapist's sexual misconduct was covered under his professional liability policy. The *Zipkin* court held that Dr. Freeman's policy, which provided coverage for damages resulting from "professional services rendered or which should have been rendered during the term of this policy by the insured," applied because the doctor's misconduct arose not from the acts of social and sexual intercourse *per se* but from his mishandling of the patient's transference.[145] According to the court's analysis, the insurer was obliged to defend and indemnify Dr. Freeman because it was aware, or should have been aware, of the risk of mishandled transference as it related to its "professional services rendered" policy.

The same result was reached in *Cotton v. Kambly*,[146] in which the court refused to distinguish between malpractice based upon an allegation of improper sexual conduct and other negligent acts, such as improper administration of a drug or a defective operation.[147] The plaintiff in *Cotton* alleged that the defendant induced her to engage in sexual relations with him as part of her therapy, thereby breaching the proper standards of medical practice. The court agreed that such conduct could be considered malpractice.[148]

The plaintiff in *L. L. v. Medical Protective Company*[149] sought treatment for her difficulty in maintaining healthy relationships with men.[150] Her psychiatrist engaged in multiple sexual acts with her, and the patient eventually sued him for malpractice. Noting that medical authorities almost unanimously considered sexual contact between a therapist and a patient to be malpractice, the reviewing court found the insurance company liable on its policy because

a sexual relationship between therapist and patient cannot be viewed separately from the therapeutic relationship that has developed between them. The transference phenomenon makes it impossible that the patient will have the same emotional response to sexual contact with the therapist that he or she would have to sexual contact with other persons. Further, by introducing sexual activity into the relationship, the therapist runs the risk of causing additional psychological damage to the patient.[151]

In *Simmons v. United States*,[152] the counselor engaged in a sexual relationship with the plaintiff, who sought his counseling services for the effects of childhood abuse. Eventually, the plaintiff began to suffer a variety of emotional problems, ranging from anxiety to depression, which worsened until she was hospitalized for psychiatric treatment and had attempted suicide. Two years after terminating therapy, she learned for the first time that her counselor's conduct had contributed to her condition.[153]

In holding the U.S. government liable for the actions of the counselor, its employee, the court emphasized that the counselor's sexual activities could not be viewed in isolation from the therapeutic context in which they originated. The court stated that the sex was inseparable from the "transference phenomenon," which is "crucial to the therapeutic process . . . [and through which the patient] becomes well."[154] In conclusion, the court noted that medical authorities consider a therapist who mishandles transference and becomes sexually involved with a patient to have committed malpractice.[155]

Insurance Coverage for Intentional and Criminal Acts

Insurers have attempted to deny coverage for sexual misconduct under professional liability policies based on two separate theories. First, insurers argue that the sexual relations were not part of the therapeutic relationship and hence did not constitute professional services ordinarily covered under malpractice insurance.[156] Second, because the therapists' sexual activities were *intentional*, or in some cases criminal, insurers argue that the therapist alone should bear the cost.[157]

As noted above, most courts have rejected arguments that state that the sexual relationship ought to be considered as existing independent of the therapeutic relationship. These courts reason that, because transference forms part of a therapeutic treatment, the mishandling of transference through engaging in sexual intercourse constitutes an insurable "occupational risk."[158] One court explained the rationale by analogy and stated that the risk of mishandling transference is not unlike the risks of driving in excess of the speed limit or driving drunk. Automobile liability carriers routinely insure these risks even though speeding or drinking and driving are considered *avoidable* risks.[159]

Insurers have also argued that sexual relations between therapists and patients are intentional, and in some states criminal, acts and therefore insurers should not cover such behavior in their malpractice policies. The insurer in *L. L. v. Medical Protective Company*,[160] for example, argued that, because its policy excluded payment of damages that resulted from the performance of a criminal act, and the therapist's sexual acts constituted crimes in that state, the conduct in question fell squarely within the policy exclusion for criminal behavior and hence was not covered.[161] Focusing on the nature of the plaintiff's claim, the court concluded that the policy did not exclude sexual acts. Specifically, the court determined that the plaintiff alleged a cause of action for malpractice, and not for an intentional or criminal act. The court stated that the plaintiff alleged "that she was damaged by [the therapist's] failure to exercise the degree of skill and care ordinarily exercised by other psychiatrists and by [his] failure to provide appropriate forms of treatment. These are allegations of malpractice, not of criminality."[162]

In *Vigilant Insurance Co. v. Kambly*,[163] the court reached the same conclusion. In that case, the court held that, although civil actions often contain elements of criminal offenses, the damages in the case were not incurred due to criminal acts but due to malpractice in a *civil action*.[164]

Public Policy Considerations
Determining the Availability of Coverage

In many cases, insurance companies have advanced the argument that policies should not cover sexual conduct. Insurers argue that, because the insured's conduct was outrageous, criminal, or outside the bounds of human decency, the insured alone should bear the burden of compensating injured patients. This argument relies on the premise that bearing the cost of his or her misdeeds will motivate the insured to confine his or her conduct to the limits of the law and thereby avoid liability. This premise, however, forsakes the compensatory function of liability insurance in favor of the deterrence function of individual liability. Policies that would not cover sexual acts, however, would deprive injured patients of financial redress for the damage they have suffered.[165]

Courts weigh public policy considerations against the injured patient's expectation of compensation to determine whether insurance policies should cover certain wrongful activity. These public policy considerations often include the following: whether the insured obtained the policy with the intent later to engage in the wrongful conduct, whether the existence of insurance coverage "promoted" the wrongful act, whether a denial of insurance coverage would make the wrongful conduct less likely to occur, whether the insured is "protected" from the consequences of wrongful behavior by the insurance coverage, and whether the victim of the wrongful act is involved in the case as a claimant for damages.[166] This balancing test is weighted in favor of patients, because they are the intended beneficiaries of malpractice insurance policies.[167] In *Vigilant Ins. Co. v. Kambly*,[168] for example, the court stated that

> coverage does not allow the wrongdoer unjustly to benefit from his wrong. It is not the insured who will benefit, but the innocent victim who will be provided compensation for her injuries. . . . In this instance there is great public interest in protecting the interests of the injured party.[169]

Insurers' Caps and Exclusions

In upholding a claim for insurance coverage in *St. Paul Fire & Marine Ins. Co. v. Love*,[170] the court implied that public policy considerations in mishandled transference cases would rarely tip the scale in favor of the insurer. The court suggested that

> [if] the underwriter does not want to provide coverage for this particular peril, it would seem it might exclude any claim for damages based on professional services in the treatment of transference which results in a sexual relationship between the insured and the patient.[171]

Many insurers have followed this advice by specifically disallowing coverage for damages involving sexual conduct or by capping the dollar amount of coverage available.[172]

In *Govar v. Chicago Insurance Co.*,[173] a psychologist's malpractice policy excluded coverage for "claims arising out of any sexual act or acts performed or alleged to have been performed by the named Insured . . . [that constitute] an essential element of the cause of action so adjudicated."[174] Although the plaintiff amended her original complaint to delete all references to sex and proceeded on the theory that her therapist had failed to exercise the degree of care and skill required by his profession, the elements of her case as proved at trial nevertheless included sexual misconduct.[175] The reviewing court held that the therapist's sexual behavior was an essential element of the cause of action and hence was excluded from insurance coverage pursuant to the terms of his policy.[176] The court did leave open the question of whether the plaintiff's claim could have been brought within the limits of the policy if she had not referred to sex when pleading her case. However, the sexual relationship between Govar and her therapist was so intertwined with her therapist's malpractice as to be inseparable. Therefore it would have been difficult for her to have alleged the malpractice without mention of the sexual relationship.

Concurrent Proximate Cause

The theory of concurrent proximate cause may allow plaintiffs to avoid malpractice insurers' exclusions or caps in some jurisdictions. In *Cranford Insurance Co. v. Allwest Insurance Co.*,[177] for example, the plaintiff alleged that the therapist both negligently mishandled his transference and abandoned him.[178] The court agreed that the doctor's mishandling of the transference process involved sexual intimacy within the meaning of the coverage exclusion in the therapist's professional liability policy, and was therefore excluded. The court determined, however, that the abandonment claim did not involve the sexual relationship and was not excluded because "under California law, where an insured risk and an excluded risk constitute *concurrent proximate causes* of an injury, a liability insurer is liable if one of the causes is covered by the policy."[179]

In *American Home Insurance Co. v. Cohen*,[180] the plaintiff sued her psychologist for professional negligence, breach of fiduciary duty, and loss of consortium.[181] She and her therapist had had sexual relations during her therapy sessions. Dr. Cohen's insurance policy contained broad clauses that limited damages arising from certain activities to $25,000 and excluded coverage for "wrongful acts."[182] The trial court found that the wrongful act provision did not exclude coverage, and focused on the applicability of the coverage cap.[183]

In allowing the limit to apply to the sexual misconduct but refusing to allow it on all the misconduct claims, the court reasoned that allowing a limit to the coverage on all the misconduct claims would permit the insurer to benefit from the existence of the sexual misconduct claim.[184] The court held that the jury should apportion the damages to the specific acts of negligence the therapist was found to have committed.[185] In the event that the jury could not apportion the damages, the court held that the insurer would bear the burden of proving that the excluded or limited act was the sole, proximate cause of the injuries.[186] It follows from this reasoning that, unless the insurer can prove that the excluded event was the sole, proximate cause of the injuries, the insurer must cover all the damages.

NONPSYCHIATRIC PHYSICIAN-PATIENT SEXUAL MISCONDUCT

While malpractice or negligence cases against sexually abusive therapists have been premised on the link between sexual relations and mishandled transference, claims against nonpsychotherapist medical care providers present different issues because the professional services provided do not usually involve patient transference. There is, however, increasing professional agreement that physicians should not engage in intimate relations with their patients, as evidenced by this 1991 statement by the AMA:

> The American Medical Association's Council on Ethical and Judicial Affairs
> . . . has concluded that (1) sexual contact or a romantic relationship concurrent with the physician-patient relationship is unethical; (2) sexual contact or a romantic relationship with a former patient may be unethical under certain circumstances; (3) education on the ethical issues involved in sexual misconduct should be included throughout all levels of medical training; and (4) in the case of sexual misconduct, reporting offending colleagues is especially important.[187]

Such ethical guidelines are useful because state licensing boards may incorporate them into licensing standards for the regulated professions. Recent decisions of administrative licensing authorities have reflected the American Medical Association's views on sexual involvement and have disciplined the offending professionals.[188] States, then, may rely on licensing standards as evidence of the standard of care and thus of the negligence of the professional who departs from them.

Common Law

Negligence

Courts have been slow to recognize sexual contact between nonpsychiatric physicians and their patients as actionable negligence. In *Atienza v. Taub*,[189] for example, the patient's malpractice suit against her doctor for sexual misconduct was dismissed by the reviewing court. In finding that the doctor's conduct did not constitute professional negligence, the court stated that

> appellant does not allege that she was induced to have sexual relations with respondent in furtherance of her treatment. Essentially, appellant complains that she had an unhappy affair with a man who happened to be her doctor. This is plainly insufficient to make out a cause of action for professional negligence under any of the theories presented.[190]

Other jurisdictions have generally followed the rationale in *Atienza*.[191]

Some plaintiffs have prevailed by alleging other malpractice, in addition to the sexual contact. In *Wall v. Noble*,[192] a plastic surgeon performed three operations on the plaintiff and engaged in a sexual relationship with her while she was under his care. While the focus of the lawsuit was on the physician's improperly performed operations, evidence of the physician-patient sexual relationship was admitted. The plaintiff testified that the physician frequently repeated the phrase, *I am your doctor—trust me,* while he made sexual advances.[193] Moreover, some of the sexual encounters occurred when the plaintiff was under post-surgical instructions not to engage in sexual intercourse. This supported the court's conclusion that the doctor was indifferent to his patient's welfare and safety.[194] The jury found the doctor liable for negligently performing the operations and negligently engaging in sexual intercourse with his patient.

In the *Wall* case, the plaintiff had originally complained that her doctor's sexual conduct was a breach of fiduciary duties of loyalty and good faith and had created a conflict of interest.[195] Breach of fiduciary obligations, however, was apparently not one of the legal theories on which the case was submitted to the jury. The jury found, as a factual matter, that the sexual relationship interfered with the physician-patient relationship.[196]

Intentional Wrongs

Courts may hold nonpsychiatric physicians liable for intentional torts such as battery and intentional infliction of emotional distress. As discussed above, however, malpractice insurance coverage generally precludes compensation to victims of intentionally wrongful conduct.

In *Smith v. St. Paul Fire & Marine Ins. Co.*,[197] a general practitioner sexually molested three teenage male patients. One of the boys subsequently attempted suicide. The reviewing court held that no insurance coverage was available under the doctor's malpractice insurance policy because the acts were not part of negligently provided medical treatment but were conducted intentionally by the doctor for his personal interests. The court stated:

> It is undisputed that [the doctor's] acts of sexual contact were not part of medical treatment [but] were solely for the satisfaction of [his] prurient interests. . . . [T]he acts of sexual contact involved neither the providing nor withholding of professional services and, therefore, the insurer's policy does not cover the damages sustained by plaintiffs.[198]

The dissent, on the other hand, argued that the court should have paid more attention to the victim's subjective impression of what occurred in the doctor's examining rooms. In his dissent, Justice Wahl argued that the incidents were part of the medical treatment that was negligently provided and not intentional acts outside of the medical context. He stated:

> All of the incidents occurred during the course of a medical examination or treatment. All of the incidents occurred solely because plaintiffs were brought to [the doctor] for medical examination or treatment. All of the incidents occurred within the context of a medical environment. Additionally, the doctor's silence surrounding each of these incidents lends credence to plaintiffs' contentions that they believed that the doctor's manipulations were somehow related to their medical treatment or examination.[199]

Courts have held insurance companies liable in sexual assault cases where the courts have found a nexus between the medical procedure performed and the sexual abuse or other injury to the patient or where the plaintiff alleges negligence other than sexual conduct. In *St. Paul Fire & Marine Ins. Co. v. Asbury*,[200] the court held that professional liability insurance covered a claim that a gynecologist wrongfully manipulated his patients' genitals during examinations because "the patients' injuries . . . were made possible only because there were professional services rendered during this time and others which should have been rendered but were not."[201]

In *St. Paul Fire & Marine Ins. Co. v. Shernow*,[202] a dentist administered an excessive dose of nitrous oxide to his patient, then sexually assaulted her while she was under its influence. Using an argument similar to that used in *Wall*, the court found that the action was covered by the dentist's policy because his administration of the nitrous oxide was negligent and had caused the patient harm.[203]

Statutory Causes of Action

Sexual assault constitutes criminal assault or civil battery in all jurisdictions. As previously discussed, some states have specific statutes imposing liability for sexual contact that occurs during the course of medical treatment.[204]

ATTORNEY-CLIENT SEXUAL MISCONDUCT

Clients have rarely sued their attorneys for sexual misconduct. Most of the recorded decisions involve disciplinary actions before state attorney licensing boards. Recently, however, several clients have brought civil lawsuits against their attorneys for damages caused by the attorneys' sexual misconduct.

In 1992 the American Bar Association's Standing Committee on Ethics and Professional Responsibility adopted a formal opinion that advised attorneys to avoid sexual contact with their clients. The committee concluded:

> A sexual relationship between lawyer and client may involve unfair exploitation of the lawyer's fiduciary position, and/or significantly impair a lawyer's ability to represent the client competently, and therefore may violate both the Model Rules of Professional Conduct and the Model Code of Professional Responsibility.[205]

The committee focused on the enhanced risk of impaired decision making on the part of both lawyers and clients due to the effect of the sexual conduct on the fiduciary relationship. It articulated these rules by stating:

> All of the positive characteristics that the lawyer is encouraged to develop so that the client will be confident that he or she is being well served can reinforce a feeling of dependence.... [There exist] a broad range of situations in which the client, by virtue of his or her emotional state, educational level, age or social status, feels particularly dependent and disarmed vis-a-vis the attorney.... Moreover, the client may not feel free to rebuff unwanted sexual advances because of fear that such a rejection will either reduce the lawyer's

ardor for the client's cause or, worse yet, require finding a new lawyer, causing the client to lose the time and money that has already been invested in the present representation.[206]

Acknowledging that no formal disciplinary rule precludes sexual relations between attorneys and clients, the committee nevertheless suggested that, due to the enhanced potential for conflict of interest, impaired judgment, and betrayal of confidences, an existing attorney-client relationship creates a climate in which sexual relations are rarely appropriate. The ABA's position goes further than many previous ethical guidelines in that it contemplates that, aside from the harm that *may* be done to a client's legal cause of action as a result of the sexual relationship, the sexual relationship itself may harm the client if it resulted from "exploitation of the lawyer's dominant position and influence."[207]

While the ABA's opinion leaves existing attorney disciplinary rules unchanged, it is an important acknowledgment that the "intangible factor" of a fiduciary relationship may adversely affect the parties' judgment, even when a client cannot prove impaired judgment or actual legal malpractice. The opinion also acknowledges the existence of what until recently has been called the profession's "dirty little secret," that is, the potentially widespread and underreported instances of sexual exploitation of clients.[208] Admittedly, however, the professional disciplinary rules provide little incentive for either clients or colleagues to report sexual conduct that the ABA has not formally recognized as clearly unethical.[209]

Both courts and state bar associations continue to rely on existing attorney disciplinary rules, which do not expressly prohibit attorney-client sexual relations, to address the most egregious breaches of professional standards. Typically, reviewing authorities view the sexual relationship as giving rise to, or exacerbating departures from, professional conduct expressly condemned by the rules.[210] While several state bar associations have issued advisory opinions or have proposed rules imposing limits on attorney-client sexual involvement,[211] the majority of these rules preclude only sexual relations that lead to or are linked with another distinct type of misconduct, or those that arise out of attorney-client dealings recognized to involve high levels of client vulnerability.

Licensing Board Actions

In *Committee on Professional Ethics v. Durham*,[212] one of the earliest decisions to censure an attorney for inappropriate sexual behavior with a client, the court focused not on whether actual malpractice had compromised the client's legal position but on whether the lawyer had misrepresented her reason for several prison visits during which she had embraced and kissed her incarcerated client.[213] "There was nothing inherently wrong," wrote the court, "with [the attorney's] activities during the visits. If [she] had not been present in a professional capacity, no violation of the Code of Professional Responsibility would have occurred."[214] Durham was ultimately found to have violated Ethical Considerations 1-5 (a lawyer should be temperate and dignified) and 9-6 (avoid the appearance of impropriety) as well as Disciplinary Rule 1-102(A)(6) (avoid engaging in any conduct that adversely reflects on [her] fitness to practice law).[215] Noting that nothing in the court record indicated that Durham's representation of her client was less than competent, the court elected not to follow an administrative recommendation that Durham be temporarily suspended from practice.[216] Instead, the court reprimanded and admonished her in its published opinion, a punishment the court thought less draconian than temporary suspension from practice.[217]

The court stated that attorneys may be held to a higher standard of care than laypersons because of the unique and learned nature of the legal profession.[218] By virtue of her special training, the attorney should have known that "sexual contact with a client in a professional context is not activity which a reasonable member of the bar would suppose to be allowed."[219] The *Durham* opinion therefore suggests that acts of a private nature between "consenting" adults are subject to regulation when one of the adults is an attorney functioning in her professional capacity, *simply because a professional relationship exists.*[220]

Eleven years later, in the *Drucker* case,[221] the reviewing court focused not on the attorney's conduct but on the potential of the attorney's conduct to injure the client. Drucker's client had sought representation in a divorce and immediately confided to him that she was agoraphobic, emotionally fragile, under psychiatric care, and on medications for her anxiety disorder. Having learned this confidential information, Drucker sat down next to her, held her hand, said he too was in a stressful marriage, embraced her, and kissed her. He apologized and said he would refer her to another lawyer, but she declined because she did not want to go through the process of telling another lawyer all the personal information she had just told Drucker.[222]

After that meeting, the client had sexual intercourse with Drucker in his office on three occasions. She was, she testified, "comforted" that her attorney cared for her "because she was so distraught about her home life."[223] When Drucker terminated the sexual relationship, the client "felt that it was another rejection in her life, but [hoped Drucker] would be attracted to her once again."[224]

The court found that Drucker had not committed malpractice in connection with his legal work on the divorce. However, by becoming sexually involved with his client, he had seriously compromised his judgment and his client's emotional well-being.[225] The client was unable "to separate her confidence in [Drucker] as her lawyer from her unrequited love, . . . [a situation that] caused her to take actions in her marriage she might otherwise have avoided."[226] As a result, Drucker caused his client and her family "mental anguish well beyond that normally associated with a difficult divorce," a result that he, as a professional, ought to have foreseen.[227] The court suspended attorney Drucker from practice for a minimum of two years for violating the disciplinary rules related to conflict of interest.[228]

The opinion suggested that the inherent coercive potential of the lawyer-client fiduciary relationship is so great that a sexual relationship in that context may be presumed to be harmful, even though the plaintiff has not proved malpractice or other harm. Because of the sexual relationship, Drucker's client lost the opportunity to make legal and marital choices free from this additional consideration.[229] Moreover, as the client testified, she felt herself to be under considerable pressure to remain in the attorney-client relationship, in spite of the sexual dimension, because she did not want to repeat the process of disclosing painful personal information to another lawyer.[230]

Common Law Negligence Actions

In both *Durham* and *Drucker*, the issue was not whether the lawyer involved would go to prison or pay damages to his or her client but whether the court would allow the lawyer to retain his or her license to practice law. In addition to licensing board actions, clients also have filed lawsuits for money damages.

In *Suppressed v. Suppressed*,[231] the client, a married mother of three, hired the defendant to represent her in a divorce action. On three occasions, first at his office, and later at an apartment, the plaintiff complied with the defendant's requests for sexual intercourse. She later alleged that her compliance was coerced by her fear that the attorney would not advocate for her and her children's interests in her divorce case if she refused to have sex with him.[232] Approximately three months after the plaintiff had hired the defendant as her attorney, she fired him, realizing that his

sexual attentions were not a necessary component of her divorce action
and were in fact contrary to her interests.[233]

The plaintiff subsequently filed a complaint against the lawyer with
the Illinois Attorney Registration and Disciplinary Commission, which
considered the complaint for more than a year and then closed the
investigation without taking any action.[234] She then filed a civil suit for
damages in court, alleging, among other things, that the defendant had
committed professional malpractice by engaging in sexual relations with
her. The court found that no malpractice had taken place and refused
to draw an analogy to cases arising under therapist-patient law. The
court concluded that the fiduciary duty owed by an attorney differs from
that owed by a psychotherapist because there is no danger of an abuse
of transference by the attorney.[235] The plaintiff lost her case once again.

The rationale for the *Suppressed* decision reflects an ingrained institutional reluctance on the part of courts generally to appear to create new
causes of action, even when such "new" causes of action can readily be
inferred from very similar cases involving other professions. "We
would," the court worried, "be creating a new species of legal malpractice action [by] holding that inherent in every attorney-client contract
there is a duty to refrain from intimate personal relationships."[236] The
court further noted that attorneys are as likely as anyone else to become
involved in activities that have "been considered wrong since biblical
times. . . . [They] are after all, human being[s] fraught with all the
frailties that the status entails."[237] The court did suggest, however, that
the client's claim might have succeeded if the attorney had actually
made his professional services contingent upon the sexual involvement
or if his sexual relations with his client had in fact adversely affected his
legal representation of the client.[238] The former allegation could be read
as a crime, the latter as a conflict of interest constituting malpractice.

Doe v. Roe,[239] which alleged sexual coercion in connection with legal
representation, demonstrates the propensity of attorneys to engage in
activities "condemned since biblical times."[240] Of interest, this case was
brought against the same attorney as in *Suppressed*.[241] The case was
dismissed from federal court because the court held that the plaintiff's
federal claim that the defendant had participated in a pattern of rack-
eteering activities was insufficient. Her other claims, which depended
upon state law, were similar to those raised in *Suppressed*.[242]

More recently, a Rhode Island jury found that a male attorney representing a female divorce client had coerced his client to have sexual
relations with him and intentionally inflicted emotional distress.[243] The
plaintiff testified that

she tolerated her lawyer's advances only because she was afraid that if she did not do as he told her, he would lose her case or stop representing her and that she would lose custody of her daughter, have her resident-alien card revoked and be deported to Spain.[244]

As a result of her lawyer's conduct, the plaintiff suffered physical injury and severe emotional distress. Testimony at trial suggested that she would require two years of counseling in addition to the two years she had already spent in therapy to recover from her injury. The jury awarded her $25,000 as compensation for her injuries and an additional $200,000 in punitive damages.[245]

The result in the Canadian case of *Szarfer v. Chodos*[246] comes closest to articulating manageable guidelines for regulating attorney-client sexual contact. In this case, the court found that attorney Chodos breached his fiduciary duty to his client, Mr. Szarfer, by having sex with Szarfer's wife.

Mr. Szarfer originally consulted Chodos in connection with a wrongful dismissal case against his former employer. In preparing for the wrongful dismissal action, Chodos learned from both Mr. and Mrs. Szarfer that the marriage relationship was strained as a result of the plaintiff's failure to obtain work and that the plaintiff and his wife had discussed separation because their interests were no longer the same.[247] Chodos was also aware that Mr. Szarfer suffered from other difficulties relating to his financial situation, past injury, lack of employment, and anxiety attacks and was aware that Mr. Szarfer was under psychotherapeutic care.[248] Mr. Chodos previously employed Mrs. Szarfer as a temporary legal secretary, and she worked with Chodos to prepare documents for her husband's case. Chodos and Mrs. Szarfer eventually began a sexual liaison that lasted until the day Mr. Szarfer saw his lawyer and his wife leaving a hotel elevator.

The day after he discovered the affair, Mr. Szarfer was hospitalized. He was discharged nine days later with a diagnosis of "neurotic depression with hysterical features" and returned home, where he subsequently attacked his wife with a knife.[249] At trial, expert testimony established that Mr. Szarfer's discovery of the affair was a severe traumatic blow that caused a posttraumatic neurosis.[250]

After hearing the evidence presented, the judge found that Chodos had violated his fiduciary duty as Mr. Szarfer's lawyer by misusing confidential information to "obtain [for himself] the delights and benefits of the affair."[251] The fiduciary relationship between a lawyer and his client, wrote the court, forbids a lawyer from using any confidential information obtained by him for the benefit of himself or a third person *or to the disadvantage of his client*. . . . It is conceded that the defendant was in a fiduciary relationship with the plaintiff and owed him all the duties of a fiduciary. The highest and clearest duty of a fiduciary is to act to advance the beneficiary's interest and avoid acting to his detriment. A fiduciary cannot permit his own interest to come into conflict with the interest of the beneficiary of the relationship.[252]

The court did not focus its analysis on the nexus between the scope of the fiduciary relationship and the conduct about which the plaintiff complained. Instead, the court's reasoning presupposed that *all* of the fiduciary's activities (affecting his client either personally or in business matters) were constrained by the existing relationship.[253] The court stated that "once the fiduciary relationship is established, as it is in this case, the onus is on the trustee to prove that he acted reasonably and made no personal use whatsoever of the confidential information."[254] This, the judge decided, Chodos had failed to do.

CONCLUSION

This chapter has examined the law's growing recognition that sexual relations between fiduciaries and their clients or patients can cause harm. As a result of professionals' breach of their fiduciary duties, patients and clients have experienced a wide range of physical and psychological injuries. Courts, legislatures, and licensing boards have begun to provide redress for these injuries by allowing injured parties to recover on various legal grounds. Additionally, courts have interpreted statutes of limitations, insurance policy exclusions, and other barriers to recovery to provide injured patients and clients with a more realistic chance of compensation or retribution.

As the law continues to recognize the harm that sexual misconduct by fiduciaries causes, more individuals will be encouraged to come forward and tell their stories, so that they may receive compensation for their injuries and begin the path to recovery.

NOTES

1. Gartrell, N., et al. (1986). A survey of physicians' attitudes & practices regarding erotic and nonerotic contact with patients. *American Journal of Psychiatry, 143*, 1126: a

nationwide survey estimating that 7% to 12% of therapists have had sexual contact with one or more patients.

2. Gartrell, N., et al. (1992). Physician-patient sexual contact: Prevalence and problems. *Western Journal of Medicine, 157*, 139. See also Kardener, S., et al. (1973). A survey of physicians' attitudes & practices regarding erotic and nonerotic contact with patients. *American Journal of Psychiatry, 130*, 1077.

3. Pitulla, J. (1992, November). Unfair advantage. *ABA Journal*, pp. 76-80.

4. Pope, K., et al. (1986). Sexual attraction to clients: The human therapist and the (sometimes) inhuman training system. *American Psychologist, 41*, 147.

5. Pope, K. (1986). Research & laws regarding therapist-patient sexual involvement: Implications for therapists. *American Journal of Psychotherapy, 40*(4), 564.

6. See Kardener et al., supra note 2, at 1077-1081.

7. See idem.

8. Gartrell, N., et al. (1986). Psychiatrist-patient sexual contact: Results of a national survey, I: Prevalence. *American Journal of Psychiatry, 143*, 1126-1131.

9. Bernard, J. L., et al. (1992, November). Dangerous liaisons. *ABA Journal*, p. 82.

10. Bouhoutsos, J., et al. (1983). Sexual intimacy between psychotherapists and patients. *Professional Psychology: Research and Practice, 14*, 185.

11. See Gartrell, supra note 8 (87% harmed).

12. See Pope, K. S., & Bouhoutsos, J. (1986). *Sexual intimacy between therapists and patients.* Westport, CT: Praeger. Also, Vinson, J. (1984). *Sexual contact with psychotherapists: A study of client reactions and complaint procedures.* Unpublished doctoral dissertation, California School of Professional Psychology.

13. Schoener, G. R., et al. (1989). *Psychotherapists' sexual involvement with clients.* Minneapolis, MN: Walk-In Counseling Center, pp. 142-143.

14. See Collins, D. T., et al. (1978). Patient-therapist sex: Consequences for subsequent treatment. *McLean Hospital Journal, 3*, 24.

15. College of Physicians and Surgeons of British Columbia. (1992). *Crossing the boundaries: The report of the Committee on Physician Sexual Misconduct.* Vancouver, B.C.: Author. Also, College of Physicians and Surgeons of Ontario, Task Force on Sexual Abuse of Patients. (1991). *Final report of the Task Force on Sexual Abuse of Patients.* Toronto, Ontario: Author.

16. See Gartrell et al., supra note 2, at 139-143.

17. Wilbers, D., et al. (1992). Sexual contact in the doctor-patient relationship in the Netherlands. *British Medical Journal, 304*(6841), 1531.

18. Feldman-Summers, S., & Jones, G. (1984). Psychological impacts of sexual contact between therapists or other health care practitioners and their clients. *Journal of Counseling & Clinical Psychology, 52*, 1054.

19. Jorgenson, L., & Sutherland, P. (1992). Fiduciary theory applied to personal dealings: Attorney-client sexual contact. *Arkansas Law Review, 45*, 459.

20. Gutheil, T., et al. (1992). Prohibiting lawyer-client sex. *Bulletin of the American Academy of Psychiatry & Law, 20*, 365.

21. See generally Jorgenson, L., et al. (1981). The furor over psychotherapist-patient sexual contact: New solutions to an old problem. *William and Mary Law Review, 32*(2), 645-732, at nn. 2-5.

22. Council of Ethical & Judicial Affairs of the American Medical Association. (1989). *Current opinions of the Council of Ethical & Judicial Affairs,* Opinion 8.14.

23. ABA Committee on Ethics and Professional Responsibility, Formal Opinion 92-364 (1992).

24. *Webster's Third International Dictionary* (unabridged). (1981).
25. See generally Jorgenson et al., supra note 21, at nn. 37-39.
26. 366 N.Y.S.2d 297 (Civ. Ct. 1975).
27. Idem at 298.
28. Idem at 300.
29. Idem at 301.
30. See, e.g., *Simmons v. U.S.*, 805 F.2d 1363 (9th Cir. 1986); *Horak v. Biris*, 474 N.E.2d 13 (1985).
31. 138 N.R. 81; 92 D.L.R. 4th 449; 34 A.C.W.S. (3d) 705 (1992).
32. 138 N.R. at 89.
33. Idem at 143-154 (McLachlin, J.), 177-182 (Sopinka, J.).
34. Idem at 116.
35. Idem at 112 (quoting from Ontario, College of Physicians and Surgeons, Task Force on Sexual Abuse of Patients, *The final report*, p. 11 (November 25, 1991).
36. Idem at 122-124.
37. 193 Cal. Rptr. 422 (Cal. App. 1983).
38. Idem at 426.
39. Idem.
40. Idem.
41. Idem.
42. Idem.
43. Idem at 432.
44. Idem.
45. Smith, J. (1986). *Medical malpractice: Psychiatric care*, sec. 1.04. Colorado Springs, CO: Shepherd's/McGraw-Hill.
46. *Bunce v. Parkside Lodge of Columbus*, 596 N.E.2d 1106, 1111 (Ohio App. 1991).
47. See, e.g., *Simmons v. U.S.*, 805 F.2d 1363 (9th Cir. 1986).
48. See, e.g., *Koren v. Weihs*, 1994 N.Y. App. Div. LEXIS 815, (Feb. 1, 1994), denying summary judgment for defendant and finding a possible departure from accepted standards of medical care because defendant had been decedent's psychiatrist and possessed detailed knowledge of her history, therefore the risk of decedent's suicide as a consequence of defendant's sexual relationship with her was not attenuated or unforeseeable.
49. 436 S.W.2d 753 (Mo. 1968).
50. Idem at 761.
51. Idem. See also Jorgenson, L., & Sutherland, P. (in press). *Liability of physicians, therapists and other health professionals for sexual misconduct with patients*. The authors state, "Therapists may also deviate from standards of care in ways other than mishandling transference. Improper regression techniques, such as those alleged in the recent Bean-Bayog case, also constitute negligence. Other acts of negligence may include a therapist's improper use of hypnosis, improper use of drugs or alcohol with a patient, failure to appropriately refer, and wrongful termination or abandonment of patients." Idem.
52. 436 S.W.2d at 758.
53. See *Simmons v. United States*, 805 F.2d 1363 (9th Cir. 1986).
54. See generally Simon, R. (1991). Psychological injury caused by boundary violation precursor to therapist-patient sex. *Psychiatric Annals, 21*, 614.
55. See *Hammond v. Lane*, 515 N.E.2d 828, 829-30 (Ill. App. 1987), holding that the plaintiff had to show that she was in fear for her own safety.
56. 770 P.2d 278 (Cal. 1989).

57. Idem at 283.
58. Idem.
59. 243 Cal. Rptr. 807 (Cal. App. 1988).
60. Idem at 810. See also *Rowe v. Bennett*, 514 A.2d 802 (Me. 1986): patient stated a claim for negligent infliction of emotional distress based on defendant social worker's involvement with the patient's partner.
61. 243 Cal. Rptr. at 809.
62. *Sullivan v. Boston Gas Co.*, 605 N.E.2d 805 (1993). But see *Shamloo v. Lifespring, Inc.*, 713 F. Supp. 14, 19 (D.D.C. 1989) ("a plaintiff cannot recover for negligently [inflicted] psychological injuries which do not result from physical injury").
63. See Simon, R. (1985). Sexual misconduct of therapists: A cause for civil and criminal action. *Trial, 21*, 46.
64. Prosser, W., & Keeton, W. *The law of torts*, sec. 9 at 39 (5th ed. 1984).
65. *See Restatement (Second) of Torts*, sec. 46(1) (1965).
66. 584 A.2d 69 (Md. 1991).
67. Idem at 77.
68. 748 P.2d 1020 (Or. App. 1988).
69. Idem at 1023-1024.
70. *DiLeo v. Nugent*, 592 A.2d 1126, 1134 (Md. App. 1991) (citing *Smith v. Rosenthal Toyota, Inc.*, 573 A.2d 418, 1990).
71. 592 A.2d 1126 (Md. App. 1991).
72. Idem at 1134.
73. See, e.g., *Sullivan v. O'Connor*, 363 Mass. 579 (1973).
74. 236 So.2d. 256 (Fla. Dist. Ct. App. 1972).
75. Idem at 257.
76. 748 P.2d 1020 (Or. App. 1988).
77. 698 S.W.2d 94 (Tex. 1985).
78. 537 N.Y.S.2d 446 (Sup.Ct.1988).
79. See generally Appelbaum, P., & Jorgenson, L. (1991, November). Psychotherapist-patient sexual contact after termination of treatment: An analysis and a proposal. *American Journal of Psychiatry, 148*, 11.
80. 537 N.Y.S. 2d at 448.
81. See, e.g., *Duffee v. Boston Elevated Ry.*, 77 N.E. 1036 (1906).
82. *Norton v. McFarland*, 818 P.2d 8 (Utah 1991).
83. See, e.g., M.G.L.A. c.207, sec. 47B as amended by St. 1985, sec. 1.
84. But see *Spiess v. Johnson*, 748 P. 2d 1020 (Or. App. 1988), applying theory of intentional infliction of emotional distress in spouses' claims against therapists.
85. 599 A.2d 1193 (Md. App. 1992).
86. Idem at 1198. See also *Harrington v. Pages*, 440 So.2d 521 (Fla. App. 1983): Florida Statute barring sexual misconduct by physicians created no right for husband to sue on what amounted to an alienation of affection theory. But see *Anclote Manor Foundation v. Wilkinson*, 263 So.2d. 256 (1972), recovery of fees paid to therapist permitted.
87. 300 S.E.2d 833 (N.C. Ct. App. 1983).
88. Idem at 838.
89. 584 A.2d 69 (Md. 1991).
90. Idem at 75.
91. This decision effectively overruled the earlier decision *Gasper v. Lighthouse, Inc.*, 533 A.2d 1358 (Md. App. 1987) in which the court held that the real basis of a husband's

claim against a therapist was the alienation of affections of his wife, a cause of action precluded in Maryland. Idem.

92. Idem.

93. Idem (emphasis added). A similar point is made in *Strock v. Presnell*, 527 N.E.2d 1235 (1988) (Sweeney, J., dissenting) ("This case does not resemble your garden variety seduction scenario. The wife did not get involved with the milkman, the mailman or the guy next door. Here, the couple's minister, under the guise of offering pastoral counselling services, abused the trust placed in him.").

94. Minn. Stat. Ann. sec. 148A (West 1993).

95. Ill. Ann. Stat. ch. 70, secs. 801-802 (Smith-Hurd 1992).

96. Senate Bill 210, engrossed May 22, 1993.

97. Cal. Civ. Code sec.43.93 (West 1993).

98. Wis. Stat. Ann. sec. 895.70(2) (West 1992).

99. See generally Jorgenson et al., supra note 21, at 703, asserting that "this type of statute is an improvement over the common law because it creates clarity and uniformity by prohibiting sexual relations in a therapeutic setting" and that "under common law, a plaintiff must still prove with expert testimony the proper standard of care and that the defendant's action fell below it."

100. Minn. Stat. Ann. sec. 148A.02; see Ill. Ann. Stat. ch. 70, sec. 802; Texas S.B. 210 art. 2.

101. Cal. Civ. Code sec. 43.94(a)(2) (West Supp. 1991); Wis. Stat. Ann. sec. 895.70(2) (West Supp. 1991); Texas S.B. 210 sec. 2.01-02.

102. Wis. Stat. Ann. sec. 895.70(2) (West 1992) (emphasis added).

103. Colo. Rev. Stat. sec. 12-43-704(q) (1992); Wis. Stat. Ann. sec. 895.70(2) (West 1988); Ill. Stat. Ann. ch. 70 sec. 801 (Smith-Hurd Supp. 1989); Minn. Stat. sec. 148A (West 1985); Texas S.B. 210 sec. 2.01-02.

104. Minn. Stat. Ann. sec. 148A.01(7) (West 1989): kissing on the mouth is not prohibited, nor is the screening of salacious films. See generally Jorgenson et al., supra note 21, at 705, arguing that the civil definition of sexual contact need not be as specific as the criminal to meet constitutional requirements; rather, "by restricting the range of prohibited behavior only to that which is also criminal, the statute[s] cannot cover even extremely sadistic acts in which touching of the genitals or other specified body parts does not occur."

105. Cal. Bus. & Prof. Code sec. 729 (West 1993); Colo. Rev. Stat. sec. 18-3-405.5 (1992); Conn. Gen. Stat. secs. 53a-65, 71, 73a (1993); Fla. Stat. Ann. secs. 491.0111-491.0112 (West 1993); Ga. Code Ann. sec. 16-6-5.1 (1992); Iowa Code Ann. sec. 709.15 (West 1992); Me. Rev. Stat. Ann. tit. 17A, sec. 253(2)(I) (1992); Minn. Stat. Ann. sec. 609.341 et seq. (West 1993); N.D. Cent. Code sec. 12.1-20-06.1 (1991); N.H. Rev. Stat. Ann. sec. 632-A:2(I)(g) (1992); N.M. Stat. Ann. secs. 30-9-10 through 30-9-16 (effective 1993); S.D. S.B. 236, enacted 1993; Tex. S.B. 210, engrossed, May 22, 1993; Wis. Stat. Ann. sec. 940.22(2) (West 1992).

106. Colo. Rev. Stat. secs. 18-3-403(h) to 18-3-404(g) (1986); Mich. Comp. Laws Ann. sec. 750.520b(1)(f)(iv) (West Supp. 1990); N.H. Rev. Stat. Ann. sec. 632-A:2(I) (g)(Supp. 1992); R.I. Gen. Laws sec. 11-37-2(D) (Supp. 1989); Wyo. Stat. sec. 6-2-303(a)(vii) (1988).

107. *State v. vonKlock*, 433 A.2d 1299, 1302 (N.H. 1981), *rev'd on other grounds* 503 A.2d 774 (N.H. 1985). Other states' similar statutes could likewise be construed to encompass the sexually assaultive behavior of mental health professionals.

108. Ala. Code sec. 13A-6-65; Mich. Comp. Laws Ann. sec. 750.90 (West 1968).

109. Wyo. Stat. sec. 6-2-303(a)(vi) (1988).

110. Colo. Rev. Stat. sec. 18-3-405.5(4)(c) (Supp. 1989); Conn. Gen. Stat. secs. 53a-71, 73a (1993); Fla. Session Law Serv. ch. 90-70 sec. 1(4)(a) (West); Ga. Code Ann. sec. 16-6-5.1 (1992); Iowa Code Ann. sec. 709.15 (West 1992) (it also describes some conduct as aggravated misdemeanors); Me. Rev. Stat. Ann. tit. 17A, sec. 253(2)(I) (1992); Minn. Stat. Ann. sec. 609.341 et seq. (West 1993); N.D. Cent. Code sec. 12.1-20-06.1(1) (1991); N.H. Rev. Stat. Ann. 632-A:2(I)(g) (1992); N.M. Stat. Ann. secs. 30-9-10 through 30-9-16 (effective 1993); S.D. S.B. 236, enacted 1993; Tex. S.B. 210 (1993); Wis. Stat. Ann. sec. 940.22(2) (West 1992). The Colorado statute was recently upheld on a constitutional challenge in *Ferguson v. State*, 824 P.2d 803 (Colo. 1992).

111. Cal. Bus. & Prof. Code sec. 729 (West Supp. 1989); Colo. Rev. Stat. sec. 18-3-405.5(4)(c) (Supp. 1989); Conn. Gen. Stat. secs. 53a-71, 73a (1993); Fla. Session Law Serv. ch. 90-70 sec. 1(4)(a) (West); Ga. Code Ann. sec. 16-6-5.1 (1992); Iowa Code Ann. sec. 709.15 (West 1992) (it also describes some conduct as aggravated misdemeanors); Minn. Stat. Ann. sec. 609.341 et seq. (West 1993); N.D. Cent. Code sec. 12.1-20-06.1(1) (1991); N.H. Rev. Stat. Ann. 632-A:2(I)(g) (1992); N.M. Stat. Ann. secs. 30-9-10 through 30-9-16 (effective 1993); S.D. S.B. 236, enacted 1993; Tex. S.B. 210 (1993); Wis. Stat. Ann. sec. 940.22(2) (West 1992).

112. Colo. Rev. Stat. sec. 18-3-405.5(4)(c) (Supp. 1989); Conn. Gen. Stat. secs. 53a-71, 73a (1993); Fla. Session Law Serv. ch. 90-70 sec. 1(4)(a) (West); Ga. Code Ann. sec. 16-6-5.1 (1992); Iowa Code Ann. sec. 709.15 (West 1992); Me. Rev. Stat. Ann. tit. 17A, sec. 253(2)(I) (1992); Minn. Stat. Ann. sec. 609.341 et seq. (West 1993); N.D. Cent. Code sec. 12.1-20-06.1(1) (1991); N.H. Rev. Stat. Ann. 632-A:2(I)(g) (1992); S.D. S.B. 236, enacted 1993; Tex. S.B. 210 (1993); Wis. Stat. Ann. sec. 940.22(2) (West 1992).

113. Consent is not a defense in California, Colorado, Florida, Georgia, Minnesota, New Hampshire, New Mexico, North Dakota, South Dakota, Texas, or Wisconsin. California imposes misdemeanor penalties on therapist-patient sexual contact, while Iowa imposes felony penalties for sexual contact with two or more patients or former patients, and misdemeanor penalties for sexual contact with one patient or former patient.

114. California, Connecticut, Florida, Iowa, Minnesota, New Mexico, and Texas.

115. See, e.g., Colo. Rev. Stat. sec. 13-25-131 (1991) and 18-3-408 (1991).

116. See Strasburger, L., et al. (1990). Mandatory reporting of sexually exploitative psychotherapists. *Bulletin of the American Academy of Psychiatry & Law, 18,* 379, discussing mandatory and anonymous reporting statutes.

117. Texas S.B. No. 210 sec. 81.006 (1993).

118. Colo. Rev. Stat. secs. 12-43-708 (b) and (c) (1988): the licensing statute does not regulate psychiatrists.

119. Wis. Stat. Ann. sec. 895.70(5) (West 1992).

120. See Jorgenson, L., & Randles, R. M. (1991). *Time out: The statute of limitations and fiduciary theory in psychotherapist sexual misconduct cases.* Also, *Oklahoma Law Review, 44,* 181, discussing policy reasons underlying statutes of limitation. Finally, Appelbaum, P., & Jorgenson, L. (1991, July). For whom the statute tolls: Extending the time during which patients can sue. *Hospital and Community Psychiatry, 42(7),* 683.

121. See idem at 187.

122. In *Lovelace v. Keohane*, 831 P.2d 624 (Okla. 1992): Plaintiff's claim that she had been sexually molested by a priest was barred because the case had not been timely filed.

123. See Jorgenson & Randles, supra note 120, at 205; *Greenberg v. McCabe*, 453 F.Supp. 765 (E.D. Pa. 1978): "Ayers' claim could not be barred because the defendant's conduct set in motion objective 'laws of nature' which prevented Mr. Ayers from ascertaining the cause of his abdominal pain: since defendant had sewn him up as part of the treatment,

'he could not open his abdomen like a door and look in' to discover the cause of his pain." Idem at 769, quoting from *Ayers v. Morgan*, 154 A.2d 788, 792 (1959).

124. Idem at 206.

125. 565 N.E.2d 780 (Mass. 1991).

126. Idem at 783.

127. Idem.

128. Idem.

129. Idem at 784.

130. Idem at 784.

131. Idem.

132. Idem at 786. See also *Shamloo v. Lifespring, Inc.*, 713 F. Supp. 14 (D.D.C. 1989). The plaintiff alleged that the psychological effects of the defendant's program prevented her "from realizing the nature and source of her problems during the years following her participation in Lifespring's training." Idem at 16. The court decided that the discovery rule applied to her case because "it might be flatly *unreasonable* to expect a person with psychological problems to identify *one* cause, injury or emotional trauma as *the* reason for a prolonged disorder. . . . Although the plaintiff was aware of [her mental] conditions, it is unreasonable to impute knowledge of an injury, or knowledge of a causal link with defendant's business on that basis." Idem at 18, n. 4. The court's reasoning in this case does not link the plaintiff's injured state of mind to the actions of the defendant, as was done in *Riley v. Presnell*.

133. *Riley v. Presnell*, 565 N.E.2d 780, 786 (Mass. 1991).

134. 568 N.Y.S.2d 250 (N.Y. App. Div. 1991).

135. Idem at 251.

136. Idem.

137. 565 N.E.2d 780 (Mass. 1991).

138. See generally *Ewing v. Beck*, 520 A.2d 653 (Del. 1987) and cases cited therein.

139. See generally idem, *The Law of Torts*, sec. 67.

140. 592 A.2d 1126 (Md. App. 1991).

141. Idem at 1133.

142. Idem.

143. See generally Jorgenson, L., et al. (1992). Therapist-patient sexual exploitation and insurance liability. *Tort & Insurance Law Journal*, 27, 595.

144. 436 S.W.2d 753 (Mo. 1968).

145. Idem at 754.

146. 300 N.W.2d 627 (1981).

147. Idem at 628.

148. Idem at 628-629.

149. 362 N.W.2d 174 (1984).

150. Idem at 175.

151. Idem at 178.

152. 805 F.2d 1363 (9th Cir. 1986).

153. Idem.

154. Idem at 1365.

155. Idem.

156. See, e.g., *St. Paul Fire & Marine Ins. Co. v. Mitchell*, 296 S.E.2d 126, 129 (Ga. Ct. App. 1982).

157. See *L. L. v. Medical Protective Co.*, 362 N.W.2d 174 (Wis. App. 1984).

158. See *St. Paul Fire & Marine Ins. Co. v. Love*, 459 N.W.2d 698, 701 (Minn. 1990). See also *Simmons v. United States*, 805 F.2d 1363, 1366 (9th Cir. 1986).

159. 459 N.W.2d at 698.

160. 362 N.W.2d 174 (Wis. App. 1984).

161. Idem at 178.

162. Idem.

163. 319 N.W.2d 382 (1982).

164. Idem at 385.

165. See generally Jorgenson et al., supra note 143.

166. See also *Aetna Ins. Co. v. McCabe*, 556 F.Supp. 1342 (E.D. Pa. 1983), articulating a similar test.

167. *Vigilant Ins. Co. v. Kambly*, 319 N.W.2d 382 (1982).

168. 319 N.W.2d 382 (1982).

169. Idem at 385.

170. 459 N.W.2d 698, 702 (Minn. 1990).

171. Idem.

172. See Jorgenson et al., supra note 143, at 607 ("Most likely, the rationale supporting the court's enforcement of liability exclusions would be equally applicable to the caps.") See also Jorgenson, L., & Sutherland, P. (1993, May). Psychotherapist liability: What's sex got to do with it? *Trial Magazine, 29*(5), 22 (used with permission). The authors state: "Exclusionary clauses and limits on insurers' liability may be challenged on several traditional grounds: they are ambiguous, they are contrary to public policy, they take unconscionable advantage of an insured, and they are contrary to the reasonable expectations of the insured or third-party beneficiaries. . . . Arguments regarding unconscionable advantage and the reasonable expectations of the insured or third-party beneficiaries may be made if the insurer . . . refuses to provide complete coverage for other negligence when sexual misconduct is alleged." Idem at 23.

173. 879 F.2d 1581 (8th Cir. 1989).

174. Idem at 1582.

175. Idem.

176. Idem at 1582-1583. See also *Sphere Insurance Co. v. Rosen*, No. 85-2654 (E.D. Pa. May 16, 1986) (WESTLAW 1986 WL 5721), denying coverage because the plaintiff's complaint suggested "undue familiarity, sexual intimacy, or assault concomitant therewith," which were excluded from coverage under the defendant's policy.

177. 645 F. Supp. 1440 (N.D. Cal. 1986).

178. Idem at 1442.

179. Idem at 1444 (emphasis added). See also Jorgenson et al., supra note 143, at 609 ("The concept of 'concurrent proximate causation' developed within the context of homeowner's and automobile insurance policies.") Cases are collected at 609, nn. 104-110.

180. 815 F. Supp. 365 (W.D. Wash. 1993).

181. Idem at 366-367.

182. Idem at 367.

183. Idem at 369.

184. Idem at 371-372.

185. Idem at 371-372.

186. See *West American Ins. Co. v. Chateau Mer II Homeowners Assoc., Inc.*, 622 So.2d 1105, 1993 Fla. App. LEXIS 8317, 9-10 (Fla. App. 1993), stating that the Florida Appellate Court approved a jury instruction that imposed upon the insurer the burden of proving that the excluded event was the sole, proximate cause of the injury; *United States Fire Ins.*

Co. v. Reynolds, 667 S.W.2d 664, 666 (Ark. App. 1984), quoting Appleman, *Insurance Law and Practice*, vol. 7A at 4501.10 (edited by Berdal, 1979, St. Paul, MN: West): burden of proof on insurer to show injury caused by excepted event.

187. Council on Ethical & Judicial Affairs, American Medical Association. (1991). Sexual misconduct in the practice of medicine. *JAMA*, *266*, 2741.

188. See, e.g., *Perez v. Bd. of Reg. for the Healing Arts*, 803 S.W.2d 160 (Mo. App. 1991): A woman having difficulty becoming pregnant sought counseling, artificial insemination, and other medical treatment by an obstetrician/gynecologist who specialized in infertility. Thereafter she had sexual relations with the doctor for six months. She later became pregnant and continued to see the doctor for another five years. The Board of Medicine found that the physician had violated the disciplinary rules by engaging in "dishonorable, unethical or unprofessional conduct of a character likely to deceive, defraud or harm the public." His license was suspended for two months followed by five years' probation. *Gromis v. Medical Bd. of Cal.*, 10 Cal. Rptr. 452 (Cal. Ct. App. 1992): Court held that there was a possibility that the doctor had misused his status as a physician to induce his patient into the relationship and had failed to refer the patient for counseling because of the existing sexual relationship.

189. 239 Cal. Rptr. 454 (1987).

190. Idem at 457.

191. See, e.g., *Jennings v. Friedman*, 875 F.2d 864 (6th Cir. 1989) (unpublished opinion), dismissing the plaintiff's malpractice claim for sexual misconduct, holding that the critical inquiry was whether a physician engaged in sexual relations with a patient under the guise of rendering professional services.

192. 705 S.W.2d 727 (Tex. App. 1986).

193. Idem at 731.

194. Idem at 733.

195. Idem at 729.

196. Idem at 731.

197. 353 N.W.2d 130 (Minn. 1984). But see *St. Paul Fire & Marine Ins. Co. v. Asbury*, 720 P.2d 540 (Ariz. 1986).

198. 353 N.W.2d at 132 (Minn. 1984); see also *St. Paul Ins. Co. of Illinois v. Cromeans*, 771 F.Supp. 349 (N.D. Ala. 1991), acts of masturbation in patients' presence and fondling patients held to be intentional acts excluded from policy coverage; *Collins v. Covenant Mutual Ins. Co.*, 604 N.E.2d 1190 (Ind. App. 1992); *Roe v. Federal Ins. Co.*, 412 Mass. 43 (1992), sexual relationship between patient and dentist not covered by policy because the only link between misconduct and treatment was that the misconduct took place in the dentist's office; *St. Paul Fire & Marine Ins. Co. v. Mori*, 486 N.W.2d 803 (Minn. App. 1992), sexual assault by gynecologist not covered by professional malpractice policy; *Snyder v. Major*, 789 F. Supp. 646 (S.D.N.Y. 1992), sexual relations with partially sedated patient are not a medical incident for insurance purposes; *Washington Insurance Guaranty Assoc. v. Hicks*, 744 P.2d 625 (Wash. App. 1987), chiropractor's insurance did not cover sexual assault of a patient because the assault was not part of the professional services rendered by the chiropractor.

199. *Smith v. St. Paul Fire & Marine Ins. Co.*, 353 N.W.2d at 133. 202.720 P.2d 540 (Ariz. 1986).

200. 720 P.2d 540 (Ariz. 1986).

201. The same judgment was reached on similar facts in *St. Paul Fire & Marine Ins. Co. v. Couch*, 1990 WL 120722 (Tenn. App. 1990).

202. 610 A.2d 1281 (Conn. 1992).

203. Idem.

204. See supra notes 94-115 and accompanying discussion.

205. ABA Committee on Ethics and Professional Responsibility, Formal Opinion 92-364 (1992). See also Jorgenson, L., & Sutherland, P. (1992). Lawyers' sex with clients: Proposal for a uniform standard. *Fairshare, 12,* 11.

206. ABA Committee on Ethics and Professional Responsibility, Formal Opinion 92-364, at 5-8 (1992).

207. Idem at 3.

208. *In re Kantar,* 581 N.E.2d 6, 12 (Ill. App. Ct. 1991). See also Gutheil et al., supra note 20, at 367-368 (citation omitted). The authors found that "preliminary results of a study conducted by researchers at Memphis State University reveal that 31 percent of attorneys surveyed knew other attorneys who had been sexually involved with their clients; only 6% reported their own sexual involvement with clients." Idem; Jorgenson, L., & Sutherland, P. (1992, June 15). Attorneys' sexual conduct with clients: An informal survey. *National Law Journal,* pp. 26-27. The authors made an informal request for information from state bar associations and found that only 90 complaints alleging attorney sexual misconduct were filed over a two-year period. Idem. See also Jorgenson & Sutherland, supra note 19, at 463-466, n. 11 (surveying state bar associations). The authors state, "The vast majority of attorneys and bar associations hold the opinion, however, that sexual contact between attorneys and their clients is not a problem. . . . Attorneys tend to turn their heads from colleagues' sexual liaisons with clients, just as mental health professionals did two decades ago." Idem at 462-463.

209. See Hazard, G., Jr. (1992, April 15). Lawyer-client sex relations are taboo. *National Law Journal,* p. 13, asserting that clients who report attorney-client sexual relations face more humiliation and possibly embarrassing publicity.

210. The following duties are derived from directives and ethical guidelines in the ABA's *Model Code of Professional Responsibility* (1980) and *Model Rules of Professional Conduct* (1991) (as adopted by the regulatory organizations of individual states) and are frequently referenced in disciplinary proceedings and court cases involving attorney sexual misconduct: "a. Duty not to breach fiduciary obligation: 'A lawyer shall not use information relating to representation of a client to the disadvantage of a client unless the client consents after consultation.' Model Rule 1.8(b); '[A] lawyer shall not knowingly . . . use a confidence or secret of his client to the disadvantage of the client [or u]se a confidence or secret of his client for the advantage of himself or of a third person, unless the client consents after full disclosure.'" *Model Code of Professional Responsibility DR 4-101 (B)(2) and (3).*

211. See Jorgenson & Sutherland, supra note 19, at 460-463, nn. 4-9, 470, n. 26.

212. 279 N.W.2d 280 (Iowa 1979).

213. Idem at 285.

214. Idem.

215. Idem.

216. Idem.

217. Idem at 286. The Court disagreed with the argument from the National Lawyer's Guild, which raised the constitutional concern that the professional standards of "temperance, dignity and propriety," when used to evaluate the impropriety of Durham's sexual conduct, were too vague a guideline to permit Durham to regulate her conduct. *Committee on Professional Ethics v. Durham,* 279 N.W.2d 280, 285 (Iowa, 1979).

218. Idem at 284.

219. Idem.

220. Idem at 285.
221. 577 A.2d 1198 (N.H. 1990).
222. Idem at 1200.
223. Idem.
224. Idem at 1199.
225. See, e.g., the *Bourdon* case, 565 A.2d 1052, 1054 (N.H. 1989): "[The attorney] knew, or ought to have known that [his client's affair with him] might have become an issue in the divorce . . . [and] might have an influence on the court's decision as to child custody."
226. 577 A.2d at 1199.
227. Idem at 1203.
228. "The respondent violated three Rules of professional Conduct: Rule 1.7(b), by representing a client when the representation was materially limited by his own sexual interest in the client; Rule 1.8(b), by using information about the client's fragile emotional state and mental disorder to her disadvantage by engaging in sexual relations with her, leading her to suffer emotional turmoil; and Rule 1.14(a), by failing to maintain a normal attorney-client relationship with the client knowing she was in a fragile emotional state and had a diagnosed mental disability." Idem at 1198-1199.
229. See also *In re Gibson*, 369 N.W.2d 695 (1985): "The public must not be subjected to unsolicited sexual conduct by attorneys in the context of an attorney-client relationship. Frequently, the client is in some difficulty and, as a result, is particularly vulnerable to improper advances made by the attorney. The client rightfully looks upon the attorney as legal advisor, one who will act in the client's best interests. Often, a client will be reluctant to terminate representation in response to an attorney's improper conduct for fear of losing time and money already invested in the attorney's representation. . . . The attorney stands in a fiduciary relationship with the client and should exercise professional judgment 'solely for the benefit of the client and free from compromising influences and loyalties.' By making unsolicited sexual advances to a client, an attorney perverts the very essence of the lawyer-client relationship." Idem at 699-700. Jorgenson & Sutherland, supra note 19, at 500: "Existing ethical code sections cover legal services rendered incompetently, but they fail to account for the fiduciary nature of the attorney-client relationship and fail to address harms to the client other than poor legal services."
230. 577 A.2d 1198 (N.H. 1990). See also *Carter v. Kritz*, 560 A.2d 360 (R.I. 1989), noting special vulnerability of clients.
231. 565 N.E.2d 101 (Ill. App. 1990), *appeal denied*, 571 N.E. 2d 156 (Ill. 1991).
232. Idem at 103.
233. Idem.
234. Idem.
235. Idem at 105, n. 2, stating: "It appears that, when imposing liability upon a psychotherapist for malpractice, courts have relied upon the fact that the psychological dependency of a patient undergoing therapy often results in a medically recognized phenomenon known as 'transference,' whereby the patient transfers feelings to the therapist. The mishandling of this phenomenon by a trained therapist, resulting in sexual involvement with the patient, has been deemed malpractice." But see Shaffer, T. (1970). Undue influence, confidential relationship, and the psychology of transference. *Notre Dame Law Review, 45*, 197, 218: "The transference itself is a perfectly natural phenomenon which does not by any means happen only in the consulting room—it can be seen everywhere and may lead to all sorts of nonsense" (quoting C. Jung, *Collected Works of Carl Jung*, 2nd ed. 1966; Gutheil et al., supra note 20, at 368: "The harm caused by an attorney's sexual intimacy with a client or client's spouse is similar to harm caused patients by therapist

sexual conduct. The similar harms may result from similarities in the relationships"). Jorgenson & Sutherland, supra note 19, at 483: "Transference is likely to exist in any professional relationship in which good rapport has been established and in which there is a degree of trust, confidence and good faith placed on the person in a position of relative authority."

236. *Suppressed v. Suppressed*, 565 N.E.2d 101, 104 (Ill. App. 1 Dist. 1990), *appeal denied*, 571 N.E.2d 156 (Ill. 1991).

237. Idem at 104-105.

238. Idem at 105.

239. 756 F. Supp. 353 (N.D. Ill. 1991), *aff'd*, 958 F.2d 763 (7th Cir. 1992).

240. 565 N.E.2d at 105.

241. Idem at 360, n. 13.

242. Idem at 354: "Although Plaintiff felt repulsed by Roe's sexual advances, she submitted because of her fear that otherwise he would not represent her and that since she could not afford a retainer fee to hire a third counsel in her divorce case, she might go unrepresented and lose both custody of her child and the opportunity for financial security for herself and her child. From 1983 to 1988 Doe continued to submit to Roe's sexual demands, at his offices, in her home, and at other locations."

243. *Vallinoto v. DiSandro* (R.I., 1992). Verdict reported in *The Providence Journal* (Massachusetts ed.) Nov. 20, 1992, at 1, jury finding that DiSandro made fraudulent representations to Vallinoto and that DiSandro and his Providence law firm committed legal malpractice.

244. Idem.

245. Idem. (Although the plaintiff conceded that DiSandro did "an excellent job" on her divorce with respect to obtaining assets, one juror noted that a legal malpractice verdict was warranted because DiSandro had "dragged out the divorce for 18 months so he could keep having sex with her.")

246. 54 Ont.2d 663 (1986), *appeal dismissed*, 66 Ont.2d 350 (1988).

247. Idem at 666. "Mrs. Szarfer [too] was vulnerable and the defendant knew it as a result of knowledge gained in relation to the claim for damages in the wrongful dismissal action." Idem at 675.

248. Idem at 675.

249. Idem at 667-668.

250. Idem.

251. Idem at 677.

252. Idem at 676.

253. Idem at 351 (opinion of reviewing court upholding the lower court's decision on appeal).

254. Idem at 677. A fiduciary cannot use for his own benefit information imparted in confidence even if that information is readily available to the public from another source. Idem at 675.

21

Employer/Supervisor
Liability and Risk Management

Linda Mabus Jorgenson

This chapter examines tort doctrines that render employers liable for the sexual misconduct of their employees. It focuses on two separate legal approaches to liability. The first is *respondeat superior*, or vicarious liability, which imputes the employee's wrongful conduct to the employer regardless of the employer's fault. The second theory is negligence, which focuses on the employer's negligence in hiring, retaining, and supervising its employees.

Nationwide, approaches to employer liability vary widely. On an identical set of facts, an employer could incur liability for employee misconduct in one state but not in another. The courts' decisions may turn upon subtle variations in their interpretation of phrases such as *scope of employment* or *intent to benefit the employer*.

In assessing employer liability, courts often consider the extent to which the employer exercises control over the employee's work. The court determines whether the therapist is in fact an employee or simply an "independent contractor" who determines whether and in what manner to perform a particular duty. Doctors in hospitals are frequently independent contractors. Imposition of legal liability on a professional association for the wrongdoing of its associates may depend on whether the association was a partnership or joint venture, or whether a patient reasonably believed that the professional association was jointly responsible for the patient's treatment.

In *Van Dyke v. St. Paul Fire & Marine Ins. Co.*,[1] the court held that medical partners are ordinarily jointly liable for the malpractice of individual partners. The court adopted a similar view in *Ruane v. Cooper*[2] but focused on "whether the three doctors . . . held themselves out to the public as a joint venture. If they had, then the doctors could be estopped from claiming that each was an independent contractor responsible only for his own torts."[3] The case law also suggests that "consultant relationships," in which one professional supervises and submits insurance forms on behalf of another practitioner, may also provide a basis for holding the consultant liable for the wrongful conduct of the supervisee.[4]

Courts have held health maintenance organizations (HMOs) liable on the following theories: vicarious liability for the wrongful acts of staff physicians,[5] apparent agency between an HMO and its staff members,[6] and "corporate negligence."[7] An effort to hold an HMO liable on the theory that it *guaranteed* the fitness of its staff, however, was rejected in *Pulvers v. Kaiser Foundation Health Plan.*[8]

Additionally, a health care employer's status as a governmental or charitable entity may determine whether the employer will be liable for wrongful employee conduct. Until recently, it has been a long-standing legal tradition that an instrumentality of the government cannot be sued for wrongdoing. Federal and state "tort claims acts" have abrogated this governmental tort immunity to a varying degree; case law has also whittled away at the immunity doctrine.[9] Further, the doctrine of "charitable immunity," which rendered certain philanthropic institutions, including hospitals, immune from suit, has also been limited by legislation in some states. The degree to which charitable immunity still applies, however, varies from jurisdiction to jurisdiction. The success of a plaintiff's efforts to obtain recovery from a charitable employer will therefore depend on the state in which the wrongful act occurred. Massachusetts, for example, abolished the charitable immunity doctrine but capped liability at $20,000 for "tort[s] committed in the course of any activity carried on to accomplish directly the charitable purposes of such corporation."[10] This cap does not apply to primarily commercial activity carried on by charitable institutions. The cap has come under attack as failing to provide sufficient compensation to render the statute financially meaningful to plaintiffs. Massachusetts courts have ruled, however, that adjustments to the cap are a matter for legislative determination.[11]

VICARIOUS LIABILITY

The doctrine of vicarious liability, also known in the context of employer-employee relations as *respondeat superior*, imposes liability on an employer for the wrongful acts of employees committed within the scope of employment. What constitutes "scope of employment" varies on a state-by-state, and even case-by-case, basis. The Restatement (Second) of Agency § 228 defines "scope of employment" as follows:

1. Conduct of a servant is within the scope of employment if, but only if:
   a. it is of the kind he is employed to perform;
   b. it occurs substantially within the authorized time and space limits;
   c. it is actuated, at least in part, by a purpose to serve the master; and
   d. if force is intentionally used by the servant against another, the use of force is not unexpected by the master.
2. Conduct of a servant is not within the scope of employment if it is different in kind from that authorized, far beyond the authorized time or space limits, or too little actuated by a purpose to serve the master.

The Restatement essentially articulates public policy that may appeal to a court's sense of equity in holding an employer responsible under a given set of facts.[12] Different courts, however, often construe the Restatement differently. Likewise, in the area of sexual torts, consistently articulated principles of law do not exist.

In deciding whether a health care provider's sexual contact with a patient was motivated at least in part by a purpose to serve the master, many courts have held that the sex was absolutely unrelated to the employment because the activity took place solely for the employee's gratification. Nothing in the record of the case, wrote the court in *Andrews v. United States*, "suggests that [the defendant] considered his sexual adventures to be a *bona fide* part of the therapy he was employed to provide. . . . [I]t is clear that [he] was furthering his self-interest, not his employer's business, at the time he seduced his patient."[13]

On a similar set of facts, however, the court in *Simmons v. United States*[14] concluded that a therapist's sex with a patient was motivated in part by an intent to serve the employer. The court held that, although the therapist was not authorized to become sexually involved with clients, the sexual contact had occurred in conjunction with legitimate counseling activities, and hence constituted an "authorized act [that was] improperly or unlawfully performed."[15] Drawing upon a line of cases standing for the proposition that sexual activity cannot be separated from the counseling relationship for insurance coverage purposes, the *Simmons* court decided that "the abuse of transference occurred within the scope of . . . employment."[16] The court's focus on "abuse of transference" as the cornerstone for imposing vicarious liability avoided issues that may otherwise have arisen in the case relating to where and when the sexual contact took place.

Minnesota has explicitly abandoned the "intent or motivation to serve the employer" test as part of the factors considered in imposing vicarious liability. In *Marston v. Minneapolis Clinic of Psychiatry*,[17] the court concluded that, even though the therapist's sexual contact with his patients was intended "to confer a personal benefit on himself," vicarious liability could be imposed on the employer because a jury could have found that the therapist's wrongful sexual conduct was sufficiently related to the employment to warrant such liability. The court also reasoned that "it is both unrealistic and artificial to determine 'at which point the [acts] leave the sphere of the employer's business and become motivated by personal animosity'—or, as in this case, an improper, personal benefit."[18]

Other states have modified the "motivation to serve the employer test" without expressly abandoning it. For example, in *Doe v. Samaritan Counseling Center*,[19] a sexual relationship between counselor and patient had predictably led to emotional harm. The center defended itself from liability on the ground that, because the counselor's "tortious acts were not motivated by a desire to serve his employer, there cannot be liability based on a theory of *respondeat superior*."[20] Embracing a line of cases that imposed liability where the wrongful activity had been "precipitated by the employee's performance of assigned duties,"[21] the court held:

> This reasoning persuades us that where tortious conduct arises out of and is reasonably incidental to the employee's legitimate work activities, the "motivation to serve" test will have been satisfied. Given the transference phenomenon that is alleged to have occurred in this case, we hold that it could reasonably be concluded that the resulting sexual conduct was "incidental" to the therapy.[22]

It was fair to impose vicarious liability on employers in cases such as this because, the court reasoned,

> the basis of *respondeat superior* has been correctly stated as "the desire to include in the costs of operation inevitable losses to third persons incident to carrying on an enterprise, and thus distribute the burden among those benefitted by the enterprise." . . . Employees' acts sufficiently connected with the enterprise are in effect considered as deeds of the enterprise itself. Where through negligence such acts cause injury to others it is appropriate that the enterprise bear the loss incurred.[23]

Another modified "motivation to serve" test was articulated in *Stropes v. Heritage House Childrens Center of Shelbyville, Inc.*,[24] which involved an attendant at a home for disabled children who sexually assaulted a patient during the course of his custodial duties. The court stated that the question of whether the employer was vicariously liable for the criminal acts of its employee was a factual matter to be decided by a jury. The court rejected a per se rule placing sexual assaults outside the scope of employment simply because they might satisfy the perpetrator's personal desires. The court argued that such a rule would "draw an unprincipled distinction between such assaults and other types of crimes which employees may commit in response to other personal motivations."[25] The court stated that the focus should be on how the employment relates to the context in which the commission of the act arose. Therefore the center should be accountable if the employee's actions were, "at least for a time, authorized by his employer, related to his employment, and motivated to an extent by [his employer's] interests."[26]

As the foregoing discussion suggests, the competing and often contradictory analyses of the respondeat superior doctrine demonstrate the relatively unsettled nature of its availability. Plaintiffs' attorneys seeking to impose vicarious liability on an employer for the sexual tort of an employee may find that they are able to exercise a degree of creativity often precluded in other, more settled, areas of the law. The ruling in the *Marston* case, for example, was predicated upon an earlier case in which a Nabisco representative assaulted a grocery store owner during an argument over shelf space for Nabisco products.[27] The ruling in *Stropes* was developed by analogy to a case in which a security officer lawfully confiscated, but then wrongfully retained, an arrestee's identification card. He later used the card to facilitate the forgery of a check. Though the employer was not held liable for the criminal act of forgery, vicarious liability was imposed on the ground that the wrongful retention of the identification took place within the scope of the security officer's employment.[28]

Inherent in the decisions in many respondeat superior cases is the notion that the cost of doing business should include the cost of compensating victims for the reasonably foreseeable, though possibly criminal, acts that result from legitimate business activities.[29] This loss-spreading function of vicarious liability, also called the "enterprise liability" theory, embodies the idea that expenses that arise due to foreseeable acts, or those within the nature of the business, should be borne by the business enterprise. For example, it is foreseeable that a security guard will misuse confiscated identification or that a personal care attendant will misuse his access to the bodies of his patients. The foreseeability of such risk, and its close connection to the nature of the business, justifies the requirement that the employer compensate the victim for the costs of the employee's wrongful conduct.

In the area of sexual relations between therapists and patients, for example, studies have revealed that as many as 12% of therapists self-report that they have had sexual contact with one or more of their patients. And 90% of those patients are damaged by the sexual contact, which is a recognized risk in therapeutic relationships.[30] The American Psychiatric Association has expressly warned practitioners that "the necessary intensity of the therapeutic relationship may tend to activate sexual and other needs and fantasies on the part of both patient and therapist, while weakening the objectivity necessary for control."[31] Therapist-patient sexual contact is a foreseeable risk of therapeutic activity. Therefore employers should bear the cost of compensating victims on an enterprise liability theory without reference to restrictive doctrines requiring, for example, the employee's subjective intent to benefit the employer.

Another legal theory imposing vicarious liability on employers is "common carrier" liability. This theory evolved in the context of railroad transportation and requires an extraordinary standard of care on the part of the employer. Common carrier theory was applied by analogy in *Stropes v. Heritage House Childrens Center of Shelbyville, Inc.*,[32] discussed above, in which the court permitted the plaintiff to proceed to trial on two theories of recovery. One focused on the employer's authority to control its employee's activity (vicarious liability) and the other focused on the plaintiff's surrender of his ability to control his environment (common carrier liability). Under the latter theory, the court noted that

the range of employee activities deemed to be under the employer's dominion is irrelevant. Liability is predicated on the passenger's surrender and the carrier's assumption of the responsibility for the passenger's safety, the ability to control his environment, and his personal autonomy in terms of protecting himself from harm; therefore, the employer can be held responsible for any violation by its employee of the carrier's non-delegable duty to protect the passenger, regardless of whether the act is within the scope of employment.[33]

Common carrier theory renders employers strictly liable for employee's wrongful conduct without inquiry into the degree of negligent or intentional culpability of either employer or employee. The basis of the imposition of liability is that, because the passenger (or patient) has surrendered the right to control his or her environment, the party in control of the environment should bear the risk of loss should any harm arise.[34]

In *Vannah v. Hart Private Hospital*,[35] the application of common carrier theory resulted in the hospital's liability for the theft of a valuable ring from a sedated patient. The surgeon, family physician, day nurse, and one of the two operating room nurses testified that they had not taken the ring. The other operating room nurse was out of the state, did not testify, and was presumed to have stolen the jewelry. The hospital was held accountable for "an act of the defendant's servants which while not in the course of the servants' employment is none the less a violation of the duty owed by the defendant under the defendant's contract with the plaintiff."[36] The contract between the hospital and the patient absolutely guaranteed that the patient receive proper treatment at a time when she was unable to protect herself. Hence the hospital was precluded from excusing itself from liability for the theft. There is a divergence of opinion in the case law as to whether common carrier liability may be extended beyond the scope of the transportation cases in which the common carrier doctrine originally arose. In *Community Theatres Co. v. Bently*,[37] the court refused, without analysis, to extend common carrier liability to impose liability on the theater for the sexual assaults by its manager.[38]

EMPLOYERS' DIRECT LIABILITY UNDER NEGLIGENCE THEORY

In addition to the vicarious liability doctrine that imputes employees' wrongful conduct to their employers, standard negligence theory often permits recovery against employers on the grounds that they negligently hired, supervised, or retained the employees responsible for committing the wrongful acts. *Darling v. Charleston Memorial Hospital*[39] established that hospitals have an obligation to provide surveillance of the quality of patient care services and also created a duty of care owed to patients. Prior to *Darling*, the law in many jurisdictions viewed hospitals as mere "facilities" that independent contractor doctors used to treat their patients. Liability for professional misconduct could not be charged to the hospital because the hospital was not deemed to be in control of the doctors who used it. The *Darling* decision, and others like it, realistically took into account the modern hospital's functions of providing more than facilities to its patients.

Hospitals and other employers may be held liable for "negligent hiring" in cases in which the hiring entity knew the employee was unfit, had reason to believe the employee was unfit, or failed to use reasonable care to discover the employee's unfitness prior to employing him or her. The liability of the hiring entity exists separately from the employee's liability for his or her negligent conduct.[40]

In *Evan F. v. Hughson United Methodist Church*,[41] the church was held liable for hiring a pastor who had been discharged from a previous position for sexual misconduct with a minor male parishioner. The pattern of wrongful sexual activity persisted in the new position. The court held that it was possible to find that the church had been negligent in its hiring practices because, even though it had no actual knowledge of the pastor's prior sexual misconduct, the church could have discovered the conduct had it made a diligent inquiry.

Liability for negligent hiring can also be imposed if the employer does not appropriately evaluate certain characteristics of the potential employee. The court in *Mary E. Moses n/k/a/ Mary Elaine Tenantry v. The Diocese of Colorado*[42] found that the diocese and bishop could be found negligent in hiring a priest they knew to possess "attributes of character" that would create an undue risk of harm to others.[43] The employee in that case was a priest who counseled parishioners. The priest's personnel file included reports of psychological tests that showed that the priest had problems with depression, low self-esteem, and "sexual identity ambiguity."[44] The court noted that liability for negligent hiring is not based on past conduct alone; it may also be based on some character attribute that would create undue risk of harm to others in the carrying out of the employee's duties.[45]

Employers who negligently supervise an offending employee may also be held liable for that employee's tortious conduct. Negligent supervision theory appeared as an additional ground for recovery in both

Andrews v. United States[46] and *Simmons v. United States.*[47] In *Andrews,* the plaintiff's vicarious liability claim was rejected on the ground that her abuser was not acting within the scope of employment when he engaged in sexual relations with her. The plaintiff's claim against the United States for negligent supervision, however, was held valid because "[the supervising doctor] was plainly acting within the scope of his employment at the time he negligently failed to provide adequate supervision."[48] In *Simmons,* it appeared that the therapist's supervisor had notice of the therapist's inappropriate sexual contact with the plaintiff for several months but took no action on that information. Accordingly, the reviewing court sustained the district court's finding of liability for negligent supervision on the basis that, had the supervisor provided closer supervision or intervened after learning of the misconduct, a significant portion of the plaintiff's emotional damages would have been averted.[49]

In *DeStefano v. Grabrian,*[50] the court held that Father Grabrian's employer, the Diocese of Colorado Springs, could incur liability for Grabrian's sexual misconduct during the course of his marital counseling activities. The court required the plaintiff to prove at trial that the diocese "knew or should have known that Defendant Grabrian was engaging in conduct which was outrageous, negligent and a breach of his fiduciary duty"[51] and that it failed to adequately supervise Grabrian.[52]

When a professional institution employs a therapist or counselor, the breach of the trust relationship may encompass not only the initial breach by the therapist but also the failure of the entity to deal appropriately with that breach.[53] In defining an institutional breach of trust, the Metro Action Committee on Public Violence Against Women and Children stated:

> When an individual who enjoys special status and bears special responsibility derived from a position within [a professional, governing, or religious] institution takes advantage of that position to commit sexual abuse, the breach of trust aggravates the wrong. When the institution does not respond in ways that recognize the abuse and its impact, respect the rights of both victims and offenders, protect and support the victim, and prevent further abuse by the same or other offenders, the original breach of trust is compounded. If it fails to care for the victim and serve her/his interests, or if it shields the offender and itself, the institution is in breach of its societal trust.[54]

A professional relationship is not a necessary prerequisite for finding the existence of a fiduciary relationship; it may also arise when one party occupies a superior position relative to another.[55]

In *Moses*, for example, the court found that sufficient evidence existed to establish that a fiduciary relationship existed between a parishioner and the Diocese of Colorado and its bishop, as well as between the parishioner and the priest who had sexually exploited her.[56] The court noted that the diocese and the bishop stood in superior positions to the parishioner and were able to exert substantial influence over her.[57] In deciding that a fiduciary duty existed, the most important factor was that the diocese and the bishop assumed a duty to act in the parishioner's best interests, and then failed in that duty.[58]

According to the court in *Moses*, the diocese and the bishop assumed a duty to the parishioner when they acted to resolve the problems that existed between the parishioner and an abusive priest.[59] "Once a member of the clergy accepts the parishioner's trust and accepts the role of counsellor, a duty exists to act with the utmost good faith for the benefit of the parishioner."[60] The parishioner came to the bishop to discuss the sexual contact between herself and the abusive priest. The bishop, acting as the representative of the diocese, told the parishioner that he would take care of it. He took no action to help the parishioner, bound her to secrecy, and then attempted to transfer the priest. Thus he breached his fiduciary duty to the parishioner. Because he and others, acting as representatives of the diocese, did nothing to help the parishioner, the diocese also breached its duty.

The *Moses* case is not only applicable to religious organizations. It shows that any organization that stands in a fiduciary relationship to a client or patient can be found to have breached that duty by failing to appropriately respond to sexual abuse charges. With the proper showing, an employer could be held liable for the harm caused by an employee when the employer should have been more diligent in supervising that employee or in dealing with problems involving that employee.

Employers cannot assume that they will be free from liability simply because they were diligent in their hiring practices. They must be as diligent in their supervisory, disciplinary, and retention practices. For example, if a hospital is aware, or should be aware, that a physician has been sexually abusing patients, it may be held liable on the ground that its failure to revoke the physician's staff privileges contributed to the harm suffered by patients the physician subsequently abused. In *Copithorne v. Framingham Union Hospital*,[61] the hospital received two complaints of sexually abusive conduct on the part of a visiting staff physician. The doctor subsequently drugged and raped the plaintiff in her apartment. The court held that these facts, if proved, would justify a jury's finding that the risk of injury to Copithorne was within the range of foreseeable consequences of the hospital's negligence in continuing Helfant's staff privileges. Where the hospital had received actual notice of allegations that Helfant had sexually assaulted patients, both on the hospital premises and off the premises in his office and in a patient's home, and yet took only the limited measures indicated, it was not unforeseeable that Helfant would continue to act in a consistent, if not worse, manner.[62]

After receiving the initial complaints, the hospital took several measures, including instructing the doctor to have a chaperon present when visiting female patients and instructing the nurses on the floor to keep an eye on Dr. Helfant.[63] Hence the hospital could be liable for failing to take appropriate remedial measures given its knowledge of the doctor's propensities.

OTHER LIABILITY CONSIDERATIONS

Supervisor/Supervisee Obligations

Another aspect of negligent supervision theory involves the relationship between supervisor and supervisee. Therapists who sign insurance forms in the capacity of the treating professional often do not actually provide treatment but instead sign as an accommodation to the therapist who sees the patient. In *Corgan v. Muehling*,[64] for example, "Muehling was not registered as a psychologist, but was able to practice psychology by having codefendant R. J. Rodriguez, M.D., a psychiatrist, submit Muehling's bills to insurance companies, including plaintiff's, for payment in Rodriguez' name."[65]

Following Muehling's sexual abuse of his patient, the patient sued, maintaining that, because Rodriguez knew Muehling was unregistered and nevertheless maintained a consultant relationship with him, Rodriguez had a duty to supervise Muehling and negligently failed to do so, causing the plaintiff injury. The trial court initially dismissed that claim and the plaintiff appealed that decision. The appellate court, however, never decided the question of Rodriguez's liability to the plaintiff because the parties settled the matter out of court.

In a case such as *Corgan*, a variety of policy arguments exist on each side. The "moral" of the case, however, is that those who sign insurance claim forms may be held to supervisory standards whether or not they have in fact undertaken a supervisory role in the counseling relationship. Any language describing the responsibilities of the signer of insurance claim forms should be carefully reviewed.

In addition, there are ethical rules relating to the duties imposed by the relationship of supervisor and supervisee. In December 1992, the American Psychological Association issued an ethical rule in *American Psychologist* that precludes sexual contact in the context of supervisor-supervisee relationships.[66]

Liability of Evaluators

In Tennessee, the local branch of the American Psychological Association attempted to establish a program for the supervision and rehabilitation of formerly sexually abusive practitioners. However, insurance carriers were reluctant to provide coverage for the program due to the perceived potential for liability.

The opportunity for exposure to liability is particularly great for those who evaluate past offenders to assess their readiness to return to the therapeutic community. In one recent case, a minister with a lengthy sexual abuse record was permitted to return to practice only six weeks after his evaluation. Obviously, in such a situation, the opportunity for recidivism is great. It offends jury members' common sense when an impaired practitioner is returned to practice only to abuse clients again. In such cases, therefore, juries are likely to find evaluators negligent.

If restrictions are placed on the practice of the former offender following an evaluation, it may well be up to the evaluating individual or body to conduct periodic reviews to ensure that those practice restrictions remain in place. If the evaluating authority fails to enforce restrictions, a good plaintiff's lawyer will be sure to argue that the restrictions were toothless and cannot absolve evaluators of liability.

Subsequent Treating
Therapists of Victims

Similarly, the subsequent treating therapist of a victim of therapist sexual abuse also has a significant responsibility to the victim. If the patient ultimately decides to file suit against the offending therapist, the patient will be required to disclose the subsequent therapist's treatment. Hence, in treating a sexual abuse victim and potential litigant, the subsequent treating therapist should always be mindful that his or her notes may become a public record. Accordingly, a complete assessment should appear in the file, along with progress notes, a treatment plan, and accounting records.

Expert Witnesses

The need for accurate documentation is especially acute when the subsequent treating therapist will be called as an expert trial witness for the plaintiff/patient. In effect, the therapist wears two hats: one to help the patient recover and one that will convince the court that the patient has suffered extreme emotional harm, may never recover from the abuse, and is entitled to monetary compensation. The perceived economic advantage of engaging the subsequent treating therapist as an expert witness is more than offset by the potential for destroying the previous therapeutic alliance. An independent forensic expert should be retained to testify at trial to the standards of care that the defendant breached as well as to the plaintiff's damages. The subsequent treating therapist should maintain the role of a fact witness to the plaintiff's course of treatment with him or her.

PREVENTION

Hospitals and others with supervisory responsibility over therapists can protect themselves from both direct and vicarious liability by (a) establishing and enforcing clear, broad-based guidelines regarding patient sexual abuse; (b) publishing personnel manuals containing detailed prohibitions on, and penalties for, specific conduct constituting sexual abuse; and (c) educating hospital and other administrators, patient advocates, all other employees, and legal counsel on their role in complying with and enforcing sexual misconduct policies.[67] Patients, too, should be advised of their rights and the complaint procedures available to deal with violations. Employers should thoroughly investigate and enforce sanctions when warranted.

As part of their routine hiring practices, "supervisory institutions" should obtain broad releases from applicants permitting extensive background checks. The investigation of candidates should include discussions with former colleagues, a check of the National Databank, and an inquiry into the reasons for gaps in employment history. Employers should explore the applicant's record for resignations, client complaints, malpractice actions, or settlements of malpractice claims before the suit was filed.

After these hiring practices and personnel policies are implemented, employers must follow them consistently. Routine in-house educational programs, including grand rounds, video presentations, newsletters, and supervisory consultations, are also advisable. It has become acceptable for therapists to discuss anger and other emotions they may feel toward their patients. Supervisors must make a forum available where practitioners may discuss transference and countertransference issues without fear of being pathologized. Therapists must learn to discuss their sexual feelings toward clients or face the consequences of their continuing silence.

CONCLUSION

The current trend makes it clear that hospitals and employers have a higher duty to assure that competent care is provided to their patients. Employers who fail to act in a responsible manner may be found liable under a negligence theory of wrongful hiring, supervision, or retention. Even if an employer has not been negligent, the employer could be held responsible under one of the theories of vicarious liability. It is in the best interests of employers, therapists, and patients to prevent sexual exploitation of patients.

NOTES

1. 448 N.E.2d 357 (Ma. 1983).
2. 127 A.D.2d 524 (N.Y. 1987).
3. Idem.
4. See infra notes 73-75 and accompanying text.
5. See *Sloan v. Metro Health Council*, 516 N.E.2d 1104 (Ind. 1987).
6. See *Boyd v. Albert Einstein Medical Center*, 547 A.2d 1229 (Pa. 1988).
7. See *Harrell v. Total Health Care, Inc.*, 781 S.W.2d 58 (Mo. 1980).
8. 160 Cal. Rptr. 392 (1979).
9. See, e.g., *Federal Tort Claims Act*, 28 U.S.C. sec. 1346(b) (1946).
10. See Mass. Gen. L. ch. 231 § 85K (1985).
11. See *English v. New England Medical Center, Inc.*, 541 N.E.2d 329 (Ma. 1989). The Massachusetts liability cap has been applied to recoveries for intentionally tortious conduct as well as negligent torts. See *St. Clair v. Trustees of Boston University*, 521 N.E.2d 1044, *review denied*, 402 Mass. 1104, 524 N.E.2d 400 (1988).
12. The Restatement (Second) of Agency § 213 (1958) provides: "A person conducting an activity through servants or other agents is subject to liability for harm resulting from his conduct if he is negligent or reckless . . . in the supervision of the activity."

13. 732 F.2d 366, 370 (4th Cir. 1984). See also *Sharpless v. State*, 793 P.2d 175 (Hawaii 1990) (following *Cosgrove* reasoning to find no purpose to serve master); *Cosgrove v. Lawrence*, 520 A.2d 844 (N.J. 1986), *affirmed*, 522 A.2d 483 (1987), finding therapist's sexual intercourse with patient not motivated by purpose to serve employer; *Bunce v. Parkside Lodge of Columbus*, 596 N.E.2d 1106 (Ohio 1991), holding sexual contact in therapeutic relationship unrelated to employer's business; *Birkner v. Salt Lake County*, 771 P.2d 1053 (Utah 1989), reasoning sexual contact prohibited by therapist's employer cannot be within scope of employment.

14. 805 F.2d 1363 (9th Cir. 1986).

15. Idem at 1369.

16. Idem at 1370.

17. 329 N.W.2d 306 (Minn. 1982).

18. Idem at 311.

19. 791 P.2d 344 (Alaska 1990).

20. Idem at 346.

21. Idem at 348.

22. Idem.

23. Idem at 349. But see *Noto v. St. Vincent's Hospital and Medical Center of New York*, 160 A.D.2d 656 (N.Y. 1990), holding hospital not liable on respondeat superior theory because alleged sexual abuse not a therapeutic treatment or diagnosis.

24. 547 N.E.2d 244 (Ind. 1989).

25. Idem at 249. The court also held that "an employee's wrongful act may still fall within the scope of his employment if his purpose was, to an appreciable extent, to further his employer's business, even if the act was predominantly motivated by an intention to benefit the employee himself." Idem at 247. Under this analysis, in the "context" of changing the patient's bed and clothing to benefit his employer, the employee took advantage of an opportunity to commit a criminal act to benefit himself. It is not necessary that the employee believe that all of the actions benefit the employer, only that there be a rational nexus between the activities.

26. Idem at 250, quoting *Gomez v. Adams*, 462 N.E.2d 212, 224-225 (Ind. App. 1984).

27. *Lange v. National Biscuit Co.*, 297 Minn. 399, 211 N.W.2d 783 (1973).

28. 547 N.E.2d 244 (Ind. 1989).

29. See Sykes, A. O. (1988). The boundaries of vicarious liability: An economic analysis of the scope of employment rule and related legal doctrines. *Harvard Law Review, 101*, 563.

30. See Schoener et al. (1989). *Psychotherapists' sexual involvement with clients: Intervention and prevention*. Minneapolis, MN: Walk-In Counseling Center.

31. American Psychiatric Association. (1985). *The principles of medical ethics with annotations especially applicable to psychiatry*, Section 2.1. Washington, DC: Author.

32. 547 N.E.2d 244 (Ind. 1989); see supra notes 24-26 and accompanying text (discussing facts and holding of *Stropes* case).

33. Idem at 253.

34. Idem at 252.

35. 117 N.E. 328 (Ma. 1917).

36. Idem at 330.

37. 76 S.E.2d 632 (Ga. 1953).

38. See idem. But see *Dickson v. Waldron*, 34 N.E. 506, *reh'g denied*, 135 Ind. 524, 35 N.E. 1 (Ind. 1893), holding theater manager liable to patron for injuries sustained at hands of theater employee.

39. 211 N.E.2d 253, *cert. denied*, 383 U.S. 946 (1965).

40. See *Joiner v. Mitchell County Hospital Authority*, 186 S.E.2d 307 (Ga. 1971), holding hospital's failure to screen employee credentials constituted negligence; *Johnston v. Misericordia Community Hospital*, 294 N.W.2d 501 (Wis. 1980): Failing to check applicant's credentials upon application may constitute negligence.

41. 10 Cal. Rptr. 2d 748 (1992).

42. No. 92SA415 (Colo., Nov. 15, 1993).

43. Idem at 37.

44. Idem at 6-7.

45. Idem at 37 n. 21 (citing *Connes v. Molalla Transport System, Inc.*, 831 P.2d 1316 (Colo. 1992)).

46. 732 F.2d 366 (4th Cir. 1984).

47. 805 F.2d 1363 (9th Cir. 1986).

48. *Andrews*, 732 F.2d at 370.

49. *Simmons*, 805 F.2d at 1371.

50. 763 P.2d 275 (Colo. 1988).

51. Idem at 288.

52. Idem; see also *Erickson v. Christenson*, 781 P.2d 383 (Or. 1989), holding church's failure to supervise, investigate, remove, or warn parishioners of pastoral counselor's abusive behavior created risk of harm; *Does v. CompCare, Inc.*, 763 P.2d 1237 (Wash. 1988), stating employer may incur liability for acts outside scope of employment if employer had knowledge of employee's dangerous tendencies.

53. Metro Action Committee on Public Violence Against Women and Children and the Ontario Women's Directorate. (1992). *Breach of Trust in Sexual Assault: Statement of the Problem Part Two: Review of Social Institutions* (Unpublished pamphlets), at 1 [hereinafter METRAC, *Part Two*].

54. METRAC, *Part Two*, at 3.

55. See *Moses v. The Diocese of Colorado*, No. 92SA415 at 22 (Colo., Nov. 15, 1993).

56. Idem at 21.

57. Idem at 24.

58. Idem at 25.

59. Idem.

60. Idem at 25-26 (citing *Destefano*, 763 P.2d at 284).

61. 520 N.E.2d 139 (Mass. 1988).

62. Idem at 142-143.

63. Idem at 142.

64. 522 N.E.2d 153 (Ill. 1988).

65. Idem at 154.

66. 1.19(b) Exploitative Relationships: "Psychologists do not engage in sexual relationships with students or supervisees in training over whom the psychologist has evaluative or direct authority, because such relationships are so likely to impair judgment or be exploitative."

67. See generally idem, *Psychotherapists' sexual involvement with clients* (1989).

22

Employer/Supervisor
Liability and Risk Management

AN ADMINISTRATOR'S VIEW

Gary Richard Schoener

As both a psychologist and the executive director of a clinic, I have had to consider risk management and prevention of sexual misconduct by counselors for more than 20 years. As a consultant to other administrators, as a member of boards of directors, and as someone who is consulted by other administrators about risk management issues, I have dealt with these issues on a regular basis insofar as they apply to a wide range of organizations.

There has been surprisingly little treatment of the issues of risk management and prevention of sexual misconduct (from the viewpoint of an organization) in the professional literature. Texts such as *Profes-*

AUTHOR'S NOTE: The Appendix at the end of this chapter is reprinted with permission from G. Schoener et al. (1989), *Psychotherapists' Sexual Involvement With Clients: Intervention and Prevention*, Minneapolis, MN: Walk-In Counseling Center, pp. 455-458.

sional Liability and Risk Management (Bennett, Bryant, VandenBos, & Greenwood, 1990) and *Psychiatry and the Law for Clinicians* (Simon, 1992a), while quite useful, are focused on the individual clinician rather than the administrator or supervisor.

W. White's (1986) *Incest in the Organizational Family* examines organizational boundary issues that may set the stage for sexual misconduct, and Edelwich and Brodsky's *Sexual Dilemmas for the Helping Professional* (1982/1991) discusses some supervision issues and issues of staff relationships. Strasburger, Jorgenson, and Sutherland (1992) also discuss supervisory and administrative issues. Menninger (1991) has written a useful description of an organizational risk management program in "Identifying, Evaluating, and Responding to Boundary Violations: A Risk Management Program." Simon (1991) has also written about boundary violation precursors to therapist-client sex, something important to understand if one is seeking to limit risks of this type of conduct. Epstein and Simon (1990) have developed an "exploitation index" as an early warning indicator of boundary violations and have also experimentally used it (Epstein, Simon, & Kay, 1992).

Supervisory and administrative safeguards were discussed at length in *It's Never O.K.: A Handbook for Professionals on Sexual Exploitation by Counselors and Therapists* (Sanderson, 1989); the state of Minnesota as well as a number of organizations have implemented a number of them.

Thus far in health care and mental health care, there is nothing to equal the videotape training packages and manuals developed for clergy and religious professionals. *Sexual Ethics in Ministry* was developed by the Department of Health and Human Issues, University of Wisconsin—Madison/Extension (1990). A Seventh Day Adventist group developed *Sexual Ethics for Church Professionals* (Ministerial Continuing Education, 1991), and the Center for the Prevention of Sexual & Domestic Violence produced *Prevention of Clergy Misconduct: Sexual Abuse in the Ministerial Relationship* the same year.

RISK MANAGEMENT
ADVICE FROM RISK MANAGERS

Over the past several years, some insurance carriers and underwriters have been examining risk management issues related to sexual misconduct by professionals. The early efforts focused on pedophilia in the church and in youth organizations and produced a few prevention tools. The American Psychological Association Insurance Trust (APAIT) funded the production of the book *Professional Liability and Risk Management* (Bennett, Bryant, VandenBos, & Greenwood, 1990), which provides some discussion of therapist-client sex.

Psychotherapists' Sexual Contact With Clients: Intervention and Prevention (Schoener, Milgrom, Gonsiorek, Luepker, & Conroe, 1989) was designed as a prevention and risk management tool and has been recommended as such by some risk managers and insurance programs. One, the Church Pension Fund, which serves the Episcopal Church, has also been very active in identifying resources and in the education of church leaders. One insurance program, the American Professional Agency, which sells insurance to a wide range of mental health professionals, offers this book to its insureds when policies are renewed. It is available to them at a reduced cost in hopes that they will use it as a risk management guide.

The most impressive effort to date, however, has been made by the Mental Health Risk Retention Group Inc. (MHRRG), a liability insurance company created by community mental health centers. They have produced a videotape as part of their "Loss Prevention Series" titled *Sexual Misconduct* (Zimmet, 1989), which features defense attorney Ronald K. Zimmet discussing risk management and prevention of sexual misconduct by professionals. Accompanying the videotape is a paper titled *Criminal and Civil Liability for Sexual Misconduct of Therapists and Other Staff of Mental Health Care Organizations* (Zimmet, 1990). The MHRRG (1990) also created "a self evaluation survey relating to sexual misconduct of therapists and other staff of mental health care organizations." This asks the manager or administrator 54 questions relative to risk management and prevention of sexual misconduct. One must credit MHRRG and its underwriting manager, J. J. Negley and Associates, for having had the foresight and courage to put this package together for their insureds. Obviously, there is a certain degree of risk in doing so in that, when a claim is made, the plaintiff could theoretically fault the insured for anything suggested in this package that was not done.

ADMINISTRATIVE SAFEGUARDS:
THE WALK-IN COUNSELING CENTER APPROACH

Our experience in organizational consultation (Schoener & Milgrom, 1989) led Jeanette Milgrom, in 1978, to develop a survey form for organizations titled "Sexual Exploitation of Clients: Its Prevention or

Remedy . . . or . . . A Look at Whether Your Agency Has Its House in Order." This was supplanted a year later by the first of a series of publications, all titled *Administrative Safeguards to Limit the Risk of Unprofessional Conduct*, which I wrote in 1979 and revised in 1986 and in 1989 (Schoener et al., 1989, pp. 453-467, 651-660). The most recent version, titled *Administrative Safeguards Which Limit the Risk of Sexual Exploitation by Psychotherapists: A Checklist*, is provided as the Appendix to this chapter.

Psychotherapists' Sexual Involvement With Clients: Intervention and Prevention (Schoener et al., 1989) includes chapters on administrative safeguards (Schoener, 1989a), hiring practices (Gonsiorek, 1989a), the role of supervision and case consultation in primary prevention (Schoener & Conroe, 1989), and sexual feelings in therapy (Schoener, 1989d). Remarkably little has been written on sexual feelings in therapy and even the excellent recent contribution by Pope, Sonne, and Holroyd (1993) is focused on trainee and clinician self-awareness rather than supervisory and administrative issues.

We have also gained experience with the issue of employer and supervisor liability and risk management through consultative work in connection with civil suits involving churches, clinics, hospitals, and so on. In these cases, issues that the expert must address are to what degree the conduct was foreseeable and to what degree reasonable precautions were taken. Such determinations are often very connected to both societal and professional awareness of the problem—something that has changed dramatically over the past 20 years. This time-frame reference is essential to a fair assessment of what should or could have been done.

A time frame may also play a role in determining what sort of precautions or safeguards might be justified by a particular fact situation, such as knowledge that a given professional has a history of a particular type of conduct. Our understanding, for example, as to what might constitute an evaluation of an impaired professional and what sort of rehabilitation might be necessary has changed considerably during the past 20 years. In some cases, churches or denominations have been poorly defended because effective testimony was not offered relative to reasonable expectations for the time period in which the decisions were made. For example, understanding of pedophilia has changed dramatically during the past 20 years. In the early 1970s, simply sending the offender to a licensed mental health professional who claimed expertise probably met the standard of care, whereas today one would expect that a specialist in sexual misconduct by professionals be used for any assessment. In some cases, early mistakes by secular professionals have led to officials making decisions that led to disasters—but these officials reasonably relied on the assertions of the professionals.

Even the seriousness of an offense may depend on the time frame in which it occurred. Standards for judging posttermination sexual relationships of psychotherapists, for example, have evolved considerably (see, e.g., Appelbaum & Jorgenson, 1991; Gonsiorek & Brown, 1989; Schoener, 1989c). Having a sexual relationship with a former client may, for example, be a more clearly deviant act in 1993 than it was in 1973.

Another source of insight into organizational safeguards has been experience helping organizations evaluate their responses to various situations. Sometimes, for example, consultation is requested to help an organization deal with the departure of a staff member who has resigned or been fired subsequent to the discovery of sexual exploitation. Usually the staff who remain are confused and, in a true sense, wounded. There may also be both shame and self-blame. As such, a review of the situation can provide for relief from this self-blame as well as for healthy introspection so as to learn from any past mistakes. In some instances, of course, one learns that mistakes were not made—that the incident might not have been preventable. There is a risk in doing this if a lawsuit ensues because one is, in effect, engaging in discovery of things that may represent negligence. However, it is essential to learn what one can from these unfortunate incidents.

RECORD KEEPING

Good records offer key protection for clinicians and administrators who have taken appropriate actions and documented them. In many sexual misconduct cases, records are lacking or sparse, leaving the reconstruction of the events and interpretation of motives to the imagination. My personal bias is to properly record one's actions and rationale, even though that may later help prove that mistakes were made. As a general rule, it is better to do one's best and document one's actions. Beyond the fact that it is far better to appear in court as a concerned and ethical professional who was honestly trying to do his or her job but who has made a mistake, cover-ups often exact a significant psychological toll. A courtroom appearance accounts for a small amount of time in one's life and career compared with the continued reanalysis and self-judgment that may occur when one looks in the mirror at home.

There are three major reasons that an item of information should appear in records or notes:

The first reason is to satisfy contractual obligations such as those to funding organizations, insurance companies or other third party payers, or governmental agencies.

The second is to document diagnosis, treatment, and so on for the purpose of doing it effectively. There is considerable disagreement as to how much documentation one needs for this purpose, but at the very least someone should be able to pick up your work in your absence and not have to begin from scratch. In the case of work being done by a trainee, additional documentation may be necessary to allow for appropriate training and supervision.

The third is to protect yourself in a situation in which an accident occurs, a risky decision is made, a client has a complaint, or you are concerned about the outcome of a situation. Contemporaneous notes and records have far more value than ones that have been written later.

There was a time when many organizations were advised by counsel to keep sparse records and to limit documentation. More attorneys seem to be recommending detailed record keeping. The notion that one can retrospectively concoct a favorable version of events is quite misguided. Physicians, psychologists, social workers, clergy, and those who oversee their work do not make effective liars. Trapped by inconsistencies in their stories, which may be tested many times during the discovery phase of a civil proceeding and then again in court, they may end up being treated very harshly by juries. The ethical and honest professional or administrator who has made an honest mistake is perceived very differently, and good record keeping is one of the common ways attorneys and juries distinguish between the two.

ADMINISTRATIVE SAFEGUARDS: HIRING

A detailed explication of the checklist of administrative safeguards, which is the Appendix of this chapter, can be found in *Psychotherapists' Sexual Involvement With Clients: Intervention and Prevention* (Schoener et al.,

1989, pp. 453-467). In this chapter, I will highlight several of the safe-guards that have played a role in a great many cases.

First and foremost are proper background checks as a part of the hiring of a psychotherapist, physician, nurse, member of the clergy, and so on. An in-depth examination of this issue can be found in Gonsiorek's (1989a) *The Prevention of Sexual Exploitation of Clients: Hiring Practices.*

The Minnesota legislature was sufficiently convinced about the importance of this issue as a result of a major task force study that it incorporated it into a civil statute, Minnesota Statutes 148A, which created a cause of action against both therapists (including clergy and others acting in psychotherapeutic roles) and their employers when sexual misconduct occurs (Sanderson, 1989). This statute requires that the employer of a therapist check back at least five years with former employers to ask if they have knowledge of sexual contact with clients or approaches to clients aimed at sexual contact. If the former employer passes such information on in good faith, he or she is protected from suit or other action by the former employee. If he or she fails to pass on such knowledge and some future client is sexually exploited and sues, the former employer can be liable for damages.

This effectively changed what had been routine for centuries—that employers were more fearful of actions by their former employees for defamation than they were about the potential for harm to future clients. It meant that negotiating "silence agreements" in connection with resignations and departures in such cases was no longer possible, unless the employer wanted to assume these risks. It had a secondary benefit in that it forced employers to investigate and decide on the validity of complaints, even when the employee resigned to avoid such an investigation. If the employer had not made such a determination and a request was received from a prospective employer via what have been termed *148A letters,* then the employer has often been obligated to investigate the incident and reach an opinion. For the first few years after the law passed, we often received calls from employers bemoaning the fact that they had in the past avoided an investigation and now had to conduct one some years later—no easy task.

In the case of the Walk-In Counseling Center as well as some other organizations who have adopted our approach, we go beyond just the use of a letter inquiring about past sexual approaches or contact. Using an approach described more fully by Gonsiorek (1989a), we obtain a release from all applicants for jobs or volunteer positions and then contact past supervisors and others by phone to obtain broad background information. The cornerstone of this undertaking is the release, which states in part:

> I authorize the Walk-In Counseling Center, its staff and representatives to consult with persons or institutions with which I have been associated and with others, including past and present employers, who may have information bearing on my *professional competence, character, and ethical qualifications.* I release from liability all representatives of WICC for acts performed in good faith and without malice in connection with evaluating my application and my credentials and qualifications. I also release from any liability all individuals and organizations who provide information to WICC in good faith and without malice concerning my professional competence, ethics, character, and other qualifications. (Schoener et al., 1989, p. 644, italics added)

Note the breadth of the inquiry allowed and the broad protection given both our staff and anyone we speak with. Note also that we are not limited to applicants' formal references.

The time of hiring is one of the few times the employer has much leverage. If the thousands of professionals who have signed this form and permitted such a check during the past 20 years have been willing to do it for the privilege of volunteering, it is obvious that those applying for positions also sign. Such a release and the use of a direct interview with the former employer, supervisor, or colleague permit one to ask about any history of boundary violations or problems in maintaining professionalism. While about 50% of the offenders we've seen have a history of some misconduct with sexual overtones, it has not always been overt sexual contact. Ideally, this sort of background check should spot at least half of the offenders as well as identify those who may have a variety of other problems or vulnerabilities.

Even the existence of Minnesota Statutes 148A and the inquiry letter it requires has led some perpetrators to leave Minnesota. A number of church officials have indicated that this has had a revolutionary impact on the hiring of clergy. However, this change has at times been bewildering to therapists and clergy who engaged in their misconduct many years ago during an era when these issues were treated more leniently and who now find that this past offense will forever stain their record. (There is no time limit as to when the offense occurred, nor is there any way to remove it, at least in theory, from one's "record" in that it should be passed on from employer to employer.)

Beyond the problem of the investigation that was never done years earlier, other problems have been created by sloppiness on the part of supervisors and employers who are unclear about the law or misconstrue its mandates. For example, in one case a hospital responded to a 148A inquiry by reporting that a nurse had engaged in some "boundary violations" with a former patient. While these violated some rules, they turned out to have nothing to do with sex and not be a proper response to this inquiry. While relevant and potentially accessible through the use of a release like ours, it was a disservice to the former staff member to pass this information on in response to a 148A letter.

We also recommend direct checks with licensure boards to be sure of licensure status and the absence of disciplinary action or license restrictions. Some attorneys and insurance programs are recommending criminal justice checks for staff—especially those who might work with children. The state of Minnesota requires chemical dependency treatment programs to have a criminal justice check done on all staff and consultants each year at the time of license renewal.

It is important to remember that in the hiring process one must focus on more than past sexual contact or sexualizing of counseling or pastoral relationships; other difficulties and vulnerabilities may be equally important. For example, the practitioner who breaks rules and does not comply with the paperwork requirements of a job can be a problem if he or she does not think that the agency's rules apply. Boundary violations in the nonsexual areas can be indicative of difficulty in maintaining professionalism and a tendency to confuse professional duties with friendship. Early warning signs range widely depending on the type of offender (Schoener & Conroe, 1989; see Chapters 11 and 12 in this volume).

Some examples of traits that might come up with a psychotherapist, a clergy member, or a physician are a tendency to hang on to clients unnecessarily, a tendency to do more "heavy psychological counseling" than the job normally entails, a tendency to socialize with clients, and a tendency toward excessive self-disclosure. In fact, excessive self-disclosure is the single most common precursor to professional-client sex in the thousands of cases we have seen. In particular, the disclosure of current problems, especially in a significant relationship, is predictive of trouble.

One must be cautious in asking about health or mental health history when hiring. However, sometimes information is volunteered and in some cases acquired as a normal part of preemployment screening (e.g., when an industrial psychology firm is used) or preordination psychological examination (e.g., required by the Episcopal Church in America). When such data are obtained, the focus must be job related but can range broadly. For example, in one case where a preordination psychological evaluation revealed that a young pastor was prone to periodic depressions due to an "endogenous depression," I recommended that there be a discussion with the supervising senior pastor and the man regarding (a) what mental health benefits were available should he need help, (b) the importance of telling his supervising pastor if he was feeling overwhelmed so duties could be readjusted, and (c) a brief discussion as to how he behaves when he is depressed and what problems might occur as well as how to give him some feedback about it. The goal is to use such information constructively to limit the risk of adverse consequences, of which one is seeking intimacy with a parishioner or counselee.

ADMINISTRATIVE SAFEGUARDS: SUPPORT AND SUPERVISION

There is nothing more damning, save for a gross hiring mistake that was preventable, than a failure to respond to an employee who is obviously having personal problems. In a health care or mental health facility in particular, when a staff member is walking around severely depressed and there is no administrative or supervisory intervention, one can expect to be held directly liable for what the impaired employee does. Many sexual misconduct cases involve situations in which the professional is depressed, going through a difficult divorce, drinking heavily, or otherwise in obvious trouble. It is the responsibility of the supervisor or administrator not only to inquire as to what is going on but to assess the impact on practice. This may relate to overall workload, to whether or not the person should handle difficult clients, whether or not he or she should deal with specific types of clients, and so on.

Given financial concerns and systems of reimbursement for health care and psychotherapy services, it is my observation that less and less supervision is being done at many facilities. In most churches, there is little or no supervision of counseling or pastoral care built into the system. The concern about sexual misconduct has brought about a review of this situation in some religious organizations. In Minnesota, the Episcopal Church now has supervision groups for priests aimed at helping them with their pastoral care and counseling challenges. In Rhode Island, there are clergy wellness groups sponsored in part by a church insurance program. I have suggested to a number of bishops that they consider having business and financial consultants available to clergy and church bodies as we have some Minnesota data showing that, across all denominations, clergy job satisfaction and stress are significantly affected by the financial condition of the clergy's church.

In psychotherapy, medicine, and religious work, the most common observable indicator of sexual misconduct is overinvolvement. This can include treatment exceeding the normal length for that type of client or for the clinician in question. It includes situations where excessive dependency is obvious, such as when there are frequent calls, letters, and unscheduled appointments. A key risk management strategy here is to make certain that there are vehicles for feedback from support staff because they often see such signs much earlier than the administration. They need to have a way of raising such concerns without fearing retribution and without having to define a clear-cut situation. At least one clinic system that had several problem situations closed their entire system down for two days and had all staff, including support staff, in a workshop done by myself and Ellen Luepker to try to bring about broad awareness and better communication.

ADMINISTRATIVE SAFEGUARDS: OTHERS

Other common mistakes are the failure to treat a complaint as a complaint and to fully investigate it. Sometimes practitioners and even their clients, when confronted, provide a quick and falsely reassuring answer to an inquiry. It is important to carefully evaluate complaints, getting back to the person who was the source and testing the validity of the response. We have seen situations in which clients and parishioners at first have issued quick denials that anything sexual was going on, trying to protect the professional or themselves or both.

Periodic workshops on professional standards and on boundaries are of great use. The approach developed by Milgrom (1992) in *Boundaries in Professional Relationships* has become a regular feature of agency in-services in a great many programs. W. White (1993) has created an excellent set of situations and vignettes for substance abuse counselors in his book *Critical Incidents*. Of a more prescriptive nature but useful in teaching situations is Villaume and Foley's (1993) *Teachers at Risk*.

In general health care, counseling and psychotherapy, and religious work, nothing has become as complex and confusing as the ever-changing standards on sexual involvement with former clients, patients, and parishioners (see, for example, Appelbaum & Jorgenson, 1991; Gonsiorek

& Brown, 1989; Schoener, 1989c). This is an area where clear staff policies and understanding of those policies are quite important.

As a final note, it is important to be clear that, although the checklist in the Appendix easily might be seen as a scorecard, it is not meant to be used that way. The items vary as to their importance by setting and situation. Nor is the list exhaustive. It is important for those in administrative and supervisory positions to be aware of the developing professional literature as well as the evolving case law discussed in the preceding chapter. It is also worthwhile to consider the benefits of legislation such as Minnesota Statutes 148A, which provides some definition of duties and some protection in discharging duties. The key to reducing risk and liability is to be proactive—to not simply wait until problems rear their head. One can benefit not only from one's own mistakes but from those of others.

APPENDIX

Administrative Safeguards
Which Limit the Risk of Sexual
Exploitation by Psychotherapists: A Checklist

STAFF SELECTION & HIRING	YES	NO
Does your job application explicitly ask about:		
Past terminations/resignations?	___	___
Past ethics complaints?	___	___
Past licensure complaints?	___	___
Past lawsuits, whether adjudicated or not?	___	___
When hiring professionals who are licensed or certified, do you directly contact licensure boards concerning areas of competency, status of the license, and the existence (or lack thereof) of complaints?		
Boards in this state?	___	___
Boards in states where previously employed?	___	___
Do you check via direct conversation (not just letter of reference) with past supervisors about the applicant's:		
Likely strengths and weaknesses working in a setting like that of your agency?	___	___
Willingness to be supervised and to be a team player?	___	___
Any history of complaints by, or problems with, other staff (e.g., sexual harassment)?	___	___

	YES	NO

Any history of client complaints?

Any concerns they might have about the person's ability to perform in your setting; any needs for special care or supervision?

If you're a Minnesota employer, do you make written requests to all employers from the past five years concerning their knowledge of sexual contact with clients or ex-clients (Minnesota Statute 148A)?

If you're a non-Minnesota employer, do you comply with the local standards for the duty of employers as spelled out in statute or case law?

STAFF POLICIES

Do you have a written policy forbidding:
Sexual contact with clients?
Sexual contact with ex-clients?
Romantic involvement with clients?

Does your policy also provide rules for support staff and other nonclinical personnel?

Do you have a policy covering sexual harassment of staff and/or romantic involvements between staff members?

Do you have a written policy for handling complaints of unprofessional conduct such as allegations of sexual contact with clients?

Do you have a plan or mechanism for the investigation of complaints by clients and others?
Do you have outside consultants who can be used to assist in such investigations?
Do you have an Ethics Committee or Professional Standards Review Committee which reviews such complaints?
Do you have a method for the filing and investigation of complaints against the Director of your program or facility?

COMPLAINT RESOLUTION

Are all complaints processed as complaints and taken seriously—not just seen as "transference" or some other therapeutic event?

Are complaining clients given reassurance and thanked for
coming forward, regardless of your initial assumptions
about the validity of the complaint?   ____   ____

Are clients given support and offered help in finding
appropriate independent resources?   ____   ____

Do you have procedures for deciding whether to temporarily
suspend a staff member pending the outcome of a review
of a complaint?   ____   ____

Are all staff involved in the investigation of complaints
clear about the limits of privacy—e.g., their reporting
duties under existing laws and rules (in Minnesota this
includes Vulnerable Adults Act, Child Abuse and
Neglect reporting, the Medical Practice Act, and the
Code of Conduct of the Board of Psychology)?   ____   ____

Is some resolution reached on all complaints, or do you
allow some of them to remain moot if a staff member
voluntarily resigns?   ____   ____

After you have decided on action relative to a complaint,
are the complainants always given feedback as to final
disposition?   ____   ____

When you receive a request for a recommendation for a
former staff member which asks about any history of
sexual misconduct with clients, do you: ____   ____
Automatically pass the information on to a Minnesota
employer as is your duty under Minnesota Statute
148A?   ____   ____
With an out-of-state employer suggest that the
employer obtain a release from the former staff
member permitting you to share all data?   ____   ____

STAFF EDUCATION

Are all staff given written copies of policies?   ____   ____

Is there a new employee orientation at which these are
explained and key policies are underlined?   ____   ____

Are there training sessions on the issue of boundaries in
psychotherapy held at least once per year?   ____   ____

Following an incident of serious misconduct, is a special
session held to discuss what can be learned from the
incident?   ____   ____

STAFF SUPERVISION/PEER REVIEW	YES	NO

Do you have regular clinical supervision or consultation?

Do you have a professional standards review system?

Is there an automatic review of:
Treatment which exceeds the usual length?
Situations in which excessive dependency is evident
  such as when clients phone frequently?

Situations in which seductive behavior is observed by
  other staff?

Is long-term treatment periodically reviewed as to:
Treatment goals and progress toward them?
Plans for termination?

Does our program have an atmosphere which encourages
  constructive questioning among staff?

Are there clear, nonthreatening pathways for making
  observations/concerns known to management, by:
Clinical & program staff?
Support staff; billing office?

When staff have obvious personal problems or are in
  distress:
Do other staff generally give them feedback?
Is there a clear mechanism, which is used, to bring
  about feedback and encourage seeking help?
Are clinical duties ever reviewed in light of obvious
  personal problems/distress?

Are there readily available interventions when therapeutic
  relationships become romanticized/sexualized:
Use of a co-therapist or consultant who may enter a
  session with the client if need be?
Referral in-house, or to another program?

CLIENTS

Do you provide new clients with information which:
Actively seeks to solicit feedback?
Identifies an easy-to-use complaint mechanism?
Provides any guidelines to evaluating therapy?

Is it general staff practice to carefully assess the client's
  view of any past treatment at your agency or elsewhere?

	YES	NO
Do you routinely survey consumer satisfaction or outcome?	___	___
Is a complaining client given the opportunity for a meeting with the therapist, with or without a mediator present?	___	___

23

The Effects of Criminalization
of Sexual Misconduct by Therapists

REPORT OF A SURVEY IN WISCONSIN

Andrew W. Kane

Beginning with Wisconsin in 1983, 13 states have enacted legislation to criminalize sexual contact between psychotherapists, counselors, clergy, or other professionals and their patients or clients (California, Colorado, Connecticut, Florida, Georgia, Iowa, Maine, Michigan, Minnesota, New Mexico, North Dakota, South Dakota, and Wisconsin). In general, this legislation is meant to serve two purposes: to punish perpetrators and to act as a deterrent to anyone who might consider becoming a perpetrator. Chapter 20 details specific legal developments.

Wisconsin initially passed a law (Section 940.22 Stats) that made it a misdemeanor to have "sexual contact with a patient or client during any

AUTHOR'S NOTE: This chapter is based in part on a presentation at the Second International Conference on Sexual Misconduct by Clergy, Psychotherapists and Health Care Professionals (Minneapolis, October 1992).

treatment, consultation, interview or examination." The statute covered "a physician, psychologist, social worker or other person providing psychotherapy services." There were numerous problems with the language of the statute, including too great a limitation on the types of professionals covered and the interpretation by district attorneys of "during any treatment" as meaning "during a scheduled therapy session for which a fee was charged." Therefore the first case prosecuted under the statute was not filed until 1987.

The statutory language was improved through legislation enacted in 1986. To the list of professionals covered were added "nurse, chemical dependency counselor, [or] member of the clergy or other person, whether or not licensed by the state, who performs or purports to perform psychotherapy." "During any treatment" was changed to "during any ongoing therapist-patient or therapist-client relationship, regardless of whether it occurs during any treatment, consultation, interview or examination." Also added was a statement that "consent is not an issue in an action under this subsection," and the penalty was raised to a Class D felony (fine not to exceed $10,000 or imprisonment not to exceed five years, or both). A mandated reporting provision was added in 1988.

To be effective, laws must be enforced through the filing of appropriate charges by district attorneys. This chapter reports on the results of a survey of the district attorneys in Wisconsin. The surveys were mailed in August 1992. A follow-up survey was sent to nonresponding district attorneys in September 1992. Data intake from district attorneys was ended as of October 1, 1992. Additional data on cases were obtained from newspaper or other official reports of adjudications through December 31, 1993.

In addition, these laws must attract the attention of the people whose behavior they seek to control, in this case those who "perform or purport to perform psychotherapy." Two ways of addressing the degree to which people pay attention to a statute are through direct questioning and a survey of behavioral changes related to the statutory prohibitions. As a sample of the "therapists" in Wisconsin, a survey with both direct and behavioral questions was sent to all 174 members of the (Wisconsin) Society of Clinical and Consulting Psychologists. In addition to being licensed as psychologists, all members of this group are listed (or eligible to be listed) in the National Register of Health Service Providers in Psychology. The register is a certification of the level of training of listed psychologists. Surveys were mailed in August 1992, with a stamped, self-addressed envelope enclosed. Data intake was ended as of October 1, 1992.

SURVEY AND RESULTS:
DISTRICT ATTORNEYS

The response rate was 61% (44 of 72). Not everyone answered every question, so the number of respondents was often less than 44 for any particular question.

1. Have you prosecuted any psychotherapists, clergy, physicians, etc. under the state misdemeanor or felony statutes (940.22) to date?

      YES: 7 (16%)   NO: 36 (84%)

2. If yes:
   a. How many cases under the misdemeanor statute, which went into effect in 1983: 2 cases.
   b. How many cases under the felony statute, which went into effect on April 30, 1986: 8 cases.

3. Have any cases been reported to your office by subsequent therapists of victims, under 940.22(3)'s mandated reporting requirement?

      YES: 5 (11%)   NO: 39 (89%)

   a. How many were first reports on an alleged perpetrator: 5 cases.
      Did you start an investigation in each case?
      YES: 2 cases   NO: victim requested anonymity: 1 case
   b. How many cases involved second or subsequent reports on an alleged perpetrator: no cases.

4. Do you believe that the criminalization of sexual misconduct by health/ mental health professionals has had a positive impact on the incidence of that misconduct?

      YES: 13 (87%)   NO: 2 (13%)

5. Do you believe that the mandated reporting of sexual misconduct by previous therapists/professionals has had a positive impact on the incidence of that misconduct?

      YES: 15 (94%)   NO: 1 (6%)

6. Have you given any information you've had regarding allegations or adjudications of sexual misconduct *to* the licensing boards for physicians or psychologists? If not, why not?

      YES: 3 (17%)   NO, nothing to report: 14 (78%)
                            NO, all anonymous: 1 (5%)

7. Have you received any information regarding allegations or adjudications of sexual misconduct *from* the licensing boards for physicians or psychologists?

      YES: 1 (3%)   NO: 36 (97%)

Discussion: District Attorneys

An analysis of cases (based on information from district attorneys, newspaper reports, and other sources; see the end of this chapter for a summary) made it evident that one additional survey question was needed: "Have you prosecuted any psychotherapists, etc. under the sexual assault statute rather than the 'misconduct by therapist' statute?" That is in fact what happened in the majority of cases on which data are presently available, which helps to explain why only 7 of the 43 district attorneys who responded to the first question said yes.

It is also evident that the "mandated reporting" statute has not had a substantial effect to date. The law requires that the subsequent therapist make a report if his or her patient/client is willing to have the report made. Only the therapist's name needs to be on the report; the victim can remain anonymous. If a second report on the same alleged perpetrator is made, the district attorney or the licensing board will then contact the reporting therapist and ask that the victim be contacted and requested to make a formal complaint. Even if all subsequent therapists were to request the victim's consent to report, however, many patients/clients do not wish to have the therapist reported. Of those who did consent, this survey found only five first reports, and in only two was the district attorney able to start an investigation.

Most of the responses to the fourth and fifth questions were along the lines of "I haven't had enough experience with this to respond." Those who did respond strongly indicated a belief that the criminalization and mandated reporting of sexual misconduct by health/mental health professionals has had a positive impact on the incidence of that misconduct.

The statute explicitly permits the exchange of information about alleged perpetrators between the district attorneys and the licensing boards. The data from this survey indicate that such exchange of information seldom occurs.

It is hoped that one result of this survey is increased awareness of the sexual misconduct statute among district attorneys and that this will lead to both increased enforcement and an increase in reporting of cases to the relevant licensing boards for licensed professionals.

Comments by District Attorneys

Many of the comments of district attorneys who responded to the survey are instructive:

Criminalization of Sexual Misconduct by Professionals

1. "[The statute] has not reduced it because laws cannot stop victims from declining to report such abuse because of embarrassment, fear of retaliation by the therapist/clergy member, fear of ostracization by their religious group, or fear of not being believed. Criminalization could, in some cases, actually hinder some victims from reporting because they 'don't want to cause trouble' for the therapist or clergy member."

2. "I believe an analogy can be made with child abuse reporting laws. I believe many mental health professionals possess beliefs not conducive to law enforcement."

3. "Criminalization alone does not have any impact on behavior. However, the prosecution of such behavior has to have an impact —which has to be positive."

4. "We had one report that was handled informally—not enough probable cause for a criminal charge."

5. "The possibility of criminal consequences, in my experience, is usually a deterrent to prohibited conduct. There are always some people who will violate anyway, but the criminal penalties will usually deter the borderline violators."

Mandated Reporting

1. "My perspective is limited but I have seen in my prosecution of clergymen for child sexual assault mental health professionals blame the victims, testify without knowing the facts, voice opinions that are biased and not supported, voice unwarranted faith in their ability to treat. I don't see them as adequate self-policers."

2. "It takes the burden of reporting off the victim in a sense. It is much easier for a victim to tell a subsequent therapist whom s/he has come to trust than to tell the police or prosecutor directly. It gives the victim automatic support: if the therapist believes him/her, s/he is more likely to be a good witness for the prosecution because s/he has more confidence."

3. "The mandated reporting creates an atmosphere of deterrence and intolerance of this behavior, which in turn increases a self-regulation within the profession."

4. "We believe it is a good law, but the infrequency of reports makes it difficult to state with any certainty its effects."

5. "Most professionals (lawyers included) will tend to give their colleagues the benefit of the doubt unless there are mandatory reporting laws. These laws also increase the probability of discovery, which acts as a deterrent."

General

"I believe that there is a general public awareness that it is unlawful to sexually assault juveniles and 'rape' (meaning force) adult victims. But I believe that there was not the same awareness that sexual misconduct by a professional was just as legally or morally wrong. I believe that the public now is seeing that sexual misconduct by a professional is an unlawful type of conduct and not to be considered a 'white collar' type of crime. That is, the public is outraged when a victim is sexually assaulted on 'the street,' and now the public may make the connection that sexual misconduct in a professional's office is just as morally and legally wrong and requires just as severe criminal consequences. . . . Maybe under 940.22 we have a 'professional sexual abuse' law."

SURVEY AND RESULTS:
PSYCHOLOGISTS

The response rate was 87 of 174 (50%).

Notes

1. "Pre-1983" = prior to misdemeanor statute
   "1983-1986" = during misdemeanor statute
   "post-1986" = after felony statute enacted
2. As part of his doctoral dissertation, Richard Brigham (Psy.D.) surveyed all licensed psychologists in Wisconsin in 1989 regarding some of the same issues relevant to the current survey. Data from his survey appear in brackets following the data from the present survey. It should be noted that his data may not be directly comparable, because his results include many psychologists who are not National Register eligible as well as master's-level school psychologists.

1. Which of the following office practices do you follow in the hope of reducing risk of frivolous sexual misconduct complaints . . . and indicate the approximate year you began the specified practice:

a. See patients only when secretary is in outer office: 38 (44%) [Brigham: 31%]
Pre-1983: 34%; 1983-1986: 34%; post-1986: 18%; no date: 13%

b. Post statement in the waiting area stating your subscription to all professional/legal prohibitions against sexual misconduct: 10 (11%) [Brigham: 6%]
Pre-1983: 20%; 1983-1986: 0; post-1986: 70%; no date: 10%

c. Refuse to see clients you may perceive as potentially seductive or receptive to sexual overtures: 16 (18%) [Brigham: 17%]
Pre-1983: 38%; 1983-1986: 31%; post-1986: 25%; no date: 6%

d. Refer elsewhere those clients with sexual issues: 7 (8%) [Brigham: 10%]
Pre-1983: 42%; 1983-1986: 42%; post-1986: 14%; no date: 2%

e. Maintain detailed notes: 68 (78%) [Brigham: 63%]
Pre-1983: 54%; 1983-1986: 26%; post-1986: 10%; no date: 9%

f. Tape-record sessions: 4 (5%) [Brigham: 5%]
Pre-1983: 25%; 1983-1986: 50%; post-1986: 0; no date: 25%

g. Make "Coalition Against Sexual Misconduct by Therapists/Counselors" pamphlets available in office: 15 (17%) [Brigham: 8%]
Pre-1983: N/A; 1983-1986: 7%; post-1986: 73%; no date: 20%

h. Work with a cotherapist when client presents with sexual difficulties: 20 (23%) [Brigham: 17%]
Pre-1983: 35%; 1983-1986: 25%; post-1986: 15%; no date: 25%

i. None of the above: 6 (7%)

j. Other:
Verbalize boundaries of therapy: 1
No physical contact other than shaking hands: 1
Supervision of problematic cases: 1
Clinic rule: Any office staff can knock once and enter the office at any time: 1
Consultation: 3

2. Do you routinely ask new clients whether they have been victims of sexual exploitation including by professionals:
NO: 55 (63%)   YES: 32 (37%)

3. If you discovered that your patient was a victim of sexual misconduct by a previous therapist, would you be willing to assist him or her through the following complaint processes:

a. Professional ethics committee: NO: 2 (2%); YES: 81 (98%) [Brigham: 96%]

b. Examining (licensing) board: NO: 2 (3%); YES: 80 (98%) [Brigham: 91%]

c. Criminal justice system: NO: 4 (5%); YES: 77 (95%) [Brigham: 84%]

4. Did your training/supervised internship adequately help you deal with seductive patient behavior:

   NO: 56 (67%)   YES: 28 (33%)

5. Did your training/supervised internship adequately help you become aware of your reactions to patient sexual material:

   NO: 47 (55%)   YES: 39 (45%)

6. Did your training/supervised internship adequately help you deal with the issue of your own attraction to patients:

   NO: 46 (55%)   YES: 38 (45%)

7. Which best describes your type of practice:

   a. Primarily institutional: 8 (9%)
   b. Primarily private practice: 73 (84%)
   c. Other: 6 (7%)

8. Have you ever had sexual contact with a patient *currently* seen by you in psychotherapy in your private or institutional practice? ("Sexual contact" means any intentional touching, either directly or through clothing, for the purpose of sexual arousal or gratification):

   NO: 86 (99%)   YES: 1 (1%)   [Brigham: YES = 6 = 1.6%]

9. Have you ever had sexual contact with a patient *formerly* seen by you in psychotherapy:

   NO: 82 (94%)   YES: 5 (6%)   [Brigham: YES = 12 = 3%]

   If yes, number of months posttherapy: one each reported 6, 12+, 16+, 36, and 48+

10. Have you had a current or past ethics committee complaint, licensing board complaint, or lawsuit, adjudicated or not, related to sexual misconduct:

    NO: 85 (98%)   YES: 2 (2%)   [Brigham: YES = 3 = .8%]

11. Have you ever encouraged a victim of sexual misconduct by a professional to file a complaint:

    NO: 31 (36%)   YES: 55 (64%)   [Brigham: YES = 40%]

12. In 1983, sexual misconduct by a therapist became a criminal misdemeanor in Wisconsin. Did you make *any* changes in the way you practice as a result of this statute:

    NO: 70 (82%)   YES: 15 (18%)

13. In 1986, sexual misconduct by a therapist became a criminal felony in Wisconsin. Did you make *any* changes in the way you practice as a result of this statute:

    NO: 69 (81%)   YES: 16 (19%)

14. Has the criminalization of sexual misconduct by therapists had any negative effect on your or your practice (increased anxiety or stress, worry about frivolous accusations, etc.):

    NO: 63 (72%)   YES: 24 (28%)

15. Since the mandatory reporting statute went into effect in May 1988, have you had a patient/client tell you of sexual misconduct by a therapist (including psychologists, physicians, social workers, nurses, chemical dependency counselors, or clergy):

    NO: 51 (59%)   YES: 35 (41%)

    If yes, did you report, as required:
    NO: 27 (77%)   YES: 8 (23%)
    (Note: Several survey responders indicated the victim did not want it reported.)

16. Has the above reporting requirement had any negative effect on you or your practice:

    NO: 79 (94%)   YES: 5 (6%)

17. Do you believe that the criminalization of sexual misconduct by health/mental health professionals has had a positive impact on the incidence of that misconduct:

    NO: 14 (21%)   YES: 54 (79%)

18. Do you believe that the mandated reporting of sexual misconduct by previous therapists/professionals has had a positive impact on the incidence of that misconduct:

    NO: 13 (22%)   YES: 46 (78%)

19. My age is:
    30-34: 3 (3%)
    35-39: 11 (13%)
    40-44: 20 (23%)
    45-49: 18 (21%)
    50-54: 10 (11%)
    55-59: 10 (11%)
    60-64: 7 (8%)
    65+: 3 (3%)
    Mean age: 48
    Median: 47

20. Number of years of psychotherapy practice to date:
    Range = 5-36 years
    Mean = 17 years

21. Gender:
    Male: 55 (68%) Female: 26 (32%)

Discussion: Psychologists

The method most often chosen to reduce the risk of frivolous sexual misconduct complaints is, by a wide margin, the maintenance of detailed notes, with 78% of respondents indicating they maintain such notes. This is 15% greater than was found by Brigham in his study of all licensed psychologists in Wisconsin, which may reflect the training level of the present sample of National Register psychologists and/or be a representation of the increased use of this method by psychologists in the four years since his survey.

In decreasing order, the frequency with which other methods are used is as follows:

See patients only when secretary is in outer office (44%)

Work with a cotherapist when client presents with sexual difficulties (23%)

Refuse to see clients you may perceive as potentially seductive or receptive to sexual overtures (18%)

Make "Coalition Against Sexual Misconduct by Therapists/Counselors" pamphlets available in office (17%)

Post statement in the waiting area stating your subscription to all professional/legal prohibitions against sexual misconduct (11%)

Refer elsewhere those clients with sexual issues (8%)

Tape-record sessions (5%)

In all but two of the above, the present data indicate a higher prevalence of use of the indicated method than was found in Brigham's study. As noted, this could reflect the greater training of the psychologists in the present sample or could be a real difference among psychologists over the ensuing four-year period.

While the data do not permit the conclusion that psychologists began to use these methods of reducing risk of frivolous sexual misconduct complaints *because of* the passage of the misdemeanor and felony statutes, there was generally a large increase in the percentage of respondents who began using these methods when the misdemeanor statute was passed and another, smaller increase when the felony statute was passed. It appears safe to conclude, at the least, that the criminalization of sexual misconduct by therapists markedly increased the awareness among psychologists of the wrongfulness of this conduct, and the consequent need to assure that they, themselves, were not accused of that misconduct.

It is unfortunate that the majority of respondents do not routinely ask new clients whether they have been victims of sexual exploitation, given the national data, which indicate that substantial numbers of people of both genders have been victims of sexual abuse at some time in their lives. In my office, the form we request everyone to fill out asks, "Have you ever been sexually assaulted," with spaces to check "yes" or "no" and to make comments. It is an easy way for patients to open up an essential area of discussion, and nearly all patients for whom this is an issue do check "yes" on the form.

It is heartening to note that nearly all the respondents would help their patients/clients through the process of complaining to ethics committees, licensing boards, and district attorneys. In the present study, as in Brigham's, there is a small decrease in the percentages who are willing to do so as the level of the complaint increases from the ethics committee to the criminal justice system.

A majority of respondents indicated that their training/supervised internship did not adequately help them deal with seductive patient behavior, become aware of their reactions to patient sexual material, or deal with the issue of their own attraction to patients. Given that the average respondent completed his or her training about 20 years ago, this is not especially surprising. It is hoped that graduates of doctoral programs and internships in the past 10 years, as the problem of sexual misconduct has been increasingly illuminated, would answer differently.

As would be expected for a sample of National Register listed/eligible psychologists, the vast majority are primarily in private practice.

Only one respondent indicated having had sexual contact with a patient while that person was in therapy. While this is much lower than would be expected on the basis of national data, it could be explained by the National Register status of these psychologists or by a decrease in willingness to respond yes to a question about sexual misconduct, even on an anonymous survey, in a state where such misconduct is a criminal offense.

The one person who did so indicate noted that the sexual contact occurred while she was an intern many years earlier. She also indicated that "my male supervisor had sex with me" during her training. This lends support to the proposition that victims have greater difficulty with a variety of boundary issues.

Five people (6%) indicated they had had sexual contact with a former patient, between 6 and 48+ months posttermination. One of these five was the woman who had had sexual contact with a patient during therapy.

Only two respondents indicated having had an ethics or licensing complaint or a lawsuit filed against them.

Nearly two thirds of respondents had encouraged a victim of sexual misconduct by a professional to file a complaint. It is not known whether those who did not so encourage the victims chose not to do so or never had a victim in their offices and so could not provide that encouragement.

In contrast with the data indicating that many specific office practices were instituted to reduce the risk of frivolous sexual misconduct complaints either between the enactment of the misdemeanor and felony statutes or after the enactment of the felony statute, more than 80% of respondents indicated they did not make any change in the way they practiced as a result of either statute. While it is possible that this is a coincidence, it is more likely that the contrast is due to increased awareness of the problem, denial, repression, or faulty memory.

About a quarter of respondents indicated that the criminalization of sexual misconduct by therapists has had a negative effect on the therapist or his or her practice. There was no consistent pattern to the comments made.

Of the respondents, 41% indicated having had a patient/client who reported sexual misconduct by a past therapist/counselor since the mandated reporting statute took effect. Of these, 77% did not report the misconduct. The most common reason stated was that the victim did not wish that report to be made. Five respondents indicated that the mandated reporting requirement had had a negative effect on them or their practice.

In addition, 79% indicated a belief that the criminalization of sexual misconduct by professionals has had a positive impact on the incidence of that misconduct. Few reasons were given by those who did not so believe.

Similarly, 78% indicated a belief that mandated reporting of sexual misconduct by previous therapists/professionals has had a positive impact on the incidence of that misconduct.

The age range of respondents was from the early thirties to more than 65 years of age, with a mean of 48 and a median of 47; 68% were male, 32% female. The range of years of practice was from 5 to 36, with a mean of 17. Members of this sample clearly have many years of professional experience. The subjects in Brigham's study were only slightly younger, with a mean age of 46. However, only 82% of Brigham's subjects had a doctoral degree, while all respondents in the present study had one. The nondoctoral respondents in Brigham's study were largely licensed for the independent practice of school psychology.

CASES

Combining cases reported to me by district attorneys with reports from newspapers or other sources regarding adjudications, I am aware of 30 cases in which a therapist was convicted of a criminal offense between the passage of the misdemeanor statute in 1983 and December 31, 1993:

The following were charged as sexual exploitation by a therapist/ counselor (Section 940.22 Stats):

1. A clergyman was charged with three felony counts. He was placed on probation for up to five years. "If exemplary probationer, defendant may petition to be discharged from probation prior to expiration of the five-year sentence." He was also incarcerated in the county jail for 90 days and was ordered to do 200 hours of community service during 1992. "It is further ordered that defendant shall not counsel females. Probation and parole will determine if defendant can counsel men."

2. A counselor was convicted on two counts. He was sentenced to prison for three years—imposed, stayed, each count; placed on probation for five years, each count, concurrent. Restitution to be determined for any out-of-pocket expenses of victims, and there was a mandatory victim/witness surcharge of $100. Incarceration in county jail for nine months. As a condition of probation, defendant must abstain from alcohol and controlled substances, must continue AA or a similar program, and cannot work as a counselor during the probation period.

3. A psychiatrist was convicted of misdemeanor sexual misconduct, sentenced to 18 months of probation, and ordered to pay $2,500 to a sexual assault treatment center.

4. A minister was charged with misdemeanor sexual misconduct. He died during open heart surgery just before his trial would have begun. The case is said to have been referred to a "higher court."

5. A chemical dependency counselor was charged with both felony sexual misconduct and fourth-degree sexual assault. Pled guilty to the sexual misconduct charge. Placed on probation for five years,

with the first year to be served in county jail. Also obligated to pay various costs, make restitution to the victim for additional counseling expenses, and undergo assessment by a sex therapist.

6. A psychiatrist was convicted of sexual exploitation by a therapist, sentenced to two years of probation, ordered to surrender his medical license and resign or retire from the medical school faculty, and to refrain from "any involvement as a therapist during probation."

7. A counselor was placed on two years of probation and ordered to spend 30 days in jail after conviction of sexual exploitation of a patient. He was also ordered not to counsel women while on probation, to pay the victim $1,619 for treatment she had received, and to seek counseling for himself.

8. A female therapist was given four years' probation for sexual exploitation by a therapist, with the first six months to be served in jail. She was also ordered to have a psychological evaluation and follow-up.

9. A chemical dependency counselor pled guilty to one count of sexual exploitation by a therapist, with additional counts being "read in" for sentencing consideration. He was placed on probation for five years, with the first year to be served in jail. He was also required to pay various costs, make restitution to the victim for her counseling expenses, and undergo an assessment by a sex therapist.

The following were charged as sexual assault (Section 940.225 Stats):

1. A member of the clergy was charged with several counts of first-degree sexual assault for having sexual contact with children under the age of 13 years and received a 17-year sentence.

2. A clergy member was convicted of fourth-degree sexual assault on a plea and placed on probation.

3. A priest was sentenced to 18 months of probation and 45 days in jail for fourth-degree sexual assault.

4. A school psychologist was convicted on two counts of fourth-degree sexual assault involving a 16-year-old boy and sentenced to six months in jail.

5. A priest was convicted on one count of second-degree sexual assault involving a 13-year-old boy. Two additional counts were read into the record. He was sentenced to seven years in prison.

The sentence was suspended and he was given nine months in jail and ten years of probation. He must seek counseling and pay costs of therapy for two victims.

6. A psychologist pled no contest to one count of fourth-degree sexual assault involving sexual contact with an adult male patient. He was ordered to surrender his license for two years, placed on two years of probation, and ordered to pay a $1,000 court assessment to the Sexual Assault Treatment Center.

7. A counselor pled no contest to an amended charge of fourth-degree sexual assault. He was placed on probation for 18 months. He may not practice counseling during the period of probation.

8. A high school guidance counselor pled guilty to having sexual intercourse with a child, in exchange for the prosecutor dropping a charge of sexual exploitation by a therapist. He was sentenced to 30 days in jail, put on 18 months' probation, and ordered to perform 180 hours of community service.

9. A priest was convicted of one count of sexual contact with a child, because of sexually touching a 12-year-old boy during counseling sessions, and was sentenced to five years in prison.

10. A priest pled guilty to second-degree sexual assault and was sentenced to one year in jail.

11. A psychiatric resident was charged with fourth-degree sexual assault for having sexual contact with a patient in the hospital. He pled no contest and was sentenced to two years' probation.

12. A social worker was charged with third-degree sexual assault. He pled no contest, was sentenced to five years' probation, and was ordered to perform 200 hours of community service.

13. A priest pled guilty to disorderly conduct involving sexual contact with a congregant and was sentenced to two years' probation.

14. A counselor was charged with two counts of sexual exploitation by a therapist and two counts of second-degree sexual assault. He pled guilty to fourth-degree sexual assault and was sentenced to two years' probation with four months to be spent in jail with work release privileges.

15. A chemical dependency counselor pled no contest to an amended charge of fourth-degree sexual assault and was placed on probation for 18 months. He was ordered to surrender any licenses he has in any counseling fields and not to reapply during the term of probation. He was not to engage in any counseling while on probation. He was also assessed costs. He surrendered his AODA (alcohol and other drug abuse) counselor certification.

16. A social worker was convicted of fourth-degree sexual assault involving a woman. He was placed on probation for two years and ordered not to engage in counseling or therapy of female clients without supervision.

17. A priest pled guilty to first-degree sexual assault of a child (a boy), a felony. He received a one-year jail sentence. He was also placed on probation for 10 years, required to participate in group therapy, ordered to have no future unsupervised contact with minors, and ordered to pay for any counseling needed by his victim and the victim's family.

18. A priest pled guilty to a charge of second-degree sexual assault of a 14-year-old boy and received a 10-year prison sentence.

19. An Episcopalian priest pleaded no contest to two counts of second-degree sexual assault of a boy and was sentenced to five years in prison.

20. A former Baptist minister was sentenced to two consecutive 10-year terms in prison for first-degree sexual assault for sexually assaulting three female students at a church-run school. He was also sentenced to 10 years of probation, to begin after his prison term, on a third count of first-degree sexual assault. The probation includes an order that he have no contact with juveniles.

21. A priest was sentenced to 10 years in prison after pleading guilty to one charge of first-degree sexual assault against a young boy. Other charges were dropped as part of a plea agreement.

CONCLUSIONS

Criminalization of sexual misconduct by therapists and counselors, including clergy, nurses, and others, has had some effect in Wisconsin, as evidenced by several known prosecutions and by statements of district attorneys and psychologists surveyed.

However, two thirds of the confirmed cases of sexual misconduct by those covered by the criminalization statutes were prosecuted as sexual assaults or other criminal offenses rather than as sexual exploitation by a therapist. In some cases, this was the result of a plea bargain; in others, it is believed that the prosecutor felt more certain of a conviction if the prosecution was for sexual assault rather than sexual exploitation. This may, however, dilute the deterrent effect of the sexual exploitation statute, because newspaper stories on convictions will be headlined "sexual assault" and potential therapist-perpetrators may assure themselves that "this doesn't apply to me."

The "mandated reporting" statute has not had a substantial effect to date. The most common reason cited for a lack of reporting was the wish of the victim that it not be reported.

Psychologists conduct a number of practices to try to prevent false accusations, with the keeping of detailed notes being by far the most common procedure. There is a clear correlation between the timing of the introduction of these procedures and the passage of the misdemeanor and felony statutes for sexual exploitation by a therapist.

Altogether, while no unequivocal evidence can be produced to prove that criminalization of sexual misconduct by psychotherapists, counselors, and others has had a significant deterrent effect, the evidence from the present surveys strongly suggests that such is the case.

APPENDIX

Wisconsin Statutes

Wisconsin Misdemeanor Statute (1983)

940.22 Sexual exploitation by therapist. (1)
In this section:

(a) "Physician" has the meaning designated in s. 448.01 (5).

(b) "Psychologist" means a person who practices psychology, as described in s. 455.01 (5).

(c) "Psychotherapy" has the meaning designated in s. 455.01 (6).

(d) "Sexual contact" has the meaning designated in s. 940.225 (5) (a).

(e) "Therapist" means a physician, psychologist, social worker or other person providing psychotherapy services.

(2) Any person who is or who holds himself or herself out to be a therapist and who intentionally has sexual contact with a patient or client during any treatment, consultation, interview or examination is guilty of a Class A misdemeanor.

History: 1983 a. 434.

Current Wisconsin Statute

940.22 Sexual exploitation by therapist; duty to report. (1)
DEFINITIONS. In this section:
(a) "Department" means the department of regulation and licensing.

(b) "Physician" has the meaning designated in s. 448.01 (5).

(c) "Psychologist" means a person who practices psychology, as described in s. 455.01 (5).

(d) "Psychotherapy" has the meaning designated in s. 455.01 (6).

(e) "Record" means any document relating to the investigation, assessment and disposition of a report under this section.

(f) "Reporter" means a therapist who reports suspected sexual contact between his or her patient or client and another therapist.

(g) "Sexual contact" has the meaning designated in s. 940.225 (5) (b).

(h) "Subject" means the therapist named in a report or record as being suspected of having sexual contact with a patient or client or who has been determined to have engaged in sexual contact with a patient or client.

(i) "Therapist" means a physician, psychologist, social worker, marriage and family therapist, professional counselor, nurse, chemical dependency counselor, member of the clergy or other person, whether or not licensed or certified by the state, who performs or purports to perform psychotherapy.

NOTE: Parameter. (i) is shown as amended eff. 5-1-93 by 1991 Wis. Act 160. Prior to 5-1-93 it reads:

(i) "Therapist" means a physician, psychologist, social worker, nurse, chemical dependency counselor, member of the clergy or other person, whether or not licensed by the state, who performs or purports to perform psychotherapy.

(2) SEXUAL CONTACT PROHIBITED. Any person who is or who holds himself or herself out to be a therapist and who intentionally has sexual contact with a patient or client during any ongoing therapist-patient or therapist-client relationship, regardless of whether it occurs during any treatment, consultation, interview or examination, is guilty of a Class D felony. Consent is not an issue in an action under this subsection.

(3) REPORTS OF SEXUAL CONTACT. (a) If a therapist has reasonable cause to suspect that a patient or client he or she has seen in the course of professional duties is a victim of sexual contact by another therapist or a person who holds himself or herself out to be a therapist in violation of sub. (2), as soon thereafter as practicable the therapist shall ask the patient or client if he or she wants the therapist to make a report under this subsection. The therapist shall explain that the report need not identify the patient or client as the victim. If the patient or client wants the therapist to make the report, the patient or client shall provide the therapist with a written consent to the report and shall specify whether the patient's or client's identity will be included in the report.

(b) Within 30 days after a patient or client consents under par. (a) to a report, the therapist shall report the suspicion to:

1. The department, if the reporter believes the subject of the report is licensed by the state. The department shall promptly communicate the information to the appropriate examining board.

2. The district attorney for the county in which the sexual contact is likely, in the opinion of the reporter, to have occurred, if subd. I is not applicable.

(c) A report under this subsection shall contain only information that is necessary to identify the reporter and subject and to express the suspicion that sexual contact has occurred in violation of sub. (2). The report shall not contain information as to the identity of the alleged victim of sexual contact unless the patient or client requests under par. (a) that this information be included.

(d) Whoever intentionally violates this subsection by failing to report as required under pars. (a) to (c) is guilty of a Class A misdemeanor.

(4) CONFIDENTIALITY OF REPORTS AND RECORDS. (a) All reports and records made from reports under sub. (3) and maintained by the department, examining boards, district attorneys and other persons, officials and institutions shall be confidential and are exempt from disclosure under s. 19.35 (1). Information regarding the identity of a victim or alleged victim of sexual contact by a therapist shall not be disclosed by a reporter or by persons who have received or have access to a report or record unless disclosure is consented to in writing by the victim or alleged victim. The report of information under sub. (3) and the disclosure of a report or record under this subsection does not violate any person's responsibility for maintaining the confidentiality of patient health care records, as defined in s.146.81(4) and as required under s. 146.82. Reports and records may be disclosed only to appropriate staff of a district attorney or a law enforcement agency within this state for purposes of investigation or prosecution.

(b) 1. The department, a district attorney or an examining board within this state may exchange information from a report or record on the same subject.

2. If the department receives 2 or more reports under sub. (3) regarding the same subject, the department shall communicate information from the reports to the appropriate district attorneys and may inform the applicable reporters that another report has been received regarding the same subject.

3. If a district attorney receives 2 or more reports under sub. (3) regarding the same subject, the district attorney may inform the applicable reporters that another report has been received regarding the same subject.

4. After reporters receive the information under subd. 2 or 3, they may inform the applicable patients or clients that another report was received regarding the same subject.

(c) A person to whom a report or record is disclosed under this subsection may not further disclose it, except to the persons and for the purposes specified in this section.

(d) Whoever intentionally violates this subsection, or permits or encourages the unauthorized dissemination or use of information contained in reports and records made under this section, is guilty of a Class A misdemeanor.

(5) IMMUNITY FROM LIABILITY. Any person or institution participating in good faith in the making of a report or record under this section is immune

from any civil or criminal liability that results by reason of the action. For the purpose of any civil or criminal action or proceeding, any person reporting under this section is presumed to be acting in good faith. The immunity provided under this subsection does not apply to liability resulting from sexual contact by a therapist with a patient or client.

History: 1983 a. 431: 1985 a. 275; 1987 a. 352. 380; 1991 a. 160.

24

Criminalization of Therapist Sexual Misconduct in Colorado

AN OVERVIEW AND OPINION

Melissa Roberts-Henry

"October 4 happens to have been my wife's birthday," he said. "I have done some lousy things in my day, but not going to bed with another woman on my wife's birthday" (Trent, 1990a). These "compassionate" words were uttered by a Colorado Springs psychotherapist who allegedly abused more than 20 patients (Pat Wyka, Colorado Springs, personal communication, 1992). He was one of several tried under Colorado's criminalization law and, as a consequence of it, was sentenced to jail.

Before highlighting the law and outlining some case histories, I want to note the major lesson learned while researching this issue. It is, perhaps, the most significant point. When asked to delineate the consequences of the Colorado statute, which criminalized sexual misconduct by a psychotherapist with a client, it appeared to be a fairly routine endeavor. We had passed the law. It seemed like the work was over; but—it is not. *We are still much closer to the beginning than I had imagined.* The passage of the new law was only the first step. It set the framework for change, but it in itself did not signify that all necessary changes had been made.

On the positive side, because of issue-related laws, the Colorado legislature has been flooded with information on abuse by therapists and its ramifications. They are sensitized and well informed. Unfortunately, the same does not hold true for some people in police departments, district attorneys' (DAs') offices, and elsewhere who work with this statute on a daily basis. We must interact more directly with these people, and we must keep working to educate.

We must convince district attorneys not to dismiss cases at first glimpse just because they are perceived as the therapist's word against the patient's. When a case is investigated, we must inform DAs of the victim's sensitivities to prevent questions and actions that retraumatize them. We must gently persuade prosecutors of the importance of using reliable expert witnesses to demonstrate the dynamics of therapy in court. Also, we must write letters to judges when they are sentencing offenders and tell them of the seriousness of this abuse, that it destroys and devastates lives, and let them know that a "slap on the wrist" is not sufficient.

Without follow-up, the law is just a piece of paper. Every step of the way, education is important *and* information needs to be disseminated *and* cases need to be tracked. Consumer groups need to work to monitor these laws and the system to be certain that they are implemented and taken seriously.

EVOLUTION OF THE COLORADO STATUTE

Having emphasized the above, the following is a brief outline of the history and content of Colorado's criminal statute. In 1986-1987 Theresa Donahue, former Director of Policy and Research for the Colorado Department of Regulatory Agencies (DORA), was asked to review and examine the mental health profession. During related hearings before legislative committees, stories surfaced involving sexual abuse by Colorado therapists (Theresa Donahue, Denver, personal communication, Spring 1988). A confidential survey by DORA indicated that, in fact, 43% of therapists were aware of sexual abuse by their colleagues in Colorado

(Brad Mallon, 1988 citation of 1986 DORA survey findings). Thus came the impetus for a bill to provide a deterrent for such behavior.

In 1988, following one failed attempt, legislation was sponsored by Senator Martinez and Representative Tebedo for the present criminalization law. After the dropping of language that would have included "former patients," arguments over the issue of consent, and a successful campaign by the clergy to be excluded, what emerged from the process was Title 18, Article 3, Part 4 (that is, C.R.S. 18-3-405.5), titled "Concerning Sexual Assault on Clients by Psychotherapists."

In essence, the law states that any psychotherapist who perpetrates sexual penetration or intrusion on a client commits aggravated sexual assault: a Class 4 felony. It classifies other sexual contact as sexual assault: a Class 1 misdemeanor. The law further stipulates that "consent by the client cannot be used as a defense."

Effective in July 1988, this law has not been significantly changed since. A 1989 amendment slightly altered the wording but not the content. In 1991 the legislature, reviewing a related law, was disposed toward refining the term *psychotherapy*. Per their request, a small group (I was included as the consumer member) convened through the Colorado Mental Health Association to make changes in the definition. In summary, our efforts and debates led to a reaffirmation of the existing definition of *psychotherapy* in the law.

GENERAL CASE DATA
SUBSEQUENT TO THE BILL'S PASSAGE

During the postpassage phase of C.R.S. 18-3-405.5, a reasonable, but not large, number of cases have been filed. According to Attorney Joyce Seelen (Denver, personal communication, July 1992), only 3 of her 50-plus civil cases have proceeded to criminal trial. She speculated that this situation is not resultant from any "criminal- versus civil-case" conflict (whereby some insurance policies contain a "criminal act exclusion" that will not permit victim compensation in civil cases also filed as criminal cases). To the contrary, in Colorado, civil case settlement payments have consistently been made in cases with both civil and criminal actions.

Therefore, in Seelen's view (personal communication, 1992), the limited number of criminal cases filed probably signifies that many of the current civil suits represent cases that predate the effective date of the criminal statute. Also, many cases involve clergy, who are exempt from the law (Seelen, personal communication, 1992). Finally, many clients are reluctant to face the stress of a second trial (Joe Epstein, Denver, personal communication, August 1992).

In any event, I was able to locate at least 20 cases that were referred to DAs' offices in Denver and surrounding counties (El Paso-Colorado Springs, Jefferson, Boulder, Arapahoe, Douglas, and Adams) since 1988. Most of these cases involved male therapists. Three related to female counselors. At least eight were directed at unlicensed psychotherapists.

The dispositions of these cases were not easily attainable. Several cases were discovered through my work with I.M.P.A.C.T. (In Motion— People Abused in Counselling and Therapy), where I have spoken with many victims and attorneys, attended trials, and gathered news accounts. The State Grievance Board provided additional assistance and data (Karen Frazzini, Denver, personal communication, August-October 1988; Claire Villano, Denver, personal communication, 1988).

Elsewhere, public information on case outcomes was not centralized and some specific DAs' offices had restrictions against providing case data. Even when data were obtainable, a few cases were filed in more than one district (i.e., both where the therapist practiced and where the abuse occurred); and some information conflicted from source to source. Instances occurred where I provided DAs with corrected information for their own cases. Other times, there was limited familiarity with the law. One charging DA (district attorney in Boulder, personal communication, August 1988), for instance, replied that she was familiar with the law and had cases filed under it 10 years ago (notably before the law existed). Considering the small number of cases and sometimes conflicting information, the following case statistics are presented as suggestive but not totally accurate.

The data from various DAs, courthouse staff and employees, attorneys, Grievance Board staff, and other sources (personal communications from R. Allott, Denver, August 1992; J. Benetin, 1989-1992; J. Epstein, Denver, August 1992; K. Frazzini, Denver, August-October 1992; D. Gilbert, 1989-1992; C. Heim, Denver, August 1992; R. Keenan, Denver, August 1992; A. Martinez, 1992; Mark Perbix, Denver, August 1992; J. Seelen, 1988-1992; Craig Silverman, Denver, August 1992; C. Villano, Denver, 1992; Dan Zook, Colorado Springs, August 1992) are as follows:

Two cases were turned down outright. Three to four cases resulted in later dismissal (or possibly were not filed due to lack of cooperation from either party, a doubting DA, the inability to locate the therapist, or the fact that the therapist moved out of state). Two cases, both in Denver, received deferred judgments such that the charges will be dropped with no permanent record if there are no further violations within a two- to four-year period. Probation was granted to two therapists with stipulations that included mandated mental health counseling, community service work, and a prohibition from working with young people. Finally, three therapists have received jail sentences. One therapist was tried by a jury and found "not guilty." Five other cases were recently filed and are still in process.

It is important to note that there are major differences as to how cases are perceived and handled from one district to another and that some districts have proven superior on this issue.

FIVE COLORADO CASES
AND SIGNIFICANT COURT OPINIONS

Below is a brief synopsis of five of Colorado's more significant case histories. They include the first four cases to fall under the statute, three of which were, notably, handled in Colorado Springs. A more recent Jefferson County case involving a female therapist is cited to illustrate that, regardless of the serious circumstances, most cases are plea bargained or given lighter disciplinary action than I believe they warrant.

The initial discussion involves a Denver case filed June 6, 1989, and tried March 26, 1990: *The People v. Whisler* (Case #323879). It was a landmark case in that it was the first criminal suit to proceed to trial in Colorado. It was therefore surprising that dozens of phone calls, seeking only to verify the trial date, yielded comments such as the following: The defendant was not listed in the computer; the prosecuting DA, present at the trial, did not exist; and the judge of record differed from the presiding judge.

Throughout the trial itself, the psychologist-minister contended that he did not violate the criminal statute because he had previously withdrawn from his therapy practice to initiate a one-on-one educational course on how psychological processes result in us becoming who we are. His course, "Being Yourself," differed from therapy in that the client did not attempt to fix a problem but instead learned a body of knowledge.

Whisler then discussed insurance billing, his management of the victim's transference, and things that did, in fact, still sound like therapy. It is my opinion that the prosecution for the trial did not sufficiently discuss the dynamics of therapy and should have brought in expert witnesses to demonstrate that Whisler was still engaged in practice. In conclusion, the jury reached the only "not guilty" verdict in a statute-related trial. The plaintiff then chose not to follow up with a civil suit (J. Seelen, personal communication, 1992). The only "punitive measure" was a five-year injunction issued by the State Grievance Board to suspend Whisler's practice (K. Frazzini, personal communication, 1992).

In the second case (1989), Lance Weldgen was accused of assaulting an alcohol-impaired patient in a hospital. He was the first therapist in Colorado Springs to be charged under the law (Trent, 1989) and the first to receive a jail sentence (*Denver Post* Staff, 1990b; *Rocky Mountain News* Staff, 1990a; Trent, 1990b). He was also, it is believed, the first to challenge (and lose that challenge to) the constitutionality of the law. His challenge asserted that the definition of *psychotherapist* was too broad, and drug and alcohol counselors were not clearly included in the statute (Trent, 1989), but the challenge was denied by Judge R. Hall based on public protection issues (Trent, 1989).

On April 15, 1990, Weldgen pleaded guilty to a reduced charge of misdemeanor therapist sexual assault on a client (*Denver Post* Staff, 1990a; Trent, 1990b). His sentence, one year in jail with no chance of work release, was purportedly, at that time, the toughest in the country for a misdemeanor (Gary Schoener, personal communication, May 1990; *Rocky Mountain News* Staff, 1990a; Trent, 1990b, 1990c). He served only 42 days, however, when Weldgen said that he needed to support his family, had a definite job, and would return to jail each night (Trent, 1990c). On this basis, the judge reversed his decision and granted him a work release; whereupon an astute reporter and DA determined that Weldgen had no such job (*Gazette Telegraph* Staff, 1990a). Nine days later, at a hearing in which Weldgen told the judge, "I really thought I had a job. I could have another one as early as today" (Trent, 1990d), the original jail sentence was reinstituted.

A civil suit was, subsequently, brought against Weldgen. It was settled out of court (D. Zook, personal communication, 1992). The Colorado State Mental Health Grievance Board was scheduled to have their hearing in October 1992 (K. Frazzini, personal communication, 1992). I have not been able to verify the outcome.

Case three, that of R. Ferguson, can be best characterized by this quote: "I meant if my hand inadvertently got in the area of her breast, I was unaware of it. I would not have done it deliberately" (*Rocky Mountain News* Staff, 1988). Ferguson, a licensed Colorado Springs psychologist who also uttered this chapter's opening quote, was the third therapist in Colorado to face charges under C.R.S. 18-3-405.5. He received the second and longest jail term under the statute and his challenge to the constitutionality of the law went all the way to the Colorado Supreme Court (1992).

Prior to passage of the criminalization statute, several complaints were made against Ferguson. Two different patients reported him to the State Board of Psychologist Examiners, and twice the board allowed him to retain his license (Paul Daraghy, Denver, personal communication, 1989; Survivor 1, personal communications, 1989-1992). In civil suits, he made out-of-court settlements for allegations of sexually abusing two patients: a mother and her daughter. He was found guilty of third-degree misdemeanor sexual assault on the 16-year-old daughter (*Rocky Mountain News* Staff, 1988), but received two years probation with 300 hours community service (*Gazette Telegraph* Staff, 1990b, 1990c; D. Gilbert, personal communication, 1990; Trent, 1990f). It was later revealed that, on the day he received that sentence, he left the courthouse, went to his office, and allegedly had sex with another patient (Survivor 1, personal communication, 1989-1992).

Under the new statute (18-3-405.5), this patient, of an estimated 20 who also alleged that he had sex with them (*Gazette Telegraph* Staff, 1990c; Trent, 1990f; P. Wyka, personal communication, 1989), filed felony criminal charges (*Gazette Telegraph* Staff, 1990b) and later settled in a civil suit. The criminal case was, in my opinion, well handled as both witnesses and evidence were used by District Attorney Gilbert.

Ferguson's defense in the criminal trial was that he did not break the law because he terminated therapy and stopped billing the woman two days before the criminal law took effect (Trent, 1990e) and it was "strictly sex after that" (Trent, 1990a, 1990f). A jury found him guilty on four felony counts of aggravated sexual assault for abuse that transpired after the law took effect (*Gazette Telegraph* Staff, 1990c) and dismissed five other counts of abuse that occurred prior to the law's effective date (*Gazette Telegraph* Staff, 1990c). He was sentenced to four, two-year jail terms (D. Gilbert, personal communication, 1991; *Rocky Mountain News* Staff, 1990b; Trent, 1990f) to be served concurrently. A civil suit settlement was subsequently paid. His license has been surrendered (June 1989) to the newly created Colorado State Mental Health Grievance Board (*Gazette Telegraph* Staff, 1990b, 1990c).

As for Ferguson's posttrial constitutional challenge (Supreme Court, State of Colorado, No. 90S497, *Ferguson v. The People*, 1992; see Colorado Bar Association, 1992), the Colorado Supreme Court used strong language in its decision upholding the criminalization law. In summary, the ruling said: (a) The law is not overbroad and does not violate Fourteenth Amendment due process privacy and associational rights, for instance, the right of therapists and clients to have consensual sex. Privacy does not mean immunity for all sexual acts; examples here are incest and prostitution. The legislature has a right to define sexual criminal misconduct to protect those whose special circumstances, as in therapy, could allow for exploitation. (b) Even though the "no consent" language is not uniformly imposed on all health care providers, there is no violation of equal protection laws. The legislature may place special restrictions on situations involving real differences; the emotional state and dependency of a client in therapy is one such circumstance. (c) Despite the "no consent" language, the law is not unfair and is not a strict liability law. There is still a burden of proving aggravated sexual assault, and the use of the term *knowingly* vis-à-vis the actions of the therapist brings mental culpability into play. Furthermore, the court affirms that consent is no more an issue in abuse by therapists than in incest.

Case four also involved an interesting decision. A Colorado Springs licensed psychologist-minister practiced what he called "simulated friendship." A therapist, he believed, can show his feelings, engage in self-disclosure, and be an ideal friend. But Oraker, unfortunately, engaged in a lot more than friendship. Again, both criminal and civil suits were filed (Gail Bell, personal communication, Denver, 1990-1992; *Gazette Telegraph* Staff, 1990d; J. Seelen, personal communication, 1990-1992). The civil suit brought into play an action by the insurance company (District Court of El Paso County, Colorado Civil Action No. 906V6483, *American Home Assurance Company v. Dr. James R. Oraker and Gail Bell*, 1992), American Home Assurance Company, which invoked its limitation of liability clause, capping sexual misconduct damage at $25,000 (but without a criminal act exclusion or absolute refusal to pay coverage).

The plaintiff's attorney, Joyce Seelen, and the victim then decided to challenge the insurance company cap applicable to the civil suit. First, they dealt with the criminal case as follows: Oraker was allowed to plea bargain to a lesser criminal charge of reckless endangerment, which shifted the focus of that complaint from sexual misconduct to other wrongful acts committed in therapy. He was fined and sentenced to 120 hours of public service—*with children* (G. Bell, personal communication, 1990-1992; J. Seelen, personal communication, 1990-1992). The Grievance Board decided that he could retain his license with the stipulation that he undergo supervision and get therapy. This requirement has been satisfied and is no longer in effect (K. Frazzini, personal communication, 1992).

The plaintiff's civil suit was then handled creatively. Plaintiff's attorney said, "I don't believe the cap holds. Give us $50,000 and file a Declaratory

Judgment with the court to see if the cap is legal. If the cap stands we'll stick with this amount. If not, our maximum request will be $25,000" (J. Seelen, personal communication, 1990-1992). Regarding the related insurance cap-based suit, it was argued that (a) given two separate wrongful acts, both should be covered, (b) the language of the contract was unclear and included two different liability clauses, and (c) the contract was "fraudulent" and in violation of public policy. All therapy has some sexual issues and therefore the contract represents an illusory promise (District Court of El Paso County, Colorado Civil Action No. 906V6483, *American Home Assurance Company v. Dr. James R. Oraker and Gail Bell*, 1992).

Under Judge M. Heydt, the verdict was determined in El Paso County District Court, where the case involving the cap was filed. He upheld the cap and reasoned that, though there were numerous wrongful acts in therapy (including but not limited to a dual relationship, improper therapeutic style, mishandling of transference, poor note taking, and sexual misconduct), these were interlinked and could not be viewed as unrelated to the sexual misconduct. On the bright side, his opinion did contain several strong statements supportive of victims and reprimanding misconduct committed in the guise of therapy.

Finally, case five, filed October 2, 1990, in Jefferson County, involved a female therapist who labeled herself a "recreational therapist." She became sexually involved with a 17-year-old male patient in a hospital alcohol treatment program and further tried to convince him to kill his parents (Finley, 1990) such that he was also brought up on charges that were subsequently dropped (Duran, 1991). Though charged with one count of felony therapist sexual assault (Duran, 1991; Finley, 1990; *Rocky Mountain News* Staff, 1990c), possibly the first felony charges against a female Colorado therapist, the therapist pleaded guilty to misdemeanor sexual assault on a child (*Denver Post* Staff, 1991a, 1991b). In August 1991 she received a mere two years of probation, a $5,000 fine, and an order to avoid further work with young people. There was also a stipulation for mental health counseling and 40 hours of community service (*Denver Post*, 1991b; Duran, 1991). A civil suit was settled (Duran, 1991).

In this case, as in many, disciplinary action has been light. The State Grievance Board has stepped in to issue sanctions in some cases of (both licensed and unlicensed) therapists facing criminal charges. However, it is likely that most of these same therapists will be allowed to practice at a later date, after applying for a license (K. Frazzini, personal communication, 1992).

VIEWPOINT OF SOME VICTIMS/SURVIVORS

Of the victims/survivors (and it is important to note that this covers only those I surveyed informally in Colorado), many feel the need for several layers of protection, and most are strongly behind the law. For one thing, it provides a strong statement to the judicial community and the public that this is a very serious offense. Additionally, Colorado press coverage of criminal cases seems to be more substantial than for past civil cases and this can act to alert others to potential abuse. Most significantly, however, the law has allowed victims/survivors to finally come to the realization that what happened to them was serious enough to sanction harshly, and that the pain and trauma they feel do indeed have a basis in fact.

As to which they would choose, if they had to decide between money from a civil suit or seeing their perpetrators sanctioned through a criminal trial (though, again, this has not been a conflict in Colorado), the consensus was divided. Of interest, some victims in Colorado have filed criminal cases in preference to civil suits. Many others, if they had the option, would choose the criminal trial because, like any other type of "rape," this is criminal behavior. Monetary compensation, if there is such a thing, is not as important as letting perpetrators know that their title does not automatically elevate them to a level that exempts them from facing the same consequences as anyone else who commits this violation. Top priority is preventing abusers from repeating their behavior. Although criminal charges do not necessarily mean heavy sanctions, there is at least that possibility.

CONCLUSION

To conclude, previously I noted that we are still too close to the beginning of dealing with this issue. Several difficulties remain despite the law's existence. These include poor treatment of victims/survivors during the investigation process or unwillingness of prosecutors to proceed with cases due to lack of understanding of abuse. Nonetheless, *the law is a significant achievement.* For, while the law may not work perfectly or be of benefit in each individual case, there have been and will continue to be benefits from the statute that accrue to society as a whole: increased public awareness, making perpetrators responsible for their actions, and, in the ideal situation, removal of abusers from the mainstream where it is likely that they will continue to do harm.

25

How Churches
Respond to the Victims and
Offenders of Clergy Sexual Misconduct

Margo E. Maris

Kevin M. McDonough

Religious leaders (deacons, priests/pastors, and bishops) upon their ordination are bestowed with the gift of power and authority associated with the sacred. As long as there have been churches, some of these religious leaders have abused their sacred power and authority for a variety of reasons. Because of the abuse of their sacred offices, people have been betrayed and deeply hurt; in some cases, their innocence and their faith have been stolen and/or profoundly damaged.

During the current time of sacred history, the religious community is being called to deal openly, honestly, and *definitively* with these actions of religious leaders. This chapter will deal with the abuse of sacred power that takes specifically sexual forms: sexual exploitation, sexual abuse, and sexual harassment and coercion. Sacred power can be abused in many other ways as well, but it is the violation of sexual boundaries in the ministerial setting that this chapter discusses. The chapter is divided into two parts. In the first section, Rev. Margo E. Maris addresses the responses of churches to victims of clergy sexual misconduct. She speaks both of the needs of those directly violated by clergy misconduct and also of the so-called secondary victims, especially congregations affected by the misconduct in their midst. The Rev. Maris is the Canon to the Ordinary of the Episcopal Diocese of Minnesota. The second portion of the chapter addresses church responses to clergy offenders. Its author is Rev. Kevin M. McDonough, the Vicar General and Moderator of the Curia of the Archdiocese of Saint Paul and Minneapolis in Minnesota. While the Reverends Maris and McDonough have produced their portions of the chapter separately, they regularly consult with one another and with other denominational leaders. Each author takes responsibility for his or her own portion of this chapter, while acknowledging indebtedness to one another and to their ecumenical and interdisciplinary colleagues in the development of these perspectives.

RESPONDING TO THOSE
HARMED BY CLERGY SEXUAL ABUSE

As an example of the degree to which this problem is acknowledged and handled, the state of Minnesota has enacted State Law 148A, which states that a cause of action against a clergy member for *sexual exploitation* exists for a counselee for injury caused by sexual contact with the clergy member, if the sexual contact occurs

during the time the person was in counseling with the clergy person or

after the time the person was in counseling with the clergy member if the person was emotionally dependent on the clergy person, or if the sexual contact occurred by means of therapeutic deception.

The law states that the person may recover damages from a clergy person who is found liable for sexual exploitation. In addition, if the congregation or diocese has knowledge of the sexual exploitation and fails to act, they too are liable.

According to Statute 148A, *sexual contact* means any of the following, whether or not occurring with the consent of the person involved with the clergy member:

- Sexual intercourse, cunnilingus, fellatio, anal intercourse, or any intrusion, however slight, into the genital or anal openings of the person's body by

any part of the cleric's body, or by any object used by the person for this
purpose, if agreed to by the clergy person

* Kissing of, or the intentional touching by, the clergy member of the person's
genital area, groin, inner thigh, buttocks, or breast or of the clothing covering
any of these body parts

Sexual contact includes requests by the clergy person for the conduct described above.

Therapeutic deception means a representation by the clergy member that
sexual contact with the clergy person is consistent with or part of the
person's counseling.

The church is also responsible for dealing with the issues of *sexual abuse*
(anyone under the age of 18 or a vulnerable adult) as well as *sexual
harassment.*

The sins of the clergy are the sexual acts or encounters themselves.
The evil in this occurs when the church fails to deal with the sins of the
clergy promptly, directly, openly, and with a clear pronouncement of
these behaviors' wrongfulness. There are no existing excuses in the
sacred world that would ever make these behaviors acceptable. Church
leaders are learning that sexual contact with anyone with whom a clergy
member has a sacred relationship (in the realm of the sacred) is always
wrong.

Various faiths have developed different strategies for dealing with
the people who have been hurt by clergy misconduct. The term *victim*
has a connotation of helplessness and powerlessness that is oftentimes
unhelpful. The term *survivor* has been used for those people who have
regained their power and authority in respect to the abuse. I will use
these terms for lack of better ones.

The role of the church must be that of a vehicle of healing and
restoring of peace. The church must not further abuse people by its
silence. Because justice and mercy are at the cornerstone of our faith,
work with the individuals who have been hurt by clergy must be centered
in their feeling that justice has been served. Most individuals who have
been hurt also seek mercy in dealing with the individual offender. It is
much more difficult for victims to ask for institutional mercy if the institution has ignored, minimized, or belittled them. Therefore the religious community (individual denominations) needs to pay close and
careful attention to the people bringing accusations.

How can religious authorities provide the feeling of safety that an
individual needs in order to bring a charge forward? First, a set of clear
policies and procedures must be developed, printed, publicized, and

distributed to all congregations and denominational institutions. (Models are available from most mainline denominations. The Minnesota Council of Churches, 122 W. Franklin, Minneapolis, MN 55404, 612 870-3600, has many of these model policies and procedures.) The leadership needs to follow these policies and procedures with as much consistency as possible. The institutional church will not feel safe to the victim if there is not consistency of action.

Once policies and procedures have been developed, there needs to be designated and publicized a list of people (advocates) available to help victims through this church process. There have been at least two interdenominational advocacy trainings since October 1991. One was held in Minneapolis, Minnesota, sponsored by the Minnesota Council of Churches, and the other, sponsored by the United Methodist Church, was held in Chicago in September 1993.

A victim assisted by a well-trained and supervised advocate is crucial to the healing process for the individual, the congregation and/or institution, and the religious institution as a whole. Two of the most important aspects that denominational leaders must pay attention to when recruiting advocates are the leaders' ability to work with the advocate in a trusting relationship, and that the potential advocate has worked through his or her own issues of victimization. Additional qualities for advocates are also available through the Minnesota Council of Churches.

What is an advocate? In a very simple way, an advocate is someone who helps the victims discover the "still small voice" inside of them that has been unable, for a variety of reasons, to learn to speak with courage and force for what they need to heal. An advocate does not speak for others but helps and encourages others to speak and make decisions for themselves.

When a "person who has been hurt," or believes he or she has been, by a member of the clergy calls or writes the religious institution, that person needs to be offered an advocate. Such people are encouraged to call the advocate themselves, after the role and the training of the advocate has been explained (either by voice or mail).

The victim calls the advocate, and the following is an outline of what an advocate *might* do.

Immediate Care

1. Call arrives in the denominational office (a) directly, (b) by referral, or (c) from someone anonymously seeking information.

a. The caller needs to know that he or she is speaking to the right person (the advocate coordinator or the advocate). *Do not* let the person tell his or her story to anyone who cannot help.

b. Advocacy people should identify themselves and their role: "My name is _____ and I have been trained to listen to stories (cases) pertaining to sexual exploitation, harassment, and/or abuse."

"I am an advocate and not a therapist or attorney or clergy/spiritual director." If the advocate is a priest/deacon/bishop, then he or she needs to be up front by identifying him- or herself with that pastoral office.

The advocate should ask the person if he or she has a therapist, spiritual director, clergy member, close friend, or attorney (this helps identify the support network). The advocate may be the first person to hear the story but should try not to be the *only* one.

2. Ask the client, "Are you in a place where you can talk to me? Do you want to set a time and place where we can talk, or do you want to begin by talking on the phone?" Describe to them the confidential nature of the interaction and any state-mandated reporting situation that might limit or waive confidentiality.

Let people know that they are free to speak anonymously, but if they want the church to act against the alleged offender, eventually they will have to

a. be known,

b. make accusations or charges in writing,

c. have a preliminary and possible meeting with the ecclesiastical authority.

3. When asked by the caller (victim) *if* and *how you* (the advocate) can help, respond in a reassuring manner, but *don't* give the message, "I can fix it."

The full story must come out in your discussions before you can begin to offer any alternatives. Exact times, dates, and places are not so important as listening and hearing the flow of the story and paying close attention to the feelings. The work done by the advocate is an attempt to help the person who has been victimized deal with his or her feelings of powerlessness and abandonment. It's important for the advocate to hear those feelings of powerlessness and abandonment flow from the story so that the advocate will know the touch points for healing. When the victim's healing has taken place, exact times and places will often be forgotten but the feelings will remain.

Do not make judgments or promises you cannot keep. Each denomination handles accusations and disciplines in its own unique way, according to the accusations. Ongoing child abuse is handled quite differently than a 20-year-old sexual exploitation case.

4. There are five basic ways that an advocate should respond to the caller. These *five words* were developed by the Illusion Theater (528 Hennepin Ave., Minneapolis, Minnesota 55414, which should be credited with the work). These words are as follows:

Believe what they are telling you

Affirm what and how they are telling you

Support them in ways they might articulate a need

Empower them to do what they need to

Refer to a therapist, spiritual director, attorney, police, child protection, and so on

Each of these actions should be done at some point in the conversations.

Don't make promises you cannot keep.

Don't put words into their mouths. Let them speak in their own voices.

Don't assume reactions or responses. Some people don't cry or get angry right away.

5. Listening to the story does not make you the investigator. You do not need all the details to have the story believed.

The advocate needs enough details of the story to truthfully be able to say:

a. I believe you.

b. It was not your fault.

c. It was wrong.

d. This has happened to others and you are not alone.

e. How may I help you?

f. Give them a vocabulary for what has happened to them (*abuse, exploitation,* and/or *harassment*)—these are *not* interchangeable words. The following are areas of concern for the advocate, but, as yet, there is not enough experience to know whether or not the advocate should keep notes or keep track of dates and times. Two other areas of concern are to whom the rules of confidentiality apply and to whom the advocate debriefs.

6. During the conversation, try to assess the immediate life situation (e.g., suicide prevention check, concurrent stressful events such as divorce or financial problems).

7. During the conversation:

    a. Stick to the story at hand of the clergy sexual abuse, exploitation, and/or harassment.

    b. Break myths surrounding other cases (large money settlements; just forgive and forget; the church does not want to hear this).

    c. Don't presume they want to pray, hear biblical stories, be told they are forgiven, and the like or be told to "gird their loins."

    d. List other resources for them, explaining that the following might be other possible actions:

        1. Do not be alone with this, if possible.

        2. Read books and articles.

        3. Participate in individual or group therapy.

        4. Do nothing.

        5. Contact attorneys.

        6. Notify agency director, supervisor, or church hierarchy.

        7. File criminal complaint.

        8. File civil suit for damages.

        9. Report to state or county authorities.

        10. Report to adult protection.

        11. Complain to the ethics committee of a professional organization.

        12. Make a licensure or registration complaint.

        13. Participate in a confrontation/processing session.

8. Keep assessing and clarifying with the client what your role is.

9. After the first phone call or until the story is clear, needs are assessed, and referrals are made, take *no* steps without the permission of the client. This is true with the exception of child abuse and other mandated reporting requirements, which vary by state.

Options in "The Wheel of Options" (Milgrom, 1989a; see Figure 27.1 in Chapter 27) will be previewed and talked about during the second meeting (victims may change their minds several times before a viable set of options emerge):

    a. File criminal complaint (states differ on this as an available option).

    b. File civil suit for damages.

    c. Report to other church bodies and/or other state licensing authorities. (For example, if a seminary is the authority involved, additional authorities to contact would be the denomination that sponsors, the authority that accredits, and/or the state agency that licenses.)

d. Report to adult protection. (This is especially important if the victim is a vulnerable adult—each state has different definitions—and/or a person who is vulnerable because of age.)

e. File a complaint to the ethics committee or professional association.

f. File a complaint to the licensing board, if the perpetrator is licensed.

g. Write or call the ex-counselor.

h. Refer to individual and/or group therapy.

i. Refer to a group that deals specifically with clergy sexual abuse, exploitation, and/or harassment.

j. File a complaint with the state Equal Opportunity Employment Commission.

k. Report abuser to judicatory head.

l. Participate in confrontation/processing session.

m. Do nothing.

All these options take varying amounts of time and energy to accomplish. The average amount of time for processing one or all of the options with a victim is about a year, although some people have processed their options in as little as five months or taken as long as two years.

The advocate for a victim must be prepared to spend the amount of time necessary to complete the process with his or her client.

It seems to work best if the victim and the advocate are not of the same denomination, because there might be issues of boundary and loyalty. It is a good idea that the advocate has available a coach/supervisor from the victim's denomination. It might be appropriate to work within the same denomination as long as the advocate and the victim are not in the same jurisdiction.

It is also *not* recommended that one advocate work with more than one victim of the same offender. Each person who has been through an act of clergy sexual exploitation has different needs. Sometimes these individual needs run into conflict with one another. Therefore each victim must have his or her own advocate to help discern his or her own primary needs and ways to get them met.

All of the options take time and have a special way of being handled. It is important that the advocate help the victim prioritize and carry out the options. The advocate must help the victim realize a process with which he or she is most comfortable. It will take different levels of awareness and healing to deal with each option.

Option 1, "Participate in confrontation/processing session," is an option I will elaborate on below. As of the writing of this chapter (February
1994), I have worked with over 500 victims of clergy abuse of power
over a period of 10 years. Over the last nine years, I have led or participated in over 50 confrontation/intervention processes. Only a very
small percentage of people want to face the offender directly.

The healing of these deep emotional, physical, and spiritual wounds
takes time. It takes time for an individual to believe that a safe place can
be provided for him or her to speak to the offender. The advocate's role
is to build the trust level between the victim and her- or himself so the
victim will believe that the setting for the meeting will be safer and the
victim will be protected.

Since 1984, when I began to realize the need for the victim to feel a
sense of powerfulness, I have suggested to victims that one of their
options is to face the offender in a safe place, surrounded by a group of
supportive people. This confrontation allows victims to return to the
offender in a way that allows them to feel a new sense of their power.
Victims begin to realize and own this sense of powerfulness by being
in the same room with the person who hurt them. What is different for
the offender is that oftentimes he or she still sees the victim as victim
and does not recognize the growth and change that has taken place.
What then can happen is that the offender accuses the advocate of
putting words in the victim's mouth. This is a point where the advocate
needs to be watchful and keep the focus on the victim's needs.

When using Option 1, I also begin, and come back to time and time
again, and end with two questions—"What do you need to heal?" "How
will you know when you are healed?"—always encouraging that still
small voice to speak from the victims' hearts and souls. I encourage
them to be self-defining within the possibilities of the options. I do not
discourage people from asking for their own set of options. But I discourage spending too much time and energy on options that are clearly
unattainable.

How to prepare a victim for the meeting. I follow a simple three-part outline:

1. Develop a chronology (timetable) of the *events* leading up to the
   sexual misconduct, including as many incidents as the victim
   needs to describe the betrayal.
2. List the effects the misconduct by the religious leader has had on
   the victim's life, including (although not a complete list of the
   possibilities)

a. emotional/psychological,
b. physical,
c. sexual,
d. economic/employment,
e. family/marriage,
f. church/faith,
g. spiritual, and
h. self-esteem.

3. Make a list of the needs you are requesting to be addressed by the denomination, congregation, the individual, the insurance company, and so on. These needs become part of the restitution process for the religious body and the individual victim. Again, the question that needs to be asked is this: "What do you need to heal?"

Who might be present at the intervention confrontation?

a. the individual victim (and possibly a family member);
b. the offender (and the offender's counselor, therapist, or spiritual leader);
c. the head of the religious body;
d. the victim's therapist (if desired);
e. the advocate; and/or
f. someone to convene and monitor the meeting.

How much time should be allotted? A meeting should last about one and a half to two hours, with some kind of a break between parts 1 and 2 in the outline above.

The victim should be allowed to speak without interruption (except for clarification) through part 1 and, if possible, part 2. The offender and the head of the religious body should be asked to respond after part 2, either before or after a break.

This meeting is *not* the appropriate place to dispute facts (a trial would be the appropriate place). The victim needs to phrase her or his comments in "I" statements. A victim is probably not ready (and therefore should not be encouraged) to do the intervention if he or she is not in control of his or her anger or rage.

What should the religious leaders be prepared to do? Apologies are appropriate, but must be sincere. It is appropriate at the end of the meeting for the head of the religious body to respond to the needs of the victim. You must respond only to the requests that you can actually promise to address. If other resources must be conferred with, tell the victim and his or her advocate, who needs to be checked with, the approximate time they will know. For example, if it will take two weeks to get authorization to cover therapy costs for a certain length of time, then that should be stated; and if that authorization has not come in two weeks, you should recontact the advocates and update them. The lack of knowing or lack of contact might undo the work of the meeting.

It is also extremely important to respond at the meeting (and in writing after the meeting) to the needs of the victim so he or she knows you have *heard* what the specific needs are. Although I encourage people to check with the denominational attorney, I would *not* encourage the letter to be written in a legally designed or guarded way but, instead, in a way that reflects the spirit of the faith in relationship to the injury that has been received. The victim came to the religious because of authority in the faith, not for legal expertise.

Because the misconduct was veiled in secrecy and shame and the victim lived in the fear of unknowing and being discovered for so long, it is critical to be on time and open with any promises the denominational head makes. *Do not make promises you cannot keep.* To the victim, any broken promise feels like another betrayal and breaks whatever trust has been built at the meeting.

Remember that the meeting is about healing the wounds of the victim. The victim needs to hear that he or she is as valuable a part of the religious institution as the ordained and/or leadership person. The denominational head is a critical bridge to helping the victim *begin* to reclaim his or her faith.

Dealing With the Other Victims: The Congregation

When sexual misconduct occurs, there are many more people who will begin to feel the victimization of the betrayal by the religious leader. The largest number will be in the congregation the leader served or in the organization he or she served. So it is critical to approach the congregation in the same way that we approach a person who is about to receive the news of the death of a loved one.

A religious leader in most cases is given the same kind of automatic trust and respect given to a parent.

It is critical, just as with the original victim, that the denomination have available a set of policies and procedures that can be presented to the leadership and the congregation before a crisis occurs. The congregation can be made to feel safe at a time it is receiving news of any kind of betrayal, and the advocate's role will be to restore order in the chaos this kind of event will cause.

When pre- and/or preventive education has not been done, the following guidelines might be helpful.

When the denominational head hears the allegation from the victim and believes that there are grounds for an investigation of the allegation of sexual misconduct, this is when the elected leadership in the congregation should be told. This is generally after hearing from the victim and confronting the clergy or leader with the allegations.

In the Episcopal Church, the two people notified would be the senior and junior wardens. The leaders need to be told of the *confidential*, private nature of the information and that it is critical to the ongoing life of the congregation that the information be received by the majority of the congregation when other safeguards are in place. The only request that denominational leaders can make is that the congregational leadership knows how important confidentiality is to the healing process. There is no way to make people keep information confidential.

The elected leadership will be critical in helping the denomination deal with the news. These leaders *must* be part of advising the denominational leadership as to the process design in informing the entire congregation.

After the clergy person has been told that he or she must go for an evaluation and/or must not be with the congregation, then the two or three elected leaders will help the denominational leaders tell the larger elected leadership. The larger leadership group *needs* to be a part of the hands-on planning to inform the rest of the congregation.

It is critical that the denominational leadership be present at the meeting when the larger elected leadership is told and the planning for the congregational meeting is being designed. The congregational leadership needs to know they are not in this by themselves. Otherwise, they will only focus on their own feelings of anger and disappointment about being betrayed and abandoned. At this critical time, congregational leaders need to think of the ongoing life of the congregation rather than their own personal feelings. To be helpful to congregational leaders, the denominational leaders should help in dealing with personal feelings.

Some of the issues that the congregational leadership needs to plan for are as follows:

1. How will the congregation be notified (by meeting or letter—both are necessary)?

2. Who will be the clergy leadership on the following Sunday (unfortunately, these events all seem to be revealed at the end of the week!)?
3. What will be said about the offender and family?
4. What will be said about the care of the victim(s)?
5. What will be said about the incidents (events)?
6. What will the leadership design be during the absence of the clergy? (If
   Grandmother Sue dies, who will be called?)
7. How will communication happen?

Because of the timing of these issues, no group of leaders feels it has
enough time to do adequate and careful planning. However much time
the leadership has to prepare, it is imperative that all members be given
the same information at the same time as much as possible. The congregation must be given the factual truth, but not necessarily in great detail.
The information must be enough for the people to wrestle with believing the truth of the allegations. If this is done correctly, the congregation
will have an easier time believing and more difficulty denying the
reality of what has been told to them.

If any preeducation has been done and the congregation has been told
of the denominational process of hearing and investigating allegations,
then more trust will be built for the action the denomination is taking.

At the point of telling the congregational leadership, a consultant
should be appointed to the congregational leadership to guide them
through this initial process. The consultant will help guide the leadership through the first few weeks of the process, including the open
congregational meetings that will be held in the initial few weeks. The
role of the consultant is not to do the work for the leadership but to
coach them and be the connector between the congregational leadership
and the denominational office.

If a further outline of this process of immediate care of the congregation is needed, I would suggest requesting one from

Rev. Chilton Knudsen
Diocese of Chicago
65 E. Huron
Chicago, IL 60611

Ms. Nancy Hopkins
Lower Falls Landing
38 Lafayette St.
Yarmouth, ME 04096

Parish Consultation Services
Minnesota Council of Churches
122 W. Franklin
Minneapolis, MN 55404

The outline of the process would help the leadership and the congregation begin to feel empowered to deal with the betrayal and to know that other congregations have gone through this process and survived.

There are two critical areas of support that are necessary for a congregation to deal with at this stage: first, to provide consistent, clear, and updated information (communication) to people, and, second, to provide consistent appropriate clergy leadership during this time. If there ever is need for "nonanxious" clergy and lay leadership in a congregation, it is now. This is the time that there should not appear to be a vacuum in leadership.

After the first few weeks, when more information is known about the fate of the clergy member, then a long-term healing process can be put in place.

At this writing, there are very few clearly healed congregations, but as congregations begin to deal openly with these betrayals, there will be more information and healing stories available. My best estimate at this point is that, depending on the many circumstances of the degree and depth of betrayal, a congregation will begin to know its own healing in about three years.

RESPONDING TO OFFENDERS

A great deal of public attention has been given to cases of clergy sexual misconduct with teenage boys. While such cases are often extraordinarily painful, it is important to note that they do not constitute the majority of sexual misconduct cases involving the misuse of clergy position and influence. The most common cases that we have investigated are, from years past, of exploitation of adult women, often involving incestlike dynamics. Each element of this description deserves some attention.

First, most complaints refer to older events. Few refer to misconduct occurring in the last five years, with many being more than 20 years old at the time of the initial report to church officials. The difficulties that this poses for investigation will be discussed below. The reasons for the predominance of old complaints is not clear. Some have suggested that this is because recent attention to the problem is now bringing forth a backlog of problems that could not have been reported in the closed atmosphere of a decade or more ago. Others have suggested there is an "incubation period" for complaints, a time during which victims work at obtaining sufficient emotional and spiritual resources to bring a complaint. Some optimists even suggest a third reason, namely, that recent publicity has reduced the incidence of clergy sexual misconduct. Perhaps another decade or so of experience will be necessary before a "normal" developmental sequence of a complaint will be evident.

Second, the majority of complaints involve sexual contact between a pastor or other clergy leader and an adult for whom he or she has pastoral responsibility. While we have seen complaints against female clergy and religious and same-sex complaints against male pastors, our most frequent complaints have been about clergymen's exploitation of a pastoral trust relationship with adult women congregants. Such complaints have often been treated with a good deal of skepticism by the general public, including congregational members. Casual comments by parish members and even by fellow clergy and denominational leaders to the effect that "at least it wasn't a boy" reflect not only a special horror for violations of children but a continued societal insensitivity to the exploitation of women. Contrary to the experience with offenses against children, in which congregants accuse denominational officials of under-reaction, denominational leaders find themselves criticized for "over-reaction" to clergymen whose involvement with adult women is viewed as "natural" and putatively consensual.

Third, the great majority of offenses appear to be most closely related to incest rather than to molestation or rape. We have dealt with few offenders accused of explicit violence against their victims. Rather, offending clergy have usually established a "familial" relationship with their victims, which may include participation in family outings, involvement in the celebrations and traumas of the extended family, and even more mundane services such as baby-sitting, home repairs, and assistance with minor household bills. As noted in the previous section, all three of these factors generate a great deal of ambivalence on the part of the complainant. They also make it more difficult for the offender to understand why his or her behavior is harmful and unacceptable.

After receiving a complaint from the victim (adult or child, male or female), the first major step in dealing with accused offenders is a confrontation. If state or local law gives priority to the involvement of public criminal or child protection officials, then denominational officials of course must wait for clearance before stepping in. These cases are rare, however, and the more usual difficulty is that of assessing an old complaint. We have learned to move as quickly as possible to confrontation in regard to all complaints, unless the complainant places restrictions on our use of the information or unless the complaint is so contradictory, either internally or with known facts, or so openly impossible as to make it seem spurious.

Most denominational disciplinary codes provide procedural protections for the rights of accused clergy. Two key issues have to be addressed at the beginning of a confrontation. First, clergy are usually entitled to, or at least well served by, the presence of a knowledgeable advocate. In cases in which civil (tort) or criminal issues may be involved, the accused clergy should have the help of an attorney immediately. In all cases, people knowledgeable in church procedures or rules should be available to the clergy. A second procedural protection is that against self-incrimination. Obvious as such a protection seems in American criminal law, it can seem foreign in a church setting. We have found that, when confronted, clergy often are eager to acknowledge their wrongdoing to the extent that they understand it as such. Our conversations with people who discipline physicians and other offending professionals suggest that clergy are different in this regard and are far more "confessional." We generally tell accused clergy that we will welcome anything they want to say, but we caution them to consider the effect that any admissions would have on their standing in the church and before civil courts.

As the primary purpose of this initial confrontation then is not that of obtaining a "confession" from the accused, why hold it at all? Especially when the confrontation is based in an older complaint, its purpose is to obtain the cooperation of the accused in a psychological assessment. Such assessments, as will be noted below, cannot establish the truth or falsehood of any particular complaint about past behavior. Frustratingly, the kinds of evidence that normally make us sure about what did or did not happen in the past, such as physical evidence and eyewitness corroboration, are generally lacking in such cases, given the secretiveness of most exploitative relationships. Friends and family of the complainant may be able to corroborate a softness of professional boundaries between the complainant and the accused, including excessive numbers of home visits, taking vacation trips together, and ongoing financial help. Short of an admission on the part of the accused, however, an older complaint only gives prima facie grounds to reexamine the safety of the current ministerial assignment or call of the accused. Denominational leaders who refuse to challenge a member of the clergy until they have proof "beyond a reasonable doubt" of the veracity of an older allegation will wind up having to dismiss nearly all complaints and will miss a critical opportunity to assess the current ministerial functioning of the accused.

We have often found it prudent to impose certain temporary restrictions on the current ministry of the accused right from the time of the first confrontation. At a minimum, this involves disclosure of the accusation to one or more coworkers. Inoffensive as such a requirement may seem, it often proves to be quite difficult for "lone ranger"-type clergy, who are accustomed to shielding major parts of their lives from close examination by anyone, including spouses and close friends. Other restrictions may include these: limitations on unsupervised contact with the alleged "target group," restrictions on the place of residence, and, in the most serious cases, temporary suspension from the ministry.

We have learned that the second phase of the process, assessment, works best when carried out by a qualified professional, or even team, specialized in this particular work. We generally ask that an assessment be performed by an individual or organization that, at least for that particular case, will not be considered subsequently as a treatment provider. There are several advantages to this approach. It places a premium on the timely completion of assessment (because therapeutic needs demonstrated by the accused during the process are referred to other professionals) and it makes clear that the assessment is done at the request of denominational officials rather than as part of a confidential, longer term therapeutic relationship. Conversely, it also protects the therapeutic relationship once that has begun, because it insulates treatment and therapy from discovery even by denominational officials. This protection of the therapeutic process is made complete when, at the conclusion of therapy, the posttreatment assessment is also done by an independent assessor, preferably the same individual or team that had performed the initial assessment.

We prefer multiaxis assessments that address a wide range of possible etiologies for distorted clergy behavior. The possibility of physical and psychiatric disorders should be examined, along with the more common addictive, immature, and other neurotic psychological profiles. In our experience, assessors use objective and projective testing as well as personal interviewing, and usually ask that a physical examination be performed by a qualified physician. Inpatient assessment facilities exist and can provide excellent assessments within a week. Their costs, which can easily exceed $5,000 per case, sometimes lead us to use less expensive outpatient providers, particularly with older complaints and fairly "straightforward" complaints.

The assessment phase is often critical in obtaining further cooperation from the accused offender. Accused clergy will often dispute the particulars of the initiating complaint, for example, acknowledging boundary violations with the accuser but denying any sexual contact. When assessments show, however, that the accused have "issues" with which to deal, they are more likely to enter cooperatively into further treatment or therapy. This is particularly so if they are permitted to maintain that participation in treatment or therapy does not constitute an admission of having committed the particular behavior described in the complaint that initiated the assessment process.

In the mid-1980s, especially when we were confronting accused child-abusing clergy, our preference was for inpatient treatment. We have come to use inpatient modalities less and less frequently. In part this is because outpatient, longer term therapy seems to be equally effective, or even more so, in dealing with exploitative behavior and boundary violations. It also reflects the fact that transition from an inpatient setting to a new, normal life pattern is often difficult. Finally, the cost of inpatient settings, and the refusal of many insurers to pick up that cost, is clearly a factor.

Whether the treatment takes place in an inpatient or outpatient setting, our experience shows that the best results are usually obtained with eclectic modalities. We generally look for providers who will give their clients opportunities both for individual and for group psychotherapy, for psychodrama and other alternatives to "talk therapy," for one or another twelve-step fellowship, and, where indicated, for drug or aversive therapies. Of course, the initial assessment is critical in making these decisions.

The duration of primary therapy differs radically from individual to individual. In some few cases, it may last only two or three months on an outpatient basis, for example, when the primary therapeutic issue is the trauma of the public revelation of behavior whose roots otherwise have been integrated successfully into the personality. On the other hand, it is not uncommon to see six- or seven-month stays in inpatient settings or two or more years of outpatient primary therapy. We generally ask treatment providers only to indicate to us that the clergy are continuing to participate in therapy. If we need a more specific update on the therapeutic process, then we ask for that directly from the clergy member, recognizing that such self-reports are limited in their objectivity and accuracy.

The transition from primary therapy to aftercare often involves a second assessment and the development of an aftercare "contract" or plan. As noted above, a separate assessment at both ends of the therapeutic process can protect the integrity of therapy and also provide well-defined information for denominational leadership. Aftercare plans usually include several elements: continued participation in individual or group therapy or in a support or twelve-step group of some type, specifics of a living situation, and restrictions on employment. A process for monitoring the plan is usually set up with an appropriate denominational official as well. We try to make such plans as concrete and specific as possible, so that ongoing monitoring is more objective for both the denominational official and the clergy member.

A particularly difficult question in most denominations is that of future ministry, whether during the aftercare period or for the long term. A consensus has emerged in recent years that clergy should not be returned to congregational ministry when it is clear that they have recently engaged in sexual misconduct with minors. No other clear consensus exists, however, on other reassignment issues. What if a fairly senior and well-respected pastor is discovered to have had sexual contact with a midteen 20 or more years ago, and no further complaints are discovered even when publicity is given to the older complaint? Clergy who are known to have repeatedly exploited congregants or harassed co-workers generally are not returned to parochial ministry, but what should be the effect of older or more isolated complaints? Sensitivities and standards of judgment will differ not only from denomination to denomination and judicatory to judicatory, but even from congregation to congregation, depending on local history. Where noncongregational assignments are possible, under what conditions are these acceptable for acknowledged offenders?

Several factors affect decisions about reassignment or outplacement, but two deserve special attention. First, no clergy member should be considered for reassignment unless he or she has made significant and consolidated gains psychologically and spiritually in regard to treatment issues. These would include the regular manifestation of empathy with victims, the addressing of family of origin issues and other issues in personal maturity and integration, the identification of unhealthy personal patterns that may lead to reoffense, regular disclosure about life issues in appropriate settings with a support network, and the willingness to submit to monitoring by denominational officials and mental health professionals.

The second factor is the particular church community's acceptance of an "impaired" leader, particularly one with an offense history, and that community's willingness to confront the return of unhealthy life patterns should they become manifest. Such acceptance and cooperation, of course, can only happen if there has been disclosure to the community. We continue to find significant resistance to disclosure on the part of offenders, denominational leadership, and the leaders and members of particular congregations. Where that resistance is overcome, however, there are significant positive gains for all involved. Victims are affirmed by the accountability that comes with public disclosure. Local congregations do not feel that they have been hoodwinked when inevitably (by rumor, litigation, or investigative reporting) past offense history already known to denominational leadership also becomes known to the congregation. To the contrary, congregations rise to the challenge and learn to address issues of sexual health and recovery in a much more sophisticated and helpful manner. For denominational leadership, congregational disclosure relieves concern about the fear that long-distance monitoring can never be entirely trustworthy or successful. It also creates bonds of trust between the judicatory leadership and the local congregational leadership, exactly opposite to the rancor and distrust created by former patterns of quiet reassignment or judicatory silence before call committees.

Finally, for the offender him- or herself, disclosure negates in large part the fear of future discovery of "the secret." Clergy have discovered that fellow recoverers step forward to provide further support for their continued sobriety and healthy living. None of this is accomplished without a good deal of pain. We expect that in the next decade or so clearer standards around reassignment or dismissal will emerge. While the quasi-judicial problems of the difficulty of proving old complaints and the very real shift in professional standards in the past two decades both call for a nuanced response, they are not the ultimate determinants of the need for further careful consideration in this area. Judeo-Christian concerns for justice, compassion, healing, the integrity of leadership, and the possibility of conversion make unacceptable the more simplistic and obvious approaches to offenders, either across-the-board permanent dismissal or a "cheap grace" forgiveness approach. They demand that we continue tracking the careers of ostensibly rehabilitated offenders and work at the same time to broaden the community's understanding of the issues involved.

26

Training for Prevention
of Sexual Misconduct by Clergy

Donald C. Houts

This chapter describes resources to help prevent sexual misconduct by clergy (see Chapters 3 and 22 for more information). Special attention will be given to videotape resources, pamphlets, handouts, and other forms of education. Passing reference will be made to the training of professionals for their work as leaders of clergy workshops. Finally, we will describe follow-up research with participants in a number of similar six-hour workshops for clergy as well as data regarding preventive efforts by numerous denominational bodies.

An increasing number of religious judicatories are taking seriously the tasks of prevention of sexual boundary abuse by their clergy. Until very recently, the public as a whole was unaware of such instances of abuse. Likewise, most persons in the church—both lay and clergy—seemed largely unaware of this problem.

Clergy have historically enjoyed a special place of honor and trust—sometimes being elevated to a superhuman image of goodness, wisdom, and selflessness. Without a doubt, personal temptation and unconscious need fulfillment through pastoral relationships have always been a factor, though a largely unaddressed one until the last 10 years. Movies such as *Elmer Gantry* once shocked viewers. However, the media and a growing number of well-publicized trials of clergy have changed all that. We are now in a crisis of trust and a growing tide of disillusionment and anger directed toward clergy.

HISTORY

My own involvement in the movement to prevent sexual abuse by clergy began about five years ago, after I had experienced the tragedy of three children who had been sexually abused by their pastor. I was deeply affected by the tragedy and became convinced that extraordinary measures would need to be taken to more nearly guarantee the safety of such children in the future.

While there have been a few persons in ministry (such as Marie Fortune and others; see Chapter 3) who have been sounding an alarm for a number of years, the movement for a thoroughgoing education of clergy is now picking up momentum. Within a month of my own heightened sense of priority, the University of Wisconsin released and promoted a new videotape designed for use with clergy of all faiths, titled *Sexual Ethics in Ministry.* Eleven brief vignettes by professional actors portray a variety of situations to which clergy can be vulnerable. A second section of the videotape deals with specific aspects of prevention. This videotape, along with a leader's guidebook, is available from the Department of Health and Human Services, University of Wisconsin, 310 Lowell Hall, 619 Langdon, Madison, WI 53703. The cost is $250.00 and it can be ordered by dialing (800) 442-4617.

After attending an initial training session in Madison, I shared the above videotape with the United Methodist bishop of the Illinois Area and his cabinet of 12 district superintendents. With their blessing, I volunteered to set up 12 mandatory district clergy conferences, which I later conducted with one of several different women as coleaders. Nearly 700 clergy have attended these and makeup sessions in succeeding years.

PROCESS

We discovered a number of things from these six-hour seminars. We learned that small table groups could effectively focus on various aspects of sexual abuse, such as power, inappropriate touch, forms of harassment, times of personal vulnerability, need for a support network, confidentiality versus secrecy, trust, and so on. We began to experience a steady stream of persons who came forward to our agency following the workshops, identifying their own vulnerability, expressing the need for help, and proposing changes within their own personal lives and professional structures.

Because our workshops were mandatory for clergy, we had the advantage of having almost all the clergy involved in one or another of the district seminars. This meant that the topic was discussed among a high percentage of clergy (nearly 90% thus far). Because we uniformly used male-female coleadership, the minority of women seemed to feel safer and the men were able to hear women's perspectives on issues with rationality and a minimum of defensiveness. Because we met in table groups of five throughout the day, many persons noted that it was the first time they had talked about such important and threatening issues with fellow clergy. We used the concept of Robert Bly and others of establishing "ritual space" in which there was a controlled and structured environment to give protection and to prevent derailment or withdrawal.

As one of our routine group experiences, we presented each group with an opportunity to share in developing a code of sexual ethics for clergy. They understood that any consensual change suggested for the document would be fed into the computer, prior to the next district meeting. Changes thus were made throughout the process of 12 district seminars so that the final product, while imperfect, represented the involvement and ownership of a large percentage of our clergy. Many chose to take the final draft, printed on parchment paper, and sign it, frame it, and hang it in the vicinity of their studies.

RESEARCH ON CLERGY RESPONSE

In a survey of 396 clergy who participated in various similar seminars using *Sexual Ethics in Ministry* materials from the University of Wisconsin, a number of findings were revealed. Of the participants, 19% reported feeling themselves to be at risk in one or more areas of sexual vulnerability. These "at-risk" participants were equally distributed by age groups, but 36% of this "at-risk" group were in the smallest parishes of 0-50 members. The implications of this fact alone are very powerful in helping judicatory leaders to understand vulnerability, support, and employment strategies.

Of the "at-risk" participants, 76% reported changes they had made in their counseling practices. Among those who found the seminar confirming to their current practice, the affirmations for "establishing professional limits, taking care of one's marriage, increasing self-awareness, and appropriate use of touch" were most often indicated. This research study is described in detail elsewhere (Sparks, Ray, & Houts, 1992).

Since completing the original 12 district workshops, we have become more interested in doing pilot workshops for various judicatories and in replicating these workshops to train new male-female coleader teams. Thus far we have conducted more than 40 workshops, using the basic model outlined in our monograph. Our evaluations support workshops led by male-female coleaders, small group interaction, and mandatory attendance.

In the United Methodist Church, we have now trained 35 such teams to work in annual conferences throughout the denomination, and a large number of those annual conferences have completed the first round of seminars for their clergy. Almost all of those conferences have set up statements regarding sexual ethics for clergy and have done additional work on sexual harassment and/or gender issues in ministry. All bishops have participated in a workshop similar to that described for clergy and are committed to perfecting documents regarding allegations against clergy, treatment for victims, intervention teams, and so on. Increasingly, attention is now being given to strategies for alerting local congregations to become more alert to prevention of boundary violations by either clergy or laity—especially in teaching, camping, and youth work positions.

DENOMINATIONAL STRATEGIES

During the fall in 1992, I surveyed the current practices of 24 denominational bodies in the United States. It is clear that each has experienced alarm, embarrassment, and shame over the appearance of denial and whitewash associated with their handling of past scandal and allegations. While progress in prevention is uneven, it is evident that most faith groups are in the process of investing in preventive strategies, with the aim of dealing forthrightly and quickly with this present crisis.

My clear impression is that church structure largely predicts a style of response to the crisis of integrity in the area of clergy sexual ethics.

Two very large denominations with congregational polity indicated that little has yet been done. Denominations with a more hierarchical structure and/or national program structure are hard at work on efforts to review and/or establish standards of sexual ethics and processes to deal with allegations against clergy. Very few indicated that they were working on policies on behalf of victims (or complainants) as yet.

While few denominations have complete and in-depth positions on child abuse, sexual harassment, and clergy violations of professional boundaries, they are nonetheless working rapidly toward completion of assigned tasks in this regard. Several were to report to their parent bodies in the spring and summer of 1993. Several others have chosen to take as long as three or four years to develop consistent policy and practice for the denomination. One of the complications is that national policies must take account of related state statutes, which vary considerably.

While it may be true that professional ethics statements for clergy have been almost nonexistent compared with other mental health professions, those statements are beginning to emerge from task forces and from the highest councils of those denominations. Our concern would be that the church could become as focused on being self-righteous in dismissing those who violate the standard as some other professional groups have shown themselves to be.

About half of the groups surveyed were gearing up for grassroots preventive education by their use of pilot seminars and their efforts to train leaders. Few had yet completed the task of involving all of their spiritual leaders, although one or two denominations have clearly stated that goal. Several denominations provide basic procedural manuals that refer only tangentially to issues of clergy sexual ethics. The more common pattern today is to set up separate manuals of policy and procedure specifically addressed to such issues as boundary violations, sexual harassment, and sexual abuse.

The increase of public suspicion of clergy motives and the decreasing clergy trust of both authorities and peers tend to stir up great feelings of defensiveness that rapidly turn into clergy complaints about feeling victimized—both by parishioners and often by "the feminist movement," which is often unfairly blamed for the crisis. It is as if the messenger were being attacked for bringing a message we do not want to hear.

Pronouncements are premature until the machinery and the leadership are in place. While some other groups have begun where they were, at the bottom and at the top and with prevention in mind, a few denominations have been working quietly to perfect policy that they expect to implement as a total package. Some denominations appear to be operating primarily from legal considerations, while others approach the task primarily from theological perspectives. Still others see the task of prevention as an existential challenge to individuals to deal with their own incipient and implicit vulnerabilities.

The machinery of the denominations and faith groups predicts marked differences in the way the functions are carried out. Therefore we see no one preferred style that will work equally well with all groups. We are convinced that, until there is a deeply sensitized laity and a clergy with consciousness raised, the lethargy of the past will be difficult to overcome. Nonetheless, as with the re-repression of infantile memories, it is already too late to attempt a new repression but it is still too early to celebrate.

My personal philosophy has been that prevention, to be most effective, must have the ownership of clergy at the grassroots level—normally those serving in parishes, chaplaincies, and mission fields. Once these clergy are convinced that there is a serious issue and begin to see their own potential vulnerability, they understand the measures that must be taken to correct past behaviors of direct sexual abuse of staff members, congregants, and children. Abuses such as sexual harassment arise from a long history of sexist thinking, a marked ambivalence of religion toward sexuality, and a gross underrepresentation of women in decision making and church discipline. This is beginning to change rapidly, not simply because of celebrated lawsuits but also in response to a raised consciousness about vulnerability, power imbalance, and the profound and lasting damage experienced by victims. Increased numbers of women clergy may help to change the paternalism and entrenched patterns of the past within a brief time.

RESOURCES

Other videotaped resources are presently available and in common use. First are the materials that are part of the training package of the Center for the Prevention of Sexual and Domestic Violence. Two videotapes, *Not in My Church* and *Once You Cross the Line*, have been used in training seminars sponsored by the center. The center has a long history of training judicatory leaders, using these and other materials they have developed over a period of time. The Center for the Prevention of Sexual and Domestic Violence may be reached at 1914 N. 34th Street, Suite 105, Seattle, WA 98103, (206) 634-1903.

A third videotape resource is titled *Sexual Ethics for Church Professionals*. This videotape features nine dramatized vignettes followed by discussions among several professional panel members. It is probably better suited to formal teaching than experiential learning. It is available for $75.00 from Ministerial Continuing Education, 12501 Old Columbia Pike, Silver Spring, MD 20904, (301) 680-6503.

A fourth videotape resource should not go unnoticed. It is called *Judgment*. This dramatized, 90-minute documentary of a child abuse case in Louisiana is superior in the quality of the dramatic portrayals and very powerful in its emotional impact on the viewer. It can be ordered from HBO Video (#90568) for $89.00.

In addition to these materials, the Mennonite Central Committee has collected folders of articles regarding sexual boundary violations, sexual abuse of children, and domestic violence. *Crossing the Boundary: Professional Sexual Abuse* is available for $5.00 from the Mennonite Central Committee, 21 S. Twelfth Street, P.O. Box 500, Akron, PA 17501-0500.

Our own experience was that we needed to develop handouts for discussion and for future reference. We matched these materials with various discussion foci throughout the workshop. They included handouts titled "First Steps in the New Parish," "Personal Touch and Hugging," "Vulnerability to Affairs," "Reminders of Our Biblical Heritage," and extensive bibliographies in sexual ethics and gender issues. Each of these handouts is discussed in a monograph titled *Clergy Sexual Ethics: A Workshop Guide*. It is available for $5.00 from the Journal of Pastoral Care Publication, c/o 1549 Clairmont Road, Suite 103, Decatur, GA 30030, (404) 320-1472.

Another valuable resource is a 16-page leaflet titled *Safety Tips on a Sensitive Subject: Child Sexual Abuse*. This leaflet is especially useful in highlighting preventive measures that can be taken in the process of employment and enlistment of volunteers within a local parish. It is available free on request from Church Mutual Insurance Co., 3000 Schuster Lane, Merrill, WI 54452, (715) 536-5577.

SUMMARY

Our perception is that having identified the seriousness and widespread occurrence of such boundary violations, denominational bodies are increasingly taking comprehensive measures to eradicate the phenomenon and to guarantee that the church will be a safe place for those who come there for fellowship, for service, and for worship. What is needed now is for expertise to be shared across denominational, international, and faith barriers as well as for building a sense of professional solidarity in eradicating this pernicious and ancient abuse. Ultimately, we shall have to go beyond this first level of "consciousness-raising" and conquer all pockets of apathy and lack of awareness to permit us to prevent the continuing exploitation of persons under the guise of caring for them.

27

The Art of Advocacy

Nancy Biele

Elizabeth Barnhill

HISTORY OF
ADVOCACY IN MINNESOTA

In 1984 the Minnesota legislature created the Task Force on Sexual Exploitation by Counselors and Therapists. For the next three years, hundreds of people from different groups such as professional organizations, regulatory agencies, women's organizations, mental health advocacy organizations, victims services agencies, and consumer groups were involved in the task force and its work groups to provide leadership in creating laws, policies, and education on sexual exploitation. The task force's accomplishments included the first felony-level law prohibiting sexual contact between clients and therapists, a bill providing civil remedies for victims of sexual exploitation, increased activity by licensure boards providing practice-related consequences for offenders, three publications, and the first national conference on sexual exploitation held in 1986 with over 200 people from 27 states. A second conference was held in 1992 with even higher attendance.

The idea of advocacy for people who have been victimized by mental health professionals and clergy was an integral part of the work in Minnesota. There are a number of reasons for this. First, much initial work was done by the Walk-In Counseling Center in Minneapolis, which has an activist philosophy regarding sexual exploitation and aiding those victimized through the maze of options, even in the years when there were fewer options. Minnesota also has had advocacy for sexual assault victims and battered women since the early 1970s, and working with victims of boundary violations was simply an extension of this work. Initially, advocacy services were created with the assumption that medical and criminal justice systems were sometimes insensitive and less than helpful when victims attempted to report sexual assault. When advocacy was expanded to sexual exploitation and complaints were made, the response sometimes ranged from denial to overt hostility. Licensure boards and ethics committees reacted with defensiveness.

DEFINITIONS

Advocacy is defined as "speaking or writing in support of." In this context, it means taking an active role in providing assistance to victims of sexual exploitation. The goal is empowerment and healing for the client. Advocates who work with those victimized by mental health professionals may be therapists, mental health or sexual assault advocates, or clergy or lay members of religious groups.

Sexual exploitation occurs in different settings and the definitions of *sexual exploitation* will vary according to the context. For example, under the Minnesota Criminal Code (1985), a *psychotherapist* means "a person who is or purports to be a physician, psychologist, nurse, chemical dependency counselor, social worker, marriage and family counselor, member of the clergy (under specific circumstances) or other mental health service provider; or any other person, whether or not licensed by the state, who performs or purports to perform psychotherapy." Under the Criminal Code, sexual exploitation is explicitly defined by sexual activity. Under the Civil Code (1986), sexual exploitation is defined by sexual activity and includes requests by the psychotherapist for sexual conduct. Because much activity that violates the sexual boundaries of a client may not fit legal definitions, the work group of the Minnesota Task Force on Sexual Exploitation by Counselors and Therapists broadly defined *sexual exploitation* to be "inappropriate sexual conversation, dating or suggestions of sexual involvement by the counselor, and/or any sexual or romantic contact between client and counselor which may include but is not limited to sexual intercourse, kissing and/or touching breasts or genitals."

While this chapter is primarily about sexual misconduct, other forms of boundary violations exist and are sometimes precursors to sexual exploitation. Professionals may abuse their power role by engaging in these types of boundary violations:

- Financial—becoming involved with business deals with clients, borrowing or loaning money, changing fee structures
- Physical—engaging in unsolicited touching, inappropriate physical closeness, seeing clients in inappropriate settings
- Spiritual—using scriptural knowledge to confuse or victimize clients
- Emotional—inappropriate self-disclosure, role reversal with clients, and having dual roles with clients

Clients may need advocacy for any of these issues as well as for sexual exploitation.

ADVOCATE SELECTION AND ISSUES

Advocates dealing with exploitation tend to be recruited from three groups: mental health professionals, sexual assault advocacy groups, and people who previously have been victimized by therapists or clergy. For all groups, sexual exploitation engenders strong feelings. There are some unique responses for each group, however.

Those that belong to the professional groups sometimes react from a sense of embarrassment and anger that someone in their profession could have abused a client. They may respond out of anger at the abusing therapist and the need to clean up their own profession, which may create an investment in reporting and in the outcome of the complaint. Professionals also may have ethical reporting requirements that go beyond any legal requirements. Clients need to be apprised if this is the case. Also, almost all helping professionals have engaged in some sort of boundary violation in their practice, and advocates may suddenly have past transgressions, no matter how small, come back to haunt them. That may cause underreaction to a client's story. There also may be fear of retaliation against the therapist or the agency if a complaint is made.

Advocates who have been in sexually exploitative situations sometimes have difficulty separating their own issues from the issues of those for whom they are advocating and may have a bias for or against specific courses of action based on their own cases. This leads to advice-giving, which is not an advocate's role. Unresolved emotions about their own victimization can also reappear in advocates, leading to confusion as to whose feelings are whose and who is the current client. Also, mistakes are sometimes made when advocates or therapists working with victims of exploitation want to be perfect to make up for the prior therapists or try to protect clients from further pain.

Initial screening of advocates is important. Can the advocates separate their own issues from the clients' issues? Does the advocate have an agenda that is about cleaning up the profession rather than advocacy? (This may be a person who can aid in training or public policy rather than advocacy.) Can the advocate allow the client to choose options even if the advocate feels those options may not be therapeutic? Can the advocate engage hostile systems and create cooperation? These are some questions to ask. There must be clear delineation between the therapeutic role and the advocacy role even when the parts are being played by the same person. Advocacy is active, not reflective. It does not involve making choices for the client but may require active participation by the advocate in carrying out the choices. Training is imperative and must include crisis intervention skills, boundary setting, and ways to advocate within systems.

Boundary setting is very important. Victims of sexual exploitation have had professionals not only *not* set boundaries but actively overstep lines between therapy and intimacy. The role of advocate is different than the role of therapist. It may involve out-of-office visits such as hearings or court appearances. It may involve longer blocks of time for personal conversation. It usually does not involve the client paying a fee for advocacy. So advocates have to be very clear about their role and the need for consistent and clear messages to the clients. Regular supervision can be a great aid in traversing the gray areas in advocacy. Advocates must be aware that, even though they are not engaging in therapy with clients, they are still in a professional role and a position of power. The relationship must always be focused on the other's interest.

STAGES OF HEALING

Clients who have been sexually exploited by counselors will go through a stage of gaining awareness of what has happened and being able to name it as abuse rather than the common myth of an "affair" with the therapist. This awareness can be triggered by a newspaper article, a television show, a chance remark by a significant other, or finding out that there are other clients engaging in sexual activity with the same counselor or clergy.

> Client A called after her husband, having done some detective work and reading a newspaper article on clergy abuse of women, confronted his wife on what he believed to be her victimization. She maintained that it was an affair and that adultery was her sin. She called first for information. Later she called for some practical help.

After gaining a sense of awareness, a client or significant people in the client's life may seek out someone to help. An assessment of immediate needs is in order.

> Client A's husband then confronted the clergy person directly (not recommended). Because Client A was the church secretary, she was fired and ostracized by a close-knit church community. Her first concerns were stabilizing the family income and dealing with her children's rejection in the neighborhood.

Assessment should include family and job-related issues and stability, medical and mental health-related needs, the need for protection against retaliation, any chemical abuse problems, and suicide risk—anything that may affect the client's current functioning.

A story of exploitation can come out in a variety of ways. It may be in a series of short, checking-out phone conversations where no names are given and only cursory information is shared. It may be clear and in chronological order. It may be a story of someone having been abused by two separate therapists so the stories have become intermingled. It may be someone concerned about a friend.

> Client B entered my office, having made an appointment the week before. She placed a notebook on my desk, asked me to read it, and said she would call me in two weeks to see if I could help her. It was a journal that recounted in great detail her exploitation by a psychiatrist.

A basic guideline in hearing the story is to avoid making assumptions about what happened; instead, explore specifically what sexual activity occurred. Also, avoid making assumptions about how the sexual involvement affected the client. There may be conflicting feelings that change over time. Focus initial intervention on crisis issues and life situations.

Advocates and therapists working with victims of sexual exploitation must expect no trust from clients at the outset. Trust has been violated at a very basic level, and these clients have no reason to trust professionals further. This may also be an important concept for other service providers to understand. Clients have fears that need to be acknowledged and validated. Sometimes a former therapist has made very explicit threats about what may happen if a client complains or files charges. A protection plan should be in place. Sometimes it is fear of personal, professional, and family exposure. It may be fear of media attention, and cautions must be offered about going public with a story. There is always concern about how long a process may take, and realistic time projections must be shared.

Get some clarity as to what the client is seeking. It may be that the client is currently seeing an exploitative counselor and needs help ending the relationship. It may be that the person wants to file a complaint. It may be a client's confusion about words or overtures in a therapeutic relationship. It may be a client wanting help in filing a lawsuit. It may be a client simply seeking information. Sometimes sending reading material on the topic is a nonintrusive way for clients to get the initial information. Sharing that sexual exploitation happens to other people helps lessen the isolation that is often felt.

When a victim of sexual exploitation seeks help, this person will need continuing support as options are explored and action is taken. Confusing and sometimes conflicting emotions may occur: shame, betrayal, and memories of pleasure in reliving the experience; sexual confusion; ambivalence about telling out of loyalty to the counselor; fear of being discounted or disbelieved, of retaliation by the counselor, and of reaction of family; distrust of any other professional; grief over the loss of the relationship; relief in sharing the experience and finding an end to the isolation; anger at the counselor and at the systems designed to intervene; inability to concentrate; suppressed rage; desire for revenge; inability to trust; self-blame; and confusion over what to do or who to tell.

There are a number of options that a client can choose; no one action is better than another. A client must ask him- or herself what it is that is most important to achieve personally. The client may be concerned about the counselor being able to exploit another client, may need compensation for future therapy, or may want to punish the counselor for the exploitation. There are advantages and disadvantages to all options, and many times more than one option can be used. A "Wheel of Options" developed by the Walk-In Counseling Center, a description of these options, and some role delineations for advocates appear later in the chapter. A warning note: While the options are not in any hierarchy, there may be potential impact of some options on later legal actions. Legal advice should be sought. If the advocate is biased toward one option or another, the client must be informed of this. The client must be in control of every decision. The advocate must always be aware that the client's healing is foremost, even if that means no action will be taken. Having a client write down the story of what happened will be helpful in most cases. It aids the client to reconstruct events and clarify their impact. Recounting the story can be traumatic for clients, and they may need emotional help in completing this task. Assumptions cannot be made that clients can read or write, so help may be needed.

With every option chosen, a different system is engaged. Each has its own governance, its own jargon, its own process, and its own time line. A major role of the advocate is to demystify the process, translate the language, and provide a schematic of what the client will encounter. After considering all the options available in a particular case, the next step will be initiating action.

Preparation is imperative. It is the advocate's responsibility to have as much knowledge as possible about the systems and to prepare the client for the event. Role-playing and having the client write about the upcoming event can be helpful. Clients' expectations must be discussed. Best possible outcomes and worst possible outcomes can be outlined. Chances are that the result will be somewhere in between. Clients sometime engage in the magical thinking that an apology from the former therapist, a guilty verdict, a large settlement, or an upheld complaint will erase the experience. Great investment is placed in the outcome of the event. The outcome is rarely that clear, and it never erases the pain of the experience. No matter what the outcome, this is when the final stage of healing can begin.

After the initial steps have been taken—complaints have been filed, lawsuits initiated, charges brought—it may be weeks or years until the resolution takes place. It is important that the advocate maintain contact with the client. There are either periods of frenetic activity (hearings, depositions, negotiations) or nothing. The client may be in therapy during this time, but often therapeutic progress means reacting to crises that the systems create. It may be helpful for the advocate and therapist to maintain some contact, with the client's permission. What clients describe is a sort of limbo, where it is difficult for them to make other important life decisions until this process is complete. Clients need to be informed of this; it may have a bearing on the options they choose to use.

It is important that the advocate not abandon the client after the final event takes place. Follow-up sessions should be scheduled so that a clear termination process can take place. Other support people should be identified all along the way. However, the advocate needs to be aware of the special role he or she has played, no matter what the outcome. And sometimes that relationship has spanned years because of the procedures involved. However, it is extremely important for the advocate to model a professional, respectful end to the relationship. It is common for the client to ask for a continuation of the relationship, to create a crisis to continue, or, because the relationship was "different" than therapy, to bargain for friendship. It is important for the advocate to be clear about the role and the need to terminate the relationship.

OPTIONS AVAILABLE FOR
VICTIMS OF SEXUAL EXPLOITATION

Filing criminal charges against the offending counselor. At least 13 states have enacted criminal laws. In Minnesota, the legal definition that was included in the Criminal Sexual Conduct Code provided for two types of sexual activity. Sexual penetration is any type of intrusion into the body of the victim (sexual intercourse, oral sex, anal sex, or penetration with an object), and sexual contact is touching by the offender of the victim's intimate parts (breasts, groin, genitals, buttocks), forcing the victim to touch the offender's intimate parts, and, in both circumstances, touching of the clothing covering the immediate area of the intimate parts. The criminal law covers the following situations: when there is a counselor/client relationship and the sexual act occurred during a therapy session, when there is a current or former counselor/client relationship and the client is emotionally dependent on the counselor, or when there is a current or former counselor/client relationship and the sexual act occurred by means of therapeutic deception (the counselor deceived the client into believing it was part of the client's treatment). (See Chapter 20 in this volume for details of various statutes.)

The criminal process begins with a report to the police and an investigation similar to that undertaken for any complaint of sexual assault. After an investigation is completed, it is the decision of the county attorney (district attorney in other states) whether or not to prosecute. Disadvantages of this choice are that it is not up to the client whether the case will go forward and the lack of control a victim has in the

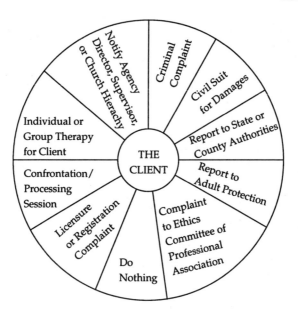

Figure 27.1. Wheel of Options

SOURCE: Adapted with permission from Walk-In Counseling Center, 2421 Chicago Avenue South, Minneapolis, Minnesota 55404.

process. Advantages are that, if prosecution is successful, the offender is held accountable and that it is a public procedure for the offender.

The role of advocate in criminal procedures will vary depending on what legal advocacy is already available through the criminal justice system.

> Client C had been exploited by a counselor for a number of years. When she initially told her story to an advocate, she wanted to confront the counselor and the counselor's supervisor (who she felt should have known what was going on). That meeting took place. The client also reported to the police. With the client's permission, the advocate was able to explain the law and its application to the police officer, who had never dealt with this type of case before. As a result, the officer was able to conduct a more thorough investigation. The advocate was able to help present the information to the prosecuting attorney, resulting in a criminal charge. There was an advocate present at the trial to help demystify the system and to translate information. Also present was a legal advocate from the prosecuting attorney's office.

Filing civil lawsuits for damages. These may be brought both against the counselor and possibly against the counselor's employer. Five states (Minnesota, Wisconsin, California, Texas, and Illinois) have enacted civil statutes specific to sexual exploitation. In Minnesota, the civil law includes the definitions found in the criminal law and also suggestions of sexual activity by the counselor. The client may sue the employer if the employer failed to take action when they knew or had reason to know that the counselor was engaging in sexual activity, if the employer failed to con- duct a background check when hiring the therapist, or if the employer failed to pass on such information to subsequent employers. There are some advantages to civil litigation:

- It can empower victims. They can be more in control in civil cases, whereas, in criminal cases, the victim is only a witness in the case.
- Recovery of monetary damages for the harm inflicted on victims both validates the victim's experience and reinforces the idea that perpetrators must be accountable for their actions.
- Civil litigation promotes enhanced safety and security practices because major lawsuits have resulted in more corporate responsibility as a way to lessen liability.
- High profile civil suits help heighten awareness of sexual exploitation.

As with any system response to victimization, there are disadvantages to civil litigation. It is a laborious, time-consuming, frustrating process. The victim may be called on to recount the victimization a number of times. Confrontation with the perpetrator will be inevitable. Anonymity may not be possible. The "gentleman's agreement" that keeps victims' names out of the media in criminal cases may not be available in civil cases. There is also no "rape shield" regarding prior sexual history or shield from prying. Virtually every aspect of the victim's life, even that which seems to have no bearing on the case, is fair game in the discovery process. This includes therapy records, medical records, and even school records. There is also the question of assessing damage. Service providers are engaged in helping victims heal. In the civil process, the attorney is trying to prove how severely and permanently damaged the victim is. Civil litigation can prove to be expensive even when attorneys take the case on contingency. Research must first be done to ascertain whether there is any money to collect. And it is a long process; it can take literally years from the time of filing a case to the time of a trial.

Often some sort of settlement is offered. A client needs to be advised of the pros and cons of a settlement. It avoids a courtroom process, which can have mixed outcomes. After mentally preparing for cross-examination and recounting the story, some clients have been disappointed at not being able to "have their day in court." On the other hand, a client may get close to what was requested without the rigors of court. Be wary of those settlements that require a gag order. It can be extremely frustrating for a client not to be able to talk publicly about what happened.

The role of an advocate in civil procedures can be multifaceted. An advocate may be used in seeking a referral for attorneys and expert witnesses, in preparation for depositions and the trial, and in debriefing after each event.

> Client D's attorney had filed a lawsuit alleging sexual exploitation by a clergy member and against the denomination that had previously employed the clergy member. The advocate made referrals for therapists and expert witnesses and worked with the attorney to prepare the client for depositions and for trials. It took four years for the case to get to trial. There were times when there was consistent contact between the client and the advocate and times when contact was more sporadic, depending on where the case was in the system. The client's most consistent contact was with the therapist.

Notification of agency director or supervisor to make a complaint. An advantage of this option is that it may bring fast action and may result in consequences for the offending counselor. However, some organizations have no procedures to deal with such complaints and need to create them as the specific complaint surfaces. In these situations, the client is a "guinea pig," an uncomfortable and often unfair role. The client obviously will be identified in a direct complaint. Having an advocate present to keep the process running and to offer suggestions for resolution can be helpful. A disadvantage may be unwillingness of the supervisor to take action. There may be denial on the part of the agency that such activity could take place.

> Client E called an agency and told the director of the sexual exploitation that had occurred in the agency a number of years prior to the director's arrival. In the first conversation, the client would not reveal the name of the offending counselor. The director sent the client a copy of the agency's complaint procedure and gave a referral to advocates at another agency. The client later identified the counselor and the circumstances. The director later helped negotiate a settlement with the insurance company.

A report to state or county authorities can be made if the clinic or facility is licensed by the state or county. Outpatient mental health clinics, residential treatment facilities, nursing homes, and licensed chemical dependency programs are examples of this type of program. Complaints could affect future licensing or funding for the agency. It makes the agency responsible for the activity of its employees; however, the victim has little control over timing and outcome.

A report to adult protection can be made if the client is a vulnerable adult. The policy of many states is to protect adults who, because of physical or mental disability or dependency on institutional services, are particularly vulnerable to abuse or neglect. Within each county, adult protective services are charged with investigation of reports and providing protection in appropriate cases. An advantage is that these services have experience in investigating complaints. In cases of abuse of a vulnerable adult, reporting is mandated by law.

A complaint to a professional association may be made. Many counselors belong to professional associations, all of which have ethical guidelines prohibiting sexual contact between counselors and clients. After an investigation is conducted, if the allegation is found to be true, the counselor can be removed from membership. An advantage is that a complaint alerts the counselor's peers to possible misconduct. Professionals have an investment in keeping their profession ethical. A disadvantage is that, because membership in a professional association is voluntary, a counselor found guilty of an ethical violation may continue to practice without restriction.

A complaint can be made to a denominational office or congregational group. For those who have been exploited by a member of the clergy, both criminal and civil options are available. In 1993 in Minnesota, the language in the criminal law was clarified to identify sexual exploitation by clergy to include that the actor is or purports to be a member of the clergy, the complainant is not married to the actor, and the sexual penetration or contact occurred during the course of a meeting in which the complainant sought or received religious or spiritual advice, aid, or comfort from the actor in private, or the sexual penetration or contact occurred during a period of time in which the complainant was meeting on an ongoing basis with the actor to receive religious or spiritual advice, aid, or comfort in private. Consent by the complainant is not a defense. Complaints may also be filed with the governing body of the local congregation or the governing body of the denomination or both depending on the structure of the denomination. Advocacy may be available from a denominational office or from advocacy groups specially trained in clergy abuse issues. The Minnesota Council of Churches first conducted a statewide training for advocates in 1991. The training provided for general training on sexual exploitation and victimization and specific training on denominational structures and responses. A second training was held in late 1993.

A licensure or registration complaint may be made. If the professional is licensed, an upheld complaint can result in the loss of the right to practice as a licensed professional. An advantage of this process is the possibility of either loss of license or restrictions on practice. It also alerts the counselor's peers. Disadvantages include the time lag between complaint and action and an intimidating hearing process.

The role of an advocate in aiding the client in reporting to supervisors, state or county authorities, adult protection, professional associations' ethics committees, or licensure boards involves preparing the client to give a statement, role-playing the event, and debriefing after the event. It must be understood that regulatory bodies are cumbersome, and their procedures are time consuming. Also, many former therapists misrepresented their credentials, licenses, or education so it is sometimes difficult to know which body to complain to. Regulatory bodies sometimes have procedures that are not written and are difficult to clarify because different members have different answers.

> Client F asked for advocacy in filing a complaint with a licensure board. The staff member of the board met with the client and the advocate to outline the procedure and the time line. A written complaint was filed and a hearing was scheduled. At the hearing, the client gave a statement outlining experiences of violation and the effects those experiences had had on all aspects of life. The counselor gave a statement as did other witnesses for both sides. While it was extremely stressful for the client, the feeling was that the board had listened with respect. The result was a one-year suspension of the license and mandated training and supervision. An important piece of the process for the client was that the results were published in the professional newsletter so that prospective clients were forewarned.

A client can choose to do nothing. Some people feel they cannot or do not want to take any specific action. The client has a right to choose whether or when to tell anyone or take any action. Some clients will call initially for information, then for validation, perhaps later for advocacy.

A client can write or call the ex-counselor. This will give a client the opportunity to express his or her feelings to the counselor that what happened to the client was not OK. This option is quick and private. However, it may also alert the counselor to other actions that may be taken and give the counselor time to plan a response. Also, the counselor may not respond in a way that is helpful and may make the client feel isolated and unsafe.

A client may engage in a confrontation/processing session. This gives the victim of sexual exploitation the opportunity to directly tell the offending counselor what the effects of the victimization were. A processing session should be done with a third party whose role is to support the victim and control the communication. An advantage of this option is that it gives the client the opportunity to tell the offending counselor the effects on the victim. A disadvantage is that expectations may not be met, resulting in disappointment and lack of accountability for the offending counselor.

The role of an advocate in a processing session would be to help the client carefully work out what is to be said, go over expectations with the client, and debrief after the event.

> Client G asked for advocacy to set up a session with a counselor who had engaged in numerous boundary violations. The client's stated need was to make the counselor understand that what had happened was serious and resulted in damage to the client. A session involving the complainant, the counselor, a support person for the complainant, and the advocate was held. It was the impression of the complaining client that the counselor simply refused to understand what the issues were about. Although the session was disappointing to the client, it also aided the client in making the decision to make a licensure complaint.

The client can engage in individual or group counseling. The original problem or concern that brought the client into therapy has probably not been dealt with. It may also be helpful to find a supportive environment to process the experience of sexual exploitation. Counseling with a supportive, ethical professional can be useful in resolving both the exploitation and any other issues. Groups set up specifically for people who have been sexually exploited by counselors can be an invaluable source of healing.

The client can network with other survivors for support and for political and educational work. The process of making the mental health profession accountable on sexual exploitation began with victims speaking out and seeking redress. Valuable service can be provided by survivors to other survivors and by having survivors attend hearings, write letters and articles, and share successes. This kind of political and educational work created the movement demanding accountability in the therapeutic community.

The client can take to the streets. If there is no adequate system response, no laws to protect victims from sexual exploitation, and nowhere else to go, a client can go public in activities that can include press releases and interviews or even picketing. Clients need to be realistic about the possible ramifications of going public to themselves and their families. They also need to know it may not engender the response they are hoping for. However, it may also create a groundswell of attention to the issue.

INTERVENTION MODEL

For those not used to an advocacy role, a short intervention model titled BASER developed by Illusion Theater may be helpful.

Believe. Advocates may think their role includes getting all the facts and making sure everything is true. Victims disclose their own reality and often disclose the least harmful parts first, looking for a supportive response. If that response is forthcoming, more details and more victimization may be revealed. Don't assume that the first disclosure is the entire disclosure. Most victims never report exploitation for fear of not being believed; they need assurance that they are believed and that sexual exploitation was not their fault.

Affirm. As described earlier, there are a wide range of feelings and reactions to being a victim. People need reassurance that all of the feelings are normal and that they have a right to express them.

Support. The amount and type of support offered and given will depend on the advocate role played. Victims of sexual exploitation need definitions and boundaries. Often, an offending therapist will have made false promises. An advocate needs to make clear the limitations of advocacy and not make promises that cannot be kept. Nor can advocates give assurances about outcomes over which they have no control.

Empower. Victims of exploitation have, in significant ways, been rendered powerless. They need to regain power. Sometimes advocates want to take over to help fix the situation. Instead, clear information and options need to be given to aid in decision making.

Refer. This is perhaps the most important point. *Refer* means for the client to be referred to whatever services may be needed—therapists, support groups, attorneys, complaint takers. Referrals can also be made for significant others for therapy or other services. It also means referral for the advocates to supervision, consultation, and support.

SUMMARY

An advocate will be working not only with the victim of exploitation but also with other service providers and professionals. It will be necessary to clarify roles. Some will be unclear about the role of an advocate and fear that an advocate is there to take over. An advocate's role is not to threaten someone's job; rather, it is to make each person accountable for his or her own job. Don't demand confidential information that cannot be shared and do not share information that has not been released by the client. Clients can sense when they are no longer in control of the decision-making process.

Advocacy is about problem solving, about empowerment, and about action. A client may be overwhelmed and not see choices or solutions. A client may need help in defining the problem, finding resources, getting support, and prodding recalcitrant systems. Advocacy encourages people to take responsibility and control back into their lives. Advocacy is about aiding a client in engaging essentially bureaucratic and insensitive systems in creating processes that result in healing.

Advocates have dual tasks. The first and most important is to aid the individual victim of sexual exploitation in whatever steps are necessary for healing. The second is systems change to demand safety and accountability from the professionals who have been entrusted with the public's mental and spiritual health. To act as an advocate on the issue of sexual exploitation is to be allowed the privilege of participating in people's healing processes. Scrupulous care must be taken to respect those processes that help people change their own identities from victim to survivor and beyond.

28

Epilogue

John C. Gonsiorek

Serious attempts to study sexual exploitation by health care professionals and clergy are no more than 20 years old. I am reminded of how different things were not too long ago. In 1980 Gary Schoener and I offered a continuing education training at the American Psychological Association on sexually exploitative psychotherapists. Despite the existence of 50 state psychology licensing boards, 50 state ethics committees, many scores of training programs and internships, and APA central office staff involved in ethics, the workshop was canceled when only three people registered. Gary Schoener contacted these three to give them the handouts we had prepared for the workshop. One of the three, a psychologist, had signed up because he thought the workshop would instruct him on how to have sex with clients.

In the early and mid-1970s, those working in this area were virtually alone, usually ignored, not infrequently vilified, and occasionally subverted by perpetrators using other professionals in attempts to entrap them into defamatory statements.

Yet, in October 1992, over 450 people from much of the English-speaking world attended the Minneapolis conference on this topic. The literature has become extensive, and a "hot topic," with the unfortunate faddishness and sloganeering that implies. A number of states and provinces have developed an impressive diversity of criminal, civil, and administrative law remedies whose effectiveness is currently being tested in the real world.

What changed? How did this about-face occur? Some, but not all, professional organizations in health care and religious denominations would have you believe that health care professionals and religious institutions saw their ethical and moral duty, and did it. If you believe that, there is a bridge in my hometown of Brooklyn, New York, that I would like to sell you.

What actually happened was quite different. A few gutsy victims, supported by equally courageous advocates, and assisted by the merest handful of mental health professionals and church personnel, in conjunction with a number of creative and aggressive attorneys, won a series of six- and seven-figure civil lawsuits. Whereupon the health care professions and religious denominations became concerned—some, deeply and truly concerned; others, more "oh so concerned," that is, concerned as this year's fad or public relations strategy.

This volume and the conference from which it sprung suggest that genuine concern is broadening and deepening, but it is important to bear witness to the true history. Catalytic change came from victims, their advocates and attorneys, with a sprinkling of professionals and clergy.

I note this pointedly not to be difficult but to caution that, despite progress in recent years, something is missing: prevention. Prevention is not educating clients about their rights or about how to spot early stages of inappropriate conduct; although these are important. Prevention is having professional abuse never happen at all. In this regard, professional training programs have generally remained as they have always been: negligent. Prevention training is a rare exception, not the rule. In the health care professions, deafening silence about ethics, professional conduct, and appropriate boundaries has typically been replaced by an obligatory, superficial, politically correct, two to three lectures over the course of many years' training.

There is little integration of ethics and professionalism throughout course work and training. These have not become, as they should be, the heart and soul of professional training but are typically mere addenda to the "real business" of technique-oriented training. Perhaps attorneys can provide the necessary motivation for training institutions to take their obligations in this area seriously, as they so ably assisted health care professionals and clergy in discovering their morality, ethics, and professionalism in recent years.

The future holds other challenges as well. We sorely need outcome research on what works and what does not, in treatment of victims and rehabilitation of offenders—not to discover the "best" way, for such a mind-set is unproductive and dogmatic, but to understand which interventions work with which people, under what circumstances, and with what limitations.

This means being responsive to the inherent diversity of the victims and perpetrators and resisting simpleminded approaches such as the "client–therapist sex syndrome" or "all perpetrators are sexual addicts." These are marketing clichés, not responsible clinical practice. Such work requires all the creativity practitioners can muster, not simple reductionist formulas that create an illusion that the world is a simple, predictable place.

We should be willing to revise or even discard our favorite theories, based on research, and then make better theories and more research. Similarly, research on what is effective and not effective in the legal arena is important. The criminal, civil, and administrative law remedies of recent years are a necessary experiment, not a final solution. It will be some years before we know which remedies provide the best balance of responsiveness and fair play to victims, due process for the accused, and protection of the public. In some jurisdictions, the pendulum has swung to the other end. Will we be as interested in fair play and due process for accused professionals (as unpopular as that is in some "politically correct" circles today) as we have been for victims?

The identified victim is not the only victim. The lives of others are diminished by effects on the primary victim. These people too need effective therapeutic vehicles to remediate their losses, as well as mechanisms for justice. Similarly, some perpetrators commit their offenses as "agents" of troubled organizations. Focusing solely on the individual at any point in the abuse spectrum often shortchanges others who have been truly hurt, and avoids necessary questions about systems that maintain exploitation. A broad, holistic context is required if we are to understand and remedy the exploitation spectrum.

We cannot pursue this work with integrity without having a commitment to justice. When victims were rarely believed, when there were no mechanisms for victims to attain justice, you would have to be crazy to make a false complaint, because even the most heavily substantiated complaints were disbelieved. My experience years ago was that false complainants were rare, and often psychotic.

However, success in changing laws has come close, in some jurisdictions, to leveling the playing field. The context has changed. There may now be motivation for false complaints where there was none before. Earlier, character-disordered therapists had no external reasons to stop exploitation; now, some character-disordered clients have an external reason to exaggerate or falsify complaints.

I continue to observe that false and exaggerated complaints are uncommon, but they are now less uncommon. How common they might become remains to be seen. Perhaps what justice really means is that the legal structures are set up so that the human capacity for wrongdoing is equally likely to occur within either party. I suggest we should be mindful that, when legal structures are changed, there is the likelihood that what was true before the change may not be true after the change. The extreme rarity of false complaints may well be such an example; there are likely to be others.

Another justice issue involves making certain that new legislative remedies are not abused. Will the greater accountability to which health care professionals and clergy are held be applied evenly, based on the features of the particular cases (as they should be), or will they be used as new vehicles for the mass pathologies of our society: racism, sexism, homophobia, religious bigotry, and others. I have observed licensing boards, ethics committees, and courts indulge in racist assumptions about perpetrators being rapacious, hypersexual, predatory individuals when they are African American or Hispanic males. Similarly, such bodies often refuse to believe that women could be perpetrators, and when persuaded that they can be, turn on women perpetrators with a ferocity male perpetrators rarely experience. I have observed gay and lesbian professionals and clergy receive discipline and punishment greatly in excess of their heterosexual counterparts for similar transgressions. Transgressions by clergy sometimes receive a media slant more related to the denomination's local "clout" (or lack thereof) than to discernible details of the case.

Some issues of justice can be hard to hear because in some areas there remains no justice for victims. The provinces and states of North America now contain everything from the most careful, thoughtful responses to this problem, to thoughtlessly written or dogmatically conceived remedies, to complete ignorance and/or denial of the issues. If, however, remedies for victims are to withstand legal challenge, as well as gain the respect of professionals, clergy, and the larger society as a whole, they must be attentive to justice and fair play for all.

A final thought: Over the past two years, I have been completing a volume on male sexual abuse with my colleagues Walter Bera and Don LeTourneau. As I reviewed the literature on child abuse, I was initially pleased by the increasing professional and lay interest in this area. Later, I was deeply disquieted. The same decade of the 1980s that witnessed increased "awareness" of child abuse has also witnessed an economic, social, and political neglect of children, such that more children are in poverty than in living memory and services for children have severely diminished. In all areas, except concern for childhood sexual abuse, the level of concern for children in the United States seems to have returned to that of the nineteenth century. What is wrong with this picture?

A grim hypothesis occurred to me: Are we really concerned as a society about children, or have we found a new vehicle with which to focus our cultural love/hate extremist relationship with sexuality?

The relationship of these somber musings to sexual exploitation by health care professionals and clergy is this: Will the "sexual" or the "exploitation" part of this problem be our touchstone? Will we have the courage to explore abuse of power and exploitation in all its forms: emotional, economic, political, social, as well as sexual? Or will we stay focused on the one area of abuse of power that is culturally "easy" for us to see: the sexual?

That is our future challenge.

References

Akamatsu, T. J. (1988). Intimate relationships with former clients: National survey of attitudes and behaviors among practitioners. *Professional Psychology: Research and Practice, 19*(4), 454-458.

Allen, C. (1991). *Women and men who sexually abuse children: A comparative analysis.* Orwell, VT: Safer Society Press.

Allen, M. (1992, November 17). Catholic officials heed protesters' cries (report). Minneapolis, MN: *Star Tribune Newspaper.*

Allport, G. (1954). *The nature of prejudice.* Reading, MA: Addison-Wesley.

American Psychological Association (APA). (1987). *Diagnostic and statistical manual of mental illness* (3rd ed. rev.). Washington, DC: Author.

American Psychological Association. (1990a). Ethical principles of psychologists. *American Psychologist, 45,* 390-395.

American Psychological Association. (1990b, June). Ethical principles of psychologists revised. *APA Monitor.*

American Psychological Association. (1991, June). Draft of APA ethics code published. *APA Monitor,* pp. 30-35.

American Psychological Association. (1992a, May). APA continues to revise its ethics code. *APA Monitor,* pp. 38-42.

American Psychological Association. (1992b). Ethical Principles of Psychologists and Code of Conduct. *American Psychologist, 47,* 1597-1611.

Amundson, J., Stewart, K., & Valentine, L. (1993). Temptations of power and certainty. *Journal of Marital and Family Therapy, 19*(2), 111-123.

Angres, R. (1990, October). Who really was Bruno Bettelheim? *Commentary,* pp. 26-30.

Apfel, R., & Simon, B. (1986). Sexualized therapist: Causes and consequences. In A. Burgess & C. Hartman (Eds.), *Sexual exploitation of patients by health professionals* (pp. 143-151). New York: Praeger.

Appelbaum, P. S., & Jorgenson, L. M. (1991). Psychotherapist-patient sexual contact after termination of treatment: An analysis and a proposal. *American Journal of Psychiatry, 148,* 1466-1473.

Applebaum, G. (1987, January). *Consequences of sexual exploitation of clients.* Paper presented at Boundary Dilemmas in the Client-Therapist Relationship: A Working Conference for Lesbian Therapists, Los Angeles, CA.

Averill, S. A., Beale, D., Benfer, B., et al. (1989). Preventing staff-patient sexual relationships. *Bulletin of the Menninger Clinic, 53,* 384-393.

Bass, A. (1989, March 5). Therapist accused of sex abuse by clients. *Boston Sunday Globe,* pp. 1 ff.

Bass, A., & Foreman, J. (1989, April 4). Therapist accused of sex abuse resigns license. *Boston Globe,* pp. 17 ff.

Bass, L. W., & Wolfson, J. H. (1978). Professional courtesy is obsolete [Editorial]. *New England Journal of Medicine, 299,* 772-774.

Bates, C. M., & Brodsky, A. M. (1989). *Sex in the therapy hour: A case of professional incest.* New York: Guilford.

Bear, E., & Dimock, P. (1988). *Adults molested as children: A survivors manual for women and men.* Orwell, VT: Safer Society Press.

Beauchamp, T. L., & Childress, J. F. (1989). *Principles of biomedical ethics.* New York: Oxford University Press.

Belote, B. (1974). *Sexual intimacy between female clients and male therapists: Masochistic sabotage.* Unpublished doctoral dissertation, University of California, Berkeley, School of Professional Psychology.

Benjamin, B. (1992). Discovering your boundary issues. *Massage Therapy Journal, 31*(3), 31-32.

Bennett, B. E., Bryant, B. K., VandenBos, G. R., & Greenwood, A. (1990). *Professional liability and risk management.* Washington, DC: American Psychological Association.

Benowitz, M. (1991). *Sexual exploitation of female clients by female psychotherapists: Interviews with clients and a comparison to women exploited by male psychotherapists.* Unpublished doctoral dissertation, University of Minnesota.

Bera, W. (1990). The systemic/attributional model: Victim-sensitive offender therapy. In J. M. Yokely (Ed.), *The use of victim-offender communication in the treatment of sexual abuse: Three intervention models.* Orwell, VT: The Safer Society Press.

Berry, J. (1992). *Lead us not into temptation: Catholic priests and the sexual abuse of children.* New York: Doubleday.

Bettelheim, B. (1983). Scandal in the family. *New York Review of Books, 30*(11), 39-44.

Bindrum, P. (1972). A report on a nude marathon: The effect of physician nudity upon the pattern of interaction in the marathon group. In H. Gochras & L. Schultz (Eds.), *Human sexuality and social work* (pp. 205-220). New York: Association Press.

Blackmon, R. A. (1984). *The hazards of ministry.* Unpublished doctoral dissertation, Fuller Theological Seminary, Fuller, CA.

Blum, H. P. (1973). The concept of eroticized transference. *Journal of the American Psychoanalytic Association, 21,* 61-76.

Bollas, C. (1987). *The shadow of the object: Psychoanalysis of the unthought known.* New York: Columbia University Press.

Bolton, Jr., F., Morris, L., & MacEachron, A. (1989). *Males at risk: The other side of child sexual abuse.* Newbury Park, CA: Sage.

Borys, D. S. (1988). Dual relationships between therapist and client: A national survey of clinicians' attitudes and practices. (Doctoral dissertation, University of California, Los Angeles, 1988). *Dissertation Abstracts International, 49,* 05B.

Borys, D. S., & Pope, K. S. (1989). Dual relationships between therapist and client: A national survey of psychologists, psychiatrists, and social workers. *Professional Psychology: Research and Practice, 20,* 283-293.

Bouhoutsos, J., Holroyd, J., Lerman, H., Forer, B., & Greenberg, M. (1983). Sexual intimacy between psychotherapists and patients. *Professional Psychology: Research and Practice,* 14, 185-196.

Braceland, F. (1969). Historical perspectives of the ethical practice of psychiatry. *American Journal of Psychiatry, 126,* 230-237.

Bradford, J. B., & Ryan, C. C. (1987). *National lesbian health care survey mental health implications.* Richmond, VA: Virginia Commonwealth University, Survey Research Laboratory.

Brown, L. S. (1984). The lesbian feminist therapist in private practice and her community. *Psychotherapy in Private Practice,* 2(4), 9-16.

Brown, L. S. (1985). Power, responsibility, boundaries: Ethical concerns for the lesbian feminist therapist. *Lesbian Ethics,* 1(3), 30-45.

Brown, L. S. (1987a, August). *Beyond thou shalt not: Developing conceptual frameworks for ethical decision-making.* Paper presented at a symposium of the 95th Convention of the American Psychological Association, Ethical and Boundary Issues for Lesbians and Gay Psychotherapists, New York.

Brown, L. S. (1987b, January). *Learning to think about ethics: A guide for the perplexed lesbian feminist therapist.* Keynote speech presented at the Los Angeles Chapter of the Association for Women in Psychology Conference, Boundary Dilemmas for the Lesbian Feminist Therapist, Los Angeles, CA.

Brown, L. S. (1988a). Beyond thou shalt not: Thinking about ethics in the lesbian therapy community. *Women and Therapy, 8,* 13-26.

Brown, L. S. (1988b). Harmful effects of post-termination sexual and romantic relationships between therapists and their former clients. *Psychotherapy,* 25(2), 249-255.

Brown, L. S. (1989, Fall). Ask Dr. practice: A column for feminist practitioners. *Psychology of Women: Newsletter of Division 35, American Psychological Association,* 15(4).

Brown, L. S. (1994). Boundaries and feminist therapy: A conceptual formulation. In N. Gartrell (Ed.), *Bringing ethics alive.* New York: Haworth.

Brownfain, J. J. (1971). The A.P.A. professional liability insurance program. *American Psychologist, 26,* 643-652.

Burgess, A., & Hartman, C. (1986). *Sexual exploitation of patients by health professionals.* New York: Praeger.

Burton, A. (1972). *Interpersonal psychotherapy.* Englewood Cliffs, NJ: Prentice-Hall.

Butler, S. E. (1975). *Sexual contact between therapists and patients.* (University Microfilms No. 76-10, 411)

Butler, S. E., & Zelen, S. L. (1977). Sexual intimacies between therapists and patients. *Psychotherapy: Theory, Research, and Practice, 14,* 139-145.

California Department of Consumer Affairs. (n.d.). *Professional therapy never includes sex.* Sacramento: Author.

Callan, S. R. (1987). *Sexual exploitation in the treatment setting: A study of female survivors.* Unpublished master's thesis, Smith College School of Social Work, Northampton, MA.

Campbell, M. L. (1989). The oath. *Perspectives in Biology and Medicine,* 32(2), 300-308.

Carotenuto, A. (1984). *A secret symmetry: Sabina Spielrein between Jung and Freud*. New York: Pantheon.

Center for the Prevention of Sexual & Domestic Violence. (1991). *Prevention of clergy misconduct: Sexual abuse in the ministerial relationship*. Seattle, WA: Author.

Chesler, P. (1972). *Women and madness*. New York: Avon.

College of Physicians and Surgeons of Ontario, Task Force on Sexual Abuse of Patients. (1991a). *Preliminary report of the Task Force on Sexual Abuse of Patients*. Toronto, Ontario: Author.

College of Physicians and Surgeons of Ontario, Task Force on Sexual Abuse of Patients. (1991b). *Final report*. Toronto, Ontario: Author.

Colorado Bar Association. (1992, February 3). No. 90S497: Ferguson v. People: Sexual assault—constitutionality of statute proscribing as a felony consensual sexual relationship between psychotherapists and clients. *Bar Association Advance Sheet Headnote*, pp. 1-2.

Colorado Revised Statutes. (1991, July 1). Civil Laws of Colorado for 1991. Title 13, Article 25, Section 131. Concerning the Admission of Evidence of a Victim's Sexual History in a Civil Action Arising Out of an Alleged Sexual Assault.

Corey, G., Corey, M. S., & Callanan, P. (1984). *Issues and ethics in the helping professions*. Monterey, CA: Brooks/Cole.

D'Addario, L. (1977). *Sexual relationships between female clients and male therapists*. Unpublished doctoral dissertation, California School of Professional Psychology, San Diego.

Dahlberg, C. C. (1970). Sexual contact between patient and therapist. *Contemporary Psychoanalysis, 6*(2), 107-124.

Denver Post Staff. (1990a, April 15). Ex-counselor pleads guilty to assault. *Denver Post*, The Region, p. 2C.

Denver Post Staff. (1990b, May 2). Counselor sentenced for sexual assault. *Denver Post*, The Region, p. 2B.

Denver Post Staff. (1991a, May 24). Therapist pleads guilty. *Denver Post*, Denver & the West, p. 2B.

Denver Post Staff. (1991b, September 2). Therapist sentenced. *Denver Post*, p. 2B.

Department of Health and Human Issues, University of Wisconsin-Madison/Extension. (1990). *Sexual ethics in ministry*. Madison, WI: Author.

Derosis, H., Hamilton, J. A., Morrison, E., & Strauss, M. (1987). More on psychiatrist-patient sexual contact. *American Journal of Psychiatry, 144*(5), 688-689.

Dimock, P. (1988). *Myths about male sexual abuse victims*. Workshop handout, Minneapolis, MN.

Disch, E. (1989a). *After sexual malpractice: What can you do?* Cambridge, MA: Boston Associates to Stop Treatment Abuse.

Disch, E. (1989b, Spring). When intimacy goes awry. *Woman of Power, 13*, 54-57.

Disch, E. (1989c). Sexual abuse by psychotherapists. *Sojourner: The Woman's Forum, 14*, 8, 20-21.

Disch, E. (1989d). One day workshops for female survivors of sexual abuse by psychotherapists. In G. Schoener et al., *Psychotherapists' sexual involvement with clients: Intervention and prevention* (pp. 209-213). Minneapolis, MN: Walk-In Counseling Center.

Disch, E. (1991). *The aftermath of sexual abuse by a health or mental health professional*. Weston, MA: Ethical Treatment in Health Care.

Disch, E. (1992a). *Is there something wrong or questionable in your treatment?* Cambridge, MA: Boston Associates to Stop Treatment Abuse.

Disch, E. (1992b). *Are you in trouble with a client?* Cambridge, MA: Boston Associates to Stop Treatment Abuse.

Disch, E. (1992c). *After sexual malpractice and when there seem to be no resources in your area.* Weston, MA: Ethical Treatment in Health Care.

Donn, L. (1990). *Freud and Jung: Years of friendship, years of loss.* New York: Collier.

Duran, M. (1991, August 29). Therapist sentenced in sex case. *Rocky Mountain News,* p. 30.

Durrant, M., & Kowalski, K. (1990). Overcoming the effects of sexual abuse: Developing a self-perception of competence. In M. Durrant & C. White (Eds.), *Ideas for therapy with sexual abuse.* Adelaide, Australia: Dulwich Center Publications.

Durrant, M., & White, C. (Eds.). (1990). *Ideas for therapy with sexual abuse.* Adelaide, Australia: Dulwich Center Publications.

Eberle, P., & Eberle, S. (1992). *The abuse of innocence: The McMartin Preschool trial.* Buffalo, NY: Prometheus.

Edelwich, J., & Brodsky, A. (1991). *Sexual dilemmas for the helping professional* (rev., expanded ed.). New York: Brunner/Mazel. (Original work published 1982)

Epstein, R. S., & Simon, R. I. (1990). The exploitation index: An early warning indicator of boundary violations in psychotherapy. *Bulletin of the Menninger Clinic, 54,* 450-465.

Epstein, R. S., Simon, R. I., & Kay, G. (1992). Assessing boundary violations in psychotherapy: Survey results with the exploitation index. *Bulletin of the Menninger Clinic, 56,* 1-21.

Epston, D., & White, M. (1989). *Literate means to therapeutic ends.* Adelaide, Australia: Dulwich Center Publications.

Eyman, J. R., & Gabbard, G. O. (1991). Will therapist-patient sex prevent suicide? *Psychiatric Annals, 21*(11), 669-674.

Felman-Summers, S., & Jones, G. (1984). Psychological impacts of sexual contact between therapists or other health care practitioners and their clients. *Journal of Consulting and Clinical Psychology, 52*(6), 1054-1061.

Feminist Therapy Institute (FTI). (1987). *Ethical guidelines for feminist therapists.* (Published by the author).

Finkelhor, D. (1979). *Sexually victimized children.* New York: Free Press.

Finkelhor, D., and Associates. (1986). *A sourcebook on children sexual abuse.* Newbury Park, CA: Sage.

Finley, B. (1990, October 4). Therapist faces sex charges. *Denver Post,* p. 3B.

Fitzgerald, F. S. (1933). *Tender is the night.* New York: Scribner.

Fortune, M. (1989). *Is nothing sacred? When sex invades the pastoral relationship.* San Francisco: Harper & Row.

Fortune, M. (1991). Betrayal of the pastoral relationship: Sexual contact by pastors and pastoral counselors. In G. Schoener, J. Milgrom, J. Gonsiorek, E. Luepker, & R. Conroe (Eds.), *Psychotherapists' sexual involvement with clients* (pp. 81-91). Minneapolis, MN: Walk-In Counseling.

Franklin, B., de Bory, G., Lavoisier, A. L., Bailly, J. S., Majault, S., d'Arcet, J., Guillotin, J., & Le Roy, J. B. (1965). Secret report on mesmerism or animal magnetism. In R. E. Shor & M. T. Orne (Eds.), *The nature of hypnosis: Selected basic readings.* New York: Holt, Rinehart & Winston. (Original work published 1784)

Freeman, L., & Roy, J. (1976). *Betrayal.* New York: Stein & Day.

Freud, S. (1953). Three essays of sexuality. In J. Strachey (Ed. and Trans.), *The standard edition of the complete psychological works of Sigmund Freud* (Vol. 7, pp. 123-245). London: Hogarth. (Original work published 1905)

Freud, S. (1958). Observations on transference-love. In J. Strachey (Ed. and Trans.), *The standard edition of the complete psychological works of Sigmund Freud* (Vol. 12, pp. 158-171). London: Hogarth.

Freyd, P. (1993). Introduction. In *False memory syndrome foundation newsletter* (Newsletter). Philadelphia: False Memory Syndrome Foundation.

Friedeman, S. D. (1981). *The effects of sexual contact between therapist and client on psychotherapy outcome.* (University Microfilms No. 8309699)

Gabbard, G. (Ed.). (1989). *Sexual exploitation in professional relationships.* Washington, DC: American Psychiatric Press.

Gabbard, G. O. (1990). *Psychodynamic psychiatry in clinical practice.* Washington, DC: American Psychiatric Press.

Gabbard, G. O. (1991a). Psychodynamics of sexual boundary violations. *Psychiatric Annals, 21*(11), 651-655.

Gabbard, G. O. (1991b). Sexual misconduct by female therapists. *The Psychodynamic Letter, 1*(6), 1-3.

Gabbard, G. O. (in press). When the therapist is a patient: Special challenges in the psychoanalytic treatment of mental health professionals. *Psychoanalytic Review.*

Gabbard, G. O., & Wilkinson, S. M. (1994). *Management of countertransference with borderline patients.* Washington, DC: American Psychiatric Press.

Gardner, H. (Ed.). (1987). *The new Oxford book of English verse 1250-1950.* Oxford: Oxford University Press.

Gartrell, N., Herman, J., Olarte, S., Feldstein, M., & Localio, R. (1986). Psychiatrist-patient sexual contact: Results of a national survey, I: prevalence. *American Journal of Psychiatry, 143*(9), 1126-1131.

Gartrell, N., Herman, J., Olarte, S., Feldstein, M., & Localio, R. (1987). Reporting practices of psychiatrists who knew of sexual misconduct by colleagues. *American Journal of Orthopsychiatry, 57,* 287-295.

Gartrell, N., Herman, J., Olarte, S., Localio, R., & Feldstein, M. (1988). Psychiatric residents' sexual contact with educators and patients: Results of a national survey. *American Journal of Psychiatry, 145*(6), 690-694.

Gartrell, N., Milliken, N., Goodson, W. H., III, Thiemann, S., & Lo, B. (1992). Physician-patient sexual contact: prevalence and problems. *Western Journal of Medicine, 157*(2), 139-143.

Gartrell, N., & Sanderson, B. (1994). Sexual abuse of women by women in psychotherapy: Counseling and advocacy. In N. Gartrell (Ed.), *Bringing ethics alive* (pp. 39-54). New York: Haworth.

Gay, P. (1988). *A life for our times* [Freud]. New York: Norton.

Gazette Telegraph Staff. (1990a, June 14). Lack of job may send counselor back to jail. *Gazette Telegraph,* City/Region, p. B5. (Colorado Springs, CO)

Gazette Telegraph Staff. (1990b, September 5). Psychologist abused trust to have sex, jury told. *Gazette Telegraph,* City/Region, p. B2.

Gazette Telegraph Staff. (1990c, September 9). Ex-psychologist is found guilty of sexual assault. *Gazette Telegraph,* City/Region, p. B3.

Gazette Telegraph Staff. (1990d, August 31). Counselor denies engaging in sex with his patient. *Gazette Telegraph,* Courts, p. B7.

Gonsiorek, J. C. (1987). Intervening with psychotherapists who sexually exploit clients. In P. Keller & S. Heyman (Eds.), *Innovations in clinical practice: A sourcebook* (Vol. 6, pp. 417-427). Sarasota, FL: Professional Resource Exchange.

Gonsiorek, J. (1989a). The prevention of sexual exploitation of clients: Hiring practices. In G. Schoener, J. Milgrom, J. Gonsiorek, E. Luepker, & R. Conroe (Eds.), *Psychotherapists' sexual involvement with clients: Intervention and prevention* (pp. 469-475). Minneapolis, MN: Walk-In Counseling Center.

Gonsiorek, J. C. (1989b). Sexual exploitation by psychotherapists: Some observations on male victims and on sexual orientation concerns. In B. E. Sanderson (Ed.), *It's never O.K.: A handbook for professionals on sexual exploitation by counselors and therapists* (pp. 95-99). St. Paul: Minnesota Department of Corrections.

Gonsiorek, J. (1989c). Sexual exploitation by psychotherapists: Some observations on male victims and sexual orientation issues. In G. Schoener, J. Milgrom, J. Gonsiorek, E. Luepker, & R. Conroe (Eds.), *Psychotherapists' sexual involvement with clients: Intervention and prevention* (pp. 113-119). Minneapolis, MN: Walk-In Counseling Center.

Gonsiorek, J., Bera, W., & LeTourneau, D. (1994). *Male sexual abuse: A trilogy of intervention strategies.* Thousand Oaks, CA: Sage.

Gonsiorek, J., & Brown, L. (1989). Post therapy sexual relationships with clients. In G. Schoener, J. Milgrom, J. Gonsiorek, E. Luepker, & R. Conroe (Eds.), *Psychotherapists' sexual involvement with clients: Intervention and prevention* (pp. 289-301). Minneapolis, MN: Walk-In Counseling Center.

Gonsiorek, J., & Rudolph, J. (1991). Homosexual identity: Coming out and other developmental events. In J. Gonsiorek & J. Weinrich (Eds.), *Homosexuality: Research implications for public policy* (pp. 161-176). Newbury Park, CA: Sage.

Gonsiorek, J. C., & Schoener, G. R. (1987). Assessment and evaluation of therapists who sexually exploit clients. *Of Professional Practice of Psychology, 8,* 79-93.

Greenberg, S. (1992, March 3). *The civil forensic examination.* Workshop handout, Los Angeles, CA.

Gross, S. Z. (1986, Summer). Ethics: Post-therapy social interaction/intimacy follow-up. *Minnesota Psychologist.* (Minnesota Psychological Association)

Grosskurth, P. (1991). *The secret ring: Freud's inner circle and the politics of psychoanalysis.* Reading, MA: Addison-Wesley.

Grunebaum, H. (1986). Harmful psychotherapy experience. *American Journal of Psychotherapy, 40*(2), 165-176.

Gutheil, T. G., & Gabbard, G. O. (1992). Obstacles to the dynamic understanding of therapist-patient sexual relations. *American Journal of Psychotherapy, 46*(4), 515-525.

Hamilton, J., & DeRosis, H. (1985). *Report of the Women's Committee to the Washington Psychiatric Society: Result of questionnaire on sexual abuse between physicians and their patients.* Washington, DC: Washington Psychiatric Society.

Harris, C. (1988). *The circuit rider's wife.* Wilmore, KY: Bristol. (Original work published as *A Circuit Rider's Wife,* 1910)

Harris, M. (1990). *Unholy orders: Tragedy at Mount Cashel.* Markham, Ontario: Penguin Books Canada.

Hawthorne, N. (1991). *The scarlet letter.* Philadelphia: Courage. (Original work published by Ticknor, Reed, and Fields, 1850)

Henderson, J. (1964). Ancient myths and modern man. In C. Jung (Ed.), *Man and his symbols* (pp. 95-157). New York: Bantam.

Herman, J. L. (1992). *Trauma and recovery.* New York: Basic Books.

Holroyd, J. C., & Brodsky, A. (1977). Psychologists' attitudes and practices regarding erotic and nonerotic physical contact with patients. *American Psychologist, 32,* 843-849.

Imber-Black, E. (1987). Families, larger systems, and the wider social context. *Journal of Strategic and Systemic Therapies, 5,* 29-35.

Jones, E. (1953). *The life and work of Sigmund Freud* (Vol. 1). New York: Basic Books.

Jorgenson, L., Randles, R., & Strasburger, L. H. (1991). The furor over psychotherapist-patient sexual contact: New solutions to an old problem. *William and Mary Law Review, 32,* 645-732.

Kalff, D. (1988). *Sandplay: A psychotherapeutic approach to the psyche.* Boston: Sigo.

Kamsler, A. (1990). Her story in the making: Therapy with women who were sexually abused in childhood. In M. Durrant & C. White (Eds.), *Ideas for therapy with sexual abuse.* Adelaide, Australia: Dulwich Center Publications.

Kardener, S. H., Fuller, M., & Mensh, I. N. (1973). A survey of physicians' attitudes and practices regarding erotic and nonerotic contact with patients. *American Journal of Psychiatry, 130*(10), 1077-1081.

Keith-Spiegel, P., & Koocher, G. P. (1985). *Ethics in psychology: Professional standards and cases.* New York: Random House.

Kerr, J. (1993). *A most dangerous method.* New York: Knopf.

Kluft, R. (1989). Treating the patient who has been sexually exploited by a previous therapist. *Psychiatric Clinics of North America, 12,* 483-500.

Kulka, R. A., Schlenger, W. E., Fairbank, J. A., Hough, R. L., Jordan, B. K., Mermar, C. R., & Weiss, D. S. (1990). *Trauma and the Vietnam war generation.* New York: Brunner/Mazel.

Kurosawa, A. (Director). (1951). *Rashomon* [Film]. RKO Pictures.

Landis, J. (1956). Experiences of 500 children with adult sexual deviance. *Psychiatric Quarterly Supplement, 30,* 91-109.

Len, M., & Fischer, J. (1978). Clinicians' attitudes toward and use of body contact or sexual techniques with clients. *Journal of Sex Research, 14,* 40-49.

Lerman, H. (1984). *Sexual intimacies between psychotherapists and patients: An annotated bibliography of mental health, legal and public media literature and relevant legal cases.* Phoenix, AZ: American Psychological Association, Division of Psychotherapy.

Lerman, H. (1990). *Sexual intimacies between psychotherapists and patients: An annotated bibliography of mental health, legal and public media literature and relevant legal cases* (2nd ed.). (Available from the Division of Psychotherapy of the American Psychological Association, 3875 N. 44th Street, Suite 102, Phoenix, Arizona 85018 for $60 in the United States and $75 outside)

Lloyd, G. E. R. (Ed.). (1983). *Hippocratic writings.* London: Penguin Classics.

Loftus, E. (1993). The reality of repressed memories. *American Psychologist, 48,* 518-537.

Lorde, A. (1984). Transformation of silence into language and action. In *Sister outside* (p. 40). Trumansburg, NY: Crossing Press.

Luepker, E. T. (1989a). Clinical assessment of clients who have been sexually exploited by their therapists and development of differential treatment plans. In G. R. Schoener, J. H. Milgrom, J. C. Gonsiorek, E. T. Luepker, & R. M. Conroe (Eds.), *Psychotherapists' sexual involvement with clients: Intervention and prevention* (pp. 159-176). Minneapolis, MN: Walk-In Counseling Center.

Luepker, E. (1989b). Time-limited treatment/support groups for clients who have been sexually exploited by therapists: A nine year perspective. In G. R. Schoener, J. H. Milgrom, J. C. Gonsiorek, E. T. Luepker, & R. M. Conroe (Eds.), *Psychotherapists' sexual involvement with clients: Intervention and prevention* (pp. 181-194). Minneapolis, MN: Walk-In Counseling Center.

Luepker, E., & O'Brien, M. (1989). Support groups for spouses. In G. Schoener, J. Milgrom, J. Gonsiorek, E. Luepker, & R. Conroe (Eds.), *Psychotherapists' sexual involvement with clients* (pp. 241-244). Minneapolis, MN: Walk-In Counseling Center.

Luepker, E., & Retsch-Bogart, C. (1980). Group treatment for clients who have been sexually involved with their psychotherapist. In A. Burgess & C. Hartman (Eds.), *Sexual exploitation of patients by health professionals* (pp. 163-172). New York: Praeger.

Lyn, L. (1990). *Life in the fishbowl: Lesbian and gay therapists' social interactions with their clients.* Unpublished master's thesis, Southern Illinois University, Carbondale.

Malyon, A. (1982). Psychotherapeutic implications of internalized homophobia in gay men. In J. Gonsiorek (Ed.), *Homosexuality and psychotherapy: A practitioner's handbook of affirmative models* (pp. 59-69). New York: Haworth.

Marmor, J. (1970). The seductive psychotherapist. *Psychiatry Digest, 31,* 10-16.

Maslow, A. (1965). *Eupsychian management: A journal.* Homewood, IL: Irwin.

Masson, J. M. (1988). *Against therapy: Emotional tyranny and the myth of psychological healing.* New York: Atheneum.

Masters, W., & Johnson, V. (1970). *Human sexual inadequacy.* Boston: Little, Brown.

Masters, W., & Johnson, V. (1975). *Principles of the new sex therapy.* Paper delivered at the annual meeting of the American Psychiatric Association, Anaheim, CA.

McCartney, J. L. (1966). Overt transference. *Journal of Sex Research, 2,* 227-237.

McGuire, W. (Ed.). (1988). *The Freud/Jung letters: The correspondence between Sigmund Freud and C. G. Jung.* Cambridge, MA: Harvard University Press.

McLean, C. (1992). Introduction. In Some thoughts on men's ways of being [Special issue]. *Dulwich Center Newsletter, 3-4,* 3-8. (Adelaide, Australia: Dulwich Center Publications)

McMurray, R. J. (1990). *Report of the Council on Ethical and Judicial Affairs.* Chicago: American Medical Association.

McPhedran, M., Armstrong, H., Edney, R., Marshall, P., Roach, R., & Long, B. (1991). *The preliminary report of the Task Force on Sexual Abuse of Patients.* Toronto, Ontario: College of Physicians and Surgeons of Ontario.

Meloy, J. R. (1988). *The psychopathic mind: Origins, dynamics, and treatment.* Northvale, NJ: Jason Aronson.

Melton, G., Petrilla, J., Poythress, N., & Slobogin, C. (1987). *Psychological evaluations for the courts.* New York: Guilford.

Menninger, W. W. (1991). Identifying, evaluating, and responding to boundary violations: A risk management program. *Psychiatric Annals, 21,* 675-680.

Mental Health Risk Retention Group (MHRRG). (1990). *A self evaluation survey relating to sexual misconduct of therapists and other staff of mental health care organizations.* Burlington, VT: Author.

Milgrom, J. (1989a). Advocacy: The process of assisting sexually exploited clients. In B. Sanderson (Ed.), *It's never O.K.: A handbook for professionals on sexual exploitation by counselors and therapists* (pp. 29-34). St. Paul: Minnesota Department of Corrections.

Milgrom, J. (1989b). Secondary victims of sexual exploitation by counselors and therapists: Some observations. In G. Schoener, J. Milgrom, J. Gonsiorek, E. Luepker, & R. Conroe (Eds.), *Psychotherapists' sexual involvement with clients* (pp. 235-240). Minneapolis, MN: Walk-In Counseling Center.

Milgrom, J. (1992). *Boundaries in professional relationships..* Minneapolis, MN: Walk-In Counseling Center.

Ministerial Continuing Education. (1991). *Sexual ethics for church professionals.* Silver Spring, MD: Author.

Minnesota Interfaith Committee on Sexual Exploitation by Clergy. (1989). *Sexual exploitation by clergy: Reflections and guidelines for religious leaders.* Minneapolis, MN: Author.

Minnesota Statutes. (1985). Criminal sexual conduct, secs. 609.341, 609.344, 609.345.

Mintz, E. E. (1969). Touch and the psychoanalytic tradition. *Psychoanalytic Review, 56,* 365-366.

Morey, A. (1988, October 5). Blaming women for the sexually abusive male pastor. *The Christian Century,* pp. 866-869.

Moss, L. E. (1987, January). *The problem of overlapping relationships with clients.* Paper presented at "Boundary Dilemmas in the Client-Therapist Relationship: A Working Conference for Lesbian Therapists," Los Angeles, CA.

Nestingen, S., & Lewis, L. (1991). *Growing beyond abuse.* Minneapolis, MN: Omni Recovery, Inc.

News Services Staff. (1990, June). Panel hears horror story stretching from street to court. *Gazette Telegraph,* p. A-11. (Colorado Springs, CO)

O'Brien, M. (1989). *Characteristics of adolescent male sibling incest offenders: Preliminary findings.* Orwell, VT: Safer Society Press.

O'Hanlon, W., & Wilks, G. (1989). *Shifting context: The generation of effective psychotherapy.* New York: Guilford.

Olarte, S. W. (1991). Characteristics of therapists who become involved in sexual boundary violations. *Psychiatric Annals, 21*(11), 657-660.

Olsen, J. (1989). *DOC: The rape of the town of Lovell.* New York: Atheneum.

Perry, J. A. (1979). Physicians' erotic and nonerotic physical involvement with patients. *American Journal of Psychiatry, 133*(7), 838-840.

Pescosolido, F. (1989). Sexual abuse of boys by males: Theoretical and treatment implications. In S. Sgroi (Ed.), *Vulnerable populations* (Vol. 2., pp. 85-109). Toronto, Ontario: Lexington.

Peterson, M. R. (1992). *At personal risk: Boundary violations in professional-client relationships.* New York: Norton.

Pope, K. (1988). How clients are harmed by sexual contact with mental health professionals: The syndrome and its prevalence. *Journal of Counseling and Development, 67*(4), 222-226.

Pope, K. (1989a). Therapist-patient sex syndrome: A guide for attorneys and subsequent therapists to assessing damages. In G. Gabbard (Ed.), *Sexual exploitation in professional relationships* (pp. 39-55). Washington, DC: American Psychiatric Press.

Pope, K. (1989b). Therapists who become sexually intimate with a patient: Classifications, dynamics, recidivism, and rehabilitation. *The Independent Practitioner, 9,* 28-34. (Bulletin of the Division of Independent Practice, Division 42 of the American Psychological Association)

Pope, K. (1991). Unanswered questions about rehabilitating therapists-patient sex offenders. *Psychology of Women Newsletter, 18,* 5-7. (Newsletter of Division 35 of the American Psychological Association)

Pope, K., & Bouhoutsos, J. (1986). *Sexual intimacy between therapists and patients.* Westport, CT: Praeger.

Pope, K., & Gabbard, G. (1989). Individual psychotherapy for victims of therapist-patient sexual intimacy. In G. Gabbard (Ed.), *Sexual exploitation in professional relationships* (pp. 89-100). Washington, DC: American Psychiatric Press.

Pope, K. S., Keith-Spiegel, P. C., & Tabachnik, B. G. (1986). Sexual attraction to clients: The human therapist and the (sometimes) inhuman training system. *American Psychologist, 41,* 147-158.

Pope, K., Levenson, H., & Schover, L. (1979). Sexual intimacy in training: Results and implications of a national survey. *American Psychologist, 34*(8), 682-689.

Pope, K. S., Sonne, J. L., & Holroyd, J. (1993). *Sexual feelings in psychotherapy*. Washington, DC: American Psychological Association.

Pope, K. S., Tabachnik, B. G., & Keith-Spiegel, P. C. (1987). Ethics of practice: The beliefs and behaviors of psychologists as therapists. *American Psychologist, 42*(11), 993-1006.

Pope, K. S., & Vasquez, M. J. T. (1991). *Ethics in psychotherapy and counseling: A practical guide for psychologists*. San Francisco: Jossey-Bass.

Quinn, S. (1988). *A mind of her own*. Reading, MA: Addison-Wesley.

Reich, W. (1945). *Character analysis*. New York: Orgone Institute.

Reid, D., Linder, R., Shelley, B., & Stout, H. (Eds.). (1990). *Dictionary of Christianity in America*. Downers Grove, IL: Intervarsity Press.

Reiser, S. J., Dyck, A. J., & Curran, W. J. (1977). *Ethics in medicine: Historical perspectives and contemporary concerns*. Cambridge: MIT Press.

Rigby, D. (1986, March). *Sexual involvement of women therapists with their women clients*. Paper presented at the 11th National Conference of the Association of Women in Psychology, Oakland, CA.

Rigby, D. N., & Sophie, J. (1990). Ethical issues and client sexual preference. In H. Lerman & N. Porter (Eds.), *Feminist ethics in psychotherapy* (pp. 165-175). New York: Springer.

Roberts-Henry, M. (1987). *Between fear and life: Personal journal*. Unpublished manuscript.

Robinowitz, C. B. (1992, May-June). Letters: More on my doctor, my lover. *The Bulletin—Area II*, p. 2. (American Psychiatric Association, Garden City, NY)

Robinson, J. (1993). *Sexual contact between gay male clients and male therapists*. Unpublished doctoral dissertation, University of Southern California, Los Angeles.

Rocky Mountain News Staff. (1988, April 8). Therapist guilty in sexual assault. *Rocky Mountain News*, p. 28.

Rocky Mountain News Staff. (1990a, May 2). Therapist jailed. *Rocky Mountain News*, Colorado & The West, p. 10.

Rocky Mountain News Staff. (1990b, November 28). Therapist sentenced. *Rocky Mountain News*, Colorado & the West, p. 10.

Rocky Mountain News Staff. (1990c, October 4). Female therapist faces sex charges. *Rocky Mountain News*, pp. 7, 32.

Roll, S., & Millen, L. (1981). A guide to violating an injunction in psychotherapy: On seeing acquaintances as patients. *Psychotherapy: Theory, Research, & Practice, 18*(2), 179-187.

Russell, R. (1984). *Sexual workers' awareness of and response to the problem of sexual contact between clients and helping professionals*. Unpublished master's thesis, University of Washington, Seattle.

Rutter, P. (1989). *Sex in the forbidden zone*. Los Angeles: Jeremy Tarcher.

Salter, A. (1988). *Treating sex offenders and their victims*. Newbury Park, CA: Sage.

Sanderson, B. (Ed.). (1989). *It's never O.K.: A handbook for professionals on sexual exploitation by counselors and therapists*. St. Paul: Minnesota Department of Corrections.

Schoener, G. R. (1989a). Administrative safeguards. In G. R. Schoener, J. H. Milgrom, J. C. Gonsiorek, E. Luepker, & R. Conroe (Eds.), *Psychotherapists' sexual involvement with clients: Intervention and prevention* (pp. 453-467). Minneapolis, MN: Walk-In Counseling Center.

Schoener, G. R. (1989b). A look at the literature. In G. Schoener, J. Milgrom, J. Gonsiorek, E. Luepker, and R. Conroe (Eds.). *Psychotherapists' sexual involvement with clients: Intervention and prevention* (pp. 401-420). Minneapolis, MN: Walk-In Counseling Center.

Schoener, G. R. (1989c). Sexual involvement of therapists with clients after therapy ends: Some observations. In G. R. Schoener, J. H. Milgrom, J. C. Gonsiorek, E. Luepker,

& R. Conroe (Eds.), *Psychotherapists' sexual involvement with clients: Intervention and prevention* (pp. 265-287). Minneapolis, MN: Walk-In Counseling Center.

Schoener, G. R. (1989d). The role of supervision and case consultation: Some notes on sexual feelings in therapy. In G. R. Schoener, J. H. Milgrom, J. C. Gonsiorek, E. Luepker, & R. Conroe (Eds.), *Psychotherapists' sexual involvement with clients: Intervention and prevention* (pp. 495-502). Minneapolis, MN: Walk-In Counseling Center.

Schoener, G. (1991, September). Memories of greatness—memories of violence. *Minnesota Psychologist*, pp. 9-10.

Schoener, G. (1992, March). Bruno Bettelheim revisited. *Minnesota Psychologist*, p. 22.

Schoener, G. R., & Conroe, R. M. (1989). The role of supervision and case consultation in primary prevention. In G. R. Schoener, J. H. Milgrom, J. C. Gonsiorek, E. Luepker, & R. Conroe (Eds.), *Psychotherapists' sexual involvement with clients: Intervention and prevention* (pp. 477-493). Minneapolis, MN: Walk-In Counseling Center.

Schoener, G. R., & Gonsiorek, J. C. (1988). Assessment and development of rehabilitation plans for counselors who have sexually exploited their clients. *Journal of Counseling and Development, 67,* 227-232.

Schoener, G. R., & Gonsiorek, J. C. (1989). Assessment and development of rehabilitation plans for the therapist. In G. R. Schoener, J. H. Milgrom, J. C. Gonsiorek, E. Luepker, & R. Conroe (Eds.), *Psychotherapists' sexual involvement with clients: Intervention and prevention* (pp. 401-420). Minneapolis, MN: Walk-In Counseling Center.

Schoener, G. R., & Milgrom, J. H. (1989). Organizational consultation. In G. R. Schoener, J. H. Milgrom, J. C. Gonsiorek, E. Luepker, & R. Conroe (Eds.), *Psychotherapists' sexual involvement with clients: Intervention and prevention* (pp. 505-516). Minneapolis, MN: Walk-In Counseling Center.

Schoener, G. R., Milgrom, J. H., & Gonsiorek, J. (1984). Sexual exploitation of clients by therapists. *Will and Therapy, 3*(3/4), 63-69.

Schoener, G. R., Milgrom, J. H., Gonsiorek, J. C., Luepker, E. T., & Conroe, R. M. (Eds.). (1989). *Psychotherapists' sexual involvement with clients: Intervention and prevention.* Minneapolis, MN: Walk-In Counseling Center.

Schwartz, M. F. (1992). Sexual compulsivity as post-traumatic stress disorder: Treatment perspectives. *Psychiatric Annals, 22*(6), 333-338.

Searles, H. F. (1979). *Countertransference and related subjects.* New York: International Universities Press.

Sell, J. M., Gottlieb, M. C., & Schoenfeld, L. (1986). Ethical considerations of social/romantic relationships with present and former clients. *Professional Psychology: Research and Practice, 17*(6), 504-508.

Sennott, C. (1992). *Broken covenant.* New York: Simon & Schuster.

Sgroi, S. (1989a). Community-based treatment for sexual offenders against children. In S. Sgroi (Ed.), *Vulnerable populations* (Vol. 2, pp. 351-393). Toronto, Ontario: Lexington.

Sgroi, S. (1989b). *Vulnerable populations* (Vols. 1, 2). Toronto, Ontario: Lexington.

Shapiro, D. (1991). *Forensic psychological assessment: An integrative approach.* Boston: Allyn & Bacon.

Shepard, M. (1971). *The love treatment: Sexual intimacy between patients and psychotherapists.* New York: Peter H. Wyden.

Shepard, M. (1972). *A psychiatrist's head.* New York: Peter H. Wyden.

Simon, R. (1991). Psychological injury caused by boundary violation precursors to therapist-patient sex. *Psychiatric Annals, 21,* 614-619.

Simon, R. (1992a). *Psychiatry and the law for clinicians.* Washington, DC: American Psychiatric Press.

Simon, R. (1992b). Treatment of boundary violations: Clinical, ethical, and legal considerations. *Bulletin of the American Academy of Psychiatry & Law, 20,* 269-288.

Simon, R. (1992c). *Clinical psychiatry and the law* (2nd ed.). Washington, DC: American Psychiatric Press.

Sonne, J., Meyer, C. B., Borys, D., & Marshall, V. (1985). Clients' reactions to sexual intimacy in therapy. *American Journal of Orthopsychiatry, 55,* 183-189.

Sparks, J., Ray, R., & Houts, D. (1992). Sexual misconduct in ministry: What clergy at risk are doing about it. *Congregations: The Alban Journal, 18*(6), 3-8.

Stark, K. A. (1989). Child sexual abuse within the Catholic church. In G. Schoener, J. Milgrom, J. Gonsiorek, E. Luepker, & R. Conroe (Eds.), *Psychotherapists' sexual involvement with clients* (pp. 793-819). Minneapolis, MN: Walk-In Counseling Center.

Strasburger, L. H., Jorgenson, L. M., & Sutherland, P. (1992). The prevention of psychotherapist sexual misconduct: Avoiding the slippery slope. *American Journal of Psychotherapy, 46,* 544-555.

Sullivan, H. S. (1954). *The psychiatric interview.* New York: Norton.

Supreme Court, State of Colorado, Case No. 90SA497—Opinion delivered by Justice Quinn. (1992, February 3). Robert E. Ferguson v. The People of the State of Colorado—Challenge to the Constitutionality of the Colorado Criminalization Statute, C.R.S. 18-3-405.5. Appeal from the District Court of El Paso County. 2-21.

Sussman, M. B. (1992). *A curious calling: Unconscious motivations for practicing psychotherapy.* Northvale, NJ: Jason Aronson.

Tallman, G. (1981). *Therapist-client social relationships.* Unpublished manuscript, California State University, Northridge.

Temerlin, M. K., & Temerlin, J. W. (1982). Psychotherapy cults: An iatrogenic perversion. *Psychotherapy: Theory, Research, & Practice, 19*(2), 131-141.

Trent, J. (1989, December 12). Judge: Law forbidding therapist, patient sex not unconstitutional. *Gazette Telegraph,* p. B2. (Colorado Springs, CO)

Trent, J. (1990a, September 8). Ex-psychologist admits affair but denies counseling. *Gazette Telegraph,* City/Region, p. B5.

Trent, J. (1990b, May 1). Ex-counselor gets jail for assaulting client. *Gazette Telegraph,* pp. B1, B8.

Trent, J. (1990c, June 12). Former counselor jailed for assaulting client will be let out to work. *Gazette Telegraph,* City/Region, p. B2.

Trent, J. (1990d, June 22). "Misled" judge sends ex-counselor back to jail. *Gazette Telegraph,* City/Region, p. B4.

Trent, J. (1990e, September 6). Woman testifies trust led to sex with counselor. *Gazette Telegraph,* p. B8.

Trent, J. (1990f, November 27). Therapist receives two-year sentence. *Gazette Telegraph,* City/Region, pp. B1, B4.

Turnbull, A. (1948). *The bishop's mantle.* New York: Macmillan.

Twemblow, S. W., & Gabbard, G. O. (1989). The lovesick therapist. In G. O. Gabbard (Ed.), *Sexual exploitation in professional relationships* (pp. 71-87). Washington, DC: American Psychiatric Press.

United Church of Christ. (1986). *Sexual harassment of clergywomen and laywomen.* Cleveland, OH: Coordinating Center for women.

van der Kolk, B. (1987). *Psychological trauma.* Washington, DC: American Psychiatric Press.

VanTuinen, I., McCarthy, P., & Wolfe, S. (1991). *9,479 questionable doctors disciplined by states or the federal government.* Washington, DC: Public Citizen Health Research Group.

Villaume, P. G., & Foley, R. M. (1993). *Teachers at risk*. Bloomington, MN: Legal Resource Center for Educators.

Vinson, J. S. (1984). *Sexual contact with psychotherapists: A study of client reactions and complaint procedures*. Unpublished doctoral dissertation, California School of Professional Psychology, Berkeley.

Waldegrave, C. (1990). Just therapy. *Dulwich Center Newsletter, 1*.

Waller, A. (1982). *Reverend Beecher and Mrs. Tilton*. Boston: University of Massachusetts Press.

Washington Council of Churches. (1984). *Sexual contact by pastors and pastoral counselors in professional relationships*. Seattle, WA: Author.

Weber, M. (1972, January). Should you sleep with your therapist? The raging controversy in American psychiatry. *Vogue*, pp. 78-79.

White, M. (1992a). Men's culture, the men's movement, and the constitution of men's lives. In Some thoughts on men's ways of being [Special issue]. *Dulwich Center Newsletter, 3-4*, 33-53. (Adelaide, Australia: Dulwich Center Publications).

White, M., & Epston, D. (1990). *Narrative means to therapeutic ends*. New York: Norton.

White, W. (1986). *Incest in the organizational family*. Bloomington, IL: Lighthouse Training Institute.

White, W. (1993). *Critical Incidents: Ethical Issues in Substance Abuse Prevention and Treatment*. Bloomington, IL: Lighthouse Training Institute.

Wolff, W. (Ed.). (1956). *Contemporary psychotherapists examine themselves*. Springfield, IL: Charles C Thomas.

Zimmet, R. K. (1989). *Sexual misconduct* [Videotape]. Burlington, VT: Mental Health Risk Retention Group.

Zimmet, R. K. (1990). *Criminal and civil liability for sexual misconduct of therapists and other staff of mental health care organizations*. Burlington, VT: Mental Health Risk Retention Group.

Additional Readings

Benowitz, M. (in press). Comparing the experiences of women clients sexually exploited by female versus male psychotherapists. *Journal of Women and Therapy.*

Brigham, R. E. (1989). *Psychotherapy stressors and sexual misconduct: A factor analytic study of the experience of nonoffending and offending psychologists in Wisconsin.* Unpublished doctoral dissertation, Wisconsin School of Professional Psychology, Milwaukee.

Bronfenbrenner, U. (1977, July). Toward an experimental ecology of human development. *American Psychologist*, pp. 513-531.

Flack, R. (1991, November 13). Appeal attacks law prohibiting sex between mental therapist, patient. *Gazette Telegraph*, City/Region/State, p. B6. (Colorado Springs, CO)

Gazette Telegraph Staff. (1989, December 1). Psychotherapist charged with having sex with patient. *Gazette Telegraph*, City/State/Region, p. B2. (Colorado Springs, CO)

Jung, C. (Ed.). (1964). *Man and his symbols.* New York: Bantam.

Mathews, R., Matthews, J., & Speltz, K. (1989). *Female sex offenders: An exploratory study.* Orwell, VT: Safer Society Press.

Milgrom, J. (1986). *Advocacy: Assisting the sexually exploited client through the process.* Minneapolis, MN: Walk-In Counseling Center.

Roback, G., Randolph, L., & Seidman, B. (1990). *Physician characteristics and distribution in the U.S.* Chicago: American Medical Association.

Robbins, A. (Ed.). (1988). *Between therapists: The processing of transference/countertransference material.* New York: Human Sciences Press.

Stern, M. (Ed.). (1985). *Psychotherapy and the terrorized patient.* New York: Hawthorne.

Index

412

About the Contributors

J. Alex Acker is a writer and lecturer. She has published several articles and is currently working on a nonfiction book and a fiction trilogy. She is in the process of completing her master's degree in creative writing from Hamline University in Saint Paul. She lives with her partner in Shoreview, Minnesota.

Elizabeth Barnhill has been the Executive Director of the Iowa Coalition Against Sexual Assault (IowaCASA) since 1990. She is a member of the Iowa Task Force on Sexual Exploitation by Helping Professionals, who persuaded the Iowa legislature to criminalize sexual exploitation by counselors. She has also worked in a residential treatment facility for abused children and as director of a battered women's shelter.

Mindy Benowitz (Ph.D.) is a licensed psychologist in private practice in Minneapolis. She has served as Vice Chairperson of Minnesota Women Psychologists. She has written and lectured on sexual exploitation by therapists, boundary issues in psychotherapy, eating disorders, sexual abuse, heterosexism, and lesbian battering. The chapter in this volume is based on her (1991) Ph.D. dissertation, *Sexual Exploitation of Female Clients by Female Psychotherapists: Interviews With Clients and a Comparison to Women Exploited by Male Psychotherapists.*

Walter H. Bera received his M.A. in educational psychology at the University of Minnesota and has worked in the field of sexual abuse and harassment assessment, treatment, and prevention since 1978. He has worked in the Family Sexual Abuse Program of the Family Renewal Center, Illusion Theater's Sexual Abuse Prevention Education Program, and the PHASE Program with adolescent sex offenders. He has produced original research, articles, plays, and videotapes; his recent works include coauthoring the video-based adolescent sexual harassment prevention curriculum *Crossing the Line* (1993) and *Male Sexual Abuse: A Trilogy of Intervention Strategies* (Sage, 1994). He is a licensed psychologist and licensed marriage and family therapist in Minnesota and a clinical member and approved supervisor in the American Association for Marriage and Family Therapy. He is completing his doctorate in family social science at the University of Minnesota on a Bush Leadership Fellowship. He maintains a private practice in Minneapolis and provides training and consultation nationally.

Nancy Biele is currently the Violence Prevention Planner for the state of Minnesota, housed in the Office of Drug Policy and Violence Prevention. She also works with the Minnesota Council of Churches' Committee on Sexual Exploitation Within the Religious Community, serving as victim advocate, advocate supervisor, congregational and denominational trainer, and consultant on issues of clergy sexual misconduct. Prior to taking the position with the state in October 1992, she was the Executive Director of the Sexual Violence Center of Hennepin, Carver, and Scott Counties and has worked for 20 years in sexual assault services advocating for victims, training service providers, and serving on the boards of directors of the Minnesota Coalition Against Sexual Assault and the National Coalition Against Sexual Assault.

Estelle Disch (Ph.D., C.C.S.) is a certified clinical sociologist who codirects BASTA! (Boston Associates to Stop Treatment Abuse). She is also Associate Professor of Sociology at the University of Massachusetts at Boston, where she teaches sociology and serves as Coordinator for Diversity Awareness at the Center for the Improvement of Teaching. She is principal investigator of a survivor/victim study titled *Sexual Involvement/Exploitation Between Health and Mental Health Care Providers and Their Clients: Effects on Clients.* She has provided workshops and consultations to victims of sexually exploitative treatment since 1984. She also provides training for professionals on sexual and other boundary issues. She was herself sexually exploited by a therapist about 25 years ago. She can be reached at Boston Associates to Stop Treatment Abuse, 528 Franklin Street, Cambridge, MA 02139, (617) 661-4667, or at the Department of Sociology, UMass/Boston, 100 Morrissey Blvd., Boston, MA 02125-3393, (617) 287-6250.

Rev. Marie M. Fortune grew up in North Carolina, where she received her undergraduate degree from Duke University. She received her seminary training at Yale Divinity School and was ordained a minister in the United Church of Christ in 1976. After serving in a local parish, she founded the Center for the Prevention of Sexual and Domestic Violence, where she serves as Executive Director. The center, located in Seattle, Washington, is an educational ministry serving as a training resource to religious communities in the United States and Canada. She is a pastor, educator, and author as well as a practicing ethicist and theologian.

Glen O. Gabbard (M.D.) is Bessie Walker Callaway Distinguished Professor of Psychoanalysis and Education in the Karl Menninger School of Psychiatry and Mental Health Services; Training and Supervising Analyst, Topeka Institute for Psychoanalysis; and Clinical Professor of Psychiatry, University of Kansas School of Medicine. He is the author or editor of eight books, including *Sexual Exploitation in Professional Relationships, Psychodynamic Psychiatry in Clinical Practice: The DSM-IV Edition*, and *Management of Countertransference With Borderline Patients*.

Nanette K. Gartrell (M.D.) is Associate Clinical Professor of Psychiatry, University of California at San Francisco, where she teaches ethics and feminist theory. She has been investigating sexual exploitation by health professionals since 1982.

John C. Gonsiorek received his Ph.D. in clinical psychology from the University of Minnesota in 1978 and holds a diplomate in clinical psychology from the American Board of Professional Psychology. He is past President of Division 44 (Society for the Psychological Study of Lesbian and Gay Issues) of the American Psychological Association and has published widely in the area of sexual exploitation by psychotherapists, sexual orientation and sexual identity, professional ethics, and other areas. His books include *Psychotherapists' Sexual Involvement With Clients: Intervention and Prevention* (with Schoener, Milgrom, Luepker, & Conroe); *Homosexuality: Research Implications for Public Policy* (with Weinrich); *Male Sexual Abuse: A Trilogy of Intervention Strategies* (with Bera & LeTourneau); and *Homosexuality and Psychotherapy: A Practitioner's*

Handbook of Affirmative Models. He is in private practice of clinical and forensic psychology in Minneapolis.

William H. Goodson III (M.D.) is in the Department of Surgery at the University of California, San Francisco.

Rev. Donald C. Houts, before his recent retirement, served successively as parish pastor, hospital chaplain-supervisor, seminary professor, and career support specialist for United Methodist pastors in the Illinois area. In the latter role, he has conducted more than 50 seminars for clergy and for church leaders in the field of clergy sexual ethics. He has written a monograph regarding the use of small group process and male-female leadership that has been widely used in the United States and Canada. In addition, he has surveyed more than 30 faith groups and has presented that research data to a number of professional groups and conferences. He currently serves as a professional consultant to the University of Wisconsin, Department of Health and Human Issues, and to the Division of Chaplains and Related Ministries of the United Methodist Church in the field of pastoral counseling. He did his undergraduate studies at the University of Iowa, his theological studies at Garrett Evangelical Theological Seminary, and his Ph.D. work at Northwestern University.

Richard R. Irons obtained his medical degree at Dartmouth College in Hanover, New Hampshire, in 1973 and has continued his medical education through training and experience in the fields of internal medicine, psychiatry, and addiction medicine. Until recently, he served as Medical Director of the Professional Assessment Program at Abbott Northwestern Hospital in Minneapolis, Minnesota (the program was formerly located at Golden Valley Health Center). He served as the first full-time Medical Director of the Washington Monitored Treatment Program and the first Physician Director of the Montana Physician Assistance Program. He has recently assumed the position of Medical Director at Talbott-Marsh Recovery Campus (TMRC) in Atlanta, Georgia.

Linda Mabus Jorgenson (J.D.), attorney, has considerable legal experience in the area of sexual exploitation by professionals. She is a partner in the plaintiffs' law firm Spero & Jorgenson in Cambridge, Massachusetts. She has handled over 300 cases of therapist-patient sexual abuse allegations. She has argued on behalf of the plaintiff in the Massachusetts Supreme Judicial Court decision applying the delayed discovery rule to psychotherapist malpractice cases, *Riley v. Presnell*, 409 Mass. 239, 565 N.E. 2d 780 (1991). She has published extensively in this area, most recently in numerous lay reviews and mental health journals including the *American Journal of Psychiatry* and *Hospital and Community Psychiatry*. She is a frequent presenter at grand rounds continuing education and at the American Psychiatric Association, the American Psychological Association, and the American Bar Association annual meetings.

Andrew W. Kane (Ph.D.) is in private practice as a clinical and forensic psychologist at 2815 North Summit Ave., Milwaukee, WI 53211-3439. He is the founder of the Wisconsin Coalition on Sexual Misconduct by Psychotherapists and Counselors, which he chaired from 1985 to 1989. He is the coauthor of *Psychological Experts in Divorce, Personal Injury, and Other Civil Actions,* published by Wiley Law Publications (second edition, 1993). He is the former President of the Wisconsin Psychological Association (WPA). He is Clinical Professor at both the Wisconsin School of Professional Psychology and the University of Wisconsin— Milwaukee and is Associate Clinical Professor at the Medical College of Wisconsin.

Hannah Lerman (Ph.D.) is a clinical psychologist in independent practice in Los Angeles. For many years, she has been involved in the special issues of women, especially that of sexual abuse of clients by therapists. She has compiled an annotated bibliography of the literature in this area and is also the author of *A Mote in Freud's Eye: From Psychoanalysis to the Psychology of Women* (Springer, 1986). She is currently working on a critical history of the psychodiagnosis of women in twentieth-century United States.

Laurel Lewis is the founder and president of Omni Recovery, Inc., a publishing company specializing in products for persons recovering from sexual exploitation. She is the coauthor of *Growing Beyond Abuse: A Workbook for Survivors of Sexual Exploitation or Childhood Sexual Abuse.* She consults with, and provides a network of support people for, survivors of sexual exploitation or clergy abuse. She can be reached at (612) 698-2781, Omni Recovery, Inc., P.O. Box 50033, Minneapolis MN 55403. She is completing (1994 graduation date) a master's degree in counseling psychology.

Bernard Lo (M.D.) is in the Department of Medicine at the University of California, San Francisco.

Ellen Thompson Luepker is a licensed psychologist, licensed independent clinical social worker, and board certified diplomate in clinical social work. She received her M.S.W. from Smith College in 1966 and a Bush Foundation Fellowship, University of Minnesota, in 1977. She has held various positions in child and adult mental health services, including Instructor in Psychiatry, University of Rochester School of Medicine, Rochester, New York; Field Instructor, Boston University School for Social Work, Boston; and Director of Group Treatment, Minneapolis Family and Children's Service, Minneapolis. Currently, she is in independent practice of psychotherapy and consultation, provides training and supervision for Walk-In Counseling Center psychology and social work graduate interns, and teaches on the continuing education faculty, Smith College School for Social Work. She is the author of numerous articles and coauthor of *Psychotherapist's Sexual Involvement With Clients: Intervention and Prevention*. She is past President, Minnesota Society for Clinical Social Work, past Secretary, National Federation of Societies for Clinical Social Work, and current Co-chair, National Committee on Clinical Social Work and the Law.

Laura Lyn completed her bachelor's degree in psychology in 1985 and a certificate in alcohol studies in 1986 at the University of California at San Diego. She earned her master's degree in counseling psychology at Southern Illinois University at Carbondale in 1991 and is now a doctoral candidate in the same program. She is writing her dissertation on supervision of counseling and psychotherapy and will graduate with her Ph.D. in 1995. She is currently working at Southern Illinois University at Carbondale as the Interim Coordinator of Women's Services and a Staff Counselor at the Counseling Center.

Rev. Canon Margo E. Maris is presently Canon to the Ordinary of the Diocese of Minnesota, after having served as rector of three parishes in the diocese. She has served on the Commission on Ministry, the Standing Committee (as president), the Diocesan Council, the Investment Committee, the Wellness Committee, and Clergy Mentoring. Prior to her ordination, she worked as a teacher in the Berkeley, California, Public School System as well as serving as executive director for five years with various nonprofit school outreach programs in Portland, Oregon, and Berkeley, California. She has degrees from Willamette University and

George Washington University, legal training at Lewis and Clark College, and an M.Div. from Church Divinity School of the Pacific. She is also a graduate of the Humphrey Institute of the University of Minnesota Reflective Leadership Training Program and is a licensed mediator.

Rev. Kevin M. McDonough currently serves as Vicar General and Moderator for the Curia of the Archdiocese of St. Paul and Minneapolis. He received his doctorate in canon law from the University of St. Thomas Aquinas in Rome in 1987. He has made national addresses on clerical sexual misconduct and seminary training in theology. Previously, he has served as Rector of St. John Vianney College Seminary in St. Paul, as Chancellor and Episcopal Vicar of the Archdiocese of St. Paul and Minneapolis, and as pastor and associate pastor.

Jeanette Hofstee Milgrom (M.S.W., L.I.C.S.W.) is the Director of Consultation and Training at Walk-In Counseling Center in Minneapolis. She has worked with victims of abuse by therapists, counselors, and clergy since 1976, providing advocacy and other services. She has done extensive training of professionals addressing this issue as well as the broader topic of professional boundaries. Her work is in part represented in *Psychotherapists' Sexual Involvement With Clients: Intervention and Prevention* (Schoener, Milgrom, Gonsiorek, Luepker, & Conroe, 1989) and in her recent training manual *Boundaries in Professional Relationships* (Milgrom, 1992).

Nancy Milliken (M.D.) is in the Department of Obstetrics, Gynecology, and Reproductive Sciences at the University of California, San Francisco.

Signe L. Nestingen (M.A.) is a licensed psychologist, a licensed marriage and family therapist, and a sandplay therapist. She is the coauthor of *Growing Beyond Abuse*, a creative arts workbook for those who have been sexually exploited or abused. She is particularly interested in creativity—her own, that of her clients, and the individual and collective creativity of all beings. In addition to lecturing and teaching, she works with children, adolescents, and adults in private practice in St. Paul, Minnesota.

Melissa Roberts-Henry was educated at Mt. Holyoke, the University of Pennsylvania, and the University of Georgia. She received her M.S. in geology at the latter. Her early interest in Remote Sensing led to participation in the ERTS and LANDSAT satellite programs. Her career transition and role as "activityist" battling abuse was a function of her experience as a victim/survivor of abuse by a therapist. Subsequent to her civil trial, purportedly the first to go to court in Denver, in 1988 she developed, administered, and funded I.M.P.A.C.T. (In Motion—People Abused in Counselling and Therapy). The PBS documentary episode "My Doctor, My Lover" focused on both and was one of many media appearances/interviews. In 1991, as cited in *Newsweek,* she initiated, coauthored, and lobbied for "The Colorado Civil Court Rape Shield Bill" to protect victims' sexual history. She has testified for numerous state bills and public hearings. Currently, she serves a governor-appointed term on the Colorado State Board of Psychologist Examiners. She continues to crusade against abuse in a variety of arenas.

Peter Rutter (M.D.) is a psychiatrist and Jungian analyst in private practice in San Francisco and Associate Clinical Professor, Department of Psychiatry, University of California Medical School, San Francisco. He is the former chair of the ethics committee of the C. G. Jung Institute of San Francisco and a holder of the Distinguished Teacher Award in Health and Medical Sciences from the University of California, Berkeley. He is the author of *Sex in the Forbidden Zone: When Men in Power— Therapists, Doctors, Clergy, Teachers, and Others—Betray Women's Trust* (Fawcett) and consults and lectures internationally on the subject of professional ethics, sexual misconduct, and sexual harassment.

Gary Richard Schoener is a licensed psychologist and Executive Director of the Walk-In Counseling Center in Minneapolis, which, over the past 20 years, has been involved in addressing more than 3,000 cases of sexual misconduct by professionals. He is coauthor of *Psychotherapists' Sexual Involvement With Clients: Intervention and Prevention, Assisting Impaired Psychologists* and many articles on the topic. He is a frequent speaker and expert witness in the United States and Canada. He is a member of the Task Force on Sexual Impropriety and the Advisory Committee on the Impaired Psychologist of the American Psychological Association. He has been a consultant to many hundreds of professional organizations about the issue of sexual misconduct, including numerous churches; the American Medical Association, the Canadian Medical Association, and the California Bar Association.

Sue Thiemann (M.S.) is a statistician in private practice.

William L. White (M.A.) is Senior Research Consultant at the Lighthouse Institute, a division of Chestnut Health Systems in Bloomington, Illinois. He has worked in and with health and human service agencies for the past 27 years as a clinician, clinical director, researcher, and well-traveled trainer and consultant. He has provided training and consultation services on issues related to sexual harassment and sexual exploitation and has conducted studies on organizational systems that have a propensity for abuses of power. He is the author of *Critical Incidents: Ethical Issues in Substance Abuse Prevention and Treatment* and *Incest in the Organizational Family: The Ecology of Burnout in Closed Systems*.

Janet W. Wohlberg, prior to teaching organizational behavior and pedagogy at Boston University's School of Management, had more than 20 years of experience in corporate and nonprofit public relations and taught courses on public relations, organizational behavior, and mass communication at Boston University's College of Liberal Arts. Her M.S., in corporate public relations, is from the College of Communication, and she is completing her Ed.D. in human development at the School of Education. She recently returned to a full-time consulting practice in which she develops, writes, and facilitates cases and experiential exercises for management training in the business and nonprofit sectors. Her materials have been published in textbooks on management, communication, and education, and many individual cases and exercises have been widely distributed for use in illustrating principles of participative management, values clarification, leadership, human resources, and so on. The most recent of her three books, *OB in Action: Cases and Exercises* was published in 1992. A fourth book, to be published in 1995, is in progress.